Informal Housing

Praise for this book

'This book by the late Kevin Tayler is an essential reference work for professionals involved with shelter and more widely with urban development in the South. It is unique in offering in-depth analysis and critique of both theory and practice from a viewpoint that is totally grounded in practical experience and on-the-ground reality gained from a lifetime's work.'

Andrew Cotton, retired Director of WEDC, Loughborough University

'This new book distils Kevin Tayler's many decades of experience and encapsulates his unwavering commitment to meeting the needs of marginalized communities in the Global South. Having worked closely with Kevin, I've seen first-hand how his practical wisdom and ethical perspectives shape his approach to pro-poor and equitable development—principles that lie at the heart of his book on informal housing.'

Dr Jonathan Parkinson, i-San consulting and Editor of IWA's Journal of Water, Sanitation and Hygiene for Development

'The 2026 World Urban Forum acknowledged that we are facing a global housing crisis. A combination of increasing demand and inequality have made access to formally approved housing increasingly inaccessible in countries at all levels of economic development. Those unable to meet official standards or regulations are increasingly forced into various forms of informal housing and these now account for more than a billion people worldwide.

Of all the reviews of this issue, none is as comprehensive and detailed as that provided by Kevin Tayler in *Informal Housing: A history of responses*. Drawing on a career covering numerous countries, Tayler takes the reader on a tour of the causes of informality and responses to it by governments, NGOs, international development organisations and other professionals. A wealth of evidence is provided in a highly engaging manner and the achievements and limitations of different approaches are assessed from a social as well as environmental and economic perspective. This book provides all you need to know about informality and how it needs to be addressed and is a fitting legacy for a distinguished professional.'

Geoffrey Payne, Housing and urban development consultant, Geoffrey Payne & Associates

Informal Housing

A history of responses

Kevin Tayler

Practical
ACTION
PUBLISHING

Practical Action Publishing Ltd
25 Albert Street, Rugby,
Warwickshire, CV21 2SD, UK
www.practicalactionpublishing.com

A catalogue record for this book is available from the British Library & Library of Congress

ISBN 978-1-78853-233-4 Paperback
ISBN 978-1-78853-235-8 Digital book

Citation: Tayler, K. (2026) *Informal Housing: A History of Responses*, Rugby, UK: Practical Action Publishing http://doi.org/10.3362/9781788532358

Since 1974, Practical Action Publishing has published and disseminated books and information in support of international development work throughout the world. All print editions are produced and distributed via ethical and sustainable print on demand global facilities.

Practical Action Publishing is a trading name of Practical Action Publishing Ltd (Company Reg. No. 01159018 | VAT 880 9924 76). All profits are covenanted back to its parent group, Practical Action (Charity Reg. No. 247257).

Cover design by: Katarzyna Markowska, Practical Action Publishing
Typeset by vPrompt eServices, India

Contents

Acknowledgements

I am grateful to all the people who I have worked with, interacted with, and learnt from over the years, on projects at conferences and through correspondence. In particular, my colleagues at Gilmore Hankey Kirke, later GHK International, especially John Kirke, who was a supportive boss who opened many opportunities for me and shared his extensive knowledge of urban development. David Gilmore who introduced me to the work of Alain Bertaud. Jim Arthur, Bruce Pollock, Mik Green, and Paul Dean, fellow engineers at GHK, provided many insights into our work while relaxing with beers during overseas assignments. Others at GHK are too numerous to mention but they know who they are.

David Allen, Ian Green, and Davids Sims of Culpin Planning introduced me to the Ismailia Demonstration Projects while we worked together on the EMS project in Cairo. David Sims has been particularly helpful in recent months in conducting a thorough review and suggesting improvements to the book. Chris Berry was the team leader for the first project in Lahore that led to the proposal for the North-east Lahore project. Geoff Read was a supportive team leader of the World Bank team supervising the project.

The ODA social development team introduced me to the concept of PRA and the local team tried hard to put the principles into practice during the Faisalabad project. WEDC's Dr Andrew Cotton and myself worked closely on publications that drew partly on experiences in Lahore and Faisalabad. Others who have provided insights into planning aspects of sites and service and upgrading processes include Dr Roger Zetter of Oxford Brooks University, Professor Pat Wakely and Babar Mumtaz of the Development Planning Unit at University College London and particularly Professor Alison Brown at Cardiff University, with whom I worked closely for many years on aspects of urban development.

I was involved with the Tamil Nadu and Mumbai sites and services projects as part of a World Bank team led by Evan Rotner, whose drive and commitment to the projects played a significant part in their eventual success. I met Barbara Evans in the course of the Tamil Nadu mission and we have shared ideas and insights on development issues for many years.

The late Parween Rahman and Arif Hasan provided Information on the Orangi Pilot Project. No doubt they would not agree with all my conclusions about the project. Similarly, Sundar Barra provided information on the Indian Alliance.

From the mid-2000s, I was part of the World Bank team supervising the Punjab Municipal Services Improvement Project, which was managed by the

Punjab Municipal Development Fund Company (PMDFC). Thanks to Shahnaz Arshad of the World Bank and the PMDFC team for helping to inspire some of the institutional ideas contained in this book. More recently, thanks to Anna O'Donnell, Sonia Sultan, and colleagues on the Low Income Communities Housing Support Programme in Bangladesh. During the course of preparation for this project, we gathered firsthand information on an earlier Urban Partnerships for Poverty Reduction (UPPR) project.

Babar Mumtaz reviewed the book for Practical Action Publishing and provided many useful comments and suggestions.

Finally, thanks to Salwa for putting up with my long absences in the office at the top of the house and to Sarah for acting as my agent in circulating the book and responding to queries as required.

Kevin Tayler (2021)

Abbreviations

ACCA	Asian Coalition for Community Action
ACHR	Asian Coalition for Housing Rights
ADS	Area Development Society
AHP	Affordable Housing in Partnership
APUSP	Andhra Pradesh Urban Services for the Poor
ASB	Anjuman Samaji Behbood
BIP	Bustee Improvement Program
BLC	Beneficiary-Led Construction
BMGF	Bill & Melinda Gates Foundation
BSUP	Basic Services for the Urban Poor
BVS	Basti Vikas Samiti
CDC	Community Development Council
CDCs	Community Development Committees
CDS	City Development Strategy
CDS	Community Development Society
CLIFF	Community-Led Infrastructure Finance Facility
CLSS	Credit-Linked Subsidy Scheme
CODI	Community Organizations Development Institute
CORC	Community Organization Resource Centre
DFID	Department for International Development
EWS	Economically Weaker Section
FAUP	Faisalabad Area Upgrading Project
FMC	Faisalabad Municipal Corporation
FSI	floor space index
FWASA	Faisalabad Water and Sanitation Agency
GLD	guided land development
HDA	Hyderabad Development Authority
IIDC	Improved Industrial Dwellings Company
ISSR	in-situ slum redevelopment
JNNURM	Jawaharlal Nehru National Urban Renewal Mission
KIP	Kampung Improvement Programme
LDA	Lahore Development Authority
LICHSP	Low-Income Communities Housing Support Project
MAPP	Municipal Action Plan for Poverty Reduction
MPA	Member of the Provincial Assembly
MPUSP	Madhya Pradesh Urban Services for the Poor
MPW	Metropolitan Planning Wing
NGO	non-governmental organization

NHG	Neighbourhood Group
NSDF	National Slum Dwellers Federation
ODA	Overseas Development Administration
OPP	Orangi Pilot Project
PDPP	Program Dasar Pembangunan Partisipatif
PMAY	Pradhan Mantri Awas Yojana
PMDFC	Pakistan's Punjab Municipal Development Fund Company
PMSIP	Punjab Municipal Services Improvement Project
PMU	Project Management Unit
PRA	Participatory Rural Appraisal/Participatory Rapid Appraisal
PRSPs	Poverty Reduction Strategy Papers
RA	Residents Association
RDDP	Revised Draft Development Plan
sDA	spatial daylight autonomy
SDG	Sustainable Development Goal
SDI	Slum/Shack Dwellers International
SHP	Social Housing Programme [Egypt]
SKAA	Sindh Katchi Abadis Authority
SPARC	Society for the Promotion of Area Resource Centres
SRA	Slum Rehabilitation Authority
SRD	Slum Redevelopment Scheme [Mumbai]
SSNS	Sparc Samudaya Nirman Sahayak
TDR	Transferable Development Rights
UCDO	Urban Community Development Office
UDC	Urban Development Corporation
UN DESA	United Nations Department of Economic and Social Affairs
UNDP	United Nations Development Programme
UPPR	Urban Partnerships for Poverty Reduction
WASA	Lahore Water and Sanitation Agency
WSC	(Hasanpura) Water Supply Committee
WSP	Water and Sanitation Program, part of the World Bank's Global Water Practice
WTs	Water Trusts
WWR	window to wall ratio

List of figures, tables, boxes, and photos

Figures

Tables

Boxes

Photos

CHAPTER 1
Introduction

Twenty-first century urban growth: an unprecedented phenomenon

Cities throughout the 'developing' world are growing rapidly. Growth rates often exceed those experienced by European cities in the 19th century and cities themselves are more numerous and generally larger than their 19th century European and North American counterparts. The result is unprecedented urbanization. The 2007 United Nations Population Fund (UNFPA, 2007) *State of World Population* Report stated that the world's urban population was set to reach 3.3 billion in 2008, for the first time in history exceeding the rural population. It predicted continued rapid growth in urban population, up to 5 billion by 2030, while rural population remains almost static, perhaps even declining slightly by 2030. Later estimates confirm this overall picture. In 2018, the United Nations Department of Economic and Social Affairs (UN DESA) assessed the world's urban population as 55 per cent of the whole, and predicted that it would increase by a further 2.5 billion by 2050, with 90 per cent of the increase taking place in Africa and Asia (UN DESA, 2018).

One aspect of rapid urbanization is the development of mega-cities such as Mexico City, Cairo, and Shanghai. In 1969, Shanghai was the only city in the developing world with a population of over 10 million (World Bank, 1990). By 2018, no less than 33 cities exceeded this population, with the number projected to increase to 43 by 2030. The problems of these large cities are obvious but official figures suggest that almost half (47.9 per cent) of the global urban population lives in towns of less than 500,000 inhabitants and over a fifth (21.9 per cent) in cities with between 1 million and 5 million inhabitants. Three countries, India, China, and Nigeria, are expected to account for 35 per cent of the growth in the world's urban population between 2018 and 2050, with India's urban population projected to grow by 416 million (UN DESA, 2019).

Urban growth is not in itself undesirable. Indeed, historical evidence suggests that rapid economic development has seldom taken place in non-urbanized economies. However, urban growth does create a demand for services, which can be difficult to satisfy. Historical records show that this was true in Britain in the 19th century. It is an even more pressing problem in the rapidly urbanizing areas of the 'South', partly because the absolute scale of growth is much greater than that occurring in the 19th century and partly because many countries experiencing rapid urbanization have weak economies. Unfortunately, municipal governments, particularly those of small towns, often lack the financial and human resources required to provide the infrastructure needed to service this rapid growth. There is also an argument, admittedly contested, that growth beyond a certain size becomes counter-productive as the diseconomies associated with size outweigh the advantages derived from economies of scale.

The causes of urban growth

Urban population growth may result from in-migration, natural population growth, and the redrawing of urban boundaries to absorb areas previously classified as rural. The relative importance of in-migration and natural population growth varies considerably between countries and perhaps between towns and cities. Where a city's boundaries remain unchanged, comparison of its population growth rate with that of the country as a whole will provide an initial assessment of relative contributions of in-migration and natural growth to its population growth. For instance, Pakistan's urban and country-wide population growth rates in the mid-1990s were around 4.6 per cent and 2.8 per cent respectively, suggesting that around 60 per cent of urban growth was due to natural population increase with the remainder accounted for by in-migration and changes in city boundaries (Tayler, n.d.). The situation in Delhi at the same time was similar, with 62 per cent of growth between 1990 and 2000 accounted for by natural growth and 38 per cent by in-migration (Chakrabarti, 2001).

Where in-migration is significant, it may be attributable to either 'push' or 'pull' factors, in other words those factors that persuade people to move from rural areas and those that encourage them to move to cities. Responses to urbanization are influenced by the relative importance assigned to push and pull factors. One school of thought, epitomized by the work of the English academic Michael Lipton, argues that policymakers and administrators in most countries have an 'urban bias', which results in a disproportionate share of available resources being spent in towns (Lipton, 1977). For Lipton, lack of investment in agriculture, particularly small-scale agriculture, is a significant cause of the exodus from the land and, by implication, of settlement of erstwhile agricultural workers in urban slums and shanty towns. This is clearly a push factor. However, Lipton's thesis, with its emphasis on the high proportion of government spending on services in urban areas, could also be used in support of the case that the better services provided in urban areas pull people into towns.

Given the hard realities of life for the urban poor, it seems that perceived opportunities for improved income rather than access to improved services are the main drivers of rural–urban migration. These opportunities are greater in cities, such as Bangalore and Hyderabad in India, that have fast growing economies, so pull factors are likely to be more significant in such cities. In situations of conflict, push factors can be very important, as can be seen in the rapid growth of shanty settlements around Khartoum, mainly occupied by Southern Sudanese, during the long war in Southern Sudan (Pantuliano et al., 2011).

To some extent, Lipton's argument has been overtaken by events. In 1977, he stated that 60–80 per cent of people in poor countries relied on agriculture for their livelihoods, but the figure in most countries is now less than 50 per cent. There is a strong argument for increased investment in rural development. However, high natural population growth rates in cities, the continued attraction of urban opportunities and the fact that most low-income migrants into cities end up in slums and poor quality informal settlements suggest a need for investment in improved housing and services for the urban poor. The challenge is to identify ways to meet this need both effectively and equitably, and this challenge is the subject of this book.

Slums, squatters, and informal development

Slums and informal areas accommodate much of the urban population growth in the countries of the South. The terms 'slum' and 'informal settlement' are often used interchangeably although their meanings are rather different. The *Oxford English Dictionary* defines a slum as 'a street alley court etc. situated in a crowded area of a town or city and inhabited by a low class or by the very poor'. It goes on to state that the term slum may also refer to 'a number of such streets or courts forming a thickly populated neighbourhood or district where the houses and the conditions of life are of a squalid and wretched character'. The United Nations defines a slum as an area in which inhabitants lack at least one of the basic conditions of decent housing, adequate sanitation, improved water supply, durable housing, and adequate living space (United Nations, 2007). Both these definitions focus on physical conditions although the Oxford Dictionary definition also reinforces the commonly held view that slums are inhabited by 'low-class' people of doubtful character.

Housing is just one aspect of the informal sector, which encompasses those activities and transactions that take place outside official rules, regulations, and norms. The term informal thus refers to the housing development process rather than the physical and social characteristics of that housing. Clearly, the terms slum and informal settlement are not synonymous: slums are usually informal but informal settlements are not necessarily slums. For example, some apartment blocks in Egypt's informal areas reach heights of 15 storeys or more. Few conform to all space and environmental standards but this does not necessarily make them slums. Even in nominally planned high-income areas, owners may add to their houses without going through official planning and building control procedures.

Some commentators avoid the use of the word slum, arguing that it is value laden and that the values it embodies are those of outsiders rather than those living in the so-called slums. Robert Neuwirth, for instance, uses the term 'squatter settlements' rather than 'slums' (Neuwirth, 2005). As with the term informal, the term squatter relates to the land settlement process, suggesting that settlers have 'squatted' on land owned by others, either the government or private individuals. Neuwirth notes that it is often associated with individuals and small groups who take possession of individual properties and that this can draw attention away from the role played by the politicians, officials, and land brokers who facilitate the occupation of the land. A more serious objection to the term is that not all inhabitants of informal settlements are squatters. Many have bought their plots from farmers or middlemen, but their activities are still strictly illegal either because the land purchase was not properly registered or because the processes by which the land was subdivided and subsequently developed were not in accordance with planning and building regulations.

Legally built housing is not necessarily of good quality, and poorly built and maintained formal housing areas may deteriorate to the point that they can be viewed as slums. Chapter 5 will give some examples. For the moment, it is sufficient to note that such formal housing is usually a small part of the overall picture.

Bearing all these points in mind, this book will use the term informal development to refer to all development that is strictly illegal in one way or another. The subdivision, sale, and development of land without reference to official regulations will be described as unauthorized land subdivision and development. The book will use the term slum with care although it cannot be avoided completely since it accurately describes some types of development and is routinely used by government in some countries, for instance India. The term squatter settlement will be used where appropriate to describe settlements that owe their existence to people squatting on land that does not belong to them.

The contribution of informal housing and slums to overall shelter needs

In 2016, UN-Habitat estimated that around 1 billion people, one-eighth of the world's population were living in slums (UN-Habitat, 2016). An earlier report estimated that the number of slum dwellers might reach 2 billion by the early 2030s (Ibid., 2003). Figures from individual cities provide further insight into the situation.

In the mid-1990s, about 2 million people in Delhi were living in 'shanty clusters' on government land and a further 1.8 million people lived in areas that government had authorized as 'notified slums'. In addition, 2 million people lived in around 1,500 unauthorized colonies with no basic services (Lal, 1996). In 2015, about 60 per cent of urban dwellers in India's Bihar State had no completion certificate for the house they were living in, and 70–80 per cent of those living in houses and apartments had no occupancy certificate. Around 55 per cent of multi-storied buildings faced vigilance cases for violation of floor area ratio (World Bank, 2015: 13). These figures clearly show that informality extends beyond so-called slums. Nevertheless, the challenges presented by slum conditions have not lessened over the years. In 2001, the estimated slum population of Mumbai was about 5.8 million. This represented nearly 50 per cent of the population of the Greater Mumbai area (*Business Standard*, 2001) but occupying only about 8 per cent of the Greater Mumbai's total area (Sharma, 2000). One settlement alone, Dharavi, may have a population of around 700,000 on a total area of 223 hectares (Sharma, 2000). This gives a population density in excess of 3,000 persons per hectare, around 11 times the density of Mumbai as a whole.

A 1981 study, carried out jointly by the World Bank and Egypt's General Organization for Housing and Building Research, estimated that approximately 77 per cent of all housing units built within Egypt between 1966 and 1976 were informal. A second study, in 1982, estimated that informal units represented 84 per cent of all units built in Cairo between 1970 and 1981. In 1993, Egypt's General Organization for Physical Planning estimated that the total population of Cairo's informal areas was 5.88 million, which compares with a total Greater Cairo population of around 12 million. These figures are rather old but the overall situation is unlikely to have changed and indeed the paper from which they are taken suggested that the rate of growth of informal settlements grew after 1986 (El Batran and Arandel, 1998). And, based on investigations of the 2006 Census of Egypt, it was estimated that 62 per cent of Greater Cairo's 16 million inhabitants lived in informal settlements (Sims, 2010). As already noted, while falling short of formal standards in many ways, Cairo's informal settlements cannot all be described as slums.

Nairobi is the largest city in East Africa with an estimated 2019 population of around 4.5 million. Many of its people live in unauthorized settlements, the biggest and best known of which is Kibera. Estimates of Kibera's population vary, from 750,000 down, but the most accurate suggest a figure nearer 250,000 (Kibera.org.uk, n.d.) In Brazil, 2010 census figures showed that Rio de Janeiro's *favelas* (informal settlements) housed more than 1.4 million people, around 23 per cent of the municipal population. A potentially more significant figure is the 28 per cent population growth in *favelas* between 2000 and 2010, as compared with a growth of 3.4 per cent for the rest of the city (Perlman, 2016).

Population densities in informal settlements can be very high. A 1994 unpublished Ministry of Local Development study estimated that the average population density in 171 informal settlements in Greater Cairo, with a total population of 4.52 million, was 780 persons per hectare. Estimated densities in some Nairobi slums exceed 1,000 persons per hectare (Mitullah, 2003). The population density in Dhaka's slums can exceed 2,500 per hectare (Islam et al., 2006). These high population densities exist because the informal settlements that typically house a high proportion of the urban population are often squeezed onto limited areas of land. In Nairobi, for instance, one estimate suggests that informal settlements house 60 per cent of the city's population but occupy only 6 per cent of its land (Kibera.org.uk, n.d.).

Rapid increases of informal housing

Not only do slums and informal housing already represent a very important part of the urban housing stock in developing countries, but there are indications that in many countries such types of housing are increasing rapidly and even becoming the dominant feature of urban landscapes. UN population projections foresee that, by 2050, 2 billion inhabitants will be added to the existing urban population of 3.5 billion found in 'less developed regions', and that almost all of this increase will occur in Asia and Africa (Satterthwaite et al., 2020: 1). Because of definitional problems of what constitutes slums and informal settlements, it is difficult to estimate what portion of this increase will be absorbed by informal urban development, but indications from many countries suggest that up to half (and sometimes more) will either crowd into existing slums and informal urban areas or will be attracted to new informal settlements and expanding fringes of existing cities. This trend towards more and more informal housing can be stark, as the case of Greater Cairo shows. Census data indicate that between 2006 and 2017 there was an increase of 4.9 million inhabitants, of which only 14 per cent were absorbed in the government new towns around Cairo, and only 11 per cent found accommodation in formal districts of the metropolis. That means that the large majority of population increase, some 75 per cent, found homes in existing informal areas or in expanding fringe informal villages in the sprawling peri-urban setting (Sims, 2018).

Such trends imply that the phenomenon of informal housing is not about to wither away, but it may well be becoming dominant, at least in some cities and towns of the South. Thus, the issues taken up in this book are not only relevant for the existing urban reality; they will become ever more pronounced.

The structure and contents of this book

There is no doubt that living conditions in informal settlements are often inadequate, with poor housing, grossly inadequate services and little if any open space. On the other hand, informal development constitutes both a resource and considerable sunk investment. Different types of development offer different possibilities. The challenge is to find out the best ways to realize those possibilities within overall low-income housing strategies. This book examines approaches to housing and service provision for the urban poor over the last 50 years, covering new housing, sites and services projects, upgrading initiatives, and more recent approaches that focus on housing finance, governance, and housing policies. It starts from the premise that some form of intervention is needed but recognizes that this intervention must be framed in the light of local realities and the existing situation.

To put later chapters into context, Chapter 2 provides a brief historical review of the development of slums and informal settlements, focusing particularly on the slums of England and the USA during the 19th century, their counterparts in colonial cities such as Calcutta and the growth of informal settlements in developing countries from around 1900 onwards. The greatly increased rate of informal housing development after about 1950 is emphasized. The last part of the chapter reviews responses to slum development, from the 19th century's 'restrictive legislation', designed to ensure minimum health and environmental standards, through to the efforts to provide public housing for the urban poor.

Chapter 3 examines thinking on informality and explores the influence of this thinking on housing policy and practice through the second half of the 20th century and into the 21st century. Almost all approaches to housing and services provision for the poor emphasize the importance of community participation and Chapter 4 explores thinking on this subject. Chapters 5 to 8 provide information on responses to the growth of the informal sector, focusing on specific countries and initiatives and, where possible, drawing on the author's own experience. Chapter 5 deals with formal housing, and the possibilities presented by prefabrication. Chapter 6 explores sites and services and core housing schemes and Chapter 7 urban upgrading. Few of the responses set out in Chapters 5 to 7 have gone to scale. Accordingly, Chapter 8 describes efforts to go beyond isolated initiatives to tackle housing problems city-wide. It examines efforts to create the conditions for successful city-wide action, including those with an emphasis on governance, financial support systems, and the development of appropriate policies.

Chapter 9 provides a review of the existing situation, summarizing the main points that have emerged from earlier chapters. It emphasizes the need to distinguish between different types of informal development, summarizes thinking on formality and informality, and explores the various factors that influence such thinking. The need to pay attention to the rental sector is emphasized and particular attention is paid to the constraints that have prevented successful pilot schemes from being taken to scale, emphasizing the importance of political and institutional constraints.

Chapter 10 builds on the points presented in Chapter 9 to explore ways forward. After setting out objectives, it examines the issues created by the gap between formal and informal standards. Possible roles for the provision of complete housing units, sites and services, and upgrading are then suggested. The suggested strategy is dependent on institutional change and the options for bringing about that change are examined. The chapter concludes with thoughts on lessons for international organizations and the need for a new professionalism.

References

Business Standard (2001) 'Greater Mumbai Has the Largest Number of Slum Dwellers with 5.8 Million People Living in Slums'. *Business Standard*, 26 November. https://www.business-standard.com/article/economy-policy/23-86-of-city-dwellers-live-in-slums-101112601077_1.html

Chakrabarti, P.G. (2001) 'Delhi's Ongoing Debate on Informal Settlements and Workplaces - Issues of Environmental Jurisprudence', *NAERUS International Workshop on Coping with Informality and Illegality in Human Settlements in Developing Cities, Leuven and Brussels, Belgium, 23–26 May 2001.* https://www.ucl.ac.uk/dpu-projects/drivers_urb_change/urb_infrastructure/pdf_land%20tenure/NAERUS_ESF_chakrabarti_Delhi_Informal_Settlements.pdf (accessed 4 September 2019; no longer available).

El Batran, M. and Arandel, C. (1998) A shelter of their own: Informal settlement expansion in Greater Cairo and government responses, *Environment and Urbanization*, 10 (1). http://eau.sagepub.com/cgi/reprint/10/1/217.pdf

Islam, N., Mahbub, A., Nazem, N.I., Angeles, G. and Lance, P. (2006) *Slums of urban Bangladesh: mapping and census, 2005*. Centre for Urban Studies, Dhaka.

Kibera.org.uk (no date) *Kibera facts and information*, https://www.kibera.org.uk/facts-info/ (accessed 5 September 2019).

Lal, A.K. (1996) *Handbook of low cost housing*, New Age Publishers, Delhi.

Lipton, M. (1977) *Why poor people stay poor: urban bias in world development*, Harvard University Press, Cambridge, MA.

Mitullah, W. (2003) *The case of Nairobi, Kenya*, Case study prepared for the UN-Habitat Global Report 2003: Understanding slums, https://erepository.uonbi.ac.ke/bitstream/handle/11295/54284/Nairobi_bw.pdf?sequence=2&isAllowed=y (accessed 13 August 2025).

Neuwirth, R. (2005) *Shadow cities: a billion squatters, a new urban world*, Routledge, New York.

Oxford English Dictionary (n.d.) Slum. In *Oxford English Dictionary* (3rd ed.). Oxford University Press. www.oed.com/view/Entry/181197 (accessed 13 August 2025).

Pantuliano, S., Assal, M., Elnaiem, B.A., McElhinney, H., Schwab, M., Elzein, Y. and Ali, H.M.M. (2011) *City limits: urbanisation and vulnerability in Sudan Khartoum case study*, ODI, London. https://odi.org/en/publications/city-limits-urbanisation-and-vulnerability-in-sudan-khartoum-case-study/ (accessed 2 September 2019).

Perlman, J. (2016) The formalization of informal real estate transactions in Rio's favelas, in E.L. Birch, S. Chattaraj, and S.M. Wachter (eds), *Slums: how informal real estate markets work*, University of Pennsylvania Press, Philadelphia.

Satterthwaite, D., Archer, D., Colenbrander, S., Dodman, D., Hardoy, J., Mitlin, D. and Patel, S. (2020) 'Building resilience to climate change in informal settlements', *One Earth* 2(2): 143–56. https://doi.org/10.1016/j.oneear.2020.02.002

Sharma, K. (2000) *Rediscovering Dharavi – stories from Asia's largest slum*, Penguin Books India, Delhi.

Sims, D. (2010) *Understanding Cairo: the logic of a city out of control*, AUC Press, Cairo.

Sims, D. (2018) 'Understanding Cairo: social cohesion, urban fragmentation, and livelihoods', El Gouna Campus, Technical University Berlin, presentation, 8 December 2018.

Tayler, K. (no date) *Infrastructure upgrading in Pakistan: lessons from experience and directions for the future*, GHK Research and Training, London.

UN-Habitat (2003) *The challenge of slums: global report on human settlements 2003*, United Nations Human Settlements Programme, Earthscan, London. https://unhabitat.org/sites/default/files/download-manager-files/The%20Challenge%20of%20Slums%20-%20Global%20Report%20on%20Human%20Settlements%202003.pdf (accessed 25 June 2025).

UN-Habitat (2016) *Slum almanac 2015/2016: tracking improvement in the lives of slum dwellers*, UN-Habitat, Nairobi. https://habnet.unhabitat.org/sites/default/files/Slum%20Almanac%202015-2016_EN_web.pdf (accessed 13 August 2025).

United Nations (2007) *The Millennium Development Goals Report*, United Nations, New York. https://www.un.org/millenniumgoals/pdf/mdg2007.pdf (accessed 2 September 2019).

United Nations Department of Economic and Social Affairs (UN DESA), Population Division (2018) *The world's cities in 2018: data booklet* (ST/ESA/SER.A/417). https://digitallibrary.un.org/record/3799524?v=pdf (accessed 25 June 2025).

UN DESA, Population Division (2019) *World urbanization prospects: the 2018 revision* (ST/ESA/SER.A/420), United Nations, New York. https://population.un.org/wup/assets/WUP2018-Report.pdf (accessed 25 June 2025).

United Nations Population Fund (UNFPA) (2007) *State of world population 2007: unleashing the potential of urban growth*, UNFPA, New York.

World Bank (1990) *Urban policy and economic development: an agenda for the 1990s*, World Bank, Washington, DC.

World Bank (2015) *India, land governance assessment: national synthesis report*, World Bank, Washington, DC. http://documents1.worldbank.org/curated/en/643361468038336423/pdf/AUS18306-WP-PUBLIC-P153485.pdf (accessed 1 January 2021).

CHAPTER 2

Informal housing in history

If responses to poor housing and informal development are to be effective, they must be grounded in reality. One aspect of this grounding in reality is the need for an understanding of the historical processes that have created informal settlements. An understanding of history is also required if we are not to endlessly repeat the mistakes of the past. With these points in mind, this chapter provides a historical review of informality and the ways in which governments and others have responded to it. A brief review of the situation prior to the Industrial Revolution is followed by summaries of informality and the responses to it in 19th century Europe and North America. The focus then shifts to low-income housing and informality in the cities of the Global South and the rapid growth of informal settlements from the mid-20th century onwards. The second half of the chapter explores the systematic attempts to analyse and deal with poor housing conditions from the 19th century through to the first half of the 20th century.

Housing prior to the industrial revolution

Poverty and the need for shelter have existed for as long as people have lived in towns and cities. Certainly, poverty and poor housing were features of ancient Rome. Estimates of the population of Imperial Rome vary but most lie in the range 400,000 to 1 million. What is not in doubt is that many of Rome's inhabitants were poor and lived in what would now be described as slums. Scobie (1986: 399–433) says that 'large numbers of destitute and near destitute inhabitants of Rome lived in squalid conditions'. He goes on to note another fact that should be familiar to observers of the divisions in modern cities: that successive administrations ignored these conditions. Most people lived in *insulae*, often poorly constructed tenements that could reach heights of up to about seven storeys. These were generally wooden-built structures and fire was an ever-present danger. Not all *insulae* were slums and indeed they were not the worst type of housing. That dubious distinction belonged to lean-to structures (*parapetasia*), located against the walls of permanent buildings and below aqueducts, and shacks (*turguria*), constructed beyond the confines of the city proper. Presaging current responses to informality, the Roman authorities tried to ban the construction of *insulae*. For instance, after the great fire in 64 CE, Emperor Nero prohibited the construction of tenements and narrow winding lanes. The effect seems to have been to drive poor quality construction to the periphery of the city rather than ending it altogether.

Another link with the common experience of those living in today's informal housing was that inhabitants of 'slum' housing had to face the possibility that the authorities would demolish their homes after declaring them illegal (Meggitt, 1998). However, many, perhaps most, were allowed to remain and were even charged rent.

Drawing on a number of sources, Neuwirth (2005: 182) notes that squatting was common in European cities during the Middle Ages. He quotes figures given by Fernand Braudel on the number of people living in 'shacks' in and around Paris; 17,000 from a total population of 260,000 in 1587, rising to 91,000 from approximately double the population 200 years later. Colin Ward explored squatting in England and Wales, focusing particularly on the concept of the 'one-night house', the idea that a house cannot be demolished if it has been built between sunset and sunrise (Ward, 2002). Most of Ward's examples were from rural areas and involved construction on waste and common land. He noted that the concept of the 'one-night house' occurs throughout Europe and it is interesting that *gekecondu*, the Turkish term for an informal settlement means 'built in one night'. He found no evidence of legal sanction for the concept of the one-night house, and this probably reflects the fact that there was no clear definition of what constitutes formal and informal housing prior to the 19th century. Indeed, it is arguable that most types of vernacular building have always been 'informal' in the sense that they do not conform to formal codes. Builders construct in accordance with widely known and accepted norms without recourse to drawings and calculations. Each step in the building process has to make sense to the builder and must be communicable through words and gestures (Dudley, 1993). This limits both what can be built and what will be considered acceptable but it also means that buildings can be constructed without recourse to regulatory institutions since everyone accepts the forms that buildings can take and what they should look like. This has implications for approaches to informality, which will be explored later in this book.

Britain in the 19th century

Britain urbanized rapidly during the 19th century, as the country became 'the workshop for the world'. Increased demand for labour, coupled with in-migration from agricultural areas, led to rapid population growth, leading to a demand for housing and basic services. Official census figures show that the population of England and Wales increased from 9.2 million in 1801 to 36.1 million in 1901, while the percentage of the population living in towns and cities grew from 26 per cent in 1801 to 72 per cent in 1891 (Upton, 2005). This represents an average urban growth rate of approximately 2.5 per cent per annum.

Accommodation for the rapidly growing workforce took the form of cheap housing, sometimes arranged in rows and sometimes around central 'courts'. To reduce costs, many houses were built back-to-back, sharing a common back wall. For all but end of terrace houses, this meant that only the building frontage faced the open air. By the middle of the century, around two-thirds of the population of Birmingham and three-quarters of the population of Nottingham were living in back-to-back houses. As late as 1920, 70 per cent of houses in Leeds were back-to-back. The courtyard arrangement adopted in Liverpool and Birmingham among others provided space for a shared water tap, washing line, washhouse, toilets, and dustbins. Toilets were invariably 'dry', requiring that excrement was collected manually and dumped at the nearest convenient location, perhaps a drain or an open ditch. The 'pan' system, first introduced in northern towns and then widely adopted across the country, closely resembles the bucket latrine system subsequently introduced to serve 'native' areas in Britain's colonies. Even where WCs existed, the absence of sewers often meant that wastewater was discharged to the nearest open ditch. Statistics from Liverpool in 1884 revealed an average of about two privies per court to serve an average of 19 houses. In Birmingham, the ratio was probably slightly better at about one privy to four or five houses (Upton, 2005). Such conditions were not confined to the larger cities. John Moore's (1945) *Portrait of Elmbury*, a lightly fictionalized description of Tewkesbury in Gloucestershire, describes the slum conditions prevailing in some of the medieval alleys that ran off the town's main street.

Poor sanitation facilities had a direct impact upon health. Residents of back-to-back houses and visitors reported on the smells emanating from badly maintained drains and overflowing cesspits. Cholera epidemics in 1831, 1848, 1853, and 1866 resulted in the deaths of thousands of people and had a direct impact upon subsequent efforts to introduce improved sanitation. At this time, faecal-oral diseases such as cholera were still thought to be spread by bad air and so reformers were keen to both improve sanitation and increase space standards so as to reduce the dangers from the noxious gases emanating from drains and cesspits. Their efforts will be explored in more detail later in this chapter.

Nineteenth century New York

In contrast to England, where most working class families lived in terraces and back-to-backs, many cities in the USA built tenements to house their low-income workers. The high densities resulted in poor ventilation. In New York's Lower East Side, blocks were divided into lots, typically 100 ft (30 metres) deep by 25 feet (7.5 metres) wide. The owners of lots initially erected single-family row houses, but these quickly gave way to tenements, up to six storeys high and housing 20 or more families. 'Building land operators', who combined the roles of land purchaser, developer, and in many cases builder, managed the development process. Some building materials suppliers expanded into speculative working class housing development in the later years of the 19th century. Builders often built quickly, using poor materials and inexperienced labourers, hired casually rather than permanently employed. The construction and ownership of tenement blocks was good business, often achieving a return on capital in excess of 12 per cent per year. The majority of Lower East Side property owners were absentee landlords, primarily former residents and hereditary property owners. Many sublet apartments to sublessees, known to the tenants as cockroach landlords, who paid a set price to the landlord and then maximized their own profit by raising rents and squeezing as many people as possible into the available space (Mele, 2000). This system has obvious similarities to Kolkata's *thika* tenancy system, which is described later in this chapter. A survey carried out in the 1860s revealed that almost half a million people, about half the population of New York, lived in tenements. In the Lower East Side, the estimated population density was about 240,000 people per square mile, almost 1,000 per hectare. In some wards, the population density was greater, averaging more than 1,600 per hectare in the 10th Ward and exceeding 2,000 per hectare in parts of the 11th Ward. Apartments typically consisted of three rooms, only one of which had access to direct light and ventilation. Again, there are similarities to conditions in today's cities, in this case to informal settlements in Cairo and other Egyptian towns and cities. One block of New York's tenements has been preserved as the Lower East Side Tenement Museum. The average floor area of its apartments is about 325 square feet or 30 square metres, similar to the floor area currently provided in Indian Government low-income housing programmes. Sanitation took the form of privies situated in the back yards of apartment buildings (Limmer and Dolkart, n.d.).

After the passing of the Tenement House Act of 1879, each inhabitable room was required to have an opening to air. To meet this requirement, developers provided narrow airshafts between buildings, creating the notorious 'dumbbell' tenement arrangement. These shafts provided little air and next to no light but were still presumably an improvement on what had gone before. The arrangement, which is similar to that now routinely adopted by Cairo's informal builders, was the inspiration for Duke Ellington's 1940 recording 'Harlem Air Shaft'. Ellington is quoted as saying that 'you get the full essence of Harlem in an air shaft, hearing people making love, praying, fighting and snoring and smelling dinner'. Unfortunately, the reality was less pleasant than suggested by his rather romantic view, as indicated by a resident who noted that an airshaft quickly became so foul, presumably because of the wastes dumped into it, that people found it difficult to sleep in the rooms facing on to it (Mele, 2000). Residents of some of Cairo's informal areas would no doubt say much the same today. Analysis of 1908 Census figures showed that half of New York's East Side families slept three to four to a room, with five or more per room in nearly a quarter of all cases (Howe, 1976). The provision of airshafts had done little to reduce high population densities and the only light and air available to most rooms was via fetid airshafts. The situation was so bad that dumbbell tenements quickly became a byword for poor quality slum housing.

Europe and the USA in the 20th century

In Europe and the USA, the extension of formal planning systems during the first half of the 20th century greatly reduced opportunities to build informally. Nevertheless, instances of informality continued to arise, albeit on a much smaller scale than during the 19th century. In the United States, informal settlements, commonly referred to as Hoovervilles, developed in some cities during the depression years that followed the 1929 Wall Street Crash (History.com Editors, 2018). Box 2.1 describes the experience of Seattle in Washington State on the west coast of the USA.

In the UK, 'plotlands' flourished in some areas between the First and Second World Wars. These were regular subdivisions, created in the institutional space left by the gaps in less than comprehensive planning regulations. They initially lacked formal services. For instance, residents of Jaywick Sands in Essex organized a system for emptying Elsan chemical toilets for around 50 years, until a sewer was built (Ward, 2004); many households in Peacehaven, a plotland development near Brighton, initially relied on toilets discharging to pits (Informal interview by author). Local councils tolerated rather than encouraged them. Over the years, some disappeared while others were absorbed into formal systems. Even today informal development is an issue in some European countries (Tsenkova et al., 2008; Potsiou and Augustinius, 2010).

Box 2.1 Hoovervilles in Seattle

Following the 1929 crash, many of those made homeless following loss of work and access to formal housing responded by building shacks on vacant public land. In Seattle, shacks appeared in many locations in 1930 and 1931 but many were destroyed by the authorities following complaints from neighbours. By the mid-1930s, informal development was concentrated in eight settlements. The city Health Department estimated their combined population to be between 4,000 and 5,000 in late 1935. The largest settlement developed on Port of Seattle property that had been the site of a shipyard during World War I but was no longer occupied. Covering 9 acres of public land with a population of up to 1,200, it existed from 1931 to 1941. It had its sympathetic public officials until the land was needed for shipping facilities on the eve of World War II. A survey of the largest settlement in 1935 found nearly 500 self-built one-room huts scattered haphazardly across the site. All but 7 of the 693 inhabitants recorded in March 1934 were men, most of whom had been born outside the USA. The city imposed modest building and sanitation rules, required that women and children not live in the Hooverville, and expected the residents to keep order. This was done by an elected 'Vigilance Committee'. The leader of the committee explained that the population fluctuated and could reach 1,200 in the winter.

Early in 1941, the Seattle Health Department established a Shack Elimination Committee to identify unauthorized housing clusters and plan their removal. A survey located 1,687 shacks in five substantial colonies and many smaller ones. In April, residents of the main Hooverville were given notice to leave by May 1. Police officers doused the little structures with kerosene and lit them (based on Gregory, 2009).

Slums in the global South

In the 19th century, Calcutta (now Kolkata) was the principal city and administrative capital of colonial India. It grew rapidly throughout the 19th century, particularly after the construction of railways and development of jute and cotton factories in the second half of the century (Kundu, 2003). Low-income rental housing settlements, known locally as *bustees*, grew up in or close to residential and industrial areas as the Bengali elite made land available so that the poor people who provided services to them could build mud huts to house themselves. For this privilege, poor families paid a nominal rent. As the number of migrants grew, intermediaries, known as *thika* tenants began to rent parcels of land on which they built huts for rent. Many *bustees* occupied poorly drained land and initially their occupants relied on water taken from local ponds, known as tanks, which also provided places for people to bathe. Since wastewater drained to these tanks, the water supply quickly became polluted. As in British cities, sanitation took the form of dry 'service privies', one or two per *thika* tenancy 'plot', from which excreta was removed manually in earthen or tin vessels. *Bustees* built for workers at mills developed into townships, which formed the core of many of the 36 municipalities that eventually fused with neighbouring townships to form the single Kolkata metropolitan area (Thomas, 1997).

The shophouse tenements of Southeast Asian cities were similar in some respects to the tenements of North American cities but were generally only two to four storeys high. Like their North American counterparts, they tended to be long and narrow, with many internal rooms that had no direct access to light and air. Rather than apartments, the tenements were divided into single rooms, little more than cubicles, averaging only about 2.5 square metres in area. Primary tenants, fulfilling a role similar to that of Calcutta's *thika* tenants, rented out whole floors, retaining a portion for themselves and subletting the remaining space. In some cases, a single family of up to seven people might rent a single room but most rooms were rented to single people who had moved into the city looking for work. Service provision in early tenements was poor but most built during the 20th century had a kitchen, toilet, and washing facilities on each floor (Drakakis Smith, 1980: 93–95).

Poor living conditions also resulted when owners subdivided erstwhile higher-income housing to provide rented accommodation for poor households. This happened in Dublin in the early 19th century and increased in scale as rural to urban migration increased during and after the great famine. Large Georgian houses were subdivided into multiple single room dwellings, which were rented to poor families (Kearns, 1994). A similar process occurred in central Cairo, where the historic core area of Al-Darb al-Ahmar, located between the Al-Azhar Mosque and the Citadel, deteriorated over time. It suffers from problems that are common in such areas, the poor state of the building fabric, a high incidence of vacant plots, partly resulting from collapsing buildings and a declining economic base. The attitude of the Cairene middle and upper classes to such areas is graphically described in Yusuf Idris's short story *Dregs of the City* (Qa'a Al Madina), which describes the journey of Abdallah, a judge, into the slums in the vicinity of Al-Azhar Mosque (Idris, 1978). Although he is 'Egyptian through and through' with poor relations in Upper Egypt and experience of many places, Abdallah is amazed by the scenes unfolding before him and feels that he is 'sinking into a bottomless pit'. The story goes on to describe these scenes in more detail, pointing to the dilapidated buildings, the smell of earth mingling with that of humanity and the poverty of the people. Abdallah sees the 'low grimy buildings' as a 'continuation of the graveyard'. Idris wrote his story in the mid-20th century but little has changed and many Cairenes still view Al-Darb al-Ahmar as a no-go area despite the best efforts of the Aga Khan Trust for Conservation to upgrade services and restore the building fabric.

The growing importance of informal development in the South

Prior to the late 1800s, there was no clear distinction between formal and informal development. Calcutta's *bustees* provided poor quality housing but were not illegal, just as back-to-back housing created slums but did not contravene existing building regulations, such as they were. Informal settlement as such appears to date from the late 19th and early 20th century, with the first *favela* (the Brazilian term for an informal settlement) in Rio de Janeiro created in the late 1890s. Like many subsequent Brazilian *favelas*, it was located on a hill, on land that was not wanted by more conventional property interests. In 1904, there were about 100 shacks on the hill and this number grew steadily to reach about 800 by 1920 and 1,500 by the early 1930s. In the meantime, other *favelas* were forming on suitably located hills. Some of the early inhabitants of the *favelas* were former inhabitants of city-centre tenement housing, demolished for sanitary reasons in the early 20th century (Neuwirth, 2005).

The first squatter settlers in Rio were former enslaved people who had served in the army but had found no suitable accommodation when they returned to Rio after their service. In a similar way, the first settlers in Kibera, Nairobi's largest informal settlement, were Sudanese soldiers from the King's African Rifles, who had been allowed to live on farmland adjacent to their training ground. In Nairobi, as in many British colonies in Africa, access to urban areas was restricted to those officially cleared to work in those areas. Families were not allowed and workers were expected to live in barracks consisting of lines of single rooms with shared toilets and cooking facilities. Africans who arrived in cities without permission from the colonial authorities had to make their own living arrangements, building huts where they could find uncontested land on the edges of towns. By the 1930s, many thousands of casual labourers were living in 'self-built hovels' on the outskirts of Nairobi. The British authorities sometimes tolerated such developments and at other times tried to remove them, an attitude found among municipal authorities to this day.

In most cases, owners of demolished huts quietly moved back and rebuilt their dwellings once the authorities had moved away (Neuwirth, 2005).

Similarly, but rather later, the large informal settlement of Ezbet El Haggana on the outskirts of Cairo initially developed to provide services and housing for Frontier Guards stationed at a nearby army base. It occupies desert land and in 1977 only about 10 hectares were developed close to the Suez road at a location known as Kilo 4.5. The settlement grew incrementally through land claims as individuals staked out boundaries and then 'sold' smaller parcels of land to other individuals, who usually built a room and a wall to confirm the extent of their holding. In 1984, the area of these plots was typically in the range 200–500 square metres. Owners in the central more consolidated part of the settlement had further subdivided their land into smaller plots, typically occupying between 80 and 100 square metres. The population at this time was perhaps a few thousand (Sims, 1984). By the mid-2010s, Ezbet El Haggana's population had grown to about 1 million (Ain Shams University, 2014). The Egyptian government has never sanctioned development in Ezbet El Haggana, although residents do have some customary rights interpreted from aspects of Egypt's civil code pertaining to land claims in desert areas.

Alexandra Township, on the north-eastern outskirts of Johannesburg, followed another route to slum status. Located on erstwhile farming land, it was established as a township in 1905. It originally targeted the white population but lack of demand led to it being re-proclaimed as a 'non-white' township with 2,300 stands, each of approximately 1,000 m^2. Settlement started around 1910. The provision in the 1913 Land Act that no further freehold land could be proclaimed for black ownership severely restricted the supply of land for black settlement, forcing people into the relatively small settlements that already existed. The result in Alexandra, as in other South African townships, was densification and overcrowding, particularly after 1939, when the outbreak of war led to an increased demand for labour and so for shelter. At this point, a previously low-density development intended for relatively well-off people began to take on many of the characteristics associated with slums. Over the years, there were various proposals to demolish or rebuild Alexandra but it remains, with a population of about 350,000 on its 800 ha. Many of these are rental units, some located in the 'back yards' of plots (Morris, 2000). Creation of larger plots followed by their later subdivision into smaller units for rent occurred in other African cities. For example, as the demand for housing in and around Nairobi increased, the retired Sudanese soldiers who had settled Kibera started to subdivide their plots, build single room huts and rent these out. Today, Kibera is the biggest informal settlement in Nairobi but some of its 'villages' continue to be dominated by descendants of the original soldiers.

Informal settlements continued to form and expand throughout the first half of the 20th century but at a relatively slow rate. A transition to much more rapid expansion occurred in many countries around 1950. In some regions, population movements driven by political events contributed to this expansion. Kolkata, for instance, received two waves of refugees, following the partition of India in 1947 and the formation of Bangladesh in 1971. Similarly, some of Karachi's oldest informal settlements developed post-partition in 1947 to meet the housing needs of migrants from India. However, the main drivers worldwide were population growth and the movement of people from rural to urban areas. As noted in Chapter 1, there is academic debate about the roles of push and pull factors in creating this movement. Whatever the causes, informal sector development could not be ignored. The last part of this chapter reviews responses to slum formation from the 19th century through to the mid-20th century, indicating where they link with the different strands of current thinking. This leads into Chapter 3's more detailed assessment of concepts and responses developed since the mid-1950s and the ways in which they have influenced housing and infrastructure policies.

Nineteenth century responses to housing need

Public health legislation

In Britain, the 19th century saw successive attempts to legislate to prevent the worst aspects of slum housing. The focus was on setting the rules to be followed by developers to achieve acceptable minimum standards and provide basic sanitary conditions. In practice, progress was slow as those who benefited from the status quo resisted the introduction of binding legislation. Edwin Chadwick's 1842 report on the 'Sanitary Conditions of the Working Classes' identified the main cause of disease among the urban working class as the atmospheric impurities caused by decomposing animal and vegetable matter, damp and filth and close and overcrowded dwellings. In response, under his considerable influence, the 1843 Health of Towns Commission recommended radical improvements in sanitation, including a change from conservancy to water flushed toilet systems, discharging to sewers. In 1844, the Metropolitan Buildings Act required that all newly constructed buildings in London located within 30 metres of a public sewer must have connections to the sewer. Parliament passed a more general Public Health Act in 1848. This established a Central Board of Health, required corporate boroughs to take responsibility for drainage and the removal of nuisances, allowed non-corporate towns to set up local Boards of Health and indeed required such Boards where the death rate exceeded the national crude death rate of 23 per thousand over a period of seven years (Fee and Brown, 2005). No new house should be constructed without a privy connected either to the sewer or, if a sewer was not available, a cesspit. Builders were required to submit plans of their houses to the Board for approval and no further 'cellar dwellings' were to be built (Lumley, 1859).

While the 1848 Act was a step forward, it had practical limitations, not least the fact that non-corporate towns were not obliged to implement its recommendations if their death rate did not exceed the 23 per thousand figure.

The Act's recommendations were to be implemented with finance raised from local rates and, perhaps not surprisingly, it faced opposition from interested parties, including town councils, developers, and builders. Further legislation followed. The 1872 Public Health Act divided England and Wales into Health Authority districts, each having a responsible sanitary authority with an appointed Medical Officer of Health. The 1875 Public Health Act required that all new housing have self-contained sanitation and water services and was followed by a number of housing acts giving local authorities powers to demolish slum housing. The 1890 Housing of the Working Classes Act broke new ground in that it gave local authorities the powers to build houses, opening the way for the more positive interventions described later in this chapter.

The various acts and the local by-laws that followed them changed the layout of low-cost housing. In Preston for instance, access to privies serving houses built before the 1848 Act was either through the house itself or via a narrow alley or 'middenstead' running between the back yards, into which residents frequently dumped waste. After the 1848 Act, lobbies running between houses provided access to privies, with one lobby normally provided for two houses. After the introduction of new by-laws in 1880, privies backed onto wide ginnels or alleys running along the backs of the yards between two rows of houses (Quiney, 1986: 113). The changes led to increased space availability around houses and improved sanitary conditions, although the biggest improvements arguably came with the introduction of sewered WCs. Examples of houses with access lobbies and back alleys still exist in some towns in northern England, as illustrated in photos 2.1 and 2.2. In photo 2.1, the waste pipes on the back walls of the houses show that in-house sanitation has replaced the outside privies.

All these acts and by-laws relate to new building. In Britain, the 19th century also saw a slow growth in the powers of local government to deal with existing poor quality housing. The 1868 Artisans and Labourers' Dwellings Act gave local authorities the power to close any house considered unfit

Photo 2.1 Rear alley access to back yard toilets, Chester

Photo 2.2 Access alley to back yard between houses, Sheffield

for habitation by a Medical Officer of Health and to demand improvement or demolition by its owner. The 1875 Artisans and Labourers' Dwellings Improvement Act allowed local authorities to demolish a whole area if either the houses were deemed unfit for human habitation or poor housing was the cause of poor health. Take up of the latter Act was initially slow as, unlike the earlier Act, it required local authorities to buy land and property at the market price and pay for demolition. Neither Act provided for the replacement of demolished homes. Indeed, one of the earliest uses of demolition powers was by Birmingham Corporation, under Mayor Joseph Chamberlain, to clear central slum areas in the city to make way for the development of Corporation Street, one of the city's main commercial streets. Initially, the Corporation offered no alternative accommodation to the inhabitants of the 855 dwellings destroyed by the scheme. Eventually, in 1889, some 14 years after inauguration of the scheme, 102 artisan houses were provided on a part of the site that had proved to be unattractive to commercial interests. However, these were offered at a rent that was likely to be unaffordable to the original inhabitants (Upton, 2005).

In North America, legislation initially focused on improving conditions in the tenements. New York State passed a series of tenement house laws between 1867 and 1901. The first of these, commonly referred to as the 'Old Law', required that one privy should be provided for every 20 people, that a connection should be made to a sewer when one was available and that interior rooms should have a 3 foot (0.9 metre) square transom or opening above their doors. The 1879 Act required that all rooms in new tenements must have access to air, a requirement theoretically met by the dumbbell design. In practice, this design hardly constituted an improvement as 10 of the 14 rooms per floor on a standard 1,000 ft × 25 ft plot had access only to the almost lightless airshafts described earlier in this chapter (Hall, 1988). The draft Act limited building coverage to no more than 65 per cent of the area of a lot but the real estate lobby insisted that a clause was added allowing builders to lobby for permission to overbuild. This nullified any effect that the Act might have had in reducing densities; indeed, the dumbbell design, which became the norm until the passing of a new act in 1901, occupied about 80 per cent of the available space. Privies were to have an 'ostensible means of flushing' and be connected to the public sewer. However, the toilets provided were not always sanitary. Commonly referred to as 'school sinks' because they were first used in public schools, they were not cistern flush toilets. A 1903 observer noted that the janitors who were meant to flush the toilets with water each day often failed to do so because the job was 'disagreeable and the stench excessive' (Limmer and Dolkart, n.d.).

As in England, conditions did improve slowly, albeit with considerable resistance from people who benefited from existing systems. The 'improved' dumbbell design was far from satisfactory and the working class tenements were still widely viewed as slums. On both sides of the Atlantic, visionaries and reformers were looking for new ways of providing housing, some of which required nothing less than the restructuring of society. Their ideas and activities are now described.

'Model' housing companies and charitable trusts

From about 1830 onwards, 'model dwelling' companies provided rental housing for low-income people. In order to reduce rents and increase affordability, they paid a restricted dividend, typically around 5 per cent rather than the 7–10 per cent paid by mainstream housing companies. Charitable trusts, funded by endowments from rich philanthropists, also started to invest in housing for the poor. The trusts sought to achieve some return on capital, typically around 3 per cent rather than the 5 per cent sought by the model dwellings companies. The model dwellings approach sought to prove that a market approach could provide housing for the poor. Their basic assumption was that the housing problem could be alleviated if suppliers were restrained in their pursuit of profit, the properties were well built and managed, and the tenants could be persuaded to lead quiet and sober lives (Malpass, 2000: 34).

Model housing companies in London included the Metropolitan Association for Improving the Dwellings of the Industrious Classes, the Improved Industrial Dwellings Company (IIDC), and the Artisans' and Labourers' General Dwellings Company, founded in 1841, 1863, and 1867 respectively. The IIDC became the largest model dwellings company operating in central London, providing about 6,000 dwellings on 40 sites over a 40-year period. Its standard designs incorporated external staircases, on the basis that these provided fire escapes and increased exposure to fresh air, so limiting the risk from infectious diseases. All allowed through ventilation, with windows at the front and back of all apartments. Sir Sydney Waterlow, its founder, was a wealthy industrialist, philanthropist, and politician who served as Lord Mayor of London in 1872–73. He successfully lobbied the Public Works Loans Commissioners for model dwellings companies to receive loans at a preferential rate of 4 per cent. The rents charged on IIDC apartments typically ranged from 5s to 6s 6d per week, comparable with the rents of 2s 6d per room and 7s 6d for a three room lodging in the notorious Nichol slum (Wise, 2009). Waterlow's biographer claims that the death rate in IIDC tenements was only 9.9 people per 1,000 per year, only just over half that for London as a whole and much less than the 30–40 deaths per 1,000 per year found in the slums (Smalley, 1909).

Unlike the model housing companies, charitable trusts did not seek to generate a return on capital. Rather, their goal was to generate enough money from rents to fund maintenance and repair and to ensure that fund finances were self-sustaining. The most notable was the Peabody Donation Fund, set up in 1862 with funds provided by George Peabody, an American capitalist resident in London. It built its first tenement block in Spitalfields in 1864 and completed six estates during the 1860s. The later developments each typically provided between 250 and 525 dwellings. To implement the

Spitalfields scheme, it entered into a partnership with the architect Henry Darbishire and the builder Cubitt, which lasted for 20 years. After 1870, it became more difficult to obtain affordable sites in appropriate locations. The passing of the 1875 Artisans' and Labourers' Dwellings Improvement Act, which required that land cleared of slums be used as working class housing, eased the situation. The Peabody Fund purchased six cleared 'slum' sites at low prices from the Metropolitan Board of Works. The Board of Works accepted Peabody's offer reluctantly, mainly because no other parties were interested in purchasing the land, but may have spent around £1.5 million in clearing land for which Peabody only paid about £200,000. Clearly, this represented a significant subsidy (Malpass, 2000: 34–36).

Octavia Hill, the co-founder of Britain's National Trust and a prominent social reformer, took a different approach, setting up what was in effect a lettings management agency for a large number of individual and corporate landlords. Hill sought to influence the behaviour of poor people, her approach involving the establishment of a social compact between landlords and tenants. The former should keep their properties in good condition, carrying out repairs promptly when needed while the latter should pay their rents and live sober, responsible lives. She believed in decentralization and treating people in a way that enhanced their self-respect and was wary of philanthropic efforts that created dependency. An important aspect of her approach was the use of 'district visitors', volunteer women assigned to specific areas and tasked with providing help with domestic budgeting, tackling bad landlords, and gaining employment. Her district visitors enjoyed considerable autonomy and Hill claimed that responsibility was so decentralized that she did not know the number of dwellings managed according to her principles. In practice, there were limitations on the decentralization of responsibilities and she maintained close oversight over finances, with decentralized managers required to bring their books to her for checking every Thursday after rents had been collected.

More than 30 model housing companies and charitable trusts were operating in London in the second half of the 19th century. Most were small in comparison with the IIDC and the Peabody Fund. Model dwellings companies existed in other English cities but the number of dwellings produced remained very low in both absolute and proportional terms. The philanthropic and model housing approaches can be criticized on the grounds of their limited impact. By about 1890, they had housed more than 72,000 people, seemingly impressive but in practice not much more than London's annual population increase. Another criticism relates to their affordability. Rents were set at levels that excluded the poorest households, with the result that they generally housed members of the regularly employed and better-paid working classes and so deviated from their original purpose of housing only the poor. They did not altogether solve the problem of overcrowding. Most apartments provided one, two or three rooms, hardly adequate for the large families that were the norm during the period. On the positive side, they demonstrated that it was possible to combine high densities with improved water supply and sanitary conditions (Malpass, 2000: 37–41, citing earlier sources). The limitations of the approach have echoes in later experience, as will become clear in Chapter 5.

Planning for Utopia: the influence of Ebenezer Howard

Public health legislation sought to enforce minimum standards and thus prevent unscrupulous developers from building poorly serviced sub-standard housing. However, it did nothing to provide better housing. During the 19th century, successive reformers including Robert Owen, Titus Salt, William Hesketh Lever, and George Cadbury had sought to develop 'model' housing projects. It is perhaps significant that all four were factory owners with a social conscience and that their initial aim was to provide decent housing for their workers. The aims of Owen and Cadbury certainly went beyond this but it is doubtful whether their schemes had a direct influence on what followed. The same is not true of Ebenezer Howard and the Garden City movement. Howard is often referred to as the father of town planning and his ideas have continued to resonate, even though many aspects of his vision were never realized. From the point of view of this book, the key point about Howard is his belief that building new towns on greenfield sites would provide better living conditions than 19th century industrial cities and, by drawing people away from those cities, reduce their population density, leading to improved living conditions for their remaining inhabitants. This belief has underpinned a series of initiatives over the years, from the original garden cities, through the British new towns of the 1940s to 1960s, to new capitals like Islamabad, Brasilia, and Chandigarh and Egypt's new cities and settlements in the desert. In all these cases, the belief has been that it is better to start afresh and build anew rather than entering into the messy business of improving and servicing poorly planned slums and informal developments.

The garden city concept brought together a number of pre-existing ideas, most of which came from those who could loosely be termed radical thinkers, who focused on the need for land reform, cooperative enterprise, and profit sharing in production. Howard believed that these were requirements for a move towards new and better forms of decentralized social organization, free of inequalities and hence of class struggle. Decentralization is clearly central to his garden city concept. Following the Russian anarchist Peter Kropotkin, Howard believed that the future belonged to small-scale cooperatives, while large cities, with their disparities in power, wealth, and opportunity, would eventually disappear (Hall, 1986: Chapter 4). In practice, only two garden cities were built, at Letchworth and Welwyn Garden City and both fell some way short of realizing Howard's vision in full. Nevertheless, Howard's ideas have been influential, most obviously in the development of new towns in the UK and other countries but also in thinking on decentralization. He certainly influenced John Turner, whose ideas are summarized in Chapter 3.

Public housing: direct intervention by the state

In the UK, Part III of the 1890 Housing of the Working Classes Act allowed local authorities to buy land and undertake building programmes in order to provide housing for people made homeless by slum clearance. The Act led directly to the early London County Council housing estates. The first of these was the Boundary Estate in the East End of London, built to replace an existing slum, the Old Nichol, which one 1896 report described as 'the blackest pit in London'. Completed in 1900, the estate consisted of five storey brick structures placed around a central circus, encircling a raised area formed with the rubble of the old slum (Wise, 2009). Other estates followed in the first decade of the 20th century, including Totterdown Fields in Tooting, White Hart Lane in Tottenham, Norbury in South London, and Old Oak Estate in West London. All these were 'cottage' estates, providing houses and low-rise flats. Their architectural style was influenced by the Arts and Crafts movement and the layouts of the later estates were influenced by the planning concepts introduced in the slightly earlier Hampstead Garden Suburb (Quiney, 1986: 133–147). To reduce costs, houses were small with the smallest units having less than 600 square feet (55.5 m^2) of floor space and some rooms were only 10 feet (3 m) square. The early estates provided around 30 housing units per acre (75 per hectare) reducing to about 25 per acre in the Old Oak Estate. Despite this, the housing was not affordable to the poorest families. The council had not consulted the residents of the Nichol on the design of the Boundary Estate. Of the 140 selected people from among those evicted who were given first refusal on a tenement in the scheme, only 10 took up the offer. It seems that the high rents and, in some cases, lack of access to the yards, sheds, and workshop facilities that they required to carry out their informal businesses deterred them. Another deterrent factor was the need to accept the rules and regulations imposed on tenement block residents (Wise, 2009). As will become clear in later chapters, all these concerns foreshadow those of informal settlement residents in the cities of the South.

A series of housing acts in the period between the First and Second World Wars provided further encouragement to local authorities in England to build affordable housing for rent. The total number of rented local authority units increased from about 24,000 in 1914 to over a million in 1939, around 10 per cent of the total housing stock (Stone, 2003).

In the USA, the idea of government involvement in housing faced more resistance than in Europe. Some housing providers adopted the 'limited dividend' approach described earlier in this chapter. Charles Abrams dismissed the limited dividend approach stating that 'The limited-dividend scheme will remain inherently unsound as long as there is a gap between the market return on speculative enterprises and the return granted to "enlightened investors"'. For this reason he believed that such schemes would continue to be mere 'demonstrations' (Henderson, 2000). In the USA and the UK, a variant on the limited dividend approach still exists in the form of schemes that allow investors to construct housing for sale on the open market if the scheme also includes a percentage of affordable or low-income housing. There are some similarities to the system in Mumbai, where increases in the 'floor space index' and the use of transferable development rights allow developers to replace existing slum areas with apartments, some of which are for sale or rent on the market. We will return to this in Chapter 5.

It was not until the New Deal in the 1930s that the US Government started to involve itself in the housing sector. One of the catalysts for change was Catherine Bauer's book *Modern Housing*, published in 1934. In the same year, the US Government established the Federal Housing Administration, which supported housing activity through guaranteed mortgages. In 1937, it followed this with the Wagner-Steagall Act, through which the federal government expressed its interest in providing public rental housing. Some momentum built up, at least in the more liberal seaboard cities, in some cases aided by the need to provide housing for workers during the Second World War. In Los Angeles, the reform-minded mayor, Fletcher Bowron, supported the development of public housing, some for resale to residents. Unfortunately, Los Angeles turned away from public housing in the 1950s. Its change of heart resulted partly from racial tension following the so-called Zoot Suit Riots in 1943. However, the main driving factor was the changing climate of opinion following the beginning of the Cold War and Senator McCarthy's witch hunt of any person or body that could conceivably be considered left of centre (Starr, 2005). The public housing that did remain into the 1960s and beyond was in many places ghettoized and stereotyped as sink housing occupied by the undeserving poor.

In contrast, the UK saw a boom in public housing from the late 1940s through the 1950s. Local authorities built new estates to replace unsatisfactory inner city slums. Glasgow provides a good example. Its new estates at Drumchapel, Castlemilk, Pollok, and Easterhouse were large and situated on the periphery of the city, several miles from the inner city areas from which their inhabitants were mainly drawn. The Glasgow estates mainly consisted of walk-up tenements but English cities often opted for apartment blocks, for instance Hulme in Manchester and Park Hill in Sheffield. Many of the architects of these new blocks were strongly influenced by the modernist movement. They believed that good design with proper services and adequate space standards would eliminate the problems associated with the old slums. One scheme celebrated at the time was Peter and Alison Smithson's Robin Hood Gardens Estate in Poplar, London. This consisted of two blocks, one of 7 storeys and the second of 10 storeys. In common with others, these schemes incorporated the 'deck access', commonly referred to as 'street in the sky', concept, in which individual apartments fronted on to wide external balconies, which acted as the 'streets'.

Disillusion soon set in. Many estates were located at the urban periphery far from job opportunities and with limited social services. Some became by-words for deprivation and social separation. Deck access walkways did not in fact function like traditional streets. Rather, the layout, with doors on one side only, encouraged people to retreat behind their front doors so that the sense of community that allows people in 'traditional' developments to work together to maintain their shared environment was lost. The inevitable result was damage, dirt, and dilapidation. The lack of basic social and recreational facilities created significant problems, even in more conventional schemes. Last, but not least, poor building construction, leading to problems such as dampness, was a feature of some schemes.

As the limitations of the new developments became evident, families moved out leaving those with few hopes or prospects to soldier on in an increasingly unpleasant environment, with high unemployment rates and many boarded up properties. The populations of the Glasgow estates fell significantly. That of Drumchapel fell from about 35,000 in 1971 to just over 13,000 at the 2001 census (Garnham, 2018). That of Easterhouse, 56,843 at the 1971 census, had fallen to 8,923 at the 2011 census. Manchester City Council demolished the Hulme blocks in the early 1990s, replacing them with low-rise housing. Rehabilitation of the Park Hill estate started in 2009, with flats revamped as up-market private apartments. Robin Hood Gardens was demolished in 2017, despite efforts to list it as a historical complex and thus save it from demolition (Braidwood, 2017).

Housing associations: moving away from the state

With the advent of the Thatcher Government in 1979, overall thinking in the UK moved sharply away from the idea that government should be a direct provider of houses. Middle and higher-income housing is now produced almost exclusively by the private sector while housing associations are the main providers of the 'social' housing that was once provided by local government. Many housing associations were formed with a specific remit to take over rental housing from local authorities. Day-to-day management duties are carried out by professional staff with oversight and guidance provided by a board, typically including representatives of the local authority and the tenants with some 'independent' members. The role of government is to regulate the sector. Local authorities provide oversight, partly through their involvement in the management boards of housing associations. Some on the right of the political spectrum argue for a greater role for the private sector and less regulation citing the high salaries earned by some housing association executives (Clark, 2015).

Relevance to low-income countries

Much of this chapter has been concerned with responses to urban housing problems in Western industrialized countries. However, these responses are relevant to housing needs in low-income countries. One reason for this is that some of the models developed in the West have been applied in the developing world. Thus, for instance, the standard building and planning codes followed in developing countries often draw directly on Western models, sometimes with rather unfortunate results. It is widely believed, for example, that the building regulations for Nairobi included a requirement for a snow-loading allowance, apparently because the building regulations for Nairobi were based on those of a town in the north of England. Whether or not this is true, it does illustrate the point that standards for colonized countries were often adapted from those in use in colonizing countries. Ebenezer Howard's thinking on garden cities presaged the efforts of governments and their consultants to deal with housing problems in existing cities by building new towns, and on occasion new societies, from scratch. We will look at this phenomenon more closely in Chapter 5 when we consider the new city and new settlement policies of the Egyptian government. Western governments have moved sharply away from any direct involvement in housing provision but some governments in developing countries have not followed their example, as will also become clear in Chapter 5. While public housing projects in developing countries have not necessarily faced the same social challenges as their counterparts in the developed world, we will see that they have been problematic in different ways. To date, the concept of housing associations has not found a place in the housing policies of developing countries but the possibilities that they offer, particularly where government intervention has proved to be ineffective, are worth considering and will be explored in Chapter 10.

References

Ain Shams University (2014) *The Integrated Case Study, Informal Areas Development Approaches in Egypt: Processes and Roles 'Ezbet El Haggana'*, Document prepared for IUSD Master's Program 2014, IUSD-ASU, Ain Shams University, Cairo. https://issuu.com/iusd.cairo/docs/ics2014_ezbet_el-haggana_presentati

Braidwood, E. (2017) In pictures: Robin Hood Gardens demolition begins, *Architectural Journal*, 7 September 2017. https://www.architectsjournal.co.uk/news/in-pictures-robin-hood-gardens-demolition-begins (accessed 1 January 2021).

Clark, R. (2015) Why housing associations are the true villains of the property crisis, *The Spectator Australia*, 25 July 2015. https://www.spectator.com.au/2015/07/housing-associations-have-failed-to-build-houses/ (accessed 13 August 2025).

Drakakis Smith, D. (1980) *Urbanisation, housing and the development process*, St Martin's Press, New York.

Dudley, E. (1993) *The critical villager: beyond community participation*, Routledge, London.

Fee, E. and Brown, T.M. (2005) The Public Health Act of 1848, *Bulletin of the World Health Organization*, 83 (11): 866–867. https://iris.who.int/handle/10665/269524 (accessed 13 August 2025).

Garnham, L. (2018) *Exploring neighbourhood change: life, history, policy and health inequality across Glasgow*, Glasgow Centre for Population Health. https://strathprints.strath.ac.uk/91042/ (accessed 13 August 2025).

Gregory, J. (2009) *The Great Depression in Washington State: Hoovervilles and homelessness*, Civil Rights and Labor History Consortium, University of Washington. https://depts.washington.edu/depress/hooverville.shtml (accessed 1 January 2021).

Hall, P. (1988) *Cities of tomorrow: an intellectual history of urban planning and design in the twentieth century*, Blackwell, Oxford.

Henderson, A.S. (2000) *Housing and the democratic ideal: the life and thought of Charles Abrams*, Columbia University Press, New York.

History.com Editors (2018) *Hoovervilles*, A&E Television Networks. https://www.history.co.uk (accessed 13 August 2025).

Howe, I. (1976) *The immigrant Jews of New York: 1881 to the present*, Routledge and Kegan Paul, London.

Idris, Y. (1978) *The cheapest nights*, Heinemann, London.

Kearns, K.C. (1994) *Dublin tenement life: an oral history*, Gill and Macmillan, Dublin.

Kundu, N. (2003) *Urban slums reports: the case of Kolkata, India*, Case study produced for the Global Report on Human Settlements, 2003, University College, London. https://www.scribd.com/document/251980727/The-Case-of-Kolkata-India-by-Dr-Nitai-Kundu-in-UNDERSTANDING-SLUMS-Case-Studies-for-the-Global-Report-on-Human-Settlements-2003 (accessed 13 August 2025).

Limmer, R. and Dolkart, A.S. (no date) *The tenement as history and housing*, Thirteen Media with Impact. http://www.thirteen.org/tenement/eagle.html (accessed 16 August 2019).

Lumley, W.G. (1859) *The new sanitary laws*, Shaw and Sons, London. https://archive.org/stream/newsanitarylaws00britgoog#page/n5/mode/2up (accessed 17 August 2019).

Malpass, P. (2000) *Housing associations and housing policy: a historical perspective*, Macmillan, Basingstoke.

Meggitt, J.J. (1998) *Paul, poverty and survival*, T&T Clark, Edinburgh.

Mele, C. (2000) *Selling the Lower East Side: culture, real estate and resistance in New York, 1880–2000*, University of Minnesota Press, Minneapolis.

Moore, J. (1945) *Portrait of Elmbury*, Bloomsbury, London.

Morris, P. (2000) Alexandra Township – A history, lesson for urban renewal and some challenges for planners. Paper presented at *SA Planning History Study Group, Planning for Reconstruction and Transformation Conference, University of Natal (Durban), May 2000.*

Neuwirth, R. (2005) *Shadow cities: a billion squatters, a new urban world*, Routledge, New York and Abingdon, UK.

Potsiou, C. and Augustinius, C. (2010) *Informal development in Europe: experiences from Albania and Greece*, UN-Habitat, Nairobi. https://unhabitat.org/sites/default/files/download-manager-files/Informal%20Urban%20Development%20in%20Europe%20%2C%20Experiences%20from%20Albania%20and%20Greece.pdf (accessed 18 November 2019).

Quiney, A. (1986) *House and home: a history of the small English house*, BBC, London.

Scobie, A. (1986) Slums, sanitation, and mortality in the Roman world, *Klio* 68 (1986): 399–433. https://doi.org/10.1524/klio.1986.68.68.399

Sims, D. (1984) 'Reconnaissance Survey: Ezbet el Haggana', Unpublished note produced during project preparation for the Extension of Municipal Services (EMS) Project in Greater Cairo.

Smalley, E. (1909) *The life of Sir Sydney Waterlow*, Edward Arnold, London. http://www.archive.org/stream/lifeofsirsydneyh00smalrich/lifeofsirsydneyh00smalrich_djvu.txt (accessed 17 August 2019).

Starr, K. (2005) 'Foreword' in D. Parson, *Making a better world: public housing, the red scare, and the direction of modern Los Angeles*, University of Minnesota Press, Minneapolis.

Stone, M.E. (2003) *Social housing in the UK and US: evaluation, issues and prospects*, research paper, Goldsmith's College, London. https://research.gold.ac.uk/id/eprint/33822/ (accessed 13 August 2025).

Thomas, F.C. (1997) *Calcutta poor: elegies on a city above pretense*. M.E. Sharpe Inc, also published by Penguin, India as *Calcutta: The human face of poverty*.

Tsenkova, S., Badyina, A. and Potsiou, C. (2008) *In search for sustainable solutions for informal settlements in the ECE Region: challenges and policy responses*, Economic Commission for Europe, Committee on Housing and Land Management. https://www.unece.org/fileadmin/DAM/hlm/sessions/docs2008/informal.notice.1.pdf (accessed 18 November 2019).

Upton, C. (2005) *Living back-to-back*, Phillimore, Chichester.

Ward, C. (2002) *Cotters and squatters, housing's hidden history*, Fig Leaves Publications, Nottingham.

Ward, C. (2004) *The hidden history of housing*, History and Policy Papers. http://www.historyandpolicy.org/policy-papers/papers/the-hidden-history-of-housing#plot (accessed 25 June 2025).

Wise, S. (2009) *The blackest streets: the life and death of a Victorian slum*, Vintage Books, London.

CHAPTER 3
Responses to informality

The previous two chapters have shown that, while largely eliminated in Western countries, informal development continues to provide most of the shelter needs of the urban poor in towns and cities across the Global South. Governments have typically responded to this situation with programmes to provide formal housing. Such programmes have been effective in Singapore and Hong Kong, both relatively small and wealthy city states, and have made a significant contribution to meeting housing needs in China. Elsewhere, formal low-income housing schemes are often isolated islands of generally poorly designed and maintained units in a sea of informal housing. Even in China, informal housing occurs in 'urban villages', although this informality is different in many respects from that found in other countries (Webster et al., 2016).

This chapter examines the development of thinking on the options for responding to the situation of pervasive informality. It first explores Jacob Crane's concept of self-help housing and moves on to the ideas of Charles Abrams and John F.C. Turner, two influential figures in the development of thinking on responses to housing needs in rapidly growing cities. Turner's ideas were contested, not least by Rod Burgess, whose detailed criticism of Turner's ideas from a Marxist perspective is examined next. Attention then turns to the World Bank's approach to sites and services and upgrading projects, as represented by one of its seminal thinkers, Alain Bertaud. Michael Stone's arguments regarding shelter poverty are briefly examined, as are the contrasting views of those who believe that housing problems are attributable to over-regulation by government. The next section provides an overview of the ideas of Hernando De Soto and his critics on the importance or otherwise of action to formalize land and property rights. It is arguable that De Soto's approach pays insufficient attention to institutional realities and so attention then turns to institutional aspects of informality, drawing on the ideas of Douglass North, Peter Evans, and Elinor Ostrom. The final section in the chapter returns to the question of property rights and land tenure, focusing on the arguments for thinking that goes beyond a simple division between formality and informality.

Jacob Crane and self-help housing

As explained in Chapter 2, some people have always built their own houses. However, formal recognition of the self-help option's role in meeting the housing needs of poor people only developed in the 20th century, starting in Sweden in 1904 and spreading to other European countries in the 1920s. Early programmes were pragmatic responses to specific historic conditions. Most were relatively short-lived and their effect on government policies was limited (Harris, 1999). The concept reached the developing world in 1939 when the Housing Authority of Ponce, Puerto Rico initiated a self-help housing scheme. This worked on the principle that slum dwellers should be encouraged to move their shacks to new sites in serviced subdivisions. In fact, most people replaced or extended their shacks, making it perhaps the first sites and services scheme. During the 1940s, aided self-help became central to Puerto Rico's housing policy with 10,000 owner-built dwellings completed by 1960. The authorities in Barbados and Jamaica adopted a similar approach. The approach was replicated in other countries, including Colombia and Peru, South Africa, the Gold Coast (Ghana's pre-independence name), Kenya, and India (Harris, 1998).

The phrase 'aided self-help' was coined in the mid-1940s by Jacob Crane, who played a large part in promoting the Ponce scheme and the policy initiatives that flowed from it, first as Assistant Director of the US Housing Administration and later at the US Housing and Home Finance Agency. Crane argued that aided self-help made sense not only on grounds of financial expediency, but also as an element of indigenous economic and cultural development. Richard Harris has described his 'Huts and Houses in the Tropics' (Crane, n.d.) as the first systematic attempt to argue for a programme of aided self-help in the developing world. In this document, Crane noted the wide range of approaches to housing provision from 'traditional' huts built by people themselves using locally available material to contractor-built housing using 'modern' materials. While 'traditional' huts provide basic shelter, they are often crowded together, with earth floors, verminous roofs and walls, and only the most basic water supply and sanitation facilities. In contrast, the 'modern' approach to housing provision produces serviced units that provide adequate shelter but at a cost that is unaffordable to individual families, even where some form of mortgage is available at a low rate of interest. For government, the financial commitment required for a comprehensive low-income housing programme is similarly unaffordable; making any form of conventional housing programme unworkable without massive external assistance.

In response to this situation, Crane proposed what he described as 'self-help plus', in which the 'plus' was governmental assistance. This assistance should take two forms, first the provision of land and utilities, which cannot be provided by individual families, and second research into new materials and processes for producing those materials. He argued that priority should be given to solving the problems of land and sanitation, his concern with the latter echoing that of 19th century sanitary reformers. Builders should use locally available materials, which should be improved where possible using industrial and semi-industrial methods. Examples of the latter might include cement-stabilized earth blocks and simple brick kilns. In addition to studying the 'materials problem' and encouraging families to use those materials, government should also assist by arranging for their storage and distribution.

Crane assumed that individual households would do most of the construction work themselves, using a combination of locally and externally sourced materials as appropriate. Government should provide simple plans, arrange for the provision of locally unobtainable materials and tools, and provide small loans, repayable over a period of up to 20 years. This would not happen automatically and Crane identified the need for a specialist ministry, department or agency to identify, engage, and train competent people, assess problems and formulate a programme to respond to those problems. He emphasized the need to deal with issues of land and utilities. While recognizing that implementing a programme would be a formidable challenge for inexperienced governments, he suggested that there was no realistic alternative and ended by posing the question, 'what are governments for unless to tackle the great problems which their people cannot cope with unaided?'

Crane's ideas are little known today but they clearly influenced later thinking on low-income housing. In particular, the World Bank's approach to sites and services projects had much in common with his concept of 'land and utilities'.

Charles Abrams and core housing

Charles Abrams was born in Tsarist-controlled Vilna, then in Poland but now in Lithuania, in 1902, but his family moved to the USA in 1904 to escape anti-Jewish persecution and settled in New York. He qualified as a lawyer in the 1920s, attending night school while working as a clerk in a lawyer's office. He was one of the primary authors of the legislation to create the New York City Housing Authority (NYCHA), created in 1934, and subsequently served as NYCHA's first general counsel, later playing a prominent role in the development of housing policy in New York and the USA as a whole. From 1952 onwards, he undertook many tasks for the United Nations, advising on housing issues in 21 countries (Henderson, 2000). On several of his missions, he was accompanied by the architect Otto Koenigsberger and together they developed a range of ideas on housing in lower-income countries (Napier, 2002). These ideas built on those of Jacob Crane and complement those of John Turner. The focus here is on his advocacy of core housing (Abrams, 1964).

Abrams' starting point was his observation that self-help works best in small communities where building traditions still prevail so that residents have the knowledge and skills required to build their own houses. Recognizing this, the developer, normally a government department, should be responsible for laying out plots, constructing core houses and providing services. Individual owners should then be responsible for extending their houses, either undertaking extensions themselves or hiring others to carry out the work.

This would facilitate 'progressive development' while providing people with secure basic shelter from the time that they acquired a plot. To achieve this aim, the core house should be a liveable minimum unit, providing one room for small families and two rooms for larger families, and allow for the possibility of future horizontal and vertical extension. The building materials required to facilitate expansion should be available through local building suppliers. Water and sanitation should be available from the time that the house was occupied (Abrams, 1964).

Napier (2002) criticized Abrams' approach, noting the requirement that extensions be built in accordance with plans provided by the project developer. He recognized that this would help to ensure that basic standards were maintained but argued that it would result in housing schemes that looked little different from other government-built mass housing schemes. He went on to suggest that core housing, as proposed by Abrams and Koenigsberger, was a highly managed and limited form of self-help and represented an essentially technical solution to the conceptual problem of bringing together formal and informal development processes. The parameters within which this partnership operated were defined by the public sector, which decided on the site and house layouts and level of service provision. Potential residents would become involved at a later stage in the process, and thus had no input into fundamental decision-making. Napier's critique encapsulates the debate, which recurs throughout this book, between those who emphasize the need to ensure that housing initiatives meet technical requirements and advocates for a more community-led and bottom-up approach to housing. Reality is arguably more nuanced than suggested by those holding extreme views on both sides of this argument.

Abrams also promoted the concept of government investment in partially complete housing units, to be completed by their owners. Government would provide those elements of a house that were more difficult to construct, typically the foundations, the roof and its supports, windows and doors, leaving owners to arrange construction of walls, finishes, and other components. This concept underlies the roof-loan schemes that were implemented in several countries and will be considered further in Chapter 5.

John Turner: housing by people

The English architect John F.C. Turner discovered the work of Patrick Geddes in 1948 while a student at the Architectural Association and was fascinated by Geddes' 'biological' approach to city planning. At a meeting in Venice, around 1950, he met Eduardo Neira, a Peruvian architect planner, and this led directly to an invitation to work with Neira in Peru, an invitation that Turner took up six years later (World Bank, 2000). Neira had been one of the founders of a new political party, Acción Popular, which was committed to providing support for genuine community-based social action. In January 1958, not long after Turner had arrived in Peru, a major earthquake hit Arequipa, the second city of Peru, damaging many houses and leaving around 100,000 people homeless. The Peruvian public works ministry had seconded Turner to work in the Oficina de Asistencia Técnica a las Urbanizaciones Populares de Arequipa (OATA), which had been created by Neira in 1955. Urbanización Popular was the term then used in Peru for informal settlements and OATA had been set up to assist the inhabitants of these settlements, perhaps the first example of formal government support to the informal sector. Turner persuaded the Mayor of Arequipa that the funds that were available for earthquake reconstruction should be used to assist the self-build housing efforts of the inhabitants of the urbanizaciones populares rather than for new housing. He and his colleagues quickly realized that their professional assumptions often failed to correspond with realities on the ground so that, despite their formal architectural training, they were reliant on the knowledge and experience of their 'clients'. The initial professionally produced designs were inadequate in some respects, with the result that the initial one-way communication, with 'clients' following the instructions of professionals, was replaced by a more collaborative approach, which utilized the knowledge of the local builder who acted as overseer and buyer and distributor of building materials.

This experience underpinned much of Turner's subsequent thinking. In an early paper (Turner, 1968, quoted by Yap, 1989) he argued that the circumstances of the user determined their priorities. Poor migrants, whom he referred to as bridgeheaders, initially looked for cheap rental accommodation, only later integrated into the city, acquiring and developing property and becoming what Turner termed consolidators. As their income increased, they became 'status seekers', who prioritized modern amenities over location and tenure. In *Freedom to Build* (Turner 1972), Turner noted that the word housing can be used as a noun or a verb. Used as a noun, it describes a commodity or product. Used as a verb, it refers to a process or activity. The way in which housing is evaluated depends on whether it is viewed as a noun or a verb. If the former, the focus will be on standards, financial costs, time, and human effort expended in producing the housing. This says nothing about whether the users of the housing believe that it either meets or frustrates their needs. Standards and other measures of material quality have their uses but it is only those who have been involved in the activity of housing themselves who can evaluate the results of that activity. There is no point in tearing down 'substandard' houses if the people who live in them have nowhere else to go. The bridgeheader-consolidator-status seeker model has since been criticized as being too simplistic. For instance, Repestro (2010) quotes the finding of Edwards (1983) that residential mobility among poor households was as much a reaction to changing conditions in the housing market as a response to changes in their demand for housing.

Turner further developed his ideas in his book *Housing by People* (Turner, 1976), in which he reiterated the point that informal housing is not a problem but rather a resource that meets the shelter needs of low-income people at a price that they can afford. Those who live in houses and occupy residential areas should play a major role in decision-making on those houses and areas. He illustrated his argument with two examples from Mexico City, which he described as the 'supportive shack' and the 'oppressive house'. The supportive shack housed a car painter and his family and was located in the back yard of a house belonging to a *comadre* (leader, translated literally as godmother) of a rag-picking community, who had been given a new house by the authorities when the shantytown next to the municipal solid waste dump had been demolished. As a *comadre* of the rag pickers, she was able to give the car painter access to the dump, so that he could make slightly more than the minimum required for subsistence living. Thanks to his rent-free living and the free access to the *comadre's* water supply and toilet facilities, he was able to save a small amount for later use in purchasing a plot of land. His relationship with the *comadre* provided de facto security of tenure. Turner commented that such relationships are rarely broken. He went on to assert that the housing matched the car painter household's priorities, meeting their immediate needs while allowing them to save for better housing in the future.

The oppressive house was occupied by a semi-employed mason, his under-employed wife, and student son. It was located in a public housing project, intended for those, such as the mason's family, who had been displaced from shantytowns. Before relocation to the housing project, the family had supplemented the mason's irregular income by running a small shop. Their low transportation and housing expenditure, estimated at only 5 per cent of income, had meant that they were able to eat fairly well and maintain a fair level of health, despite their low income. The move had allowed them to live in a vastly improved modern house but at a considerable cost. Because vending was not allowed from their new location, their income had decreased while their rent and travel costs had increased, with 55 per cent of their income spent on rent and utility costs and a further 5 per cent on transport to work. Turner observed that the result was a decrease in their food budget and suggested that the 'improvement' in the family's housing had led to a significant deterioration in their circumstances, as assessed in human and economic terms. He concluded that the use value of the supportive shack more closely matched the needs of its occupiers than did that of the oppressive house, despite the fact that the market value of the latter was clearly higher.

Based on these and other similar examples, Turner concluded that standardized processes cannot meet the diverse needs of poor people. Rather, there is a need for housing processes that recognize the interaction between people, their activities, and the housing that allows them to undertake those activities. Once this is accepted, it becomes clear that approaches based on local control are preferable to centralized approaches, not least because the latter require forecasts of demand, which will always be wrong. Centralized housing programmes will inevitably result in a standardized 'one-size-fits-all' approach to housing, which minimizes variety and cannot address the different needs of different households and changes in those needs over time. The result will be a mismatch between households' housing priorities and the housing that they get. As the mismatch increases, so will user dissatisfaction, leading to a decrease in user investment and an increasing reliance on outside resources (Turner, 1976: 51). When these resources are not available, as will often be the case, deterioration in the housing fabric will inevitably occur. Harris (2003) believed that the emphasis on local control and user autonomy was Turner's most important contribution to the housing debate. Even here, he had been preceded to some extent by Jacob Crane, who referred to the desirability of local control in his later writings but did not develop the concept as far as Turner.

Turner recognized that local autonomy is dependent on the availability of resources. Building materials and equipment, manual and managerial skills, building land, and financial credit, must be accessible and their users must be free to employ them in ways that meet their requirements, without inhibiting the freedom of others. He argued that the role of higher levels of government is not to provide housing but rather to pass and administer appropriate laws and ensure access to basic resources. Prescriptive law, defining what must be done, may be necessary in some fields, for instance the design and installation of major utility systems. However, the aim should be to maximize use of proscriptive laws that set limits on what can be done but leave individual actors freedom to make their own decisions within those limits. The use of a proscriptive approach will facilitate the development of variety in responses to housing needs.

Turner distinguished between relatively centralized and monolithic formal systems and informal systems, which 'are networks of independent local builders and suppliers, generally contracted by small proprietors and individual households' (Turner, 1976: 129). He suggested that, while citizen participation in centrally administered housing programmes requires more time and money per unit than for units provided in a 'conventional' top-down way, this is not the case for locally self-governed systems. The key question is then 'whose participation in whose decisions?', or to put it another way, who has the power to decide? In urban areas, water, electricity, and other utility services are usually supplied from a central source through a more or less hierarchical system. In order to ensure equitable supply, the overall network has to be centrally planned and administered. However, centralized service providers do not attempt to provide facilities within the plot boundary, recognizing that this is best left to individual households. There is similarly room for intermediate organizations, perhaps associations of consumers, to take responsibility for the local systems that connect central systems to individual consumers. Turner notes that this option is both relatively common and highly desirable in localities with low incomes or difficult terrain. Only in exceptional circumstances should central authorities provide local goods and services. These ideas prefigure the philosophy of NGOs such as the Orangi Pilot Project in Pakistan and Slum Dwellers International, which are considered in Chapters 7 and 8, and the World Bank's concept of 'unbundling' of responsibilities for service provision.

Rod Burgess: a Marxist response to Turner

Turner's views have attracted criticism, particularly from left-wing thinkers. One of the most trenchant critiques is that of Rod Burgess, who approached Turner's work from a Marxist perspective (Burgess, 1982). Burgess argued that informal housing was cheap because of the structural and organizational features of its system of construction, which were determined by the prevailing capitalist mode of production rather than issues of technology and managerial and legal organization. In a similar critique, Hans Harms argued that self-help housing had always emerged as a policy solution to housing problems in capitalist societies when there was a crisis in capitalism (Harms, 1982).

A key feature of Burgess' critique is his argument that, in focusing on the use value of housing, Turner pays insufficient attention to the fact that housing is also a commodity with a market or exchange value. In relation to the self-help house he posed the question, 'can it best be understood ... as a use value for its producer, or do we have to take into account those instances where it acquires exchange value?' (Burgess, 1982: 60). His own answer to the question was clear: viewing housing and land primarily in terms of use values alone ignores the possibilities that the producer may view the house as a commodity and that one person's use value may be another person's exchange value and vice versa. While self-help housing differs from other commodities in that self-builder producers construct a house for their own use, they do have the option of offering it for sale on the market.

Burgess also criticized Turner's distinction between centralized bureaucratically controlled and autonomous self-managed forms of production. He argued that Turner was incorrect in assuming that the low cost of informal housing is primarily a consequence of technology and managerial and legal organization. Rather it depends on the manipulation of these elements by the dominant capitalist mode of production. The self-builder reduces costs by avoiding administrative overheads and finance capital costs, making their own materials or buying them from petty commodity sources and using cheap and unprotected labour. In doing so, they reduce their costs while increasing their potential profit if they sell or rent the house produced. By operating in a petty commodity production mode, the self-builder has not escaped capitalism but is merely operating in a specific part of it. So, Turner is mistaken in locating the origins of the housing problem in a bureaucratically and technologically top-heavy system rather than in the operation of the capitalist mode of production. In essence, Burgess's argument is that Turner is focusing on symptoms of the deeper inequalities that are inherent in the capitalist system rather than the structural causes of those inequalities. The differences between self-help and institutional housing relate to form rather than substance because the commodity status of both will remain as long as the capitalist mode of production continues.

Burgess proposed an alternative framework for understanding housing provision, based on the distinction between industrialized, manufactured, and self-built forms of housing first postulated by Emilio Pradilla (Pradilla and Jimenez, 1976). His framework expanded Pradilla's analysis from the level of the individual house to that of the settlement and emphasized the need to identify the relationships between the three forms of housing in terms of the relationship between dominant capitalist and dependent petty commodity modes of production (Burgess, 1982: 68). Burgess characterized the three forms of housing as follows:

- *Industrialized housing*: dependent on mechanisms of commercial exchange, to produce an industrialized and standardized product, with exchange mediated through formal intermediaries such as estate agents. Its dominance is established through allocation of national and urban housing budgets to the provision of finished housing units, the use of components produced by an industrialized building materials industry dominated by large foreign monopolies, and its reliance on land supplied by large property companies dominated by state and finance capital.
- *Manufactured housing*: produced by petty contractors for sale to others. It relies mainly on manual labour and locally manufactured materials and produces housing mainly for middle and upper income groups. Its survival is dependent on low wage levels and poor working conditions. Burgess suggests that limited access to capital and low levels of labour productivity limit the capacity of this form of production. It relies to a significant extent on land that has been made available through clandestine subdivision by small- and medium-scale land speculators.
- *Self-built housing*: for which the producer is also the user, although paid labour may be used when necessary. Burgess argues that this form of housing derives from the under-valorization of labour, endemic to 'Third World' capitalist development, and the requirement of low-income groups for some form of shelter. Housing is required for the maintenance and reproduction of the labour force and the dominant capitalist mode of production is happy to allow self-production of housing, with the consequent reduction in living costs and hence in pressure for wage increases.

Burgess's argument that the petty contracting procedures that predominate in the informal sector must inevitably be less efficient than 'industrialized' procedures receives some support from the work of La Porta and Shleifer (2014). Focusing on the manufacturing sector, they found that both the productivity and the size of informal sector firms were usually much lower than those of their formal sector counterparts. The average formal sector firm employed 126 people, as against 4 for the average informal sector firm. Few firms were able to either make the transition from informality to formality or grow and improve over time. They were hampered by lack of access to finance, which was rooted, at least partly, in their inability to provide the formal accounts and control systems required by commercial banks. La Porta and Shleifer concluded that these weaknesses were likely to lead to the relative and later absolute decline of the informal sector. The extent to which their conclusions apply to the housing sector, which arguably lends itself to fragmentation more than the manufacturing sector, is debatable and requires further investigation.

Burgess agreed with those who contend that planning always has a political dimension (see for instance Friedmann, 1998 and Jasper, 1998). For him, Turner's call for radical changes in economic and technical systems lacked credibility because Turner failed to recognize that such changes were dependent on changes in political systems. In trying to legislate to guarantee low-income groups' access to land, finance, and materials, Turner was asking the interests of industrial, financial, landed, and property capital to legislate against their own interests. Burgess stated that 'Turner's recommendations represent nothing less than the now traditional attempts of capitalist interests to palliate the housing shortage in ways that do not interfere with the effective operation of those interests' (Burgess, 1982: 86). Actions taken within existing systems would only delay the revolutionary change that must precede effective action on housing.

Burgess criticized Turner's proposals for community trusteeship of land as unworkable, dismissing them as a reactionary attempt to revive pre-capitalist forms of land tenure. While superficially simple, providing legal security of tenure to the urban poor can be complex and difficult and is a process that the capitalist mode of production is often reluctant to concede. He was similarly unconvinced by Turner's arguments for relaxed minimum standards and proscriptive legislation, stating that minimum standards had always been used to reinforce the class segregation of the urban habitat. Applying a proscriptive approach to standard setting would result in further lowering of acceptable standards and so increase the class-based division in living standards. Noting that low-income groups in many countries routinely ignore or circumvented existing standards, he concluded that relaxation of standards would have little impact on efforts to satisfy the housing needs of the poor. Turner's proposed shift from prescriptive to proscriptive standards would thus have little effect as long as gross inequality remained. It is worth noting that standards tend to be proscriptive in any case, setting minimum values for criteria such as street width and minimum plot sizes, and maximum values for criteria such as housing and population density. One important exception to this rule is the prescriptive requirement that houses and services must be in place before people move in. Despite this, the issue is arguably not whether standards should be prescriptive or proscriptive but rather whether generally proscriptive standards are set at the right levels.

The last part of Burgess's critique was aimed as much at the sites and services approach as at Turner per se. He saw little hope of the approach being implemented on the scale required for success. Even if successful, he suggested that it would have drastic and deleterious consequences for low-income groups. Government-guaranteed access to housing resources for low-income groups would represent a massive diversion of investment from middle-class consumption and would thus divert them away from growth. The price of the materials used by the poor would increase as demand for them increased, as would the price of land while the demand for infrastructure would be greatly increased. From a broader economic perspective, he argued that assistance to self-help housing involved an investment in consumption and unpaid labour and so would have very limited multiplier effects. Finally, he argued, in common with Michael Lipton (1977), that there is a link between urban living conditions and urban–rural migration. Any improvement in low-income urban housing would increase the rate of rural–urban migration, leading to the return of housing shortage and renewed informal development.

Burgess's critique of Turner is itself open to criticism. Most obviously, his assumptions about existing systems appear to be rooted in Marxist ideology rather than conditions on the ground. The prevalence of informal development in many cities suggests that 'manufactured' housing produced informally by petty contractors plays a much bigger role in housing provision than he allows. His assumptions that 'industrial' housing is the predominant mode of production and that foreign monopolies play a major role in producing it are, to say the least, questionable. Government policies in India and Egypt, two countries considered in some detail in Chapter 5, do promote 'industrialized' approaches to housing. However, in neither country is this approach predominant, despite the clear wish of government that this should be so. In neither country do foreign companies play a major role in housing provision, despite the attempts of the Egyptian Government to enter into agreements with large housing companies from the Gulf States. His dismissal of attempts to introduce minimum standards as nothing more than a means to reinforce class segregation is arguably a simplification of a complex reality. It is true that minimum standards are mainly proposed for use in low-income areas but the promotion of such standards is surely a response to class segregation rather than one of its causes. Burgess is correct in noting that minimum standards legislation has had a limited effect on the building activities of low-income groups, who have largely ignored or circumvented them but this is something with which Turner would agree.

Whatever the theoretical merits of Burgess's approach, the reality is that most countries are a long way from achieving the radical changes that it requires. Even Russia, a country that enjoyed or endured, depending on your viewpoint, over 70 years of communist government, was not particularly successful in providing adequate housing for all. Communal apartments, in which households shared kitchens, toilets, and other common areas, were the dominant housing type from the 1930s through to the 1990s (Gerasimova, 2000, quoted by Vihavainen, 2005). In the 1950s and 1960s, President Khrushchev started a programme, based on the provision of five storey apartment buildings, which was intended to end the housing shortage within 10–12 years. The apartments were built quickly, at minimum cost, providing small (40–45 m^2) apartments with low ceilings. The construction quality was poor and the apartments were largely disliked and required frequent repair (Lebina, 2003, quoted by Vihavainen, 2005). There is much that is useful in Burgess's analysis. However, the response to the issues that he identifies must surely be to ascertain the options that are available in the imperfect world as it exists, assessing their potential benefits while being alive to the need for meaningful political change.

Alain Bertaud and the World Bank: efficient design and cross-subsidy

From the early 1970s through to the late 1980s, 'sites and services' and upgrading were important components of the World Bank's urban initiatives. The basic principle of sites and services is very simple: government or its agents provide serviced sites for sale to individual householders who then build or arrange construction of their own houses. Upgrading also starts from recognition of the value of informal sector development and focuses on regularizing tenure and providing infrastructure services, the tasks that individual householders find difficult to do themselves. There are obvious echoes of John Turner's thinking here and Turner certainly interacted with and influenced World Bank staff at this time. However, there were significant differences in their concerns and philosophes and Turner was critical of the World Bank approach. He and his supporters started from the needs and aspirations of low-income people and recognition of the vibrancy of the informal sector. The World Bank theorists, on the other hand, were concerned with the efficient use of scarce government resources. Although they attempted to assess and respond to demand for housing, their approach was essentially supply based. This meant that sites and services and upgrading projects tended to involve citizen participation in centrally administered housing programmes. In this respect, their approach was diametrically opposed to that promoted by Turner.

In order to ensure efficiency, World Bank staff members and consultants sought to maximize the amount of saleable land while minimizing the length and hence cost of infrastructure lines and connections. They sought further savings through adoption of appropriate planning standards, in particular through reduced minimum rights of way, recognizing that most households in low-income areas do not own cars so that vehicle access to every house is not necessary. Together, efficient layouts and appropriate access standards could increase the percentage of land available for sale as plots, from around 40 per cent to around 70 per cent. The replacement of large and difficult-to-maintain public open spaces and wide streets with smaller semi-public open spaces and local access lanes would facilitate maintenance and produce a more attractive living environment.

In an attempt to match supply to demand, schemes provided a range of plot sizes. The theory was that the price of smaller plots, intended for low-income households, would be subsidized from profits generated by charging premium prices for larger plots in prime locations. In some cases, costs were further reduced by providing basic service levels, for instance water supply to public taps rather than individual house connections, in the first instance.

The potential savings of this approach are set out in a World Bank discussion paper (Bertaud et al., 1988). This describes the Bertaud Model, a computer-based analytical tool, intended to allow the cost implications of using different planning and design standards and different combinations of plot sizes and prices to be quickly assessed. The paper argues that the model facilitates an integrated design process that addresses planning, engineering, and financial and affordability issues together rather than in sequence. This, in turn, helps to avoid the outcome that a scheme is designed and engineered and then found to be unaffordable to the intended beneficiaries without significant levels of subsidy. Bertaud's intention was that modelling could be used by regulatory authorities as a tool for exploring more appropriate and affordable standards and regulations and at the project level to enable designers to make more effective use of available land and, through cross-subsidy, provide affordable plots for the urban poor.

Bertaud claimed that his model provided a means of both reducing costs and ensuring a high level of user satisfaction, which he equated with value. User satisfaction was not assessed directly but related to a range of factors, including plot size and frontage, the quality of infrastructure and social facilities provided, the possibilities for deriving income from the plot, for instance by using part of it as a shop or building additional rooms for rent, and the social status attached to the plot. While cost per unit would decrease with increased street length, there would be a point at which increasing length results in a loss of a sense of community so that people's willingness to pay decreases. Layouts should provide larger 'commercial' plots along main roads, with smaller plots grouped around short cul-de-sacs that afford their residents 'semi-private space'. Bertaud contended that mathematical functions could be used to represent the relationship of value to different sizes of plot with different levels of infrastructure provision and in different configurations. His examples were generic with fairly simple layouts. In practice, as John Turner would no doubt point out, accurate assessment of real subdivisions is likely to be very difficult. Indeed, Bertaud recognized the importance of professional judgement when choosing designs to maximize value to beneficiaries. Whether or not the more detailed aspects of Bertaud's model were used in practice, the examples from India described in Chapter 5 show that the general principles were applied with some success.

Shelter poverty: lessons from the USA and the UK

All countries of the Global South face the challenge of closing the gap between the cost of housing and the amount that poor people can afford to pay for it. Jacob Crane saw self-help as one option for closing this gap. John Turner went further, emphasizing the role of informal systems and relationships in reducing the cost of housing. The sites and services approach favoured by Alain Bertaud and his World Bank colleagues combined their insights with an emphasis on rational design, reduced plot sizes, and cross-subsidy. However, the challenge of reaching the poorest remained and seemed all but insoluble. Michael E. Stone's work on shelter poverty examines this challenge in relation to housing in the USA (Stone, 1993). His analysis of the history of poverty in the USA and its effect on shelter affordability from the mid-19th century to the 1990s led him to the conclusion that there had never been a time when a significant proportion of lower-income households had not experienced what he termed shelter poverty. He defined this in terms of a household's ability to meet shelter costs when outlays on other basic needs are subtracted from its income. His analysis showed that food rather than shelter was the main consumption expenditure for most of the USA's population throughout the century preceding the Great Depression of the 1930s. Over most of this period, the problem faced by poor people was not so much the high housing costs as the non-availability of anything other than 'minimal or miserable' housing. The low level of incomes meant that the private sector did not have a profit incentive to provide better housing (Stone, 1993: 88). At times when national economic systems were under strain, for instance the period following the great stock market crash of 1929, the housing options for low-income households became even more constrained. Despite his focus on a rich industrialized country, Stone's methodology is applicable anywhere. Indeed, his conclusion that shelter poverty had been and remained a problem in a rich country such as the USA has obvious implications for the impact of poverty in poorer countries.

Stone is not alone in recognizing that housing involves more than physical shelter. The residential environment encompasses not only the dwelling unit but also the site and setting, neighbours and community, and public services, among others. Those who cannot afford secure housing will not have access to the various benefits associated with it. Stone's main innovation was his approach to determining ability to pay for housing. Rather than the conventional assumption that every household can afford up to a certain percentage of income for its housing, he used a sliding scale of affordability that took account of differences in household composition and income to assess 'shelter poverty'. This led him to the conclusion that low-income and larger households might not have sufficient funds to pay for minimum levels of non-shelter necessities even if they paid a relatively small proportion of their income for shelter. His analysis of shelter poverty in the USA for the year 1991 showed that over 40 per cent of all renters and 20 per cent of homeowners were shelter poor. Shelter poverty was disproportionately experienced by African American and Latino households, of which around 50 per cent were shelter poor, as compared with a figure of 25 per cent for white households.

Assessment of the situation in the UK reveals a similar situation. There, as in other countries, housing costs constitute the most important and most direct impact of housing on poverty and material deprivation. Failure to take account of housing costs results in a significant underestimate of the risk of poverty and material deprivation for workless households, minority ethnic groups, single people, and renters. For example, one estimate suggested that the proportion of private tenants classed as being in poverty increased from 18 per cent to 38 per cent once allowance had been made for paying housing costs (Tunstall et al., 2013).

If rich countries such as the USA and UK have faced such difficulties in providing formal housing that is affordable to low-income households, it is not surprising that the countries of the Global South have faced and continue to face similar difficulties. Any serious attempt to respond to informality must recognize the fact that it exists partly as a result of the inability of formal housing systems to provide housing that meets the aspirations of poor households at a price that they can afford.

The problem is government: the solution is freer markets

The triumph of neoliberal thinking in the 1980s led to several decades in which Western governments sought to reduce the role of government and privatize public services. Housing was not immune to this movement. In the UK, local authorities lost their role as housing providers and housing supply was increasingly left to large private sector house builders. House prices rose more rapidly than income growth and it became increasingly difficult for first-time buyers to enter the housing market. Advocates of the free market argue that the problem lies in planning regulations, which restrict the supply of housing. The solution lies in liberalizing the planning regime: the more permissive a local authority's approach to planning, the broader its tax base will be and the greater its capacity to lower local tax rates, and/or invest in better local public services (Niemietz, 2012). For Peter King (2008), the basic issue was one of choice. Like Turner, he argued that people should have the ability to determine their own ends and have access to the resources required to achieve them. Government's role should be limited to facilitating activity through the guaranteeing of resources and the enforcement of property rights. King echoed Turner in other respects. He emphasized the need for local control of housing processes and referred approvingly to Turner's advocacy for proscriptive rather than prescriptive planning approach. He cited Robert Whelan's 'demonstration' of the impact of local level voluntary activity on 19th century housing conditions and his argument that state action undermined this voluntary involvement in housing provision, driving non-government providers from the field.

Advocates of a free market approach also concerned themselves with housing issues in the countries of the South. Writing about the African context, Karol Boudreaux (2008) argued that a maze of regulations and administrative barriers had imposed high transaction costs on formal sector housing entrepreneurs, raising the cost of providing low-income housing.

These barriers, together with direct government intervention in low-income housing provision, were driving housing entrepreneurs either out of the housing market altogether or into the informal sector. Governments should recognize informal settlements, accepting the fact that, however imperfectly, they met the needs of their residents. Rather than carrying out enforced evictions and relocations, city officials should work closely with slum dwellers associations and other local groups to identify cost-effective mechanisms to increase tenure security and empower local residents to upgrade slum infrastructure and provide services such as clean water and sanitation. Such actions should be accompanied by efforts to reduce the regulatory and administrative burdens placed on formal sector developers. This would leave government free to focus on efforts to control inflation and improve the institutional environment in order to provide the poor with improved access to housing microfinance and other financial tools. For Boudreaux, as for King, the key to solving housing problems lay in giving the poor the resources that they required to make their own decisions and choices.

Boudreaux advanced the standard neoliberal argument that government action to provide a good or service will tend to crowd out the private sector. In fact, government housing programmes are usually implemented by private sector contractors and it would therefore seem that they actually increase the opportunities that are available to those contractors. The issue is perhaps not so much crowding out of the private sector as the lack of opportunities for contractors working in the informal sector to engage in formal sector work for government and private sector developers. Regardless of this, the evidence from the field is that there will always be a role for government. A 2004 World Bank working paper stated that 'the foremost lesson we have learned is that ... a targeted and limited public role is a sine qua non for a well-functioning housing sector. At the same time, there is no mysterious, straightforward capitalist panacea that can address all of the shelter problems faced by low-income families in developing countries' (Buckley and Kalarickal, 2004).

Whelan's argument that state intervention in 19th century Britain crowded out effective voluntary sector involvement in housing provision is open to challenge. As shown in Chapter 2, the impact of voluntary housing providers on 19th century housing provision, though far from negligible, fell a long way short of addressing overall needs. The majority of poor households that could not access the housing provided by the various voluntary bodies and trusts were left to rely on the wholly inadequate accommodation provided by the unregulated private sector. Stone's work on shelter poverty shows that this failure to meet housing needs, particularly those of the urban poor, has been a consistent feature of Western experience. Another problem relates to the nature of the housing market and the degree to which it provides people with real choice. In the UK, house production has become increasingly dominated by large companies. The number of smaller active house-building companies fell from around 12,200 firms, responsible for nearly 4 in 10 new home completions in 1988, to around 2,400 companies responsible for just 12 per cent of new builds in 2014. A report to the UK's House of Lords stated that the business model operated by the large private builders made commercial sense for them but did not deliver an increase in the supply of new homes on the scale required. The market had oligopolistic characteristics with the eight largest builders building more than 50 per cent of new homes and smaller builders finding it difficult to operate (House of Lords Select Committee on Economic Affairs, 2016). The main concern of the large builders is with profit rather than need. The UK government requires that each scheme includes a specified number of affordable houses: typically, between 30 per cent and 50 per cent of the total number built. House builders frequently deploy viability assessments, conducted after they have obtained planning permission, to argue for a reduction in the number of affordable units to be included in a scheme (Akehurst, 2017).

A final point is that the neoliberal approach, as set out by Boudreaux and others, makes little distinction between the regulations and standards required to protect public health and provide acceptable living conditions and those resulting from unnecessary bureaucratic interference in the market. The public health legislation outlined in Chapter 2 certainly changed 19th century housing markets but most would now see these changes as necessary modifications rather than distortions. If this is accepted, the challenge is to bridge the gap that will often exist between the minimum standards required to provide safe, decent housing conditions and those that are affordable to low-income people. The issue then becomes when it is reasonable to accept informal sector activity. Acceptance might be reasonable where informal subdivisions are laid out to reasonably generous standards, as in Karachi's unregulated subdivisions. However, it is much harder to justify where poor people are housed in substandard accommodation with narrow access lanes, a complete lack of light and air, and minimal service standards. These points will be considered further in Chapters 9 and 10.

Hernando De Soto and the mystery of capital

One of the defining characteristics of informality is the absence of officially recognized land and property rights. In the 1960s and 1970s, John Turner and others had emphasized the need to recognize the legitimacy of informal development. Through the 1980s, various projects and programmes included reference to the need to regularize land tenure arrangements. Many internationally funded upgrading projects required that residents of upgraded areas paid at least part of the cost of land and services in return for some form of formal land title. The World Bank emphasized the need to develop and enforce property rights and formal land markets, arguing that registration of property rights in squatter settlements gave occupants legal protection, encouraged the buying and selling of houses, and enabled households to move to a dwelling that more closely suited their needs and budget (World Bank, 1993).

The emphasis on the need to integrate informal sector activities into formal market systems is the central message of Hernando De Soto's book *The Mystery of Capital* (De Soto, 2000). De Soto's central argument is that a lack of clear property rights prevents 'Third World' and former communist countries from using the capital represented by property to fund their transformation into successful capitalist economies. He cites Egypt and Haiti as examples of countries in which the value of savings among the poor is many times greater than the sum of all recorded foreign investment. Most of these savings are 'locked up' in property, which cannot be traded because it is held through a multitude of property systems, mostly poorly documented and with varying degrees of legality. This means that house owners cannot either trade their property outside narrow local circles or use it as collateral on a loan. The value of property thus remains dormant and cannot contribute to exchange and capital growth. Granting formal property rights will allow transformation of property into collateral, collateral into credit, and credit into income. By thus unlocking the potential contained in its informal sector housing stock, a country can transform its economic performance. Based on this 'insight', De Soto makes the case that rapid urban growth presents an opportunity rather than a problem. He is at one with Burgess in recognizing the importance of housing as a commodity although their conclusions as to the implications of this recognition are very different.

His thesis rests on three key assumptions:

- The investment capacity of low-income households living in informal settlements is hindered by credit constraints, which can be overcome by formalizing tenure.
- Low-income households will pledge their land and shelter as collateral in order to finance business activity.
- Financial institutions will provide mortgage credit to low-income households and accept their properties as collateral for loans.

In practice, there are problems with all these assumptions. There are situations in which formalizing tenure arrangements has resulted in improved access to formal loans. For instance, Gilbert (2002) quoted the finding of Conger (1999) that 45,000 out of a total of 300,000 new title holders in Lima, Peru, had taken out loans guaranteed by their property. Examination of data from the same scheme suggested that approval rates for loans from public sector institutions were as much as 12 per cent higher for those with formal land title than for those without. However, there was no evidence that titles increased the likelihood of receiving credit from private sector banks, although interest rates were significantly lower for applicants with land title (Field and Torero, 2006).

Such positive outcomes are not guaranteed. Indeed, it is not even certain that people will welcome formalization. The direct cost of obtaining a title to land may exceed a household's average annual income. Even if spread out over time, this is likely to be a significant burden for low-income households.

For instance, a study in Guayaquil, Ecuador, showed that the cost of obtaining title represented an average of 102 per cent of annual household income (Lanjouw and Levy, 2002, quoted by Gilbert, 2002). In addition to these immediate costs, entry into the formal system may trigger increased ongoing costs, a point stressed by Turner. Owners of formally recognized properties may have to pay property taxes and tenants may be charged increased rents to cover the direct and indirect costs of formalization. At worst, renters may be evicted following the regularization process. Gilbert concluded that poor households' access to adequate housing is constrained not so much by the legality or otherwise of property ownership as by their ability to afford property. Rakodi and Leduka (2004) noted that, by increasing the value of urban land, formal land titling makes it less affordable for low-income groups.

Williamson (2011) argued that De Soto's work is based on two testable hypotheses:

1. Property rights impact development by altering the ability and incentives for capital formation.
2. Land titling provides the means to secure property rights.

Based on her review of the literature and the findings from fieldwork in Peru, Williamson concluded that secure property rights do lead to an increase in development, access to credit, and gross capital formation. However, a top-down, one-size-fits-all approach to land titling would tend to downplay local knowledge and might not therefore be the best option for achieving secure property rights. She concluded that government land titling programmes should not automatically be preferred to options that utilize existing local institutions. This, in turn, led her to argue that De Soto's assumption that the need is for formal tenure, based on centrally defined and administered property rights, is misplaced.

Turning to the willingness to use owned property as collateral for loans, Gilbert's research in Bogota, Colombia suggested that possession of a legal title made little or no difference to the availability of formal finance. His review of studies from other places revealed a similar picture (Gilbert, 2002). This is partly due to supply-side constraints, as explained in the next paragraph. However, another relevant factor is the understandable reluctance of poor people to pledge their major asset as collateral for what may be a risky business proposition. This is particularly true for low-income households, who are unlikely to mortgage property to release capital, partly because of the high priority that they assign to ensuring livelihood security and providing for the future housing needs of their children (Rakodi and Leduka, 2004).

On the supply side, bank lending is normally income rather than asset based and difficult to access for those who depend on uncertified and irregular incomes generated in the informal economy. This is true even when they possess clear land title (McLeod, 2003). Lenders also take account of the type of property offered as collateral for a loan. It is difficult to obtain a mortgage for a property that diverges from the norm in terms of construction or location, regardless of the legal status of that property. Gilbert (2002) noted that even Colombia's Colmena, a bank more progressive than others in lending to the poor, listed many types of settlements in which it would not offer loans. For example, its argument was that the severity of the inclines on which the settlements were built made investment in housing risky. Unfortunately, many low-income settlements are built in just such areas. One consequence of this difficulty is that the market value of properties is likely to be much less than the replacement value used by De Soto to calculate the amount of 'dead' capital tied up in property. Another is that poor people are the most likely to be living in properties that are marginal in terms of either construction or location and therefore the most likely to be excluded from efforts to widen the availability of credit.

These constraints limit the number of house sale and purchase transactions in low-income areas. Gilbert's study of four low-income settlements in Bogota, all more than 20 years old, found that households had lived in the same property for an average of 19 years. Out of 276 households surveyed, only 14 had moved in the previous 5 years. The market for property was flat, even in areas that had been granted formal property rights. Other studies support the view that conferring legal tenure does not necessarily increase the likelihood of property sales. Gilbert (2012) cites a 2007 Finmark Trust study in three cities in South Africa, which found that settlements with the most secure form of title had the lowest rate of transactions. Conversely, he quotes a study in Andhra Pradesh, India (Banerjee, 2002), which found that a quarter of the residents in one settlement in which government had issued non-transferable *pattas* (legal documents providing proof of ownership) to residents had subsequently sold their lots. The sales were illegal but this had not constrained either buyers or sellers.

A central feature of De Soto's argument is his contention that the complexity of existing land registration procedures deters people from seeking to formalize their living arrangements. To support this view, he quotes his finding that a person wanting to acquire and legally register a lot on state-owned desert land in Egypt had to comply with at least 77 bureaucratic procedures involving 31 different agencies in a process taking anything from 5 to 14 years. Acquiring and building on agricultural land would require 6 to 11 years or more of 'bureaucratic wrangling'. In such circumstances, it is difficult for a person to 'stay legal', even if they start by seeking to follow the formal procedures. His response to this is to argue for the development of new formal systems, based on existing informal sector systems. Property arrangements work best when people have developed a consensus about the ownership of assets and the rules that govern their use and exchange. Attempts to create a unified property system that do not take account of the shared understanding that underpins existing informal property arrangements will be bound to fail.

This seems eminently reasonable. However, as De Soto recognizes, integration of existing informal systems into new formal systems requires political will. Unfortunately, the political will required to make the radical changes that he advocates is absent in most countries. The situation is complicated by the fact that responsibilities for registration of property transactions are often shared between several ministries and government departments. For example, land administration in Bangladesh involves three ministries (Hasan, 2017). The resulting fragmentation leads to discrepancies and hence increases the potential for conflict. Even where political will exists, it must be supported by effective systems to define and confirm ownership. Unfortunately, formal regulatory systems often lack the capacity to survey and register large numbers of individual titles (Rakodi and Leduka, 2004). This is particularly true where existing land ownership arrangements are complex and poorly defined. For example, individual plots in Egypt are often the result of multiple divisions of land over decades, with each transaction governed by a simple contract signed by two witnesses. None of these transactions are reflected in official land records (Sims, 2002). Land records in South Asia often date from the Colonial period, pre-1947, and have never been updated so that they bear no relationship to land subdivisions on the ground (Mishra and Suhag, 2017). Colonial-era cadastral maps were often at a small scale. In Bengal, India, for instance, land holdings were mapped at a scale of 16 inches to a mile (1:3,960), increased to either 32 inches or 80 inches to a mile (1:1,980 or 1:792) in congested areas. Urban settlements have expanded greatly over the years so that urban development, including informal areas, now covers many areas that were originally mapped at the 1:3,960 scale, which is arguably too small for accurate recording of land holdings in congested urban areas. Furthermore, in Bengal the Colonial-era maps are rarely geographically accurate. Each map related to a specific *mouza* (village). Theodolite traverse methods were used to fix the boundaries and the internal detail was then filled in using plane table methods. Efforts to geo-reference and digitize these maps are complicated by the fact that the mapped boundaries of adjacent *mouzas* do not fit each other precisely (Paul, 2014; Sengupta et al., 2016). Taken together, these factors suggest that the situation on the ground is likely to be significantly different from that suggested by formal records. The situation is a long way from that required for the operation of effective cadastral systems: unambiguous definition of land units, the rights and interests associated with each unit, and the persons enjoying rights to that unit (Barry, 1999).

Dealing with this situation requires a comprehensive exercise to accurately record present land ownership and resolve disputes regarding ownership in order to update land records to reflect current realities. Only then, will it be possible to implement De Soto's simplified land registration procedures. To do this for a whole city or country is a huge task, requiring first a significant change in government attitude to informality and then considerable political commitment to bring in legislation to make the proposed changes possible. De Soto assumes that the conditions required to allow the creation of formal property rights are already in existence, whereas the reality is that the absence of these conditions is a major reason why achieving effective formal property rights is so difficult.

One further point on De Soto's thesis is that he pays insufficient attention to the ways in which informal relationships are embedded in nominally formal procedures. Investigations in Tanzania found that informal contractors played an important role in formal house construction, providing services to larger formal sector contractors through labour-only subcontracts. No less than 97 per cent of small formal sector contractors and 82 per cent of large and medium contractors interviewed said that they used such contracts. Many used materials obtained from informal sector suppliers (Mlinga, 2001). Such arrangements are likely to be found in many other countries.

More generally, De Soto is open to criticism on the grounds that he pays insufficient attention to the political and economic context within which land and property transactions take place. Drawing on his extensive experience in Mozambique, Paul Jenkins suggested that 'the formal land market in many developing countries will not act in the foreseeable future on behalf of the urban poor' (Jenkins, 2001: 642). Regularizing informal systems may do nothing more than provide systems for recognition of land rights which are limited and corrupt, and exacerbate social exclusion. He argues that efforts to bring the poor into the mainstream must be based on the cultural values and social mechanisms that actually operate, adapting the formal system to the informal reality (Jenkins, 2002: 4). De Soto would no doubt say that he agrees with this but his proposals for bringing informal sector activity into the formal mainstream take little account of such institutional realities. Based on their review of the literature, Mooya and Cloete (2008) found that there were situations in which title had had positive effects on housing market activity but that there were many other cases in which the anticipated benefits had not materialized. They concluded that the varied effects of title on market activity could probably be explained by differences in institutional environments and arrangements. With these points in mind, we now turn to the insights of Douglass North and other proponents of the need for an institutional approach to informality.

Institutional aspects of informality: North, Evans, and Ostrom

Douglass North is well known in economic circles for his championing of 'the New Institutional Economics'. He defined institutions as the 'rules of the game' or, more formally, 'the humanly-devised constraints that structure human interaction' (North, 1993). They include both formal rules, including laws and regulations, and the informal conventions and norms that structure social relationships and help to reduce the influence of uncertainty on human exchange. Informal institutions do not exist in isolation or as appendages to formal ones, but are derived in part from formal institutions and actors' perceptions and experiences. Effective institutions reduce transaction costs, which are rooted in information asymmetries between the parties to the exchange. Well-defined, secure, and well-enforced property rights reduce transaction costs by: clarifying property boundaries, validating ownership rights, and making those rights easily transferable (Lanjouw and Levy, 2002).

Institutions are not static entities and the way in which they develop, which North terms institutional path dependence, depends on both internal and external factors. Individuals and organizations that wield power under the existing institutional framework have a stake in the continued existence of that framework. This makes them resistant to change. This point is important, suggesting a need to examine both overall objectives and the possible paths to be taken and the attitudinal and other constraints to be overcome to achieve those objectives.

One obvious constraint is the difficulty in linking formal and informal systems. The former usually operate through hierarchical structures in which roles and responsibilities are clearly defined. In contrast, informal systems tend to be organic, involving many stakeholders who act independently through structures that are loosely defined and contingent. In practice, these differences are less clear-cut than is apparent at first sight. For instance, 'formal' is often equated with 'planned', while 'informal' equates to 'unplanned'. In practice, the situation is more complicated. Much formally approved housing is built without reference to an overall plan while many informal sector developers produce subdivision plans for the land that they have assembled. Similarly, while it is often assumed that all formal housing is legal in all respects, the reality is that not all formally approved housing complies with all official rules and regulations. Conversely, while informal housing has no legal status when it is built, it is possible that it will be awarded that status in the future. Indeed, there are examples of informal subdivisions being laid out in accordance with formal standards in order to facilitate their later formalization. North provides a useful insight here, arguing that informal institutions do not exist in isolation or as appendages to formal ones. Rather they are derived in part from formal institutions and people's perceptions and experiences, which give rise to the 'mental models' that underpin their beliefs and actions. Individuals typically act on incomplete information and with subjectively derived models, which are often erroneous. The information that is available and the ways in which people interpret it are typically insufficient to correct these subjective models.

Recognition of the difference between formal and informal institutional systems creates a need to assess possible paths from informality to formality. North argues that change is a consequence of the choices made by individuals within organizations. While most are routine, some require alteration in existing 'contracts' between individuals and organizations. This can sometimes be achieved within the existing structure of property rights and political rules. At other times, new contracting forms will require an alteration in the rules and this will require more than the formal changes advocated by De Soto and others. North recognizes that existing informal behavioural norms guide exchanges and will require modification if change is to be sustained.

Modifications occur when individuals perceive that those modifications will benefit them. The key point here is that, while it is possible to change formal rules quickly, informal norms change only gradually. Since these norms provide the essential 'legitimacy' of any set of formal rules, the impacts of 'revolutionary' change are never as great as expected by its promoters and performance is likely to be different than that anticipated (North, 1993: 7).

The concept of coproduction, developed in the mid-1990s, most notably by Peter Evans (1996) and Elinor Ostrom (1996), provides a theoretical basis for assessing interactions between the formal and informal sectors. Rejecting the idea that relationships between the public and private sectors embody a clear division of labour, based on the contrasting properties of public and private institutions, Evans argues that relationships between citizens and public officials often incorporate ties that connect them across the public–private divide. He refers to this phenomenon as 'embeddedness', quoting Judith Tendler's work on health programmes in Ceará State in Northeast Brazil to illustrate his thesis (Tendler, 1997). Tendler found that health workers hired for the programme had been willing to go beyond their prescribed duties. This helped to build relationships of trust with the communities with which they worked and this in turn was a major factor in ensuring the success of the programme. One explanation for the good performance of the workers was that they had been hired at the centre. This reduced opportunities for patronage and ensured that workers were hired on merit. However, Evans' main interest is in Tendler's observation that the success of the health workers stemmed in large part from the fact that they had become 'embedded' in the communities that they served.

Ostrom defined coproduction as 'the process through which the inputs used to produce a good or service are contributed by individuals who are not "in" the same organization'. Drawing on a study of school performance in four villages in Nigeria, she found a positive correlation between good performance and the value placed by parents on education, which influenced their willingness to provide support to their primary schools. In the villages with poorly performing schools, teachers were incapacitated and demoralized in the absence of parental support. She concluded that successful provision of public services requires inputs from users of those services and that top-down and unresponsive administrative systems that discourage such inputs are likely to undermine efforts to provide effective services. Her investigation of condominial sewer systems in low-income urban communities in Brazil led her to conclude that success depends on 1) organization of citizens to enable them to fulfil promises to undertake collective action, 2) good teamwork within the public service delivery agency, and 3) effective coordination between citizens and the agency. Using Tendler's terminology, she described the first as social capital outside government and the second as social capital inside government. She quoted the view of Gabrielle Watson that good agency performance results not from strengthening public sector agencies but from increasing their responsiveness to customers. Watson argued that engaging people during the implementation of condominial systems and the negotiation with government that this requires fosters an 'active, vocal constituency that puts in motion the accountability mechanisms needed for good agency performance' (Watson, 1995).

Ostrom suggests a number of conditions for coproduction to be possible and worthwhile. First, the technologies used must provide possibilities for complementary actions by government and civil society. Second, the parties to proposed action must have the legal right to carry out the activities required of them. A related point, not specifically mentioned by Ostrom, is the need for conformity between official standards and norms and those used by the community. Third, participants need to be able to build a credible commitment to each other so that they can match each other's output. Clear and enforceable contracts between government agencies and citizens can reinforce this credibility. Fourth, there is a need for appropriate incentives to encourage inputs from both officials and citizens. She suggests that the last three conditions are more likely to apply in what she calls a polycentric political system, in which rules applying to overall systems can be drafted in a way that provides scope for decisions pertaining to specific parts of the system to be made at the local level.

Ostrom goes on to argue that coproduction of many goods and services normally considered to be public goods by government agencies and the organization of citizens in polycentric systems are crucial requirements for the achievement of higher levels of welfare in developing countries, particularly for the poor. In order for this to happen, public officials and citizens have to be able to bridge the 'great divide' that presently exists between them. As will become clear from the case studies described in later chapters, this is rarely an easy task.

Perez (2011) argues that Ostrom's thinking provides an opportunity to overcome a fundamental contradiction in De Soto's approach, his insistence on one hand that efficient institutional arrangements are already in place through the informal sector and on the other that there is no alternative to individual property rights. Ostrom, in contrast, suggests the possibility that meaningful trust relationships among economic actors can allow them to change the rules of the game from the bottom up, with the options for change grounded in a sound understanding of local circumstances. If De Soto's theory is to be free from internal inconsistencies it must explicitly recognize the possibility of working with institutional arrangements other than narrowly defined individual private property rights. This will allow his vision of a bottom-up approach to formalizing the informal to include institutional arrangements other than narrowly understood private property or government management.

Property rights and secure tenure: beyond simple duality

Adoption of an institutional approach leads to recognition of the need to move beyond a simplistic distinction between formal and informal systems. Recognizing that informal systems will continue to provide an important mechanism for poor people to access urban land, Colin Marx (2009) argued that informal land markets must be viewed on their own terms rather than as a reflection of formal systems. All too often, attempts to move beyond binary formal–informal concepts of housing markets have only succeeded in creating new binary distinctions. In response to this situation, Marx distinguished between what he termed 'legalist' and 'structuralist' approaches to the analysis of informality. He defined legalist approaches as those based on the view that divisions between formal and informal practices are legal and bureaucratic rather than the structural outcome of economic and political forces in society. Because they define informal land markets in terms of the absence of formal laws and standards, they tend towards the complete removal of the state from the analysis. In contrast, he suggested that structuralist approaches emphasize the political economy of informality, focusing on the social and political dynamics that structure economies in specific and exploitative ways. In doing so, they recognize the involvement of state actors in seemingly unregulated development. Marx argued that most approaches to informal development have been grounded in a legalist approach to property rights and have emphasized the role of clearer property rights in increasing the number of transactions and leveraging assets to reduce poverty. De Soto clearly adopts this approach, which implicitly assumes that informal land markets are similar to formal land markets. Drawing on research in three South African cities, Marx noted that land markets, far from excluding the state, depend on state interventions, including:

- Service provision, which often follows some form of enumeration and registration of both dwellings and population.
- Assurances, provided by ward councillors, that a seller has the right to sell the property; hence, confirming the legitimacy of the sale. No less than 70 per cent of interview respondents in Cape Town and 55 per cent in Durban stated that councillors and municipal officials could make the process of buying and selling informally simpler.

Marx pointed to the interactive nature of the relationship between state systems and the social networks, social identities, and claims that determine the nature of informal land transactions. Box 3.1 summarizes the findings of investigations in Brazil and India that illustrate the existence of interactive relationships.

Marx's focus is on institutions and the way in which they operate. Others have focused specifically on the variety of ways in which informality affects tenure security. Payne (2002) identified nine levels of tenure security, encompassing pavement dwellers, squatter tenants, squatter 'owners', tenants in unauthorized subdivisions, owners in unauthorized subdivisions, legal owners but with unauthorized construction, tenants with contract, leaseholders, and freeholders. Durand-Lasserve and Selod (2007) referred to a 'continuum in land tenure rights', provided by a range of tenure situations, and represented

Box 3.1 Interactive relationships in Rio de Janeiro, Brazil, and Guhawati, India

Janice Perlman described the role of residents associations (RAs) in registering land transactions in favelas in Rio de Janeiro. RAs are municipally recognized organizations that act as the government's arm within favelas. She further records what she refers to as the bizarre arrangement by which the signatures of RA presidents are registered in the Cartótio de Registro de Titulos e Documentos (Registry for Titles and Documents) in the district where the RA is located. In the past RA presidents were well known, trusted, and openly elected community members. Unfortunately, many RAs are now controlled by drug gangs, which routinely use violence to achieve their ends. Perlman notes that the quasi-legalization of extra-legal property transfers blurs the boundaries between legitimate and illegitimate transactions, creating what she describes as a 'perverse formalization of the informal sector, which leaves the urban poor without protection of the law while offering a veneer of legitimacy' (Perlman, 2016).

Perlman also refers to local service centres, called *pousos,* which were established from 1996 onwards to help regularize the right to occupy dwellings in favelas. The *pousos* were staffed by city-paid specialists, including architects, engineers, and social workers, whose main task was to verify that houses met safety standards and provide an occupancy permit, known as a Habite-Se. This is not a title and does not provide security of tenure but it does obligate the city to provide replacement housing in the event that there is a need to remove the house.

Property rights in India are conferred through *pattas*, documents specifying bundles of freehold, leasehold or licence based rights provided to the beneficiary under certain conditions for a specific purpose and period. *Patta* acts in the various Indian states provide time-bound protection from eviction for people living in informal settlements on public land (Vinodia and Garg, 2015). Desai and Mahadevia (2014) describe formal and semi-formal tenure regularization systems in Guwahati, the capital of Assam. Government issues two types of *patta*, which provide different levels of tenure security. By far the most commonly used is *miyadi patta*, a lease given for 30 years and transferable through both inheritance and sale/purchase. It is given in return for a one-time payment to the land revenue department of the state government and is considered to be as good as permanent land tenure. Unfortunately, this path to tenure security is not available to many poor households. Increases in the fee charged by state government for a *miyadi patta* have made them inaccessible to the poor. At the same time, fearful of the possibility that Bangladeshi migrants will obtain *pattas*, the state government has made the procedures for obtaining a *patta* much more stringent. Poor households follow another path to tenure security. This path starts when the land revenue department levies a penalty, called a Tauzi fine, on a household that occupies government land illegally. The household pays the fine, obtains a receipt, which provides proof of occupation of the land from the date that the fine was issued. Although less secure than a *patta*, this arrangement provides some tenure security and is a stepping stone towards an application for a *miyadi patta*. As in the Rio de Janeiro case, this provides an example of government interacting with residents of informal areas in ways that only partly comply with formal procedures.

the relationship between these rights and situations in a matrix, which is reproduced in rearranged form in Table 3.1.

Within the continuum represented by Table 3.1, it is possible to distinguish between:

- administrative recognition of property rights, which is normally time-limited, given to an individual, and non-transferable; and
- land titling, which confers transferable rights, which may be either freehold or leasehold.

Table 3.1 Continuum of land tenure rights

Tenure status		Level of rights: *No rights*	*Rights limited to legal or administrative protection against evictions*	*Access to limited range of rights to use (including right to inherit and sub-let)*	*Access to full bundle of rights (to develop, transfer, inherit, mortgage, etc.)*
Squatters (Including pavement dwellers and tenant in squatter settlements)	Not protected against forced evictions	■			
	With temporary protection against forced evictions		■		
Occupants in unauthorized land subdivisions	on sites unsuitable for development	■	■		
	on sites eligible for upgrading		■	■	
Holders of temporary permits to occupy				■	
Holders of long-term or renewable permits to occupy				■	
Leaseholders	with no formal contracts			■	
	With formal contracts (short-term renewable leaseholds)			■	
Long-term leaseholders (registered leaseholds)					■
Freeholders					■

Source: Durand-Lasserve and Selod, 2007

Administrative recognition of property rights takes many forms. *'Urfi'* contracts are commonly used in Egypt. These are simple sales contracts, made between two people and witnessed by a further two people. For additional security, it is possible to have a contract endorsed in the court under either the *saha towqia* procedure or the more stringent *da'wa saha wa nafaz* procedure, both of which can be arranged by any lawyer for a small fee (Sims, 2016). In India, ownership may be established through a registered sale deed, which records the transaction between the buyer and the seller. However, this does not guaranteed title to the property and responsibility for checking past ownership records of a property rests with the buyer. Land ownership, as determined by such sale deeds, is presumptive in nature, and subject to challenge (Mishra and Suhag, 2017).

A similar continuum of arrangements exists in relation to customary land tenure. In Africa, customary systems, in which land is communally owned and, typically, administered by village chiefs and head-men, co-exist alongside formal land titling systems. Leduka (2004) described the variety of such systems in Africa and of government responses to them. The latter ranged from confrontation with tribal land owners around Gaborone in Botswana to tacit acceptance of informal land registration arrangements using letters of agreement in Eldoret, Kenya. In Gaborone, the courts had usually found in favour of tribal land owners who had subdivided their land for sale rather than the land tribunals that opposed their right to do so. In Indonesia, many residents of *kampongs* (informal 'villages') hold land in accordance with traditional '*adat*' law, which provides semi-formal individual and inheritable ownership rights (Reerink, 2011). Where customary tenure has legal status and most land transactions take place in the context of customary systems, as is the case in Ghana, there is arguably no such thing as pure informality. Customary procedures originated in rural contexts, where their role was to confer communal rights to a group sharing the same cultural identity. Problems are particularly likely to arise when they are applied in rapidly growing urban areas, where those requiring land are often outsiders. In such circumstances, customary land delivery processes may be modified and combined with other formal and informal practices. Individuals usually sell, as market commodities, more rights than they have initially received. These new practices can be labelled neo-customary (Durand-Lasserve, 2005).

Advocates of administrative recognition to informally held land argue that it provides a reasonable level of protection against eviction and, unlike expensive and time-consuming tenure regulation programmes, can be implemented relatively easily through simple regulatory and normative measures. As such, it can represent the first step in an incremental process of tenure upgrading. Others argue that it may prove to be an inadequate measure, which may postpone residents' access to full legal ownership indefinitely (Durand-Lasserve and Royston, 2002).

References

Abrams, C. (1964) *Man's struggle for shelter in an urbanizing world*, MIT Press, Cambridge, Massachusetts.

Banerjee, B. (2002) Security of tenure of irregular settlements in Visakhapatnam. In: A. Durand Lasserve and L. Royston (eds.), *Holding their ground: secure land tenure for the urban poor in developing countries*, Earthscan Publications, London. https://www.taylorfrancis.com/chapters/edit/10.4324/9781849771566-14/security-tenure-irregular-settlements-visakhapatnam-banashree-banerjee (accessed 9 February 2019).

Barry, M.B. (1999) *Evaluating cadastral systems in periods of uncertainty: A study of Cape Town's Xhosa-speaking communities*, Faculty of Engineering, University of Natal, Durban.

Bertaud, A., Bertaud, M. and Wright, J. (1988) *Efficiency in land use and infrastructural design*, World Bank Report INU 17, World Bank, Washington, DC. http://documents.worldbank.org/curated/en/572091468739300255/pdf/multi-page.pdf (accessed 26 July 2019).

Boudreaux, K. (2008) *Urbanisation and Informality in Africa's housing markets*, Blackwell Publishing, Oxford. https://www.mercatus.org/sites/default/files/d7/uploadedFiles/Mercatus/Events/Urbanization%20and%20Informality%20in%20Africa's%20Housing%20Markets.pdf (accessed 2 May 2019).

Buckley, R.M. and Kalarickal, J. (2004) *Shelter policies for the urban poor: idiosyncratic and successful but hardly mysterious*, World Bank Policy Research Working Paper 3427, October 2004. http://documents1.worldbank.org/curated/en/382611468761683337/pdf/wps3427.pdf (accessed 15 January 2021).

Burgess, R. (1982) Self-help housing advocacy: a curious form of radicalism. A critique of the work of John F.C. Turner, in P.M. Ward (ed.) *Self-help housing: a critique*, Mansell, London.

Crane, J.L. (no date) Huts and houses in the tropics. FAO. http://www.fao.org/3/x5350e/x5350e04.htm#TopOfPage (accessed 24 July 2019).

Desai, R. and Mahadevia, D. (2014) Diversity and dynamics of informal rental housing in a mid-sized city in India, *Environment and Urbanization Asia*, 5(2) 285–301. https://doi.org/10.1177/0975425315577173

Durand-Lasserve, A. (2005) Land for housing the poor in African cities: are neo-customary processes an effective alternative to formal systems? in N. Hamdi (ed.) *Urban futures: economic development and poverty reduction*, Practical Action Publishing, Rugby.

Durand-Lasserve, A. and Royston, L. (2002) International trends and country contexts – from tenure regularization to tenure security, in A. Durand-Lasserve and L. Royston (eds) *Holding their ground: secure land tenure for the urban poor in developing countries*, Earthscan, London.

Durand-Lasserve, A. and Selod, H. (2007) The formalization of urban land tenure in developing countries, paper prepared for the World Bank's *2007 Urban Research Symposium, May 14–16, Washington DC.* https://www.foncier-developpement.fr/wp-content/uploads/urban-land-tenure-formalisation.pdf (accessed 3 August 2025).

Edwards, M. (1983) Residential mobility in a changing housing market: the case of Bucaramanga, Colombia. *Urban Studies* 20(2): 131. https://doi.org/10.1080/00420988320080281

Evans, P. (1996) Government action, social capital and development: reviewing the evidence on synergy, *World Development*, 24 (6): 1119–34. https://doi.org/10.1016/0305-750X(96)00021-6

Field, E. and Torero, M. (2006) *Do property titles increase credit access among the urban poor? Evidence from a nationwide titling program* [Online] https://scholar.harvard.edu/files/field/files/fieldtorerocs.pdf (accessed 24 October 2019).

Friedmann, J. (1998) The new political economy of planning: the rise of civil society, in M. Douglass and J. Friedmann (eds) *Cities for citizens*, Wiley, Chichester.

Gerasimova, K. (2000) Istoriya kommunal'noi kvartiry v Leningrade. https://www.iied.org/sites/default/files/pdfs/migrate/10613IIED.pdf (accessed 3 August 2025).

Gilbert, A. (2002) On the mystery of capital and the myths of Hernando De Soto: what difference does title make? *International Development Planning Review* 24: 1–20. https://doi.org/10.3828/IDPR.24.1.1

Gilbert, A. (2012) De Soto's *The Mystery of Capital*: reflections on the book's public impact, *International Development Planning Review* 34(3). https://doi.org/10.3828/idpr.2012.15

Harms, H. (1982) Historical perspectives on the practice and purpose of self-help housing, in P.M. Ward (ed.) *Self-help housing: a critique*, Mansell, London.

Harris, R. (1998) The silence of the experts: 'aided self-help housing', 1939–1954, *Habitat International*, 22 (2): 165–89. https://doi.org/10.1016/S0197-3975(97)00038-6

Harris, R. (1999) Slipping through the cracks. The origins of aided self-help housing 1918–1953. *Housing Studies* 14, 3: 281–309. http://dx.doi.org/10.1080/02673039982803

Harris, R. (2003) A double irony: the originality and influence of John F.C. Turner, *Habitat International*, 27 (2): 245–69. http://dx.doi.org/10.1016/S0197-3975(02)00048-6

Hasan, M.T. (2017) Land administration in Bangladesh: problems and analytical approach to solution, *International Journal of Law*, 3 (2): 44–49. http://www.lawjournals.org/archives/2017/vol3/issue2/3-1-39 (accessed 29 October 2019).

Henderson, A.S. (2000) *Housing and the democratic ideal: the life and thought of Charles Abrams*, Columbia University Press, New York.

House of Lords Select Committee on Economic Affairs (2016) *Building more homes*, House of Lords, London. https://publications.parliament.uk/pa/ld201617/ldselect/ldeconaf/20/20.pdf (accessed 25 April 2020).

Jasper, J.M. (1998) Reviewed work: *Rationality and Power: Democracy in Practice*, Bent Flyybjerg. *Social Forces* 78(2): 806–808. https://doi.org/10.2307/3005579

Jenkins, P. (2001) Strengthening access to land for housing for the poor in Maputo, Mozambique. *International Journal of Urban and Regional Research* 25(3): 629–48. https://doi.org/10.1111/1468-2427.00333

Jimenez, E. (1984) Tenure security and urban squatting, *The Review of Economics and Statistics*, 6 (November): 556–67. https://documents1.worldbank.org/curated/en/802041468915281113/pdf/Tenure-security-and-urban-squatting.pdf (accessed 3 August 2025).

King, P. (2008) Editorial, housing for the poor: the role of government, *Economic Affairs*, June. Institute of Economic Affairs, London. https://iea.org.uk/wp-content/uploads/2016/07/upldeconomicAffairs336pdf.pdf (accessed 26 April 2020).

La Porta, R. and Shleifer, K. (2014) Informality and development, *Journal of Economic Perspectives*, 28(3): 109–26. https://doi.org/10.1257/jep.28.3.109

Lanjouw, J.O. and Levy, P.I. (2002) *Untitled: a study of formal and informal property rights in urban Ecuador*, Yale University, Economic Growth Center Discussion Paper No. 788.

Lebina, N.B. (2003) Zhil'e: Kommunizm v otdel'noi kvartire. In N.B. Lebina and A.N. Chistikov, *Obyvatel' i reformy. Kartiny povsednevnoi zhizni gorozhan.* Dmitrii Bulanin, Sankt-Peterburg.

Leduka, R.C. (2004) Explaining informal land delivery systems and institutions in African cities: conceptual framework and emerging evidence, paper presented in a workshop on *The Perpetuating Challenge of Informal Settlements Organized by the Housing Studies Programme, University of the Witwatersrand 8–10 November 2004.* https://assets.publishing.service.gov.uk/media/57a08c4540f0b649740010ee/R8076LedukaClement.pdf (accessed 27 April 2020).

Lipton, M. (1977) *Why poor people stay poor: urban bias in world development* Temple Smith, London.

Marx, C. (2009) Conceptualising the potential of informal land markets to reduce poverty. *International Development Planning Review* 31(4): 335–53. http://dx.doi.org/doi:10.3828/idpr.2009.1

McLeod, R. (2003) Urban myths. *Insights Issue #48.* https://webarchive.nationalarchives.gov.uk/20090704123504/http://www.id21.org/insights/insights48/index.html (accessed 24 January 2019).

Mishra, P. and Suhag, R. (2017) *Land records and titles in India*, PRS Legislative Research. https://prsindia.org/policy/analytical-reports/land-records-and-titles-india (accessed 3 August 2025).

Mlinga, R.S. (2001) *Collaboration between the formal and informal construction sectors: Towards a new national policy for Tanzania*, PhD thesis, University of Cape Town, South Africa. https://open.uct.ac.za/items/a8ff2324-de3e-4860-ad90-611335dad528 (accessed 3 August 2025).

Mooya, M.M. and Cloete, C.E. (2008) Land tenure and urban poverty alleviation: theory, evidence and new directions, paper presented at *Integrating Generations FIG Working Week, Stockholm, Sweden, June 2008.* http://fig.net/resources/proceedings/fig_proceedings/fig2008/papers/ts07a/ts07a_03_mooya_cloete_2757.pdf

Napier, M. (2002) *Core housing enablement and urban poverty: the consolidation paths of households living in two South African Settlements*, PhD thesis, CARDO, University of Newcastle upon Tyne. https://theses.ncl.ac.uk/jspui/bitstream/10443/2052/1/Napier%20PhD%202002.pdf (accessed 25 July 2019).

Niemietz, K. (2012) *Liberating housing: a free-market approach* [blog], 16 October, Institute of Economic Affairs. https://iea.org.uk/blog/liberating-housing-a-free-market-approach, (accessed 12 March 2020).

North, D.C. (1993) *The new institutional economics and development*, Economic History 9309002, University Library of Munich, Germany. https://econwpa.ub.uni-muenchen.de/econ-wp/eh/papers/9309/9309002.pdf (accessed 29 October 2019).

Ostrom, E. (1996) Crossing the great divide: coproduction, synergy and development, *World Development*, 24 (6): 1073–87. https://doi.org/10.1016/0305-750X(96)00023-X

Paul, A. (2014) Mouza map updating by high resolution satellite images and GIS, *Journal of Geomatics*, 8(2). https://isgindia.org/JOG/abstracts/October-2014/JOG-VOL08nO2-Oct2014_pg23%20-27.pdf (accessed 7 December 2018).

Payne, G. (ed.) (2002) *Land rights and Innovation: improving tenure security for the urban poor*, Practical Action Publishing, Rugby, UK.

Peattie, L. and Aldrete-Hass, J. A. (1981) "Marginal" settlements in developing countries: research, advocacy of policy, and evolution of programs. *Annual Review of Sociology*, 7: 157–75. https://doi.org/10.1146/annurev.so.07.080181.001105

Perez, A. (2011) Yet another path: another path: expanding De Soto's framework using Ostrom's insights, in E. Chamlee-Wright (ed.) *The Annual Proceedings of the Wealth and Well-Being of Nations, 2011-2012, Volume IV*. https://www.beloit.edu/live/files/125-upton-annual-proceedings-volume-iv-2011-2012

Perlman, J.E. (2016) The formalization of informal real estate transactions in Rio's favelas, in E. L. Birch, S. Chattaraj, and S. M. Wachter (Eds.), *Slums: How informal real estate markets work* (pp. 58–82). Philadelphia, PA: University of Pennsylvania Press.

Pradilla, E. and Jimenez, C. (1976) Notas acera del problema de la vivienda, *Ideología y Sociedad, Bogota*, 9 (January–March): 77–108.

Rakodi, C. and Leduka, R. (2004) *Informal land delivery processes and access to land for the poor: a comparative study of six African cities*, Policy Brief 6, International Development Department, University of Birmingham, England and Department of Geography, National University of Lesotho.

Reerink, G. (2011) *Tenure security for Indonesia's urban poor: a socio-legal study on land, decentralisation and the rule of law in Bandung*, Leiden University Press, Leiden, the Netherlands. https://openaccess.leidenuniv.nl/bitstream/handle/1887/18325/Nieuwste%20pdf%20Tenure%20Security%20bijdruk%20binnenwerk%20met%20omslag.pdf?sequence=1 (accessed 7 February 2019).

Repestro, P. (2010) Moving in – selling out: the outcomes of slum rehabilitation in Mumbai, paper presented at the *International Conference on Applied Economics 2010 (ICOAE 2010), Athens, Greece*. https://core.ac.uk/download/pdf/51233221.pdf (accessed 3 August 2025).

Sengupta, A., Lemmen, C., Devos, W., Bandyopadhyay, D. and van der Veen, A. (2016) Constructing a seamless digital cadastral database using colonial cadastral maps and VHR imagery – an Indian perspective, *Survey Review*, 48(349): 258–68. https://doi.org/10.1179/1752270615Y.0000000003

Sims, D. (2002) What is secure tenure in urban Egypt, in G. Payne (ed.) *Land rights and innovation: improving tenure security for the urban poor*, ITDG Publishing, London.

Sims, D. (2016) Securing land tenure in Egypt: who needs registered titles? *Métropolitiques*, 14 June. https://www.metropolitiques.eu/Securing-Land-Tenure-in-Egypt-Who-Needs-Registered-Titles.html (accessed 30 January 2019).

De Soto, H. (2000) *The mystery of capital: why capitalism triumphs in the West and fails everywhere else*, Basic Books, Bantam Press/Random House, New York/London.

Stone, M. (1993) *Shelter poverty: new ideas on housing affordability*, Temple University Press, Philadelphia, PA. http://www.jstor.org/stable/j.ctt14bt4bs

Tendler, J. (1997) *Good government in the tropics*, Johns Hopkins University Press, Baltimore, MD.

Tunstall, R., Bevan, M., Bradshaw, J., Croucher, K., Duffy, S., Hunter, C., Jones, A., Rugg, J., Wallace, A. and Wilcox, S. (2013) *The links between housing and poverty: an evidence review*, Joseph Rowntree Foundation. https://www.york.ac.uk/media/chp/documents/2013/poverty-housing-options-full.pdf

Turner, J.F.C. (1968) Housing priorities, settlement patterns and urban development in modernizing countries, *Journal of American Institute of Planners*, 354–63. https://doi.org/10.1080/01944366808977562

Turner, J.F.C. (1972) Housing as a verb, in J.F.C. Turner, and R. Fitcher (eds), *Freedom to build: dweller control of the housing process*, Collier Macmillan, New York. http://www.communityplanning.net/JohnTurnerArchive/pdfs/FreedomtoBuildCh7.pdf (accessed 3 January 2021).

Turner, J.F.C. (1976) *Housing by people: towards autonomy in building environments*, Marion Boyars, London.

Vihavainen, R. (2005) Housing in Russia – policies and practices, paper presented at a *Workshop in St Petersburg, April 24–26 2005*. https://blogs.helsinki.fi/respublica/files/2008/08/rp05_interim_housing.pdf (accessed 8 April 2019).

Vinodia, A. and Garg, Y.K. (2015) Tenability scanner: a theoretical framework for classification of slums in India. *International Research Journal of Social Sciences*, 4 (7): 70–77. http://www.isca.in/IJSS/Archive/v4/i7/12.ISCA-IRJSS-2015-129.pdf (accessed 10 March 2020).

Watson, G. (1995) *Good sewers cheap? Agency-customer interactions in low cost urban sanitation in Brazil*, World Bank Water and Sanitation Division, Washington, DC. https://coilink.org/20.500.12592/q2v9nz (accessed 3 August 2025).

Webster, C., Wu, F., Zhang, F. and Sarkar, C. (2016) Informality, property rights and poverty in China's 'favelas', *World Development*, 78, February 2016: 461–76. https://doi.org/10.1016/j.worlddev.2015.10.007

Williamson, C. (2011) *The two sides of De Soto: property rights, land titling, and development*. https://papers.ssrn.com/sol3/papers.cfm?abstract_id=1940201 (accessed 3 August 2025).

World Bank (1993) *Housing: enabling markets to work*, World Bank policy paper, Washington, DC. http://documents.worldbank.org/curated/en/387041468345854972/Housing-enabling-markets-to-work (accessed 24 January 2019).

World Bank (2000) *Interview with John F.C. Turner* [online]. http://siteresources.worldbank.org/INTUSU/Resources/turner-tacit.pdf (accessed 24 October 2019; no longer available).

Yap, K.S. (1989) Housing priorities, expenditure patterns and the urban poor in third-world countries, *Netherlands Journal of Housing and Environmental Resources*, 4(1). http://dx.doi.org/10.1007/BF02498027

CHAPTER 4

Participation in theory and practice

The received wisdom among development professionals who work for international agencies and NGOs is that participation is the key to successful settlement upgrading. Accordingly, all internationally funded upgrading projects now include provision for some form of community participation. Most aim to engage residents of informal settlements in participatory structures and processes that have been developed by professionals from outside their communities. The same is true, although less obviously so, for projects and programmes initiated by national NGOs and organizations such as Slum Dwellers International (SDI). These are likely to be closer to the communities that they seek to serve but still rely on the insights and commitments of their leaders and staff who are rarely residents of the informal settlements that are the focus of upgrading.

Recognition of the desirability of participation in shelter projects is not new: Jacob Crane's self-help plus concept required government participation to support the activities of informal self-builders. John Turner stressed that low-income people should be central actors in the housing process, providing their own houses with government providing support. The early World Bank-funded Lusaka upgrading project assumed the need for community involvement in decision-making. It established community structures to first assist in aspects of project design and then ensure effective operation and maintenance of the facilities provided (Jere, 1984). Projects such as the Ismailia Demonstration Projects and Khuda ki Basti, which will be considered in later chapters, also emphasized the need for participation. However, despite good intentions, many projects implemented in the 1980s were essentially top-down, partly because the need for quick implementation left little time and space for participation and partly because of government resistance to the idea of involving users in the project design and implementation process.

The 1990s brought renewed interest in the need for community participation in the planning, design, and implementation of infrastructure services to serve low-income communities. This chapter summarizes the thinking that underpinned this interest and provides examples of how this thinking has been translated into practice.

Theories of participation

Arnstein and the ladder of participation

Sherry Arnstein's seminal 1969 paper on the ladder of participation has influenced much of the subsequent thinking on the subject (Arnstein, 1969). For Arnstein, participation should be a means to redistribute power and allow 'have-not citizens, presently excluded from the political and economic processes, to be deliberately included in the future'. She identified eight levels of participation, ranging from manipulation to citizen control with intermediate levels including placation, consultation, informing, partnership, and delegated power. For her, the only worthwhile forms of participation were partnership, delegated power, and citizen control. For partnership to work well, the community should be well organized, leaders should be accountable, and adequate resources should be available to pay leaders an honorarium for time taken up by committee activities. Delegated power should normally relate to specific plans and programmes while full citizen control might take the form of a neighbourhood corporation with no intermediary between it and the source of funds. Full citizen control equates to John Turner's local autonomy and self-governance, with government participating in the people's programme rather than people in the government's programme.

The objectives of participation

Caroline Moser distinguished between participation as a means to an operational end, for instance the provision of an improved water supply, and participation as an end in itself, leading to increased empowerment and thus enabling people to take an increasingly meaningful role in development processes (Moser, 1983). Later, taking a more nuanced view, she suggested that the distinction between participation as a means and participation as an end was 'mechanistic and limited in its applicability'. The key question was whether participation as a means had the capacity to develop into participation as an end (Moser, 1989).

Taking a more instrumental approach, Tayler and Cotton (1993) suggested that the objectives of participation in infrastructure provision can extend to one of three levels. A basic level of participation is required to ensure that the services and facilities provided are appropriate to needs and properly used. At the next level, participation may lead to a reduction in costs and/or an increased rate of implementation. At the third level, participation can seek to strengthen community organization and capabilities, achieving the first and second level objectives in the process. Unless the first level is achieved, there is no guarantee that services and facilities will be used. However, the aim, wherever possible, should be to move beyond this to the second and third levels. The third level is not too far from Moser's concept of participation as an end although she might argue that it was still instrumental rather than truly participatory. Samuel Paul (1987) adopted a similar approach, identifying five possible objectives for community participation: cost sharing, improving project efficiency, increasing project effectiveness, building beneficiary capacity, and empowerment. The focus on project efficiency and increased project effectiveness perhaps reflects the fact that Paul was a World Bank employee and was drawing upon World Bank experience.

Schübeler and types of participation

Peter Schübeler (1996) distinguished between community-based, area-based, collaborative functionally based, and process-based approaches to participation in service delivery and infrastructure management. For Schübeler, community-based approaches constitute the most elementary form of participatory development. However, their simplicity and local focus limit their ability to link locally developed infrastructure systems to municipal networks. Area-based approaches normally involve the provision of a multi-sectoral package of infrastructure improvements and are usually directed by government institutions. While they are better than community-based approaches at channelling significant resources into low-income areas, levels of participation may be limited. In Turner's terms, they may be seen as an attempt to involve the people in the government's approach. However, quoting the example of Indonesia's Kampong Improvement Program (KIP), Schübeler noted that supply-driven programmes with a modest level of participatory decision-making may function well with minimal community development inputs. The functionally based approach devolves more responsibility to the community than the area-based approach in that communities, through user groups or community-based organizations (CBOs), assume full responsibility for managing local infrastructure facilities and at least partial responsibility for financing those facilities. The key concept here is collaboration, as government takes responsibility for higher-order facilities while the community manages its own local services. This is essentially the approach advocated by the Orangi Pilot Project (OPP) in Pakistan, which will be explored further in Chapter 7. Schübeler suggests that it requires a relatively high level of technical and organizational capacity on the part of CBOs and clear guidance on the way in which responsibilities for different parts of the infrastructure system are to be allocated. Its implementation normally requires 'external' primary and secondary municipal networks to which community managed local facilities can connect. It is clearly dependent on good coordination between the organizations that are responsible for higher level and local infrastructure facilities. This in turn implies that government authorities are willing and able to interact with community organizations and allow them to take responsibility for infrastructure provision at the local level.

Schübeler viewed process-based strategies, involving decentralization, as the ideal. He argued that decentralization 'implies a double movement: the shift of decision-making and management functions toward local levels, and the opening of these processes downwards, thus making them more responsive and accountable to the users'. A process-based strategy requires the flow of information to local decision-making bodies and a basic planning and programming capacity at the community and district levels. While admitting that these requirements rarely apply in practice, Schübeler argues that this weakness may be overcome through capacity-building measures assisted by continued application of collaborative and area-based strategies. The key point here is that, while identifying an ideal situation that is close to Arnstein's partnership and citizen control, Schübeler recognizes that less complete forms of participation may be required to pave the way towards eventually achieving that ideal situation.

John Abbott's areas of participation

Like Schübeler, John Abbott (1996) recognized that the approach to participation must take account of the nature and the scale of the task to be accomplished. He argued that initiatives that only involve the community can only achieve local, fairly limited objectives. When dealing with more complex situations, there is a need to move from a community-dominated approach to one that promotes community involvement in broader decision-making processes. In such situations, the outcomes of participatory activities are greatly influenced by the 'community participation surround' – the political, institutional, and cultural circumstances in which participatory activities take place. Abbott goes on to suggest that the community participation context can be broken down into 'arenas', which reflect different relationships between communities and the government systems that surround them. Figure 4.1 is based on his diagrams showing these arenas, their relationship to system complexity and government openness, and the possibilities that exist in each arena.

The boundaries between the different arenas will usually be hard to define in practice. Despite this, the diagram is useful in that it illustrates the following important points:

- Meaningful community participation will be difficult or impossible where government is closed to the possibilities of participation.
- The possibilities for participation increase with increased government openness to the idea but complete citizen control and community management, as envisaged by Arnstein and favoured by Turner, will only ever be possible for relatively local facilities and services.
- When considering more complex situations involving higher level facilities and services, there is a need to develop systems and mechanisms for linking communities with government. This point links with Eleanor Ostrom's emphasis on the need for public officials and citizens to come together to bridge 'the great divide'. Action within the Arena of Consensus is clearly dependent on the existence of mechanisms to facilitate coproduction.

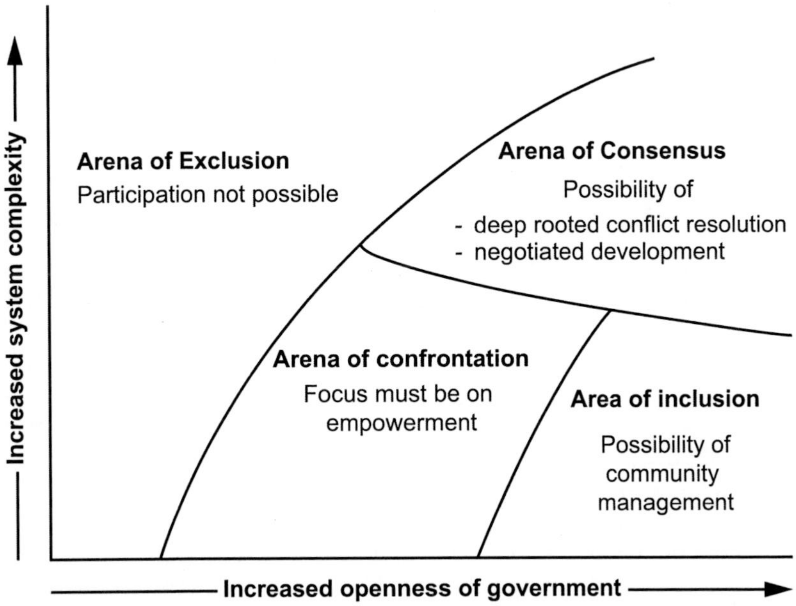

Figure 4.1 Abbott's diagrammatic representation of the different arenas of participation

Chambers and participatory appraisal

From the mid-1990s onwards, the thinking of Robert Chambers had a significant impact on development theory and practice. In particular, many international organizations adopted his Participatory Rural Appraisal (PRA) approach. As the name suggests, PRA was initially used in rural contexts but it has also been used in urban contexts, leading to a change in name to Participatory Rapid Appraisal. Chambers argued that professionals often have a partial, indeed a biased, view of development issues and stressed the need to take account of the knowledge and concerns of local people. His approach is encapsulated in his frequently quoted reference to 'handing over the stick' – the stick being the instrument used to draw on the ground in the course of a participatory mapping exercise. The phrase derives from the rather naïve assumption that poor people from rural communities will be more relaxed if community plans are drawn in the sand rather than using paper and pens. In practice, PRA exercises in urban areas invariably use the latter. In essence, Chambers is calling for professionals to hand over the power to control the stick, real or metaphorical, to community members.

Chambers (1992: 1) described PRA as a 'family of approaches and methods to enable rural people to share, enhance and analyse their knowledge of life and conditions, to plan and to act'. It shares important principles with rapid rural appraisal (RRA), including the direct learning from local people, offsetting biases, optimizing trade-offs, triangulating (cross-checking facts using different methods), and seeking diversity. The major difference between the two lies in the fact that RRA involves the eliciting and extraction of information by outsiders, while PRA gives ownership of the appraisal process itself to local people. It recognizes that poor people are creative and capable and should therefore be involved in much of their own investigation and planning. Outsiders should not lead but should act as convenors, catalysts, and facilitators. For Chambers, PRA was a philosophy as much as a methodology but he did list the methods commonly used in PRA exercises. These included participatory mapping and modelling, transect walks, matrix scoring, well-being grouping and ranking, institutional diagramming, trend and change analysis, and analytical diagramming, all undertaken by local people (Chambers, 1994).

Chambers claimed that PRA could be used to plan, implement, and evaluate community-led initiatives. In practice, most references to it in the literature relate to the planning stage of the project cycle. It has also been used for evaluation, as illustrated by the example in Box 4.1.

Chambers claimed that PRA can provide information on existing conditions and facilities more quickly and using fewer resources than conventional social survey methods. The findings may not be suitable for statistical analysis in the same way as those obtained from carefully designed social surveys but will usually give a reasonably accurate view of the overall situation. Over the years, most assessments of PRA have been written by its advocates and emphasize its achievements. One exception, a review of PRA use in Gambia (Brown et al., 2002) gave a rather more nuanced view. It found some positive

Box 4.1 The use of PRA to evaluate performance of a rural water supply scheme

Johnson (1992) describes a participatory evaluation of a rural water supply scheme in Mysore District Karnataka, India using PRA tools. Initial focus group discussion members of community organizations suggested that there had been no problems in the two years that the system had served the community. People had not resorted to using river water since the system was built and there had been no problems with breakdowns. While these discussions were ongoing, other members of community organizations produced a map showing all the taps in the village. The group presented the map to the community, stimulating a lively discussion of its contents by all members of the community, including upper and lower castes, men and women, young and old. The visual nature of the information presented allowed all to participate. This discussion revealed a rather less satisfactory situation than that suggested by the initial discussions. Three taps were broken and two had been moved from their original location. A meeting next day with the man who was responsible for cleaning the water tank and doing minor repairs revealed that the water pump had broken down a few months previously. Pressure from the community had led to the government repairing the pump. During the repairs, everyone had had to use the river. The government had now taken over responsibility for managing the system. Further discussions revealed large variations in access to the water points. The lowest caste community was using one functioning tap for 80 families and 75% of this group were still using the river. Elsewhere, the ratio was 10–15 families per tap. The two-day PRA exercise had revealed information about the performance of the scheme that might not have been picked up by a more conventional evaluation method.

effects, particularly on the government agency side, where it instilled a spirit of enquiry. However, there was some uncertainty as to whether this spirit could be sustained over time. Drawbacks included concerns about data quality and cost-effectiveness and the high transaction costs of PRA use, particularly for villagers. PRA had encouraged the participation of poor people in data collection and making choices on the direction of project initiatives. However, its value as a community mobilization tool was reduced by its idealization of the 'community' and focus on literate community members. Overall, the authors concluded that there was little evidence that PRA was effective in empowering the poor or challenging long-term power relations.

Social capital

The 1990s saw increased interest in the concept of social capital, the idea that a person's family, friends, and associates constitute an important asset. Communities that are endowed with strong social networks and civic associations will be in a stronger position to confront poverty and vulnerability. Social capital resides in relationships and complements the human capital that resides in individuals. Together, they increase the ability of literate and informed citizens to organize, evaluate information, and express their views in constructive ways (Woolcock, 2001).

Social capital can be subdivided into bonding, bridging, and linking social capital. Bonding social capital is that which exists within a community of individuals such as those residing in a particular neighbourhood. Bridging social capital occurs when members of one community develop ties with people from other communities in order to seek access or support or to gain information. Linking social capital provides vertical ties to persons with power and resources. Bonding social capital is necessary if low-income communities and the individuals that live in them are to survive and join together to address neighbourhood-level problems and issues. More importantly, its presence enables individual communities to move on to more powerful forms of bridging and linking social capital (Larsen et al., 2004). When communities come together in networks, they increase their ability to gain access to decision-makers and are thus able to reject patron–client ties in favour of collective action. However, the combined impact of bonding and bridging social capital is strongly influenced by the institutional context in which networks of the poor are embedded (Archer, 2009).

Archer investigated the intra-community and inter-community ties and state–community linkages created through Thailand's Ban Mankong programme. She found that upgrading had positive but temporary effects on community action within individual communities. This suggests that people saw participation primarily as a means to achieving the ends of better housing and improved services rather than an end in itself. Her findings are in accord with the author's experience of community initiatives in Faisalabad and elsewhere. Together, they suggest that it is not sufficient to talk about participation as an abstract concept but rather to ask what participation is intended to achieve.

On the subject of inter-community ties, she argued that slum networks, representing inter-community relations, are essential if settlement upgrading is to be scaled up to the city level. However, government bureaucracy was a barrier to effective cooperation, and trust in officials remained low. The removal of this barrier is clearly necessary if a move is to be made from Abbott's area of exclusion to his area of consensus.

Voice

In the context of urban housing and services, voice can be defined as the collective attempts of members of an organization or group to improve their living conditions by lobbying those with power to change those conditions. Most of the literature on voice refers to its potential role in lobbying for improved services, although it could clearly include demand for government action to provide improved housing. Voice can be exercised through either direct user pressure or indirect pressure from politicians and individuals and divisions within outside agencies, acting on behalf of those demanding services (Hirschman, 1970). New Social Movement analysts pointed to the emergence of urban social movements from the late 1970s onwards and their role in developing new forms of mobilization that were internally democratic, free of state and party manipulation, and capable of bringing about democratic transformation within the state. However, they noted that mobilization for service improvements often brought limited one-off victories and created dependent relationships with local politicians.

Watson (1992) studied the role of voice in bringing about improvements in water and sanitation services in São Paulo's *favelas*. Political liberalization following the removal of the repressive military regime had allowed Brazil's citizens to voice demands and criticisms without fearing government reprisals, and provided progressive politicians and bureaucrats within government with more latitude to respond to these demands. This combination of greater openness from above and growing participation from below helped to facilitate public agency responsiveness to unmet user needs. The remarkable increase in water and sewer service between 1979 and 1985 coincided with a wave of popular mobilizations for urban services that emerged with the gradual democratization process in Brazil. Though these mobilizations were not solely responsible for transformations within SABESP, the São Paulo water and sewerage service provider, they did influence the pace, timing, and nature of that organization's policy and programme initiatives. This suggests a movement from Abbott's areas of confrontation and exclusion to those of consensus and inclusion. Watson went on to make the important point that user pressure can only achieve results if citizens can exercise their rights to protest and petition government, pointing out that much of the literature on voice ignored this important factor. The clear implication is that governments and those who control them play a dominant role in deciding where the limits of the areas of consensus and inclusion lie.

Watson found that water and sanitation struggles in São Paulo had involved waves of active mobilization, followed by periods of less visible activity. Despite the rather intermittent nature of community activities, she found considerable continuity of both leadership and community participation from one struggle to the next. Women played an active role, helping to ensure leadership continuity and cumulative learning through periods of active mobilization and relative inactivity. Neighbourhood associations periodically developed informal district-level networks, learning from one another's successful strategies and occasionally mounting joint campaigns, achieving significant victories without forming formal movement federations. They progressed from strictly protest and demand-based strategies to negotiation and limited participation in service extension tasks. Rather than representing time-limited one-off struggles, as suggested by the New Social Movements literature, Watson argued that these discrete waves of mobilization resulted in increased demand-making capacity, more effective demand articulation, and a transformation in communities' relationship with government. In the case of both water and sewerage services, neighbourhood associations were able to engage with SABESP in ways that were not open to individuals acting independently of one another. Watson found a high degree of continuity in community leadership. In all three of the communities that she studied, activists had been involved directly in struggles to improve water and sewerage services for over 5 years and in other forms of community activity and mobilization for over 10 years.

Neighbourhood associations played a central role in bringing communities together, bringing large numbers of neighbourhood residents to agency doorsteps to bang pots and pans, deliver petitions, stage sit-ins, and demand that agency representatives visit their communities to see how people were living. This generally positive view must be tempered by Janice Perlman's finding, set out in Box 3.1, that many residents associations in Rio de Janeiro's *favelas* are controlled by drug gangs. This suggests a tendency for attempts to exert voice to be either replaced by or transformed into patronage relationships, controlled by local politicians and community 'leaders'. De Wit and Berner (2009) state that many relatively established electoral democracies in the South are perceived as 'patronage democracies'. Even in the case of 'public goods' and collective services, poor people are more likely to contact intermediaries and politicians than to organize rallies to voice their demands. Their position is logical. Investing in collective action is problematic, time-consuming, and fraught with free-rider problems. The use of an intermediary or broker is therefore perceived as a better option for both seeking an improved service and gaining protection against a threat. Brokers or patrons are more effective if they are linked to political actors such as local councillors and, through them, to members of parliament. They go on to argue that collective action and slum-wide organizations inevitably reflect local divisions and inequalities and tend to be controlled by local elites. This suggests a need to be sceptical about 'grassroots-led urban development', slum federations or CBO alliances if the benchmark is the actual participation by and benefit to all or a significant majority of slum residents. At worst, the CBO label may be used by local leaders and entrepreneurs to obtain benefits which are not widely shared. In such circumstances, the relationships between municipalities and communities will tend to be based on frequently politicized vertical relationships, mediated by individuals, rather than horizontal, collective relations rooted broadly in communities.

De Wit and Berner (2009) claim that mobilization and organization of people collectively on the basis of horizontal ties and common interests does not appear to work well in most places. Indeed, it appears to work less well the poorer and more dependent people are. They suggest that there is evidence that the urban poor are not 'naturally' inclined to engage in horizontal organizations or get involved in collective actions, often preferring to rely on vertical patronage. The brokers of such patronage will be more effective if they are part of the political machinery. Once they lose an election, their ability to provide services to their supporters is limited, since the political machinery is now controlled by another party.

Participatory models

Since the 1980s, many internationally funded projects have used an approach to participation that builds on small groups, often of women and typically comprising 20–40 individuals. Each group meets to produce a plan of its immediate neighbourhood and list and prioritize its needs. Representatives of the groups then meet to produce an overall 'action plan' for their settlement. In some cases, these action plans are combined into a town or city-wide action plan. The settlement action plan usually consists of a list of priority projects, which typically include street paving and drainage, sanitation, and water supply improvements. There may also be proposals for new community centres, solid waste collection, and street lighting among others. Where possible, the aim is to implement these schemes through some form of community contracting, whereby community members themselves carry out the required work, typically in accordance with agreed unit rates developed by local government engineers. Two versions of this basic approach are described here, Sri Lanka's CDC model of participation and the Kerala CDS model. The latter has been widely adopted beyond Kerala and is used in many projects supported by international and bilateral agencies.

Sri Lanka's CDC model of participation

In the mid-1980s, Colombo Municipal Council (CMC) introduced the concept of community-based self-help groups, known as community development councils (CDCs). As part of their remit to improve public health, they implemented small-scale community programmes focusing on local environmental and sanitation improvements. From 1984, the Million Houses Programme (MHP) used the CDCs to launch programmes to upgrade substandard houses and facilities and by 1998, CDCs had been established in 636 of the 1,504 settlements in and around Colombo. Each CDC was governed by a committee, elected by its members and consisting of a president, vice-president, secretary, assistant-secretary, treasurer, and other committee members (Dayaratne and Samarawickrama, 2003). In some, but it seems not all cases, several CDCs, typically representing different areas within a single settlement, joined together to form a CDC Federation. The Federation was made up of the officers of its constituent CDCs and led by a committee, consisting of a president, vice-president, secretary, assistant-secretary, treasurer, and around eight other members (Fernando et al., 1987).

The CDC system was linked with existing administrative and political structures through a three tier system, which involved:

- Monthly meetings between CDCs and officers of concerned government agencies.
- Bi-monthly ward-level meetings of presidents and secretaries of all CDCs in the ward, chaired by the elected representative for the ward.
- Bi-monthly meetings of a district-level housing and community development council, comprising CDC leaders and under the leadership of the district engineer and medical officer of health.
- Consideration of unresolved issues at a monthly city-level housing and community development committee, chaired by the mayor.

This system was designed to give CDC leaders and members confidence that they had access to all levels of the urban administrative system, including the mayor. This, in turn, helped to ensure that CMC officers liaised with communities rather than ignoring their concerns (Dayaratne and Samarawickrama, 2003). In theory, the initiative sought to develop broad-based CDC leadership, with leadership roles regularly rotated among members of the CDC. It was hoped that this would break traditional leadership monopolies in participating communities.

A community action planning (CAP) approach, using a microplanning procedure, was developed to help CDCs to identify priorities and implement improvements. This was intended to be problem-driven and incremental, with each action identified leading to subsequent actions. The aim was to allow local participants to contribute to both the content and the structure of the programme. Only the broadest of intentions and policy prescriptions were to be determined by outsiders, leaving community members to craft these into workable programmes through the action from the bottom up (Goethert and Hamdi, 1988). Local infrastructure improvements identified through CAPs were to be implemented using community contracting procedures.

CDCs were encouraged to take part in programmes and activities of other agencies that could potentially enhance the activities and respond to the challenges identified by the CMC. The programme was implemented through the administrative structure of the CMC, including ward structures.

The theoretical strength of the CDC model lies in its emphasis on linking CDCs into municipal administrative and political structures. If implemented as intended, the regular schedule of meetings would have integrated community structures into broader municipal structures, facilitating 'sharing the stick' between community members and municipal professionals. This would have increased the likelihood that the actions identified by communities formed part of overall municipal plans rather than comprising isolated, and hence less effective, local actions. Little information is available on how this worked out in practice. The NGO Sevanatha still uses a CDC model but it is doubtful whether this includes the link to municipal structures envisaged in the original model. Similarly, the Kerala government's Kudumbashree programme, which aims to empower women, uses a three tier system. Again, the emphasis is on promoting savings and there does not appear to be a strong link with municipal structures. The issue here is arguably that the original CDC model was intended to operate within Abbott's Arena of Consensus but, in the absence of the necessary institutional support from government, mainly operates within his Arena of Inclusion. Thus, the original bold concept has been reduced to something close to the Kerala CDS model, which is examined next.

The Kerala CDS model

The community development society (CDS) model was developed in the Indian state of Kerala in the early 1990s, with UNICEF assistance, and shares many features of the CDC model. The model was piloted in seven wards in Alleppey (or Alappuzha) and was later extended, first to the whole of Alleppey and then to 58 municipalities in Kerala. It was later adopted by a succession of Indian Government urban poverty alleviation programmes, including the Swarna Jayanti Shahari Rozgar (SJSRY) Programme, launched in 1995, and the National Slum Development Programme (NDSP), launched in 1996 (de Cleene, n.d.). The process started with identification of poor households, using an index based on nine non-economic indicators. Women from these households were formed into neighbourhood groups (NHGs), consisting of not more than 40 women with an average group size of 25. Groups of NHGs, typically 10 to 15 in number, were formed into area development societies (ADSs). In the initial Alleppey initiative, there were several ADSs, one for each ward, but the link with wards was not considered essential (The Kudumbashree Story, n.d.). The ADSs, in their turn, were federated into a town level CDS, which was registered as a society under the Charitable Literacy Act.

Each NHG elected one woman as the resident community volunteer (RCV) and their leader. Another woman was elected president and three other volunteers were elected to carry out the responsibilities relating to community health, community infrastructure, and community income generation.

Together, these five women formed the NHG Committee (NHC). The governing body of the ADS was made up of the committee members of all its constituent NHGs. A committee, comprising a chairperson, a vice-president, and seven other members was then elected from among the wider body. A community organizer, appointed by the municipality, acted as the ADS committee member secretary. At the town level, the general body of the CDS included the chairpersons, vice-chairpersons, and member secretaries of all the federated ADSs. The general body members elected a governing body, comprising a president, vice-president, seven members, and several non-executive members and community organizers. NHG and CDS activities were to have been supported by ward and town level advisory committees, chaired by the ward councillor and mayor respectively and including representatives of various municipal departments. Unfortunately, these committees proved to be ineffective (The Kudumbashree Story, n.d.).

Thrift and credit societies (TCSs), another important feature of the CDS approach, were first introduced in 1994. By mobilizing their members to save small amounts and giving members small loans, they acted as informal banks for the poor. Support from India's National Bank for Agriculture and Rural Development (NABARD) underpinned their activities and helped to ensure the success of the initiative. This led to TCSs being seen as synonymous with NHGs, with savings and credit becoming an essential function of the latter.

Many subsequent programmes have adopted one or more of the key features of the CDS approach, including its three tier community development structure, the emphasis on the savings and credit activities of NHGs, and a CAP approach. So, for instance, Thailand's Community Organizations Development Institute (CODI), which will be examined in detail in Chapter 8, stresses the importance of savings and credit. The Faisalabad Area Upgrading Project (FAUP), examined in Chapter 7, attempted to introduce a model based on multi-purpose community organizations (MPCOs), in effect NHGs.

The settlement action plan usually consists of a list of priority projects, which typically include street paving and drainage, sanitation, and water supply improvements. Other proposals might cover new community centres, improvements in solid waste collection, and street lighting among others. As already noted, these are normally implemented through community contracting procedures, typically in accordance with agreed unit rates developed by local government engineers.

Critiques of participation

Who holds the stick?

Most participatory processes assume that communities will take the lead in identifying their needs and determining their priorities. This assumption is explicitly contained in Chambers' emphasis on the need to hand over the stick. It can be criticized on the grounds that it removes any role for professional experience and knowledge. It is true that communities know more about their local situation than outside professionals. However, their choices are constrained because:

- They lack knowledge of the wider context and the ways in which contextual issues should influence their choices.
- They know what they know but not what they don't know and so tend to fall back on what they have already seen and experienced. This reduces the scope for trying out innovative responses to problems and needs.

Outsiders can introduce new ideas and approaches. While there is no guarantee that these will be appropriate in the local situation, they should increase the range of options to be considered. Even where inappropriate in their initial form, there is always the possibility that a better way forward will emerge from dialogue around ideas put forward by both community members and outsiders. This suggests that the aim should be to ensure that the stick is shared in a way that allows community members to state their ideas and concerns and outside professionals to respond to them. That response might involve courses of action that would never have occurred to community members on their own.

The role of the facilitator

The focus and findings of participatory exercises in urban settings can be strongly influenced by key actors in the process, particularly the facilitators. In theory, they act as neutral enablers, encouraging all participants to express their views and share their knowledge. In practice, they have the power, wittingly or unwittingly, to affect the evolution, and hence the outcomes, of participatory processes. Box 4.2 illustrates this point by describing a PRA exercise conducted in the course of the Calcutta Environmental Management Strategy and Action Plan (CEMSAP) project in the mid-1990s.

The case study from Mysore summarized in Box 4.1 highlights the risks associated with quick evaluations by outsiders but it also illustrates the extent to which the outcomes of participatory exercises depend on facilitator skills. In this case, the true story emerged following efforts to check and triangulate the information initially provided by community members. However, the information about the pump breakdown required a meeting with an individual – the man responsible for system maintenance. This could easily have been missed in an exercise that focused only on the 'community'.

Asking the right questions can depend on the interviewer having the relevant specialist knowledge. For instance, local water supply systems in South Asian informal settlements frequently break down because the pump motor burns out. This is often the result of low voltage in the electricity supply system. It is common practice to repair the motor in a local workshop, replacing the motor armature windings. Unfortunately, this invariably reduces the motor performance and makes the pump set vulnerable to further burn

Box 4.2 PRA exercise in ARP Basti, Howrah, India

Like other jute mills, the mill on whose land ARP Basti is located provided basic housing for its workers on part of its land. The mill closed in the 1960s but the workers living on company land refused to move and were still there when the PRA exercise was conducted in 1996. In the meantime, the mill company had sold the land to a third party and an uneasy stalemate existed. The landowner had an obvious interest in removing the settlements from the land, which had considerable redevelopment value. However, it seemed that the residents were able to stall this process, partly because they were supporters of the ruling Communist Party of India (Marxist) and received support from local politicians. However, it is doubtful whether this support would have been sufficient to allow them to continue to occupy land on which they had in effect squatted unless the law provided some backing for their position. On the other hand, the irregular nature of their land-occupancy meant that the landowner was able to block any attempt to provide improved services to the settlements. The result was that, although the conditions in the settlements were, in many respects, better than those in adjacent *thika* tenancies, most noticeably in the relative lack of crowding and availability of open space, the settlements were very poorly serviced. Residents were reliant on water brought from tubewells located outside the company compound at some distance from their houses. Sanitation was non-existent.

The facilitator of the PRA exercise, which lasted 5 days, was a doctor. On the first day of the exercise, the residents produced a detailed map of their settlement. On the subsequent days, the exercise focused increasingly on health issues. The land ownership and tenure issues were hardly touched upon. There is little doubt that the facilitator had unconsciously directed the exercise in directions that interested her. While these might have had some importance, they were as nothing compared with the tenure stand-off that affected every aspect of the residents' life. The settlement is no longer visible on Google Earth and it is likely that the owners did eventually succeed in evicting the residents.

out incidents. In one case in Sindh, Pakistan, pump operators said that they had filed down the impellors on the pump in order to reduce the load on the motor. This was only revealed because the engineers assessing the system realized that the pumps were not performing at their rated capacity and questioned the operators about the reasons.

Two key points emerge from this brief review of the role of facilitators:

1. It is important to ensure that facilitators are aware of the ways in which they, consciously or unconsciously, can influence the outcomes of participatory processes. The key to successful action is to ensure that they are aware of this and are able to make informed decisions on the ways in which they exert that influence. It will often be the case that initial open-ended exploration of issues should lead to more focused exploration of specific issues.
2. When dealing with any type of 'technical' issue, facilitators should either have direct knowledge of that issue or have access to specialists who do have that knowledge. This suggests a need for collaborative working, with team members coming together to review and, where necessary, build on the findings of participatory processes.

Do participatory processes pay sufficient attention to power structures?

Participatory processes have been criticized on the grounds that they pay insufficient attention to the power structures that exist within society. Berner (2010) cited the view of Cooke and Kothari (2001) that mainstreaming participation within development programmes depoliticizes it, making it a technical instrument and facilitating the illegitimate and/or unjust use of power. It is perhaps no accident that devolved, participatory approaches to government in Pakistan have tended to flourish during periods of military rule. Thailand's CODI is an example of a participatory initiative that has survived periods of military government. On the other hand, Kerala's participatory initiatives were instigated and supported by a state government that was clearly intent on devolving power to the people. The lesson here is perhaps that it is important to understand the context within which participatory approaches are being promoted.

Berner went on to say that the frame of reference of donors and policy-makers, constrained as it is by a fixed timeframe and the need for tangible and measurable results, with output indicators known in advance, is not compatible with any real influence of beneficiaries on relevant decisions. John Turner would no doubt agree with this, seeing this approach to participation as a means of fitting people into the agency or government's programme rather than tailoring that programme to their expressed needs.

Berner further argued that much of what is considered participatory is in fact a process whereby large numbers of people are represented by a relatively small number of participants (Hickey and Mohan, 2005). Quoting Guijt and Shah (1998), he argued that, in failing to consider power relationships within the community, many nominally participatory initiatives oversimplify reality and thus act as obstacles to the proper examination of local power systems. Bottom-up approaches to development need to start from recognition of the fact that exploitation and marginalization can take place within poor communities. Existing inequalities along gender and other lines are likely to be reproduced in participatory processes.

Advocates of PRA would argue that methods such as wealth ranking provide understanding of the divisions within society. This may be true but there is a danger that the information gained through a wealth-ranking exercise will be appropriated by the outsider who commissioned the exercise, while community members continue to accept the structures that it reveals.

The focus of participatory processes

PRA, and participatory methods in general, start from the view that all aspects of community life are up for discussion and analysis. When prompted to explore a specific subject with a community, one of the community organizers for the FAUP, which will be considered in Chapter 7, rightly reminded the author that PRA required that the subjects for discussion should be identified by the community rather than the outsiders. In practice, projects and initiatives often have limited scope and a clearly defined aim. Where this is the case, there is no point in extending participatory activities that will not be covered by the project. Taken together with the need to make space for professional knowledge, this suggests the need for a modified approach, designed to ensure wide-ranging community engagement but recognizing the value of professional input and the need to focus on project objectives. This might be termed guided PRA.

The CDS model, which is perhaps the most widely adopted model in internationally funded projects, is further open to the criticism that it assumes that local communities are able to identify both the problems that they face and the best solutions to those problems. The first may be true but the second is debatable. The model relies almost exclusively on local knowledge, producing lists of small local initiatives, but providing no vision of how those local initiatives can be brought together to create a greater whole. Box 4.3 provides two examples to illustrate this point, both taken from the author's experience.

The Brazilian condominial approach offers more limited options for community choice. Only one service delivery option is offered, sewerage in the case of excreta and wastewater disposal, and connection to the networked system in the case of water supply. The choices offered to the community are limited to service location (back of plot, front of plot or sidewalk) and level of involvement in ongoing maintenance. As noted in Chapter 7, the choice of service location is often further constrained by existing building on plots while few households have wanted to take over maintenance responsibilities for condominial systems.

Box 4.3 Disjointed results of participatory planning in Indonesia and Bangladesh

In 2000, the US Agency for International Development (USAID) supported the Program Dasar Pembangunan Partisipatif (PDPP) in Indonesia, in order to support a participatory medium-term development planning process.[1] While not concerned exclusively with informal areas, it throws light on the participatory processes implemented in those areas. While engaged in project preparation for a proposed Asian Development Bank project in Kediri, East Java, the author attempted to assess the proposals included in the town's PDPP plan. The plan included a list of proposed projects but no map was available to show the locations of those projects. Without this, any proposals for improved drainage and connections to the municipal water distribution system were meaningless. Another example from the author's experience is a series of community plans for informal settlements in Bangladesh, which identified drainage priorities in the form 'Faridul's house to Gonazor's house'. The emphasis was on short lengths of drain and there is no concept of an overall drainage system. Clearly, this disjointed approach will not work for facilities that are designed to link into wider networked systems. This has obvious immediate consequences for the nature and quality of services in informal areas. Its less obvious consequence is a reinforcement of the assumption that informal settlements are detached entities, separate from the formal urban fabric.

The limited success of bottom-up approaches in going beyond local improvements to improved access to networked services such as piped water arguably reflects the difficulty faced in moving into Abbott's area of inclusion, in which action requires collaboration between community members and service providers. The Orangi Pilot Project is regularly cited as an example of an organization that has been successful in facilitating this collaboration, but, as will be shown in Chapter 7, it has often faced difficulties in engaging with formal service providers. Regardless of this, the examples given in Chapter 8 show that it is hard for purely bottom-up initiatives to go to scale, particularly when they are dependent on inputs from formal sector service providers.

Participatory processes introduced by external agencies are hard to sustain

The PDPP process described in Box 4.3 was devised and guided by USAID. When asked about planning processes, government officials in Kediri invariably referred to the government's pre-existing hierarchy of development plans and made no reference to the PDPP plan. A study of PDPP activities in Maros District, South Sulawesi, found a higher level of integration, with at least some PDPP proposals incorporated into district government plans and budgets (Nachuk and Hopkins Leisher, 2006). However, relatively few of the PDPP proposals were implemented. PDPP implementation depended heavily on Forum Warga, the project's local partner. Unfortunately, Forum Warga's limitations reduced the chances that the process would be institutionalized. In the event, USAID's withdrawal at the end of the set period assigned for the project left the process dependent on inadequate local government funds. Follow up investigations found that villager awareness of the process varied greatly; in some villages no one was aware that the planning process had taken place. Surprisingly, this was true of village leaders who had been recorded as being facilitators of the process.

Despite the clear problems with direct community management, it is still widely promoted, in most cases by international agencies. A particular challenge is that of developing the capacities required to successfully manage piped sewerage systems. Schübeler argued that it was desirable for functionally based approaches to participation to eventually lead to more comprehensive process-based approaches and build the capacities of a user who is considered a 'citizen' rather than merely a 'client' (quoted in Neto and Ily, 2013).

An important but rarely recognized point is that international agencies promote participatory processes that tend to focus on individual settlements. This limits opportunities to explore the context within which those individual settlements are located, in particular the existence of other informal settlements close to the focus settlement. This has practical implications in that it ignores the opportunities for providing shared off-site infrastructure. The cost per household of off-site infrastructure to serve one settlement is likely to be higher than that to serve several settlements in the same area.

This increases the cost of networked infrastructure and may result in a preference for on-site solutions such as pit latrines and tubewells. This may perpetuate the assumption that informal areas are detached from the formal city, resulting in the exclusion of informal area residents from participation at the municipal level.

Note

1. See https://ash.harvard.edu/wp-content/uploads/2024/02/10600.pdf (accessed 3 August 2025).

References

Abbott, J. (1996) *Sharing the city: community participation in urban management*, 1st ed. Routledge, Abingdon.

Archer, D. (2009) *Social capital and participatory slum upgrading in Bangkok, Thailand*, PhD thesis, Sidney Sussex College, University of Cambridge. https://www.repository.cam.ac.uk/bitstream/handle/1810/244821/Diane%20Archer%20thesis.pdf?sequence=1 (accessed 19 August 2020)

Arnstein, S.R. (1969) A ladder of citizen participation, *JAIP*, 35 (4), July 1969: 216–24. http://lithgow-schmidt.dk/sherry-arnstein/ladder-of-citizen-participation.html

Berner, E. (2010) Participation between tyranny and emancipation, in G.M. Gomez, A.A. Corradi, P. Goulart and R. Namara (eds.), *Participation for what: social change or social control?* (pp. 1–7). ISS/Erasmus University Rotterdam. https://www.researchgate.net/publication/254805460_Participation_for_what_social_change_or_social_control (accessed 24 July 2020).

Brown, D., Howes, M., Hussein, K., Longley, C. and Swindell, K. (2002) *Participatory methodologies and participatory practices: assessing PRA use in the Gambia*, Agricultural Research and Extension Network, Network Paper No. 124. https://odi.org/en/publications/participatory-methodologies-and-participatory-practices-assessing-pra-use-in-the-gambia/ (accessed 3 August 2025).

Chambers, R. (1992) *Rural appraisal: rapid, relaxed and participatory*, IDS Discussion Paper no. 155 Institute of Development Studies, Sussex. https://www.ids.ac.uk/download.php?file=files/Dp311.pdf (accessed 3 August 2025).

Chambers, R. (1994) The origins and practice of participatory rural appraisal, *World Development* 22(7): 953–969. https://doi.org/10.1016/0305-750X(94)90141-4

Dayaratne, R. and Samarawickrama, R. (2003) Empowering communities in the peri-urban areas of Colombo, *Environment and Urbanization*, 15 (1): 101–110. https://journals.sagepub.com/doi/pdf/10.1177/095624780301500101 (accessed 11 October 2019).

de Cleene, S. (no date) *Community learning information and communication case study*, Kerala Community Development Society, Working Paper 105, Development Planning Unit, London. https://www.ucl.ac.uk/bartlett/development/sites/bartlett/files/migrated-files/wp105_0.pdf (accessed 19 August 2020).

de Wit, J. and Berner, E. (2009) Progressive patronage? Municipalities, NGOs, CBOs and the limits to slum dwellers' empowerment, *Development and Change* 40 (5). https://doi.org/10.1111/J.1467-7660.2009.01589.X

Fernando, S., Gamage, W. and Dharmawansa, P. (1987) *Navagampura and Aramaya Place: two urban case studies on support based housing*, NHDA, Colombo, Sri Lanka.

Goethert, R. and Hamdi, N. (1988) *Making microplans: a community based process in programming and development*, IT Publications, London.

Hickey, S. and Mohan, G. (2005) Relocating participation within a radical politics of development, *Development and Change* 36: 237–262. https://doi.org/10.1111/j.0012-155X.2005.00410.x

Hirschman, A.O. (1970) *Exit, voice, and loyalty*, Harvard University Press, Cambridge, MA.

Jere, H. (1984) Lusaka: local participation in planning and decision-making, in G. Payne (ed.), *Low-income housing in the developing world: the role of sites and services and settlement upgrading*, pp. 55–68, Wiley, Chichester.

Johnson, D. (1992) 'Evaluation: a participatory partnership using PRA tools and techniques for evaluation' [online], MyradaPRA – PALM Series, Paper 10, Myrada, Bangalore. https://myrada.org/evaluation-a-participatory-partnership-using-pra-tools-and-techniques-for-evaluation/

The Kudumbashree Story (no date) Evolution of the CBO Idea – The Alappuzha Model. https://kudumbashreestory.in/index.php/history-and-evolution/the-kudumbashree-idea/the-kerala-model/the-alappuzha-model (accessed 13 August 2025).

Larsen, L., Harlan, S.L., Bolin, B., Hackett, E.J., Hope, D., Kirby, A., Nelson, A., Rex, T.R. and Wolf, S. (2004) Bonding and bridging: understanding the relationship between social capital and civic action, *Journal of Planning Education and Research*, 24(1). https://doi.org/10.1177/0739456X04267181

Nachuk, S. and Hopkins Leisher, S. (2006) *Making services work for the poor: a synthesis of nine case studies from Indonesia*, Harvard University. https://www.google.com/search?client=safari&rls=en&q=ash+centre+harvard&ie=UTF-8&oe=UTF-8 (accessed 3 August 2025).

Moser, C.O.N. (1983) The problem of evaluating community participation in urban development, in C.O.N. Moser (ed.), *Evaluating community participation in urban development projects*, pp. 3–11, Working Paper No. 14, Development Planning Unit, London.

Moser, C.O.N. (1989) Community participation in urban projects in the Third World, *Progress in Planning*, 32(2): 71–133. https://doi.org/10.1016/0305-9006(89)90010-X

Neto, A. and Ily, J. (2013) *'Choosing and Implementing Small-Bore Sewers': Case Study BRAZIL*, pS-Eau. https://www.pseau.org/sites/default/files/fichiers/r_d/case-study_non-conventional-sewers_brazil.pdf (accessed 3 August 2025).

Paul, S. (1987) *Community participation in development projects: the World Bank experience*, Discussion Paper 6, World Bank, Washington, DC.

Schübeler, P. (1996) *Conceptual framework for municipal solid waste management in low-income countries*, Urban Management and Infrastructure, SKAT (Swiss Centre for Development Cooperation in Technology and Management). https://es.ircwash.org/sites/default/files/Schubeler-1996-Conceptual.pdf (accessed 3 August 2025).

Tayler, K. and Cotton, A. (1993) *Urban upgrading: options and procedures for Pakistan*, 1st ed. Water, Engineering and Development Centre (WEDC), Loughborough.

Watson, G. (1992) *Water and sanitation in São Paulo, Brazil: Successful strategies for service provision in low-income communities*, Master's thesis, Department of Urban Studies and Planning, Massachusetts Institute of Technology, Cambridge, MA. https://dspace.mit.edu/handle/1721.1/12804 (accessed 3 August 2025).

Woolcock, M. (2001) *The place of social capital in understanding social and economic outcomes* [online]. https://faculty.washington.edu/matsueda/courses/590/Readings/Woolcock%20Soc%20Cap%20Development.pdf (accessed 3 August 2025).

CHAPTER 5

Housing the poor

As explained in Chapter 2, successive British governments implemented public housing programmes through most of the 20th century, particularly in the period 1920 to 1970. Other European governments also had extensive public housing programmes, with direct public investment in housing reaching a peak in the two decades following the end of the Second World War. Most European colonies achieved independence towards the end of this period, and it is perhaps no surprise that their initial response to housing need was to provide public housing, often at a subsidized price. Despite the later emergence of other approaches to housing and service provision, public housing is still central to the policies of many governments in developing countries.

The first part of this chapter examines public housing provision in India and Egypt, two countries that have invested and continue to invest heavily in public housing. During the 1950s and 1960s, both had left-of-centre leaders, who believed that the state could and should play a role in most aspects of life, including housing. Politically, both have since moved to the right and now emphasize the role of the private sector in housing provision. Despite this, both have continued to implement mass housing programmes, albeit with significant private sector participation and a greater acceptance of the role of markets in housing provision. This chapter reviews the development of policy in each country.

Most public housing programmes provide limited opportunities for involving their intended beneficiaries. Many face difficulties in accessing the finance required to implement housing projects that meet the needs of the urban poor. Various individuals and organizations have attempted to overcome these drawbacks. This chapter examines one notable example of an effort to support their activities, the Community Led Infrastructure Finance Facility (CLIFF) in India.

Prefabrication is often promoted as an option for housing the urban poor. The last part of the chapter examines the experience of prefabrication, from the 1950s onwards, and assesses its potential role in the housing programmes of the future.

Egypt: apartments in the desert

Over the years, Egypt's approach to housing has encompassed rent control, provision of new housing units, mainly in apartments, and the development of new cities and settlements on desert sites. The focus here is on the efforts to provide new housing, both in existing urban areas and in new towns and cities.

In the late 1950s, two low-income housing options were open to the Egyptian Government. One was to build on the approach pioneered by the Egyptian architect Hassan Fathy in the 1940s in the village of New Gourna, near Luxor. The existing Gourna village was located over pharaonic-period tombs and its inhabitants made a living from digging up and selling antiquities, a practice that was unacceptable to the Department of Antiquities. Accordingly, the government decided to move the inhabitants to a new village, located well away from the tombs, and commissioned Fathy to design the village. Drawing on the lessons that he had learnt from Nubian masons, Fathy designed a scheme using local materials, mainly mud, and depending on natural ventilation and orientation to ensure that houses were acceptably cool in summer and warm in winter. He believed that his 'traditional' approach would be both more suitable for the climate and cheaper than 'modern' building methods. Recognizing that each family's needs were different, he suggested the need to plan on the basis of thorough socio-economic and ethnographic investigation. In practice, the authorities were unwilling to provide the resources required for this investigation and eventually the design was based on Fathy's 'own knowledge and intuition, based on a sympathetic understanding of peasant life' (Fathy 1973).

Although New Gourna is a well-recorded landmark in the history of ideas on planning and housing, it was never completed and was only briefly occupied by some of its intended inhabitants. Not surprisingly, the people of Gourna resisted any attempt to move them from a location that allowed them to engage in their lucrative but illegal trade. The failure of the scheme ended any hope that the government would adopt Fathy's approach to housing the poor. Rather, it opted for the second option, the construction of standardized walk-up apartments. Both informal sector builders and government used the same construction techniques, constructing walk-up apartments with reinforced concrete frames and floor slabs, with brick infill walls. The idea of using 'traditional' materials and building techniques might appeal to romantics and architectural theorists but the inescapable reality was that concrete with brick infill was cheaper and allowed provision of more housing units on a given area of land.

Thereafter, Fathy's ideas would be of interest only to the rich, an outcome that was far from that which he had intended. The state would house the poor, using standardized designs and 'modern' materials. When a Master Plan for Cairo was published in 1956, shortly followed by the launching of a public housing programme, its emphasis was on providing cheap housing units in tenement apartments. By 1965, Cairo Governorate, the largest of the three Governorates within which Greater Cairo is contained, had built almost 15,000 low-income units (Abu-Lughod, 1971: 231, quoted by Sims, 2003). These units typically provided a floor area of between 45 m^2 and 65 m^2. Later public housing schemes included larger units, intended for higher-income households. Public housing invariably consisted of 4–5 storey walk-up apartments, which typically provided 2–4 housing units per floor (Sims, 2010). Tipple (2000) quotes an average figure of 20,000 'low-cost' housing units per year during the 1980s, but it is likely that some of these units were unaffordable to truly low-income families. Sims (2010) gives a figure of 625,500 public housing units built in Greater Cairo between 1982 and 2005, an average of about 27,000 housing units per year, which is about 35 per cent higher than Tipple's figure. Whatever the exact figure, the continued growth of informal sector housing is an indication that formal housing provision was failing to meet the housing needs of poor households.

Early public housing schemes were located on land within or close to existing urban areas, but from the mid-1970s onwards, the Egyptian Government's response to the country's housing needs was to create new cities and settlements in the desert. The New Cities programme began in 1976 and by 2010, eight 'new cities' existed within the bounds of Greater Cairo. Over 200,000 subsidized public housing units were built in new city areas between 1982 and 2005, with at least a further 208,000 planned in the period up to 2011 (Sims, 2010).

With the exception of 15th of May, which is located close to the southern industrial suburb of Helwan, the new cities were located some distance from existing built-up areas. The design populations for individual cities initially lay in the range 250,000–500,000 with 6th October, the largest within the Greater Cairo area, designed for a population at the upper end of this range. Subsequent expansion of the new city areas led to large increases in target populations, in the case of 6th October to no less than 5.5 million. The early 1980s saw plans for a further nine satellite settlements close to the route of the planned Ring Road, each of which was intended to house around 250,000 people and to provide 10,000 public housing units in the first instance. Work started on five of these settlements but all were subsequently absorbed into New Cairo and Sheikh Zayed City, two of the later new city projects. Most development in both New Cairo and Sheikh Zayed City catered for middle and higher-income households, in some cases in gated communities. The author's site visits to New Cairo and inspection of satellite images reveal only small pockets of affordable public housing.

The emphasis on building subsidized apartment blocks, mainly on relatively remote desert land, has continued regardless of the political complexion of government. In 2005, Mubarak's government announced a new National Housing Program (NHP), which aimed to build and distribute 500,000 affordable housing units over a six-year period, almost half of which were to be in Greater Cairo, almost exclusively in the new cities. The units were either standard 63 m^2 two-bedroom units or 35–40 m^2 basic units, intended for rental to the very poor. By mid-2009, most had been budgeted and construction had commenced (Sims, 2010: 162). As with many such projects, information on performance is limited. An unconfirmed analysis suggests that the programme delivered about half the intended 500,000 units over the planned six-year period and that around 50,000 of these units were not connected to utilities and infrastructure (Shawkat, 2014a). The NHP did include a component, *Ebni Beitak* (build your own house), that was aimed at individual owner-builders. The intention was that 89,000 150 m^2 plots, 17.8 per cent of the total provided under NHP, would be sold at subsidized prices with a requirement that purchasers construct a single storey 63 m^2 unit within the first year. The purchaser could extend the unit incrementally up to a maximum of three floors (Shawkat, 2014a). All the plots were located in new towns. The *Ebni Beitak* initiative fell well short of its objectives, for reasons that included the remote locations of the new towns, failure of infrastructure provision to keep pace with the rapid pace of land allocation and construction, inflexible and complicated bureaucratic procedures and slow 'build-out' rates. Not surprisingly, subsequent programmes have not attempted to repeat the approach (Sims and Abd-El Fattah, 2016).

In 2011, the government committed itself to deliver an additional 1 million housing units to lower-income households in Egypt under the Social Housing Programme (SHP). After the hiatus caused by two changes of government in rapid succession, the new Sisi government relaunched this programme in 2014. The stated target group is 'low-income' households although it offers housing across the income spectrum. It only offers finished apartment units, most of which are sold with a very limited number of rental units. At 75 m^2 for two-bedroom apartments and 90 m^2 for three-bedroom apartments, the floor areas of standard apartments are greater than those provided by previous schemes (Shawkat, 2018). Greater Cairo is the main beneficiary of the programme, with 254,328 units planned for 6th October and a further 244,440 units planned in the other new cities (Invest-gate, 2016). The Built Environment Observatory (Shawkat, 2018) used figures from various sources, including Ministry of Petroleum and Mineral Resources (MoP) plans, CAPMAS (Central Agency for Public Mobilization and Statistics) reports, and the Guarantee Subsidy Fund (GSF) and Social Housing Fund (SHF) annual reports, to assess year-on-year SHP performance in terms of the number of housing units built and delivered to beneficiaries. Its assessment suggested that, for Egypt as a whole, the number of units built would approximate to 50 per cent of the planned number by 2017/18. Performance in delivering completed units to owners was good in the three governorates that make up Greater Cairo, but this did not mean that units were occupied quickly. For reasons to be explained later, Cairo has a very high proportion of unoccupied housing units and this will certainly be the case for recently completed units on desert land.

The Sisi government has also provided low-income housing through its Tahya Masr Fund, which it launched in 2014. In Greater Cairo, the fund supported a 'model' housing scheme, located in Asmarat at the eastern end of the Moqattam plateau, some 11 km east of central Cairo. The stated intention of the Asmarat scheme was to rehouse the residents of 'unsafe' informal districts in Greater Cairo and government saw it as the first stage in a comprehensive programme to eliminate unplanned 'shantytowns' within 10 years.

In practice, the government also used the scheme to rehouse people from areas that had been earmarked for redevelopment, in particular the Maspero Triangle in the historic Boulaq area just north of the original Egyptian Museum. Responsibility for construction, which was scheduled to take place in three phases, lies with the Cairo Governorate and the Armed Forces Engineering Authority. The first two phases, providing almost 11,000 housing units, were complete by 2018, and the planned third phase will increase this number to over 18,000. (Mounir, 2018). The scheme provides standard 63 m^2 apartments with two bedrooms, a small living room, a kitchen, and a bathroom. All housing units are fully furnished, and the residents are not permitted to bring furniture from their old homes. The apartments are located in six-storey blocks and analysis of Google Earth images shows that clearances between the blocks range from about 6 m to 10 m. In addition, the scheme was to provide 281 commercial units and 'dozens of service and entertainment areas', designed to raise the living standard of more than 80,000 citizens. Social objectives were to be achieved through literacy and adult education classes and regular campaigns to inform young people of the danger of drug abuse (Tahya Misr Fund report quoted in Al-Youm, 2018). Residents complain of high rents (Egyptian pounds (LE) 300 per month).

Alongside the commitment to provide new housing in the desert, the Egyptian Government appeared to take a harder line on informal development, in particular that on state-owned desert land. In April 2014, the Housing Minister was reported to have said that Sadat City, one of the original new cities situated on the Cairo to Alexandria Desert Road, had seen illegal encroachment and settlement on 70,000 feddans (about 29,400 ha) of state land. He said that this was affecting the future development of the whole Nile Delta and called on the Interior Ministry and the army to remove the blatant encroachments in and around Sadat City. People living in the informal developments were to be housed on 685 feddans of land in Sadat City, as part of the housing initiative described in the previous paragraph (quoted by Esterman, 2014). Either the Minister was overstating his case or the government has already taken action to remove informal development around Sadat City. Inspection of Google images reveals only two obvious informal areas close to Sadat City, with a combined area of less than 25 ha.

The limited government action to provide better housing in Cairo's informal settlements invariably involves redevelopment. Take, for instance, the Rawdat Al-Sayeda scheme in the Sayeda Zainab area in central Cairo. The scheme covers 7.5 feddans (3.15 ha) and comprises 16 six-storey housing blocks, which provide 815 residential units and 344 commercial units (*Egypt Today*, 2018). The housing and population densities are thus 258 units and around 1,100 persons per hectare. While high, these figures are lower than those found in some informal housing areas. The Rawdat Al-Sayeda scheme has a generally regular layout, modified as necessary to suit the irregular shape of the site, with clearances between blocks varying from about 7 metres to about 15 metres.

Despite its size, Egypt's public house building programme has not stemmed the growth of informal settlements on agricultural land around Cairo. In 2006 about 63 per cent of the population of Greater Cairo lived in informal areas, which constituted approximately 39 per cent of its built-up area (Sims, 2010). Estimated contributions of the public, private, and informal sectors to housing production over the period 1996–2006 were 10.5 per cent, 24.3 per cent, and 65.2 per cent, and the contribution of informal housing has increased significantly since 2006 (Sims and Abd-El Fattah, 2016). Analysis of Ministry of Agriculture data suggests that the rate of loss of farmland to illegal construction since 2011 has actually increased, and is around 40 per cent greater than the average rate over the period 1983–2011 (Masri and Abdelaty, 2018).

There are several reasons why the public housing programme has failed to meet the housing needs of low-income people and so replace informal development on agricultural land. The most important of these relate to affordability, location, and the absence of social networks. Despite subsidy, the housing units are relatively expensive. Sims (2010) stated that, prior to the launching of the NHP in 2005, subsidies ensured that monthly instalment payments were affordable to all but the lowest income families. However, prices have increased significantly since then. Shawkat (2014b) stated that the cost of a subsidized apartment increased by 270 per cent, from LE 50,000 to LE 135,000, between 2005 and 2014. Official press releases gave the minimum monthly mortgage payment for housing units provided under the SHP as LE 480 per month. It was estimated that this would require a household income of LE 23,000 per year. According to the CAPMAS 2012/2013 Household Income, Expenditure and Consumption Survey, households with this income would fall into the middle-income bracket. In 2014, it was estimated that around 10 per cent of low-income families would be unable to afford the LE 225 per month rent for one of the 10 per cent of SHP units reserved for rent (Egyptian Initiative for Personal Rights, 2014). Recent schemes have provided larger and hence more expensive units, 75 m^2 and 90 m^2 in the case of the SHP, further reducing affordability. The low proportion of rental units also reduces affordability. The proportion of rental units in Egypt as a whole halved between 1986 and 2017, from 29 per cent to 14 per cent. (Shawkat, 2018). Wide roads, designed for cars that low-income residents are unlikely to be able to afford, and generous provision of public open space increase both construction costs and the need for subsequent maintenance of public spaces.

One important result of these factors is that a very high proportion of the housing stock lies vacant. Analysis of 2006 census data suggests gross vacancy rates in Cairo and Giza Governorates of 28 per cent and 34 per cent respectively, compared with gross vacancy rates in informal areas ranging from 15 per cent in Matariya to 24 per cent in Embaba (Sims and Abd-El Fattah, 2016). These figures exclude apartments that are vacant because their owners are working overseas but do include apartments in buildings that are under construction. Whatever the exact figures, they do clearly indicate that formal units are less likely to be occupied than informal units.

The challenges posed by location and the lack of social networks are related. Almost all government housing schemes are located on desert land, in places that are usually remote from the target population's work and existing social networks. The influence of these factors, always great, has increased as Cairo has grown and the focus of government housing programmes has shifted to the new cities. Problems associated with distance from workplaces are likely to be greatest early in a settlement's existence, when public transport links are poor or non-existent. Experience in Greater Cairo and elsewhere suggests that some people are prepared to live with such problems. Sims (2010) reported the existence of new informal settlements on desert land 12–30 km south of Helwan and 35–54 km from Cairo city centre. Nevertheless, it is reasonable to assume that people will generally prefer to live close to their work and their social networks.

Another important factor is the lack of variety offered by formal housing schemes. Most offer something similar to the Asmarat scheme's living room, two bedrooms, kitchen, and bathroom and thus fail to provide an adequate response to the range of household sizes and types seeking accommodation. In older schemes, people sometimes responded to this situation by extending their apartments, as described in Box 5.1. Their action represents what is,

Box 5.1 Occupier ownership and investment: two public housing schemes in Cairo

Tipple (2000) provides information on housing unit 'transformations' in two housing schemes in Greater Cairo. The Gamal Abdel Nasser public housing scheme in Medinet Nasr (Nasr City) provided 1,200 apartments, the first of which were allocated in 1967. Householders acquired apartments through what was in effect a hire purchase agreement. Tenants paid a monthly instalment and ownership passed to the occupier when the 180th monthly payment had been made, 15 years after the apartment had been occupied. The selling prices were low and subsidized. The Economic Housing scheme in Worker's City, Helwan, constructed in the early 1960s to provide housing for workers in nearby heavy industry, was larger, comprising 2,460 five-storey apartment blocks. In both developments, construction consisted of reinforced concrete frames with brick infill walls. Standard blocks were built in rows with public space between.

In both locations, occupants of apartments invested heavily in extensions once they owned their properties. The process appears to have started around 1980 and was well established by the mid-1980s. In Helwan, the occupants of ground-floor apartments were the first to act, building load-bearing brick extensions. These could not support many storeys and so brought no significant benefits to people living in the apartments above. A new form of construction evolved as households living in apartments vertically above and below one another cooperated to build framed extensions extending the full height of the block. The depth of these extensions, typically 3–4 metres, was limited by the distance between blocks. Extensions typically occupied areas in the range 10–30 m^2, with a median increase of over 20 m^2, of which 15–16 m^2 was habitable space. The occupants of corner apartments, who had the option of extending to the side of their apartment as well as in front of it, invested in the largest extensions. In extending apartments and reducing the distance between blocks, occupants were following the example of informal sector builders, who generally provide a relatively narrow right of way, usually 6 metres or less, between housing blocks. Tipple (2000) and Sibley-Behloul (2002) provide further information on the process, including photographs.

in effect, informal extension of formally acquired properties. Such action is more difficult in recently constructed schemes, partly because they provide less space between blocks than the older schemes and partly because of the increased enforcement of planning and building regulations. Restrictive rules further constrain people's choices. Although schemes such as Asmarat include provision for shops, workshops, and *ahwas* (traditional coffee/shisha houses), these facilities are often unoccupied, perhaps reflecting the high rental and purchase prices for such facilities. People do set up informal shops and workshops in schemes such as Asmarat, but risk fines for undertaking such 'illegal' activities (Mohie, 2018).

Key points to take from this overview of housing policy and practice in Egypt in general and Greater Cairo in particular are as follows.

1. Poor construction quality and lack of regular maintenance mean that many older units built through public housing programmes are in poor condition.
2. The overall quality of the housing stock, including that built informally, is reasonably good and most Egyptian families, whether living in formal or informal areas, on erstwhile agricultural land or government-owned desert land and whether renting or owning housing units, enjoy relatively secure tenure (Sims and Abd-El Fattah, 2016).
3. Many formally provided apartments are in new towns and 'new communities' located in the desert far from the places where poor people now live and work, and are thus often uninhabited.
4. These units are only affordable to poor people when highly subsidized.
5. Despite the best efforts of the Egyptian Government and formal sector private developers, investment in formal housing has not stemmed the growth of the informal housing sector.

India: from slum clearance to slum redevelopment?

The pioneering role of Mumbai and Maharashtra

Since independence in 1947, India has experienced rapid urban growth, much of which has been in informal settlements. Informal development in India takes two basic forms, illegal occupation of vacant, often government, land and unregulated subdivision of private land. The Indian Government refers to congested settlements with poor infrastructure as slums. Not surprisingly, given its negative view of such settlements, its initial focus was on slum clearance, a point that is well illustrated by the case of Mumbai. In 1954, an amendment to the Bombay Municipal Corporation Act empowered the municipal corporation to clear slums. Central Government's Slum Areas (Improvement and Clearance) Act followed in 1956. However, no significant clearance occurred in Mumbai prior to 1967, when the municipal corporation launched its development plan, which included provision for slum clearance. In 1969, it created the Slum Improvement Cell, with a remit to clear and resettle slums located on municipal land. Enactment of the Maharashtra Slum Areas (Improvement, Clearance and Redevelopment) Act in 1971 equipped government with wider powers to notify slums and implement clearance schemes (Risbud, 2003). Similar developments were occurring in other Indian states, many of which set up slum clearance boards. As in Egypt, the focus was on providing standardized walk-up apartments. Despite the fact that apartments were smaller than those in Egypt, poor households could not afford the housing provided without subsidy, the provision of which placed a severe strain on limited government resources.

Local politicians and municipal authorities have always provided funds for service improvements in low-income informal areas. However, their activities have usually been piecemeal and uncoordinated. From the 1960s onwards, international multilateral and bilateral agencies supported efforts to promote the sites and services and services upgrading schemes that will be the subjects of Chapters 6 and 7 respectively. In the 1990s, international agencies moved away from the sites and services paradigm and emphasized the role of government as an enabler rather than direct provider of services. Faced with the challenge of finding the considerable financial resources required to provide the required housing units, national, state, and municipal government bodies in India followed suit, focusing on the potential role of the private sector in housing the poor. Mumbai's Slum Redevelopment Scheme (SRD), initiated in 1991, invited private developers to rehouse slum dwellers in small apartments, with a minimum of 180 square feet (16.7 m^2) carpet area. (The term carpet refers to the floor area excluding external and internal walls.) In return, the developer could use a floor space index (FSI) of 2.5 on slum plots instead of the 1.0 prevailing in the suburbs and 1.33 in the island city. Box 5.2 explains the concept of FSI, also known as floor area ratio (FAR). In addition to the slum rehabilitation units, the developer was free to construct shops and apartments for sale, with the profits on sales used to cross-subsidize the dwellings of the erstwhile slum dwellers. Slum dwellers were also required to pay the builder a minimum of Rs. 15,000 of the projected Rs. 75,000 cost of a 180 square foot tenement. In return, they received 30-year renewable leases but were not allowed to transfer ownership during the first 10 years of the lease. Schemes could only proceed with the approval of 75 per cent of the registered slum dwellers living on the site and developer profit was limited to 25 per cent of the scheme cost.

The scheme had limited success for reasons including:

- slum dweller distrust of developers and the reluctance of developers to engage in the difficult task of working with slum dwellers;
- difficulties in obtaining the consent of 75 per cent of slum dwellers, which were intensified by the existence of political factions which often supported rival developers;
- related to the last, problems with provision of temporary transit accommodation during construction;

- developer preference for projects on un-encroached land, with the prospect of higher profits than the 25 per cent maximum allowed in the SRD; and
- difficulties in meeting eligibility criteria – many residents had lived in their houses for less than the residence period of almost a decade required by the scheme rules (Jagdale, 2014).

Box 5.2 Floor space index, floor area ratio, and transferable development rights

The floor space index (FSI), also known as the Floor Area Ratio (FAR) is the ratio of the total covered area on all floors of all buildings on a plot to the area of the plot. This normally includes the area occupied by walls. Different FSIs may apply in different zones. The FSI determines the maximum feasible building height. For instance, if the building occupies 80 per cent of the plot area, a three-storey building will have an FSI of 2.4, permissible if the maximum allowable FSI is 2.5 but too high if the maximum allowable FSI is 1.33.

Slum Transferable Development Rights (slum TDR) are generated when a landowner or developer surrenders land to allow construction of tenements for slum dwellers, either those already living on the site or those who are displaced by development projects. The owner of the land must provide 'ground plus 5' or 'ground plus 7' apartments for existing residents and is then granted a TDR certificate that allows the holder to build an additional 1.0 m^2 of housing for each 1.0 m^2 of replacement slum housing built. This additional development right (ADR) must be used on the site until a minimum density of 500 dwelling units per hectare, as prescribed by the National Building Code, is reached. Beyond that, the developer can transfer the ADR to another site until the FSI reaches the maximum prescribed value for the area containing the slum site. Zoning rules define the areas in which TDR can be used.

Source: Based mainly on Chandy, 2007

Following a change of government in 1995, the Slum Rehabilitation Scheme (SRS) replaced the SRD. It removed the Rs.15,000 beneficiary contribution requirement and 25 per cent cap on profit and increased the minimum carpet area to 225 square feet (20.9 m^2). It still required the consent of 75 per cent of affected slum dwellers, subsequently reduced to 70 per cent. In 1995, the Maharashtra State Government created the Slum Rehabilitation Authority (SRA) to implement the SRS. This was to serve as the local and planning authority for all slum areas in Greater Mumbai. The inclusion of the term rehabilitation in its title is misleading since the SRA's remit is one of redevelopment, replacing existing informal housing with medium or high-rise tenement apartments. It makes no explicit provision for low-rise housing, either in the form of complete units or through the provision of serviced sites. Like the SRD, the SRS relies on an increased FSI to allow construction and sale of additional apartments to subsidize the cost of rehousing slum dwellers. Apartment blocks provided under the scheme have increased in height over the years, to 12 storeys or more, creating a need to provide lifts. In September 2018, the Government of Maharashtra announced that illegal hutment dwellers who were notified after 2000 and before 2011 would have to pay the full cost of apartments provided through SRA projects (Suryawanshi, 2018).

Maharashtra's current (2019) planning rules allow the FSI sanctioned for a slum rehabilitation scheme to exceed 3.0, increasing to 4.0 where the existing housing density exceeds 650 dwelling units per hectare (DU/ha). Other small changes were made, but the planning rules and rehabilitation schemes continue to be difficult to apply and implement.

National housing programmes

Later national programmes incorporated aspects of the Maharashtra approach, adopting similar space standards and focusing on the provision of apartments. The Basic Services for the Urban Poor (BSUP) component of the Indian Union Government's flagship Jawaharlal Nehru National Urban Renewal Mission (JNNURM) programme ran from 2005 to 2014. BSUP typically provided apartments in 4–5 storey blocks with walk-up access, although some schemes rose to eight storeys or more, with lifts provided. As in Mumbai, the floor space provided increased over time from 180 square feet (16.7 m^2) to 225 square feet (20.9 m^2), sufficient to provide two rooms and basic WC and bathing facilities. Standard designs grouped apartments around one or more stairwells. In most cases, blocks were evenly spaced with open space between them.

From 2009, the Rajiv Awas Yojana (RAY) scheme complemented and eventually replaced BSUP. This 'Housing for All' scheme aimed to prevent further slum creation by providing slum dwellers with appropriate housing with long leases. In 2015, it was replaced by a new low-income housing scheme, Pradhan Mantri Awas Yojana (PMAY). The change in name reflects a change in government rather than a change in approach. PMAY's stated aim was to ensure that every Indian family has a house built from permanent and durable materials, with a water connection, toilet facilities, and 24 hours a day electricity supply by 2022, the 75th anniversary of India's independence. With this in mind, its initial target was to construct 10 million housing units in urban areas, subsequently revised upwards to 11 million, by 2022 (Singh 2018). PMAY initially targeted low-income households, but by early 2017, its scope had been expanded to include middle-income households. The scheme has four components (MoHUPA, 2016):

1. *In situ slum redevelopment (ISSR component) using land as a resource and with the participation of private developers*. This option is possible on Central and State Government land, urban local body land and private land that is already occupied by slum housing. It involves construction of new multi-storey apartment blocks by a private sector partner, selected through an open bidding process. In order to ensure the financial viability of ISSR, the PMAY guidelines allow the FSI to be increased to 4.0, if the developer hands over a proportion of the apartments provided, typically 50 per cent, to government. The assumption is that this allows landowners to provide additional units, which they can then sell on the open market to finance the rehousing of the existing low-income residents.

2. *Credit-linked subsidy scheme (CLSS component) to increase access of poor households to affordable housing.* The scheme provides a subsidy on the interest rate charged on loans of up to Rs. 600,000, equivalent to about US$8,500, thus reducing the amount that the borrower has to pay back. The subsidy is available to 'Economically Weaker Section' (EWS) households, Low Income Group (LIG) households, for housing units with carpet areas of 30 m^2 and 60 m^2 respectively. (EWS households are those with an annual income less than Rs. 300,000 ($4,300) and LIG households are those with annual incomes between Rs. 300,000 ($4,300) and Rs. 600,000 ($8,600).) The subsidy is available for the period of the loan, up to a maximum of 15 years. Those wishing to take a loan must be able to produce a recognized form of identification, such as a government identity card, a voter card or a certificate of house ownership.
3. *Partnerships with public and private sector actors to provide affordable housing* (affordable housing in partnership (AHP) component). Houses are provided in mixed schemes that deliver at least 250 houses, of which at least 35 per cent are intended for EWS households. Under this component, Central Government can provide a subsidy of up to Rs. 150,000 (about $2,100) per housing unit to States, Union Territories, and other organizations for units intended for EWS households.
4. *Subsidies for beneficiary-led construction or enhancement of individual houses* (BLC component). This option is available to households living in houses built with non-permanent materials in settlements for which there are no plans for *in situ* redevelopment. To be eligible for a subsidy, a household must have a carpet area of less than 21 m^2, the additional floor area should not be less than 9 m^2 and the floor area of the completed house should not exceed 30 m^2 (MoHUA, n.d.).

The PMAY guidelines state that the contribution of each of the four components should be determined in response to the demand for housing, as determined by a demand survey and set out in a 'Housing for All Plan of Action' (HFAPoA) for each city (MoHUPA, 2016). However, ISSR is the preferred option for settlements with 'low' (350 DU/ha) and 'medium' (500 DU/ha) housing densities. Where the state government has a TDR policy and the ability to implement that policy, the ISSR approach can be used for higher densities. It is worth noting that the suggested densities for ISSR exceed those found in many informal settlements in India and elsewhere. The AHP, CLSS, and BLC options can be considered where the ISSR mechanism is not viable (MoHUA, n.d.).

Support for the focus on ISSR is provided by the findings of an exercise to compare the costs and benefits of the ISSR, AHP, and BLC. For Rajasthan, the benefit to cost ratios were 2.20 for ISSR, 1.49 for AHP, and 1.20 for BLC (Kundu and Kumar, 2018). Similar benefit to cost ratios were found for Andhra Pradesh. Regardless of ISSR's clearly higher benefit-cost ratio, it has had a very limited impact. Its benefits thus remain more theoretical than real.

The default position of government through all these changes in housing policy has been that slums are a blight on the city and stand in the way of progress towards the 'beautification' required to achieve 'world class' city status (Dupont, 2008). In the early years after independence, this no doubt reflected the socialist philosophy of the Congress Government, but governments of all hues have adopted the same approach, despite the fact that India is now a market economy. The success or otherwise of this approach can be assessed in terms of performance against its output targets, success in meeting the needs of the urban poor, and the quality of the living environment created, each of which is briefly considered below.

Performance against output targets

Despite the relaxation of some of the SRD requirements, the initial impact of the SRS was limited. By March 2000, only 3,486 units to house slum dwellers were complete, although 75,000 slum households had expressed interest in having their settlements redeveloped (*Times of India*, 2000, reported by Mukhija, 2001). By 2007, the implementation rate had increased with a construction rate averaging between 10,500 and 15,000 dwelling units per year over a 10-year period (Chandy, 2007). A more recent *Times of India* report suggests that the slum TDR area generated in Mumbai has reduced over the years, from a maximum of about 1 million m^2 in 2004 to 200,000 m^2 in 2015, 97,155 m^2 in 2017, and just over 70,000 m^2 in 2018. The report suggested that the decline could be explained partly by the stagnant property market and partly by the state government's delay in implementing new development control rules (Bharucha, 2018).

Patel (2013) reports the findings of investigations in 11 of the 63 cities covered by the BSUP scheme, chosen to ensure diversity in terms of location, size, approach, and implementation progress. In 9 of the 11 cities investigated, investigators found that the proportion of slum households covered was low, ranging from 3 per cent to 16 per cent with the proportions in most cities clustered around 13 per cent. In all but one case, completion rates lay within the range 0 per cent to 43 per cent, mostly at the lower end of the range. Figures for ongoing construction varied from almost zero to 50 per cent. The one exception to this scenario was Visakhapatnam in Andra Pradesh, where all units were either completed or ongoing, but even there only 10 per cent of the completed units were occupied.

PMAY progressed slowly at first but has accelerated over time. By mid-2018, about 4 million houses had been sanctioned countrywide under its urban component, PMAY(U) (Jadhav, 2018). In March 2018, the Union Minister for Housing and Urban Affairs stated that work had started on about 1.8 million housing units and that about 400,000 units were complete. Of the units that were under construction, reports suggested that 55 per cent were at ground level, 12 per cent at foundation level, and the remainder at various stages of construction (Moneycontrol News, 2018). At about the same time, a parliamentary oversight committee report noted low dispersal of funds sanctioned for the programme and concluded that 'all is not well with the implementation of the scheme and the progress of PMAY has been disappointing' (quoted in Makkar, 2018). By late May 2019, the total number of housing units sanctioned had reached about 8.1 million. The Ministry of Housing and Urban Affairs website claimed that work had started on 4.603 million units, that 2.569 million units were complete and that 2.373 million units were occupied (MoHUA, 2019). The figures for houses started and occupied included 170,000 houses started under the earlier JNNURM scheme. Another source, quoting MoHUA data presented in the Lok Sabha (the Indian Parliament) in February 2019, gives the much lower figures of 1.44 million houses constructed under PMAY(U) and 1.39 million houses occupied up to 31 January 2019 (Saldanha and Salve, 2019). These totals amount to less than 20 per cent of the 7.6 million sanctioned units and suggest that PMAY was some way from achieving its stated objective of providing housing for all.

Whatever the exact figures on housing units started and completed, there is no doubt that the AHP and BLC components provide the bulk of the units sanctioned under PMAY. An answer to the Lok Sabha in December 2018 gave the number of units provided through the different 'pillars' of the PMAY programme as 314,703 units through CLSS, 452,137 units through ISSR, excluding units carried over from previous schemes, 2.188 million units through AHP, and 3.590 million units through BLC. The ISSR contribution of about 7 per cent of all housing units delivered under PMAY(U) was clearly much smaller than envisaged in the PMAY guidelines. Of the units provided under ISSR, almost 50 per cent were in Maharashtra. Andhra Pradesh had the highest number of AHP units, followed by Maharashtra, Karnataka, and Madhya Pradesh (Yuvaonline, 2019). The figures suggest that developers prefer the AHP's relatively simple option of providing tenement blocks on previously undeveloped land. The lack of ISSR schemes outside Maharashtra suggests that developers have faced difficulties in transferring the FSI/TDR mechanism from high-density cities like Mumbai to lower density cities.

Another constraint on implementation is the reluctance of many slum dwellers to move from their existing houses into new tenement blocks. Because of their requirement that at least 70 per cent of slum dwellers agree to the proposed redevelopment scheme, this is particularly important for ISSR schemes. Box 5.3 summarizes the findings of investigations in Ahmedabad in Gujarat, Berhampur in Odisha, and Nagpur, the third city of Maharashtra. All revealed slum dweller resistance to redevelopment. Many residents had already invested in buildings constructed from permanent materials and were reluctant to write off this investment. In some cases, rehoused households would be giving up moving from a larger plot to a smaller apartment.

Success in meeting the needs of the urban poor

The success of official housing programmes in meeting the needs of the poor depends on the interest and ability of formal providers to deliver housing that poor people want, in places where they want to live at prices that are

Box 5.3 Three examples of resistance to redevelopment

Detailed investigations in one slum in Ahmedabad revealed initial resident fears that the promise of new apartments was nothing more than a ploy to evict them from their present location. Some residents resisted the scheme because they did not have the formal documentation required to prove that they met the residence requirements to be allocated an apartment. The engagement of a local NGO to liaise with residents helped to overcome some of the resistance and the developer prepared a scheme and submitted it to the municipal corporation. However, those who had not agreed to the proposed scheme continued to oppose it and demolition of existing hutments stalled as opponents challenged the scheme in the courts. Multiple individual cases reached the Gujarat High Court, which eventually ruled that the development should continue (Mahadevia et al., 2018).

In 2013, Berhampur Municipal Corporation (BMC) in Odisha surveyed slums in the city while preparing a 'Slum Free City Plan of Action' (SFCPoA) as part of the Rajiv Awas Yojana (RAY) programme. This identified 163 slum settlements, housing 16,400 households, with more than 50 per cent of the dwelling units built from permanent materials and a further 27 per cent classed as semi-permanent. Plot sizes varied from 15 m^2 to 45 m^2 and 44 per cent of households had a *patta* (legal document providing proof of ownership) giving them residential rights. Based on the SFCPoA findings, BMC proposed redevelopment of 25 slums, housing 5,012 households. All schemes involved complete clearance of the slum and construction of four-storey walk-up apartments. Most households in the selected slums possessed a *patta* and some had already constructed houses from permanent materials and had paved access and a municipal water supply. By 2017, work had started on only nine slums, partly because of resident resistance to demolition and rehousing (Mahila Housing SEWA Trust, 2017).

A 2017 survey of more than 3,000 households, carried out in nine notified and five non-notified slums in Nagpur, found that carried out by Youth for Unity and Voluntary Action (YUVA) joined the Indian Housing Federation (IHF). Almost 90 per cent of interviewees from notified slums and 94 per cent of those from non-notified slums wished to improve their existing dwellings rather than move into new apartments. Most were interested in adding another room and many desired improved sanitation. The findings suggest that the BLC component of PMAY would be the preferred option for most interviewees. However, about 57 per cent of those favouring upgradation of their existing house had a house with a floor area greater than 300 sq ft (27.9 m^2), and so would not theoretically be eligible for subsidy through BLC. No less than 87 per cent of those wanting new housing had accommodation with a floor area of less than 300 sq ft.

Almost all the surveyed slum dwellers had an Aadhaar card, a 12-digit unique identity number that Indian residents can obtain, based on their biometric and demographic data. However, many lacked other important documents required from those seeking to benefit under the BLC and CLSS verticals of PMAY. In particular, only 8.8 per cent had a property tax receipt, a basic requirement for accessing the BLC and CLSS components of PMAY (YUVA, 2018).

affordable to them. Like the Egyptian approach, the Indian approach offers a limited range of house units, configured in ways that are not conducive to many of the home and locally based activities found in informal areas. Turning to location, India's emphasis on *in situ* redevelopment does overcome one of the problems with Egypt's housing programme, the remoteness of new housing from people's work and social networks. Unfortunately, it does this at the expense of considerable disruption to people's day-to-day life and requires that the residents of an area are rehoused while redevelopment is in progress. In practice, as already noted, *in situ* redevelopment accounts for a far smaller proportion of the housing units provided under PMAY than was intended by the scheme's planners. One reason for this is that developers are primarily interested in profit, which can be maximized by building apartments for slum dwellers in remote suburbs, where land prices are low, using the construction rights generated on units for higher-income households in prime locations such as Bandra and Juhu. Their schemes reduce the already limited land area available to the poor residents of informal areas (Indorewala and Wagh, 2016).

Even if suitable formal housing is provided where people want to live, it is unlikely that the poorest people can afford it. Agarwal et al. (2013) suggested that the maximum that a household in the government's EWS category could afford would be Rs295,000, Rs265,000 short of the Rs560,000 required to build the minimum 25 square metre unit stipulated by government. A household would have to have an income placing it at the top end of the government's LIG category to be able to afford a house without subsidy. This helps to explain the figures given in the Lok Sabha answer quoted above, which show that the subsidized AHP component of PMAY has been much more successful than ISSR in providing housing units. However, developers only need to target 35 per cent of these units at EWS beneficiaries, so it is likely that AHP mainly benefits higher-income households, who may or may not have previously lived in informal areas.

The findings of the investigations summarized in Box 5.3 and the relative success of the AHP component suggest that there is a strong demand for *in situ* upgrading of existing houses. In Nagpur, a high proportion of the demand for house improvements under BLC came from households who already owned a house with a floor area of more than 300 sq ft (27.9 m^2). Those wishing to benefit from BLC should have an existing floor area of less than 322 sq ft (29.9 m^2), so it would seem that many of those favouring upgrading of their existing properties were theoretically ineligible for BLC funding. Taken together with the prominent role of BLC in the overall PMAY portfolio, this suggests that local authorities take a relaxed view of the BLC eligibility rules, with the likely result that those benefiting from BLC grants are not among the poorest inhabitants of informal settlements.

Eligibility to benefit from government schemes also affects the schemes' ability to meet the needs of the urban poor. Requirements for eligibility include proof of identity, which will be available for most through an Aadhar Card, proof of address, proof of income, and possession of relevant property documents. To be eligible for rehabilitation under the ISSR component of PMAY, potential beneficiaries must be able to produce evidence that they were resident in the slum since before a cut-off date. Decisions on cut-off dates are the responsibility of individual states/urban bodies, most of which update the cut-off date from time to time. For instance, surveys carried out in Ahmedabad, Gujarat, revealed that many residents did not possess the formal documentation required to prove their period of residence, despite the fact that they had lived in their present home for more than 10 years. The state government reacted positively by:

- setting a cut-off date of 1 December 2010 in 2018, significantly later than Mumbai's then date of 1 January 2000, which had only recently been revised from a 1995 date; and
- extending eligibility to include hutments that had been allocated a unique Household Identification Number (HIN) during a 2010 socio-economic survey (Mahadevia et al., 2018).

Gujarat's eligibility rules are relatively generous. In Maharashtra, the cut-off date for occupants of hutments certified as eligible by the 'competent authority' is 1995 later extended to 2000 (Jog, 2014). Regardless of the cut-off date, they must be able to prove either that they were resident or that they had inherited or bought their property from someone who was resident before that date. Those who cannot provide proof will not have a place in the redeveloped settlement and will have no option but to move to unauthorized slums (Zhang, 2016).

In Kolkata, the Thika Tenancy Act prohibited changes in land-use patterns in slum areas and the use of *thika* land for commercial purposes. For many years, informal sector developers ignored these provisions of the act, replacing hutment dwellings with walk-up apartments. The normal practice was to house existing tenants in small apartments on the ground floor and to rent out the larger apartments provided on higher floors (author's observations in late 1990s). In 2019, the Government of Bengal amended the Thika Tenancy Act to allow *thika* tenants to replace hutments with buildings up to five storeys in height (*Times of India*, 2019).

Quality of the living environment

The poor condition of older apartment-based public housing in both Egypt and India is likely to be a result of both poor construction and inadequate maintenance. However, high housing densities are a potentially greater problem in recent Indian slum redevelopment schemes. As explained in Box 5.4, redevelopment schemes that include housing for higher-income groups further reduce the already limited land area available to low-income households and can only work with very high housing densities. Zhang (2016) points out that, without adequate planning and construction standards, there is a danger that rehabilitation buildings will become 'vertical slums'.

The reality is that standards do exist. The issue is not therefore a lack of standards but rather the ability of existing standards to ensure liveable conditions in redevelopment and new-build schemes. This is particularly true of standards for the minimum space between buildings. In Mumbai, the 2016 Revised Draft Development Plan (RDDP) specifies two sets of building envelope standards, the first for general use and the second for use in rehabilitation and resettlement (R&R) projects. While the general standards tie allowable building

Box 5.4 How FSI can result in greatly increased densities in previously informal areas

K East Ward is located just north of Mumbai International Airport. About 60 per cent of its households, 90,000 in all, live in informal settlements, which occupy 270 hectares or 11.2 per cent of the ward area. The Revised Draft Development Plan (RDDP) for Mumbai, reserves 33.7 hectares, 1.4 per cent of the ward's land area, for rehabilitation and resettlement (R&R) schemes, to be implemented with an FSI of 4.0. Indorewala and Wagh (2016) assumed a mean apartment size of 25 m^2 and an FSI of 4.0 and calculated that it would be possible to provide 54,000 tenement units at a density of 1,600 units per hectare on the 33.7 hectares. Under this scenario, about 36 per cent of the ward's poorest households would be crammed onto only 1.4 per cent of the ward's area. Later, they quote an RDDP requirement for a minimum tenement density of 325 units per hectare for every 1.0 FSI, noting that for an FSI of 4.0, this would mean that every R&R scheme should contain not less than 1,300 dwelling units per hectare! Their calculation applies the FSI calculation to the whole area, including the area required for public spaces and roads and assumes an FSI figure of 4.0 rather than the 3.0 figure specified by the Maharashtra Government for on-site redevelopment. Assuming that plots cover 70 per cent of the total area and taking an FSI of 3.0, the housing density reduces to 840 units per hectare. Even this reduced figure is 1.68 times the maximum residential density of 500 units per hectare prescribed by the National Building Code norms for low-income housing. It would allow provision of about 28,300 units on the 33.7 hectares reserved in the RDDP. An approximate calculation, based on sets of four tenement blocks, each providing 12 apartments per floor, surrounded by 9 m roads, with set-backs as per the 2014 Mumbai Urban Development Project (MUDP) Notification, gives the housing density achievable as about 155 units per floor per hectare, far short of the 325 dwelling units per floor per hectare figure given in the RDDP. To achieve the 840 units per hectare figure, blocks should have between five and six floors.

Source: Based on Indorewala and Wagh, 2016

heights to the width of the road that fronts them, the standards for redevelopment schemes allow any height of building on roads of 9 metres width and more. To the front and rear, the minimum space between buildings up to 30 metres in height is 6 metres (Indorewala and Wagh, 2016). These standards conform with those set out in the 2014 Maharashtra Urban Development Department (2014) Notification, which requires at least 6 metres between two rehabilitation buildings up to 40 metres in height, increased to 7.5 metres for buildings between 40 and 50 metres in height, and 9 metres for buildings above 50 metres in height. The key point here is that constructing high blocks in such close proximity must lead to situations that deprive most if not all their inhabitants of light, air, open space, and privacy. In this respect, they result in conditions that are similar to those found in informal settlements in Cairo.

Space standards are not the only problems with R&R housing in India. For example, one study has highlighted the fact that new slum rehabilitation housing layout designs are frequently problematic, leading to dramatically increased consumption of electricity by households, with negative effects on both total energy consumption and household budgets (Almeroth-Williams, n.d.).

There have been some attempts to improve the design of apartment housing. For instance, the award winning Mumbai-based architect Charles Correa retained the 20.9 square metre apartment size but arranged the units in clusters of four, separated by staircases and arranged so that each unit faced the open air on two sides (Correa, 2000). Nirman, the building arm of the Indian Alliance, made some changes to the basic design, increasing the width of access corridors to 6 feet (1.83 metres) and improving the internal layout of apartments. However, they, like all those working on SRA schemes, have to work within the parameters set by SRA.

Beneficiary control over the process

The PMAY guidelines refer briefly to the need to consult with organizations that represent slum dwellers while formulating redevelopment projects, but provide no guidance on how to carry out this consultation. Rather, they adopt a technical approach, which emphasizes the need for computer-based management information systems for tracking project progress and recording details of project beneficiaries. A study of two slum communities in Nagpur, one scheduled for *in situ* redevelopment and the other a redevelopment site, found that residents were neither informed nor consulted and had no influence over critical decisions. The guidelines on community participation were vague and there was no 'political' culture of participation. NGOs had been employed to facilitate implementation but their main role was to generate community consent for execution of standardized projects, conceived by others. The authors of a paper describing the study concluded that market-oriented urban governance negatively influences the implementation of fully fledged community participation during public housing schemes (De Geest and De Nys Ketels, 2019).

Community-led housing: the CLIFF initiative

Despite the references to consultation, India's slum redevelopment schemes provide limited scope for beneficiary participation. An investigation in 11 cities covered by the BSUP scheme found that consultants or municipal engineers had prepared most city development plans and detailed project reports. Scope for input from intended beneficiaries had been at best limited (Patel, 2013). Even if the process provided for greater levels of participation, it is difficult to see how this could lead to significant design changes, given the prevalence of the apartment block model. The dependence on conventional contracts further limited the scope to ensure accountability to beneficiaries. In almost all the 11 sites investigated, Patel found that residents were dissatisfied with the new housing and often in conflict with the authorities. In some cases, the apartments offered were smaller than the homes that people were being forced to vacate.

Since 1986, the Indian Alliance, which comprises the NGO SPARC (the Society for the Promotion of Area Resource Centres) and two community-based networks, the National Slum Dwellers Federation (NSDF) and Mahila Milan, has sought to put the urban poor at the centre of housing planning and delivery processes. Founded in 1974, the NSDF now claims to have 750,000 members in over 70 towns and cities throughout India. Mahila Milan (women together) is a network of women's savings groups. SPARC was formed in 1984 to support the ideas and priorities of the urban poor. In 1998, the Alliance created the not-for-profit company Sparc Samudaya Nirman Sahayak (SSNS) to manage building and construction projects that it had initiated. By the end of the 1990s, the Alliance had developed a number of housing and infrastructure projects, which it believed could and should have a strong influence on policy and practice. Once these projects were complete, the Indian Government would reimburse 70–80 per cent of the cost, allowing the Alliance to reinvest the funds in further development. However, lack of finance for these projects had emerged as a major issue. The Alliance had built up a 'bridge finance' fund to provide funds to cover the period between expenditure on construction and reimbursement by government, but this was not large enough to service the growing number of projects that were being identified (SSNS website).

From 2002, the Alliance's programmes received financial and other support from the Community Led Infrastructure Finance Facility (CLIFF), an initiative of the British NGO Homeless International (now Reall – Real Equity for All) supported by the Department for International Development (DFID) and Swedish International Development Cooperation Agency (SIDA). One of CLIFF's central aims was to leverage financial resources from government and the private sector to facilitate scaling up and replication of the initiatives that it supported. Starting from the fundamental assumption that projects should emerge from strategies developed by organizations of the urban poor and reflecting their relationships with local authorities and municipal officials, it aimed to provide affordable finance to its implementing partners in order to allow them to develop financially viable housing projects for their low-income communities. Its activities would support scaling up of community-driven slum development, rehabilitation, and infrastructure initiatives in towns and cities characterized by high levels of poverty, with the ultimate aim of achieving reductions in urban poverty. However, its more immediate concern was with what it termed 'flagship' projects, which would provide examples of good practice and set a precedent for future scaling up. These must build on established organizations created by poor urban communities and must actively include and benefit the most poor and marginalized community members (World Habitat, 2014). One way of achieving the last objective was to channel construction work through community organizations and community entrepreneurs. The contract arrangements appear to have been informal, with little or no formal documentation. It appears that most were for finishing works such as plastering and painting. Nirman employed a female civil engineer to build the capacities of community contractors and supported those contractors by providing facilities such as a children's day care centre, health facilities, and housing for construction workers (WSP, 2010).

In order to achieve its objectives, CLIFF provided technical assistance grants, capital grants for projects, knowledge grants designed to support exchange visits and workshops, and grants for core administrative costs for partner organizations. Over the first five years of its existence, capital grants accounted for about 75 per cent of CLIFF's expenditure. CLIFF also provided an avenue for Homeless International's Guarantee Fund to be used to provide financial guarantees to underwrite some of the risks taken by banks when lending to projects. The aim was to support revolving funds with repayments on loans being recycled as projects were completed and revenues were received. While the concept of revolving funds was not new, the idea that organizations of the urban poor should control them certainly was. CLIFF's objective of levering financial resources from others was at least partially achieved as it convinced Citibank and India's National Housing Bank to provide loan financing for housing schemes. CLIFF-supported schemes also benefited directly from government funding for schemes to rehabilitate and rebuild informal areas.

In its first years, CLIFF supported projects in Mumbai, Bangalore (now Bengalaru), and the Maharashtra town of Solapur. Most involved slum redevelopment and resettlement, achieved through the construction of medium-rise apartment buildings. In Mumbai, CLIFF tapped into the SRA's Slum Rehabilitation Scheme. Its first slum redevelopment initiative was located in Rajiv Indira and Suryodaya, adjacent settlements that form part of Dharavi, Mumbai's biggest slum. Other early schemes included Milan Nagar, a resettlement scheme designed to house pavement dwellers, and Bharat, Janata, a redevelopment scheme. The Rajiv Indira Suryodaya and Milan Nagar schemes had predated CLIFF but the involvement of CLIFF enabled them to overcome funding constraints. All these schemes were modest in size and the Alliance's next move was to collaborate with a landowner and developer to build two much larger schemes in Oshiwara, north of the centre of Mumbai. Table 5.1 provides information on CLIFF-supported schemes in Mumbai and Pune.

Table 5.1 shows that, with the exception of the Oshiwara 2 project, none of the schemes provided more than 1,000 units. Viewed in relation to the scale of housing need in India, these figures are very modest and slow implementation further reduced CLIFF's impact. Table 5.1 shows that several projects remained incomplete in 2013, 15 years after the Alliance's initial engagement with Rajiv Indira Suryodaya, and around 10 years after commencement of several other projects in its Mumbai portfolio. Some of the delays were attributable to factors beyond the control of the Alliance and its CLIFF partners. Others resulted from problems that, despite being foreseeable, were difficult to deal with. For instance, work at Oshiwara stopped at one point because the site had been encroached. This created a dilemma for the Alliance – if it acted like a developer and removed the

Table 5.1 Summary of CLIFF schemes in Mumbai and Pune

Project name	*Project type*	*Households benefiting*	*Units for sale*	*Start date*	*Planned completion*	*Projected actual completion 2009*
Rajiv Indira Suryodaya	*In situ* redevelopment	209	27 + commercial	1998	2003	Four buildings complete 2013. For-sale unit not started. FSI reduced from 2.5 to 1.33 because of CRZ II rules
Milan Nagar	Resettlement	327	201	2001	2004	One of four units complete 2013
Bharat Janata	*In situ* redevelopment	147	50 + commercial	2003		3 out of 5 G+7 buildings complete in 2013. FSI reduced from 2.5 to 1.33 because of CRZ II rule
Oshiwara Phase 1	Resettlement/*in situ* redevelopment	780 G+7	38 + commercial	2004	2004	No information available after 2006. Said to be complete December 2006 but it may have been subsumed into Oshiwara 2.
Oshiwara Phase 2	Resettlement//*in situ* redevelopment	2564 G+7	120	2004	2006	In 2013, 7 out of 8 Phase 1 buildings were ready for occupation. 11 buildings to be provided under Phase 2 had not started
Jollyboard	Resettlement	101			2006	Scheduled late 2008
Pune incremental housing	*In situ* upgrading	750		2009		Carried out with funds from BSUP

Source: Information taken from several sources, including CLIFF annual reports and http://sparcnirman.org/projects.html
Note: CRZ is Coastal Regulation Zone

encroachers, it would run the risk of betraying its own commitment to poor people living in informal settlements.

A 2010 assessment of CLIFF activities in India identified other problems, including weak project management, a lack of clarity regarding the roles of implementing partners, and a lack of clear strategy. It found that a tension existed between the desire to pilot and demonstrate ideas and approaches in order to influence policy and the desire to tackle more and larger projects in order to take programme activities to scale. The Indian Alliance view was firmly on the side of piloting and demonstrating, a reasonable approach provided that there was at least an outline of a vision of where the piloting and demonstrating were intended to lead. The focus of CLIFF activities shifted over time, from *in situ* redevelopment to development on greenfield sites to upgrading of building structures *in situ*. While this contributed to the perceived lack of strategic direction, it could also be viewed as a flexible response to the opportunities created by changes in government policies and funding streams. Issues identified in relation to implementation included informal contractor selection procedures, the limited pool of community entrepreneurs to carry out community contracts and the difficulties and delays experienced in receiving government funding for schemes that depended on those subsidies (WSP, 2010).

Homeless International extended its activities to Kenya in 2005 and the Philippines in 2007, in both cases working with local federations of homeless people falling under the general umbrella of the organization Shack Dwellers International (SDI). A later phase of the CLIFF programme expanded to include activities in Nepal and several countries in Africa. Unlike the first phase, this phase included links with some organizations that were not part of SDI. DFID funding for CLIFF ended in 2015 although some CLIFF activities appear to have continued beyond that date. Overall, the initiative provided over 23,000 housing units over the 13 years of its existence (Majale et al., 2017). Overall, the impact of the CLIFF initiative was limited. It is arguable that one factor contributing to its limited impact was its inability to bridge the gap between formal and informal institutions and procedures. The 2010 Water and Sanitation Program (WSP) evaluation team were unable to find much contract documentation, particularly for subcontracts with community contractors. It appeared that main contractors were chosen because Alliance members knew and trusted them. Contracts were lump sum rather than measured, appropriate for small contracts with petty contractors but arguably unsuitable for the relatively large and complex schemes executed under CLIFF. Community contractors, perhaps better described as community entrepreneurs, were all Mahila Milan members, apparently selected without competition (WSP, 2010). In all these aspects, SSNS procedures diverged from those formally required for government contracts. SSNS acknowledged the tension. In its 2015–2016 Annual Report (SSNS, 2016), it referred to the duality that exists because of the parallel needs to ensure that people participate in the development process and to follow stringent government procedures. This duality could become problematic when state implementing agencies saw their relationship with non-state implementing agencies purely in terms of contractual obligations. The Annual Report referred to 'a series of complaints, show cause notices and blacklisting notices on performance default' (p. 13). It went on to identify a range of issues that 'are not accommodated within the sub-contracting norms that presume a cordial environment before assigning timeline and cost estimates' (p. 13). Navigating through these issues on contractual terms is 'something that simple subcontractors will never be able to handle' (p. 13). In making these points, the Annual Report attempted to explain and justify implementation delays, which clearly affected the relationship between SSNS and the government bodies with which it worked, particularly in Odisha State.

A final point is that the extent to which projects implemented by SSNS, including those financed through CLIFF, were truly community led is not clear. CLIFF reports do indicate that the impetus for early *in situ* redevelopment schemes came from community members but it is harder to see that this would be the case for new development schemes such as Oshiwara.

Prefabrication: the 'modern' way forward?

Conventional housing built to appropriate standards is expensive and is often unaffordable to poor households unless heavily subsidized. Over the years, many have argued that prefabrication can reduce construction costs and hence improve affordability. Prefabricated housing systems were introduced in the early 20th century but the idea really came into its own in the years after World War II. For instance, around 160,000 single storey 'prefabs' were constructed in the UK in the late 1940s and early 1950s. These houses fulfilled a need at a low price and most lasted for considerably longer than their planned 10-year lifespan. In the 1960s, several British cities invested in prefabricated apartment blocks. This investment came to an abrupt halt in 1968 with the collapse of the 22-storey Ronan Point block in Newham, East London, following a gas explosion in one of the apartments. The Ronan Point collapse resulted from a basic design fault: the floors relied on wall panels for support and collapsed when the explosion blew these out. Regardless of the prospects for rectifying this design fault, enthusiasm for fully prefabricated housing reduced after Ronan Point. Some specialist housing suppliers continued to produce more or less complete building systems, but the bulk of housing in developed countries has continued to be provided using 'traditional' building techniques.

The mid-20th century saw attempts to introduce prefabricated systems in Ghana, India, and Pakistan among others. These were not a success. The number of units produced was low, some systems relied on components imported from overseas and most, if not all, were more expensive than traditional construction using local material (Abrams, 1964: 165–68). Studies in Egypt reported in the early 1990s found that the cost of heavily prefabricated dwellings was about 40 per cent more than that of load-bearing brick construction and about 25 per cent more than concrete framed construction (Hassan, 1992). One important factor, perhaps neglected by those promoting prefabrication, was the low cost of labour in low-income countries, which must have favoured *in situ* building methods using relatively traditional methods.

The failure of these complete prefabricated systems led to renewed emphasis on conventional and self-help housing construction methods. A United Nations team, comprising Charles Abrams, Vladimir Bodiansky, and Otto Koenigsberger, visited Ghana, and recommended that government should facilitate the provision of components for roofs, doors, and windows. The effect was to shift the emphasis from prefabrication of whole buildings to that of key building components. Initiatives to provide prefabricated building components have continued over the years, often involving informal and semi-formal materials suppliers. In Pakistan, for instance, many small casting yards produce a roofing system consisting of precast concrete slabs spanning between pre-stressed concrete beams. The author used this system to provide roofs for a core housing scheme for a housing society formed to provide affordable housing for sweepers and other low-income members of the Christian community in Peshawar. The system is cheap but only suitable for roofs. Those wishing to build two or more storeys will normally elect to use *in situ* concrete frame and brick infill construction. In Bangladesh, many residents of informal areas use precast concrete door and window frames in preference to *in situ* wood construction. Bangladesh is also one of several countries in which residents of low-income settlements build with corrugated steel sheeting. While the system is cheap, the poor insulation qualities of the sheeting results in a poor living environment, with extreme high temperatures in summer and cold temperatures in winter.

Interest in complete fabricated housing systems has ebbed and flowed but has never disappeared. For instance, during the 1980s, one international NGO promoted prefabricated concrete dwellings as a solution to the housing needs of Afghan refugees living in Pakistan. The dwellings were circular in plan and thus quite inflexible. They provided little insulation and were therefore hot in summer. Not surprisingly, the initiative did not get very far. In 2014, prefabricated housing was being proposed as a solution to India's housing problems. The assumption was that by moving much of the construction process off-site, factory-based prefabrication would remove the need to temporarily rehouse residents while redeveloping informal settlements, which would in turn remove disincentives for developers to engage with the redevelopment of slums (Villaitramani and Hirani, 2014). The obvious flaw in this argument is its failure to recognize the need to relocate people while demolishing existing dwellings, building the foundations for the prefabricated units, and finishing those units once the basic prefabricated structure is in place. The paper shows no advance from

1950s thinking in that it assumes that demolition and redevelopment is the only option for Mumbai's slum settlement (ibid.).

Over the last few years there have been many studies and proposals for low-cost prefabricated housing systems that could be applied in developing countries. Some of these have focused on prefabricated components and kits, while others have promoted complete prefabrication systems. However, claims of dramatic cost reduction and thus improved affordability have proven unrealistic, and in any event very few schemes have resulted in more than a handful of prototype pilot units. Some schemes were simply impractical and utopian, some of the concepts seemed to represent wishful thinking, and many appear to have sunk without a trace.[1] For Charles Abrams, prefabrication was a term with a range of meanings. He noted that individual building components have been prefabricated since the beginning of urban civilization. For instance, the burnt bricks used in the Indus Valley Civilization cities of Moenjadaro and Harrapa around 5,000 years ago were prefabricated components, made and fired at one place and used in another. The question is not whether or not to use some prefabricated components but rather whether complete prefabrication of the house structure is desirable. Abrams' answer was yes to the first and no to the second. The brief survey of prefabrication initiatives over the last 50 years given above provides no grounds to revise his conclusion. There is a strong case for exploring options for improving production methods for individual building components. However, clever ideas for prefabricating complete buildings are unlikely to contribute much to meeting low-income housing needs for many years to come. This is particularly true of ideas conceived in the USA and Europe, where material and labour availability and price will normally be very different from those found in the towns and cities of the South.

Note

1. These schemes include those of the TATA Housing Group (2011), a $300 unit design challenge (Govindarajan and Sarkar, 2010), the Menlo Capital Group steel high rise (Suri, 2011), and most recently India's Ministry of Housing and Urban Affairs Global Housing Technology Challenge (https://ghtc-india.gov.in/Content/Guide-to-GHTC.html).

References

Abrams, C. (1964) *Housing in the modern world*, Faber & Faber.

Abu-Lughod, J. (1971) *Cairo: 1001 years of the city victorious*, Princeton University Press, Princeton, NJ.

Agarwal, A., Jain, V. and Kramchandan, A. (2013) *State of the low-income housing market: encouraging progress and opportunity to realize the dream of millions*, Monitor Deloitte. https://muthoot.com/pdf/Low-Income.pdf (accessed 27 June 2025).

Almeroth-Williams, T. (no date) Fixing India's slum rehabilitation housing, University of Cambridge [online]. https://www.cam.ac.uk/stories/indias-slum-rehabilitation-housing (accessed 3 August 2025).

Al-Youm, A.M. (2018) Tahya Misr Fund provides housing for 250,000 citizens, *Egypt Independent*, 26 December. https://ww.egyptindependent.com/tahya-misr-fund-provides-housing-for-250000-citizens-to-combat-slums/

Bharucha, N. (2018) Mumbai: Decline in slum TDR sharpest in 20 years, *Times of India*, 17 December. https://timesofindia.indiatimes.com/city/mumbai/mumbai-decline-in-slum-tdr-sharpest-in-20-years/articleshow/67120509.cms (accessed 7 June 2019).

Chandy, M. (2007) The Use of ADRs and TDRs in Slum Upgrading, Presentation at *World Bank Fourth Urban Research Forum, May*. http://siteresources.worldbank.org/INTURBANDEVELOPMENT/Resources/336387-1269364687916/6892589-1269394486592/chandy.pdf (accessed 7 June 2019; no longer available).

Correa, C. (2000) *Housing and urbanisation*, Thames and Hudson, London.

De Geest, F. and De Nys-Ketels, S. (2019) Everyday resistance: exposing the complexities of participatory slum-upgrading projects in Nagpur, *Housing Studies* 34(10): 1673–1689. https://doi.org/10.1080/02673037.2018.1562056

Dupont, V. (2008) Slum demolitions in Delhi since the 1990s: an appraisal, *Economic and Political Weekly*, 12 July 2008. https://www.academia.edu/5326192/Slum_Demolitions_in_Delhi_since_the_1990s_An_Appraisal (accessed 31 May 2019).

Egypt Today (2018) Construction works at Rawdat Al-Sayeda project finished, *Egypt Today*, 24 September. http://www.egypttoday.com/Article/1/58046/Construction-works-at-Rawdat-Al-Sayeda-project-finished (accessed 29 May 2019).

Egyptian Initiative for Personal Rights (EIPR) (2014) Discrimination against the poor and support for the undeserving: EIPR analysis of the new conditions for the Social Housing Programme, Press release, 10 April 2014. https://www.eipr.org/en/press/2014/04/discrimination-against-poor-and-support-undeserving-eipr-analysis-new-conditions (accessed 31 October 2019).

Esterman, I. (2014) Egypt's steep learning curve in national housing projects, *Mada Masr*, 15 April. https://madamasr.com/en/2014/04/15/feature/economy/egypts-steep-learning-curve-in-national-housing-projects/

Fathy, H. (1973) *Architecture for the poor: an experiment in rural Egypt*, University of Chicago Press, Chicago.

Govindarajan, V. and Sarkar, C. (2010) The $300 house: a hands-on lab for reverse innovation? *Harvard Business Review*, 26 August. https://hbr.org/2010/08/the-300-house-a-hands-on-lab-f (accessed 3 August 2025).

Hassan, M.M. (1992) Low cost housing finance in developing countries; with reference to Egypt, in L. Kilmartin and H. Singh (eds), *Housing in the third world: analysis and solutions*, pp. 317–28, Concept, New Delhi.

Indorewala, H. and Wagh, S. (2016) Discriminatory living standards: FSI, tenement densities and building controls for low income housing in RDDP 2016, BlogURK, Reimagining Cities in the Global South. https://theblogurk.wordpress.com/2016/08/18/discriminatory-living-standards-fsi-tenement-densities-and-building-controls-for-low-income-housing-in-the-rddp-2016/ (accessed 9 August 2019).

Invest-gate (2016) *Social Housing Report 2016.* http://invest-gate.me/wp-content/uploads/2016/06/Social-Housing-Report-2016-2.pdf (accessed 31 October 2019).

Jadhav, R. (2018) PM Awas Yojana: Only 8 per cent target met under urban housing scheme, *Times of India*, 22 March. https://timesofindia.indiatimes.com/india/pm-awas-yojana-only-8-target-met-under-urban-housing-scheme/articleshow/63405544.cms (accessed 17 January 2018).

Jagdale, R.H. (2014) *An Overview of Slum Rehabilitation Schemes in Mumbai, India*, Report prepared in partial fulfilment of Master's degree requirement, University of Texas at Austin, https://repositories.lib.utexas.edu/server/api/core/bitstreams/e604b708-d179-4f7b-b065-696774fcef84/content (accessed 3 August 2025).

Jog, S. (2014) 'Maharashtra passes Bill to change cut-off date', *Business Standard*, 1 March, https://www.business-standard.com/article/current-affairs/maharashtra-passes-bill-to-change-cut-off-date-114022801016_1.html (accessed 13 August 2025).

Kundu, A. and Kumar, A. (2018) *Cost-benefit analysis of housing vertical interventions for the urban poor in large cities of Rajasthan*, Copenhagen Consensus Center. https://www.copenhagenconsensus.com/sites/default/files/raj_social_housing_formatted_sm.pdf (accessed 11 November 2019).

Mahadevia, D., Bhatia, N. and Bhatt, B. (2018) Private sector in affordable housing? Case of slum rehabilitation scheme in Ahmedabad, India, *Environment and Urbanization ASIA*, 9 (1): 1–17. https://doi.org/10.1177/0975425317748449

Maharashtra Urban Development Department (2014) *Notification No. TPS 1212/121/CR-162/13/UD-12, dated 11th September 2014*, https://cihab.in/wp-content/uploads/2021/06/SRA-Thane.pdf (accessed 3 August 2025).

Mahila Housing SEWA Trust (2017) Report submitted to the Inclusive Cities Partnership Programme, GIZ, http://www.mahilahousingtrust.org/wp-content/uploads/2017-05-12_Land-Tenure-Study_MHT.pdf (accessed 15 February 2019; no longer available).

Majale, M., Sigvaldsen, E. and Murray, P. (2017) *Community Led Infrastructure Finance Facility (CLIFF): Milestone evaluation of CLIFF2b.* https://iati.fcdo.gov.uk/iati_documents/50375580.pdf (accessed 3 August 2025).

Makkar, S. (2018) 4 years of Modi govt: NDA's 'housing for all' project falls short of target, *Business Standard*, 18 May. https://www.business-standard.com/article/economy-policy/4-years-of-modi-govt-nda-s-housing-for-all-project-falls-short-of-target-118051800058_1.html (accessed 14 June 2019).

Masri, L. and Abdelaty, A. (2018) Egypt's poor bear brunt of crackdown on farmland building, *Reuters*, 27 November. https://www.reuters.com/article/us-egypt-agriculture-housing/egypts-poor-bear-brunt-of-crackdown-on-farmland-building-idUSKCN1NW163 (accessed 29 December 2018).

Ministry of Housing & Urban Affairs (MoHUA) (no date) *Preparation of Housing for All Plan of Action (HFAPoA).* http://mohua.gov.in/upload/uploadfiles/files/HFAPoA per cent20Module-Final per cent20Draft.pdf (accessed 11 June 2019).

MoHUA (2019) *Pradhan Mantri Awas Yojana (Urban) Housing for All (HFA) State wise Progress (Since 2014)* [As on 27 May 2019]. http://mohua.gov.in/upload/uploadfiles/files/4(14).pdf (accessed 16 June 2019).

Ministry of Housing and Urban Poverty Alleviation (MoHUPA) (2016) *Pradhan Mantri Awas Yojana: Housing for All (Urban) Scheme Guidelines, March 2016*, MoHUPA, Government of India, https://mohua.gov.in/upload/uploadfiles/files/18HFA_guidelines_March2016-English.pdf (accessed 3 August 2025).

Mohie, M. (2018) Asmarat: The state's model housing for former 'slum' residents, S. Khalifa (tr.), *Mada Masr*, 18 June. https://madamasr.com/en/2018/06/18/feature/politics/asmarat-the-states-model-housing-for-former-slum-residents/ (accessed 27 December 2018).

Moneycontrol News (2018) Govt to meet target of 11mn homes under PMAY before 2022: Puri, 23 March. https://www.moneycontrol.com/news/business/real-estate/govt-to-meet-target-of-11mn-homes-under-pmay-before-2022-puri-2534983.html (accessed 14 June 2019).

Mounir, S. (2018) Social housing: Better homes in Egypt, Al Ahram online, 16 February 2018. http://english.ahram.org.eg/NewsContent/1/1189/291088/Egypt/ElSisis-Balance-Sheet/Social-housing-Better-homes-in-Egypt.aspx (accessed 27 December 2018).

Mukhija, V. (2001) Enabling slum redevelopment in Mumbai: policy paradox in practice, *Housing Studies* 18(4): 213–22. https://doi.org/10.1080/02673030120090548

Patel, S. (2013) Upgrade, rehouse or resettle? An assessment of the Indian government's Basic Services for the Poor (BSUP) programme, *Environment and Urbanisation*, 25(1): 177–88. https://doi.org/10.1177/0956247812473731

Risbud, N. (2003) *Urban Slum Reports: The case of Mumbai, India*. https://archive.org/details/mumbai-slum-case-study (accessed 3 August 2025).

Saldanha, A. and Salve, P. (2019) Half finished, behind schedule: PM's promise of housing-for-all by 2022, *FactChecker*, 23 April. https://www.factchecker.in/half-finished-behind-schedule-pms-promise-of-housing-for-all-by-2022/

Shawkat, Y. (2014a) Mubarak's promise, social justice and the National Housing Programme: affordable homes or political gain? *Égypte monde arabe*, 11: 203–33. https://doi.org/10.4000/ema.3318

Shawkat, Y. (2014b) *EIPR housing policies paper II drafting a fair housing policy for Egypt*, Egyptian Initiative for Personal Rights, Cairo. https://eipr.org/sites/default/files/reports/pdf/housing_policy_paper_english_.pdf (accessed 29 December 2018).

Shawkat, Y. (2018) A million houses for whom? Six facts about the Social Housing Project, Built Environment Observatory. http://marsadomran.info/en/facts_budgets/2018/05/1543/#_ftn8 (accessed 31 December 2018).

Sibley-Behloul, M. (2002) Informal transformations of formal housing estates in Algiers and Cairo, *GBER* 2(3): 32–41. https://pdfs.semanticscholar.org/8639/c77cf79da678a672c2d502f6008c33bb91e3.pdf (accessed 30 May 2019).

Sims, D. (2003) *The Case of Cairo, Egypt*, Case study produced for the Global Report on Human Settlements, https://web.archive.org/web/20040514070713/http://www.ucl.ac.uk/dpu-projects/Global_Report/pdfs/Cairo.pdf (accessed 17 December 2018).

Sims, D. (2010) *Understanding Cairo: the logic of a city out of control*, The American University in Cairo Press, Cairo and New York.

Sims, D. and Abd-El Fattah, H. (2016) *Egypt housing profile*, United Nations Human Settlements Programme (U-Habitat), Nairobi. https://unhabitat.org/sites/default/files/download-manager-files/1525977522wpdm_Egypt per cent20housing per cent20EN_HighQ_23-1-2018.pdf (accessed 30 April 2020).

Singh, T. (2018) Tracking the progress of Pradhan Mantri Awas Yojana, QRIUS, 28 March, https://web.archive.org/web/20210518211455/https://qrius.com/tracking-the-pradhan-mantri-awas-yojana/ (accessed 19 September 2025).

Sparc Samudaya Nirman Sahayak (SSNS) (2016) *Annual report: 2015–16*, SPARC, Mumbai. https://sparcindia.org/pdf/ssns_annual_reports/ssnsar2016.pdf (accessed 18 September 2025).

Suri, S. (2011) The $300 house: the urban challenge [blog], *Harvard Business Review*, 24 February. http://blogs.hbr.org/cs/2011/02/the_300_house_the_urban_challe.html

Suryawanshi, S. (2018) No more free houses in SRA projects: Maharashtra government, *DNA India*, 9 September. https://www.dnaindia.com/mumbai/report-no-more-free-houses-in-sra-projects-maharashtra-government-2660941 (accessed 3 June 2019).

Times of India (2019) Thika Tenancy Bill passed: new law on the cards to legalise encroachments, *Times of India*, 10 July. https://timesofindia.indiatimes.com/city/kolkata/thika-tenancy-bill-passed-new-law-on-the-cards-to-legalise-encroachments/articleshow/70150378.cms (accessed 3 August 2025).

Tipple, G. (2000) *Extending themselves: User-initiated transformations of government-built housing in developing countries*, Liverpool University Press, Liverpool.

Villaitramani, K.R. and Hirani, D.P. (2014) Pre-fabricated construction for mass housing in Mumbai, *International Journal of Innovative Research in Advanced Engineering (IJIRAE)*, 1(9). https://www.ijirae.com/volumes/vol1/issue9/OCCE10087.22.pdf (accessed 31 July 2020).

World Habitat (2014) Community-Led Infrastructure Finance Facility (CLIFF), World Habitat Awards. https://www.world-habitat.org/world-habitat-awards/winners-and-finalists/community-led-infrastructure-finance-facility-cliff/ (accessed 6 August 2019).

WSP (2010) *CLIFF Review of small overseas development projects, appendix 2 India – country report*. https://assets.publishing.service.gov.uk/media/57a08af640f0b652dd0009e4/TI_UP_Consultancy_Jun2010_CLIFF_India_Country_Report.pdf (accessed 11 November 2019).

YUVA (2018) *Housing Needs of the Urban Poor in Nagpur – Assessing the Applicability of the PMAY Housing for All Mission*, City Say, Youth for Unity and Voluntary Action and Indian Housing Federation, Mumbai, https://yuvaindia.org/wp-content/uploads/2023/04/Housing-NeedsofUrban-Poor-in-Nagpur.pdf (accessed 3 August 2025).

Yuvaonline (2019) How the PM's affordable housing scheme went from promising to dysfunctional, *Medium*, 18 May. https://medium.com/@yuvaonline/how-the-pms-affordable-housing-scheme-went-from-promising-to-dysfunctional-3be18e46ae32 (accessed 1 July 2019).

Zhang, Y. (2016) Building a slum-free Mumbai, Wilson Center Urban Sustainability Laboratory, Washington, DC. https://www.wilsoncenter.org/article/building-slum-free-mumbai (accessed 10 August 2020).

CHAPTER 6

Sites and services, core housing, and land pooling

The 1970s saw a growing realization of the problems with conventional housing programmes in developing countries. They required governments to invest large sums in housing construction and, as explained in Chapter 5, produced standardized housing units that were usually unaffordable to poor people without high levels of subsidy and were extremely costly for cash-strapped governments. Drawing on the ideas of Jacob Crane, Charles Adams, Otto Koenigsberger, and John Turner, international agencies turned to the concept of serviced plots of land, with or without core accommodation, as an affordable and accessible option for housing for the urban poor. The basic principle of 'sites and services' is very simple: government or its agents identify suitable land, subdivide it, and offer serviced sites for sale to individual householders, who then manage the construction of their own houses. In providing services, government does what it is well equipped to do while, recognizing Turner's insights, it leaves house building to the private self-build sector.

The logic seems impeccable but the concept is now almost completely ignored by most governments and international agencies. One possible reason is that sites and services schemes have not, on the whole, been very successful. The number of plots that they have delivered has fallen well short of need and subsequent uptake of completed plots has often been slow. In many, probably the majority, of cases, plots have been acquired by those with higher incomes than the target population. Despite these difficulties, there are examples of relatively successful sites and services projects, albeit on a relatively small scale in relation to demand. The main part of the chapter describes some of these in some detail, starting with the Ismailia Demonstration Projects in Egypt and moving on to consider World Bank projects in Tamil Nadu and Mumbai in India. Subsequently the Khuda ki Basti scheme on the outskirts of Hyderabad in Pakistan is examined, which took a rather different approach to the challenge of ensuring that plots go to those who need them, rather than speculators.

At the end of this chapter the use of other land development mechanisms – guided land development and land pooling – are reviewed to see to what extent they have succeeded in providing suitable land for poorer families to create their own housing.

Early schemes

The UN promoted a small number of core housing schemes in the 1950s, several in African countries and mostly prior to independence. These schemes were small in scale and their impact was very limited. In some countries, for instance Ghana, momentum was lost as the leaders of newly independent countries saw the core housing concept as a relic of discredited colonial policies and focused their efforts on building complete new houses and apartments (Arku, 2009). Newly independent governments did initiate some early sites and services schemes. For instance, the government of recently independent Zambia started a programme of 'Aided Self-Help Site and Service' schemes in 1967. Its Second National Development Plan, which covered the period 1972–76, introduced a new policy of upgrading selected informal areas and providing new housing in sites and services schemes. However, a worsening of Zambia's economic situation in the early 1970s meant that World Bank assistance was required to implement the policy (Rakodi, 1989). This was a period when the World Bank took the lead in promoting and financing sites and services schemes, and other early World Bank-supported projects included the Metroville scheme in Karachi, the Dandora scheme in Nairobi, and projects in Dhaka and Jamaica. Many of the World Bank's projects, for instance the Lusaka project described in Box 6.1, included both sites and services schemes and upgrading of existing settlements. Between 1972 and 1980, the bank helped 29 countries to provide about 310,000 serviced plots, an average of almost 40,000 per year (Baum and Tolbert, 1985). By 1990, it had provided or was providing support to 116 sites and services schemes in 55 countries, many of which were linked to upgrading initiatives in adjacent settlements (Pugh, 1995).

Box 6.1 Sites and services in Lusaka, Zambia

World Bank-supported projects in Lusaka drew on the experience of previous Zambian government schemes and was also influenced by the ideas of the pressure group SAIL (Social Action in Lusaka). This had been formed in 1970 with the aim of establishing a demonstration project to improve the residential environment of what was then called Kapwepwe Township (Seymour, 1975). The project included services upgrading, off-site infrastructure, and community facilities in addition to its sites and services component. The overall aim was to provide 25,000 households, about 35% of all households in Lusaka at the time, with improved living conditions. There were problems with land acquisition, which led to delays of more than two years in some phases of the project (Bamberger et al., 1982). Nevertheless, Jere (1984) reported that 18,579 houses had been completed in the sites and services schemes by 1974. This suggests that the project was successful in terms of achieving its intended outputs. However, the outcomes achieved were less satisfactory. A World Bank review of the project noted that, despite being better than that achieved for many locally led urban development corporation (LUDC) housing programmes, cost recovery was poor (Bamberger et al., 1982). Reasons for the poor performance included inadequate debt collection machinery, inability to pay, lack of willingness to pay because of poor maintenance of facilities by the responsible authorities, and non-delivery of some promised services (Jere, 1984).

Early assessments of these schemes were positive. For instance, an evaluation of first generation World Bank-supported sites and services and upgrading projects in El Salvador, the Philippines, Senegal, and Zambia, carried out between 1975 and 1980, concluded that they had been remarkably successful (Keare and Parris, 1982). Project impacts on the housing stock had generally been greater than expected and the housing provided had been affordable and generally accessible to the target population. The evaluation did identify problems with cost recovery, delays in implementation, and a need for more rental accommodation, but concluded that they could be overcome if standards and costs could be pushed lower, with explicit opportunities provided for rental arrangements. Unfortunately, this conclusion proved to be premature and by 1990 the sites and services approach was falling out of favour with the World Bank and other international agencies. This was partly due to the limited size of the schemes implemented as compared with overall demand. The author's assessment of the 1972–80 figures given by Baum and Tolbert suggests that World Bank-assisted sites and services schemes had provided less than 1 per cent of the total requirement for low-income housing worldwide.

Low coverage was not the only problem with the early schemes. Many sites and services projects were designed but never implemented, mainly because of land acquisition difficulties. Because the projects that were implemented were small in relation to overall demand, they tended to be 'captured' by higher-income groups, either because the intended beneficiary sold his or her plot, invariably to someone in a higher-income group, or because plots were acquired directly by higher-income people, cutting out the intended beneficiaries completely. In many cases, plots were bought as investments and some were left vacant for many years. The Metroville programme in Karachi illustrates some of these problems. It was intended to provide 40,000 plots per year over a period of 10 years from 1974 but only four Metroville schemes were implemented, providing a total of about 15,500 plots (Siddiqi, 1983). In 1979, five years after the first plots in Metroville 1 had been allocated, only 11 of its 5,800 plots had been occupied. By 1984, 2,700 plots had been occupied in all four schemes, occupied mainly by middle-income households. Around 2,200 of the plots in Metroville II had been used to house Bihari refugees and only two plots were listed as being occupied in Metroville III, with no plots occupied in Metroville IV (Kool et al., 1988). These authors suggest that a few undeveloped plots remain. By the early 2000s, much of Metroville I consisted of residential houses, typically three storeys high and often divided into apartments (Collective for Social Science Research, 2005). Satellite images show that the whole area is now fully developed.

The Metroville experience was repeated in the slightly later Gujjarpura sites and services project in Lahore. When the author visited the site in 2008, around 20 years after implementation began, there were still a few undeveloped pockets, although recent Google Earth images suggest that

Photo 6.1 Unoccupied core units in the Gulshan-e-Shahbaz scheme

these have since been developed. A 2009 visit to the Gulshan-e-Shahbaz scheme in Hyderabad, Pakistan, found the site, begun in 1981, almost empty (Photo 6.1). None of the 11,280 plots allotted through conventional processes had been developed, apart from some core housing, constructed at considerable cost but unoccupied and rapidly deteriorating. Satellite images from January 2019 suggest that little had changed since 2009. The one exception to this general rule was the area reserved for the Khuda ki Basti initiative, which involved serious efforts to ensure that plots went to the poor people for whom they were intended. This initiative is described and assessed later in this chapter.

As described, the sites and services approach was largely abandoned by donors in the early 1990s. Yet, some projects were successful and the concept does in theory allow for partnership between government and low-income households, providing a means of using resources in a more effective way than would be possible if the parties acted independently. There is a strong case for revisiting the approach in order to understand what worked, why it worked, and to identify the constraints that prevented more widespread success. With this in mind, and drawing on the author's personal experience, the rest of this chapter examines in some detail relatively successful sites and services projects in Egypt, India, and Pakistan and explores the reasons for their lack of subsequent impact.

Ismailia: implementing Turner's ideas?

Like many internationally funded projects from the 1970s, the Ismailia projects in Egypt were conceived as demonstration projects and combined upgrading and provision of serviced sites. They are generally regarded as successful although there were important limitations on their success.

The need for sites and services and upgrading interventions was identified in the course of the Ismailia Master Plan Study, which commenced in 1974 and was produced by Culpin Planning, part of the UK architectural practice Clifford Culpin & Partners. The study was part of a reconstruction programme for the Suez Canal zone initiated by the Egyptian Ministry of Housing and Reconstruction following the cessation of hostilities with Israel after the 1973 war. Funds were provided through a grant from United Nations Development Programme (UNDP). The Master Plan Study predicted that the population of Ismailia would grow from around 150,000 in 1977 to around 500,000 in 2000 and suggested that the existing government policy of providing subsidized accommodation for sale or rent could not cope with this rate of growth. It recognized that the informal sector was adding appreciably more units to the national housing stock than all public efforts combined at costs significantly lower than those achieved for officially approved housing. Accordingly, it recommended an approach to housing design that would involve erstwhile informal sector actors, with government subdividing land and providing basic infrastructure and plot-holders taking responsibility for house construction.

In May 1977, following approval of the Master Plan, the Ministry commissioned the Ismailia Demonstration Projects to facilitate implementation of the Master Plan's housing-related recommendations. The intention was to formulate proposals for schemes capable of early implementation with minimum subsidy, while maintaining the momentum achieved during the preparation of the Master Plan. The Demonstration Projects included both upgrading of existing areas and provision for new development. Plans for newly developing areas to the north of the city included blocks, each containing a hierarchy of semi-private areas, neighbourhoods with sub-centres, and a new main centre to serve old and new areas. Sub-centres were to have local services such as health clinics and junior schools while the main centre in El Hekr, which was renamed Hai el Salaam, was to have a large Friday Mosque, polyclinic, social centre, and market. The design assumed that small workshops would be accommodated on residential plots with special areas provided to accommodate 'bad neighbour' uses. In contrast to many sites and services projects, suitable public land was available. Implementation on-site started in late 1978.

Hai el Salaam was the first and larger area covered by the project. It covered an area of 226 hectares of desert land, of which 132 hectares had already been partly developed by the informal sector at the beginning of the project. Like all desert land in Egypt, undeveloped land was owned by government and did not have to be purchased. The name El Hekr had originated in the fact that people had been allowed to build houses in the area once they had paid a small charge (*al hekr*) to the city. Rakodi and Leduka (2004) suggest that informal development is often characterized by poor layouts and inadequate services and that these deficiencies can be addressed by recognizing such areas and working with subdividers and sellers to improve layouts and facilitate the early provision of basic services. In practice, the layouts developed by informal developers are often rational since the objective of developers, to maximize the area of saleable private land, can best be achieved by providing a simple grid layout. This was clearly the case in the pre-existing development in El Hekr. Accordingly, the layout adopted for the subdivision and development of vacant land was essentially a rationalization and extension of that in the already developed area.

Most plots were sized in the range 72 m^2 to 162 m^2, with 65 per cent falling in the range 108–135 m^2. A small number of larger plots, between 360 m^2 and 576 m^2 in size, were provided along main roads. These were to be auctioned in order to provide some cross-subsidy of the cost of other plots. Plot sizes and shapes were designed to allow the patterns of use observed on existing plots, with prices set at levels that would ensure that plots would be affordable to the target population, while raising sufficient money to pay for services. Affordability considerations led to the adoption of fairly basic infrastructure standards. Water was to be supplied to standpipes located at 150 m intervals and sanitation was to be on-site. The water supply design allowed for future upgrading to full house connections. In the event, USAID extended its support for city-wide water supply and sewerage network extensions, which had originally omitted El Hekr, to cover the project area. It was driven to do this by the existence of the project, after some lobbying from the consultants (Davidson, 1984; David Sims, personal communication). The process followed in Abu Atwa, the second Demonstration Project site south-west of Ismailia, was similar, albeit at a smaller scale and in a less urbanized location.

Because the Ismailia Governorate had limited experience of the proposed approach, semi-independent project agencies, headed and staffed by local officials and technicians, were set up to manage activities in El Hekr and Abu Atwa. The agency offices were located in the two project areas. Each agency was authorized to buy and sell land within its area and to use the proceeds for infrastructure provision and management. The agency managers enjoyed considerable discretion on technical issues but all decisions with cash flow implications needed the approval of a steering committee chaired by the Governor (Matteucci, 2006). The project was to be largely self-financing, with income from land sales covering the costs of administration and service provision. This aim was achieved, with development costs covered mostly by income from the sale of larger plots along the main streets. Two factors contributed to the financial success of the project:

- *The limited reliance on external funds.* The reliance on its own funds created a situation in which the project had to be financially sustainable.

The British Ministry of Overseas Development, the forerunner of today's Foreign, Commonwealth & Development Office, provided limited grant funding, £60,000 for Hai el Salaam and £40,000 for Abu Atwa, to cover initial site preparation and provision of an office in Hai el Salaam. In addition, the British Government and the Egyptian Ministry of Housing provided funds for Culpin Planning to provide a small technical assistance team to set up and support the project agencies.

- *The decision to provide only basic service levels in the first instance.* This meant that the project was designed to follow the informal sector sequence of Land – People – Housing – Infrastructure, rather than the Land – Infrastructure – People – Housing sequence followed by most donor-supported projects. In this respect, it was closer to Turner's thinking than most subsequent sites and services projects.

The retention of the Master Plan study consultant for the preparation of the Demonstration Projects allowed the technical assistance team to develop a strong relationship with Ismailia Governorate officials. These officials had been living with the idea of informal sector involvement for four years, had accepted it, and saw the approach not as something imposed from outside but rather as the result of joint decisions by Governorate staff and consultants. Given the general antipathy to informal sector activities found in Egyptian political and professional circles, this was immensely important.

The consultants proposed that land prices should start at LE 1.76 per m^2. This was based on affordability and was higher than the LE 0.5/m^2 price of government land but significantly less than the LE 10–15/m^2 market price of land with freehold tenure. In fact, the lowest land price was set at LE 2.25/m^2, little different from the proposed price when inflation was taken into account. The original proposal for a 30 year pay-back period was reduced to 5 years, with a 25 per cent down payment for the cheapest plots, rising to 50 per cent and 100 per cent for plots on larger roads. The rationale was that this would give the project agencies an adequate cash flow in the early years and this proved to be the case (Davidson, 1984: 142). Arandel and El Batran (1997) suggested that subsequent increases in land prices led to a black market in the sale and purchase of land but gave no details. They did note an increase in rents, from an average of LE 10 for three rooms in the old area to LE 120–150 plus LE 5,000 'key' money (up-front money paid to the landlord) by 1994. During this time, Egypt's yearly inflation rate was mostly in the range 15–20 per cent. Taking this into account, the rent increase amounted to only about 50 per cent of the original figure.

The original design located low-cost plots on 6–9 m wide streets, designed to replicate traditional layouts in order to allow play and communal use but to discourage through traffic (Davidson, 1984). Agency staff and, it seems, residents rejected this approach in favour of straight streets, which they perceived as being more modern. Arandel and El Batran (1997) suggested that this was one of the factors that led to an increase in land prices, taking the price of accommodation beyond that which was affordable to low-income families. This conclusion is debatable. In January 2019 Google Earth shows very little difference between street layouts in the pre-existing and sites and services areas of Hai el Salaam other than a major east to west street through the sites and services area. Parts of Abu Atwa are distinguished from surrounding areas by their regular street layout. In both demonstration project areas and in both upgraded and new areas, the layouts are much closer to those found in Egypt's informal settlements than to those of more conventional housing developments in Ismailia. A more likely constraint on the involvement of poor households was the Ismailia Governorate's requirement that houses should be constructed using 'modern' materials. Arandel and El Batran (1997) noted that inhabitants were directed to build using 'skeleton' structures (reinforced concrete frame and floors with brick infill) rather than load-bearing walls. In fact, concrete-framed construction is ubiquitous in informal developments around Egypt's cities. Nevertheless, the requirement that incremental development should start from a defined minimum standard is likely to have excluded the poorest households.

The requirement for 'modern' materials was one of several ways in which project implementation differed from project design. The original proposal to give leasehold tenure was superseded by a delayed freehold system. Under this system, freehold would only be granted when plot assignees had completed all the required payments and had built an inhabitable structure. Unfortunately, this requirement was first bypassed and then removed, so removing an important constraint on land speculation. In a similar way, the original requirement that plots should be assigned mainly to households from El Hekr was dropped after the first plot award lottery. These changes suggest that government officials were less committed to ensuring access to the poorest households than the British consultants. This is consistent with the picture that emerges throughout this book of the widely differing views of development professionals and local politicians and government officials on possible responses to informal development.

How successful was Ismailia as a demonstration project? This question can be answered in relation to both the project areas themselves and the impact of the project on thinking in Egypt and beyond. Various surveys and reports provide information on the situation in the project's areas. A 1985 survey found that the number of inhabitants in the project areas had reached 70,000, exceeding the projections made at the time of project design (GOHBPR, 1985, quoted by Arandel and El Batran, 1997). This was despite the fact that another source, apparently based on the same survey, states that 30 per cent of assigned plots were not yet built-up and an even higher percentage of dwellings (over 43 per cent) were not occupied (Metwally, 1987, quoted by Matteuci, 2006). Whatever the situation in the early years after implementation, satellite images show that the project areas are now completely developed. Matteucci (2006) describes a study carried out in Hai el Salaam in the mid-2000s. This involved initial definition of the main typologies of buildings and public spaces, followed by 14 case studies, selected to obtain a representative sample of the living conditions found in the area. Its key findings included the following:

- The majority of buildings in Hai el Salaam had been constructed incrementally and were occupied mainly by extended families of owner-builders. Residents were generally the same people who had bought the land from the project agency. The population had increased as new storeys were added and new households formed within extended families.
- Some plots had been developed with tall buildings divided into rented apartments, suggesting that the land had been sold on to speculative builders.
- The highest benefits in the upgraded part of the scheme had tended to go to households with enough resources to invest in improving their properties. The poorest had benefited the least.
- Households living in the sites and services development were generally wealthier and more able to invest in good quality buildings than those living in upgraded areas. While the project had effectively reached the proposed target population in the upgraded area the generally wealthier occupants of housing units in the sites and services area had displaced the poorest assignees. While this indicated a higher degree of speculation than in the upgraded area, the differences between the two areas were insufficient to suggest that gentrification had taken place.

The investigation revealed poorer and richer zones in both sites and services and upgraded areas, none of which were isolated from the adjacent neighbourhoods. Hai el Salaam had become a lively part of the city, containing many economic activities, with main streets filled with shops, workshops, and food and drink outlets. Its population was diverse, ranging from qualified professionals to unskilled manual workers. Overall, the study concluded that the Ismailia Demonstration Projects had had positive outcomes for both their inhabitants and the city as a whole.

The many papers and articles on the Ismailia Demonstration Projects are an indication of their influence on the thinking of urban development professionals. The approach and design principles underlying the project were set out in the *Urban Projects Manual* (Davidson and Payne, 1983), which ran into two editions. The project also influenced the thinking of Egyptian government officials and international agencies, but arguably in a more limited way. In Ismailia, after facilitating the formation of the project agencies for Hai el Salaam and Abu Atwa, the consultants helped the local administration to create the Ismailia Planning and Land Development Agency. The agency's staff were drawn mainly from the two Ismailia Demonstration Project teams (Matteucci, 2006, quoting an earlier Davidson paper). This agency does not appear to have had a lasting influence. By the mid-1990s, international agencies were focusing on the New Urban Agenda and the United Nations Centre for Human Settlements (UNCHS) were supporting a new initiative, the Sustainable Ismailia Project (SIP), which ran from 1991 to 1995. This had been formulated using the UNCHS 'Sustainable Cities Programme' approach, which stressed the importance of inter-agency cooperation and the need to involve government, the private sector, and NGOs in a participatory action planning approach (Khoury, 1996). Khoury's review of the SIP refers to the Ismailia Master Plan but is rather dismissive of it, suggesting that it paid insufficient attention to the availability of government human and financial resources and, in some respects, lacked an understanding of local social and economic dynamics. A more positive interpretation would note that the SIP followed the Ismailia Demonstration Projects in emphasizing the importance of local management and working with local resources. Certainly, continuity was facilitated by the fact that the team leader for SIP had previously been a key member of the Ismailia Development Projects team. However, the overall conclusion must be that government commitment to the Demonstration Projects approach lacked depth and was discontinued when another international agency came along offering funds to support the latest externally formulated 'solution' to urban development problems. The consultants did approach UNDP to provide a small budget to support the promotion of the Ismailia model in other Egyptian governorates but UNDP chose instead to give funding to Egypt's General Organization for Physical Planning (GOPP) to establish regional planning centres (David Sims, personal communication).

Beyond Ismailia, the Demonstration Projects had a strong influence on the approach proposed for the World Bank-funded Extension of Municipal Services (EMS) project in Greater Cairo. This is not surprising, given that Culpin Planning were the lead consultants for the project and that many members of their team had previously worked in Ismailia. The EMS project objective was to provide an alternative to the widespread but illegal informal development on agricultural land around Greater Cairo. It aimed to do this by identifying suitable sites on desert land that could be subdivided, serviced, and developed using planning and infrastructure standards that were both affordable to low-income households and acceptable to government. The intention was to go beyond individual projects to pioneer an approach to development that could co-opt informal sector builders and eliminate new development on agricultural land. If successful, it would have initiated a rolling programme of subdivision and development. Unfortunately, it failed to reach the implementation stage, for reasons that will be all too familiar to those with experience of efforts to implement sites and services initiatives. The most obvious of these was inability to secure land. Despite the fact that all desert land in Egypt is owned by government, it proved extremely difficult to find suitable sites in reasonable proximity to the city. Part of the problem was that huge swathes of land were controlled by the Egyptian army, which had absolutely no interest in relinquishing its control. If development was to occur, it would be on the army's terms and would provide the type of development that privileged army officers and the middle and upper classes thought was appropriate. On the west bank of the Nile, the only desert land close to existing development was within the area surrounding the Great Pyramids and thus protected against further development. The project was assigned land in some of the new settlements referred to in Chapter 5 but this arrangement was far from satisfactory because of the distance of the settlements from the city and their lack of services. Underlying the land issue was the fundamental fact that Egyptian politicians and decision-makers never accepted the premises underlying the project, instead remaining wedded to the apartments in the desert approach already described in Chapter 5. In one meeting, the Governor of Cairo, an ex-army general, referred to the threat posed by poor people encircling the city if the project was implemented as planned. The Culpin Planning team had temporarily changed perceptions in Ismailia because of the close relationship that they had been able to develop with the leaders of a relatively small governorate. No such relationship was possible in the much larger and politically important arena of Greater Cairo. Without political support, the project was bound to fail and, as has already been explained in Chapter 5, government housing projects continued to provide conventional apartments in medium-rise blocks.

Tamil Nadu and Mumbai

Between 1973 and 1997, the World Bank financed 11 projects in India with sites and services components, covering approximately 3,200 hectares and providing approximately 280,000 plots across 27 cities. These figures give an average of 87.5 plots per hectare and, assuming that 35 per cent of the available land was used for access, open space, and public facilities, an average plot size of about 75 m^2. Seven projects were assessed as satisfactory, with the remainder deemed unsatisfactory, mainly because of land acquisition problems. Between 1977 and 1994, the World Bank supported projects that invested US$200 million on 13 sites in Chennai, providing 57,000 plots, and 15 sites in Mumbai, providing 88,000 plots and 17,000 apartments (Owens et al., 2018). The sites varied in area, in Chennai from 20.9 to 141.9 hectares and in Mumbai from 7 to 180 hectares. The schemes were implemented under a series of World Bank projects. The author visited both cities in 1991 and returned to Chennai in 1992 as a member of World Bank supervision missions. At this time, planning and construction were proceeding under the First Tamil Nadu Urban Development Project (TNUDP), which included Chennai and some other towns in Tamil Nadu, and the Bombay Urban Development Project.

Land acquisition is one of the most difficult challenges faced by sites and services projects. The earlier Gujjarpura sites and services project in Lahore had addressed this problem by giving landowners back an area of land in the form of serviced land equivalent to a percentage of their original land holding as part payment for their land. The Indian schemes took a different approach, developing schemes almost if not entirely on government-owned land. In Tamil Nadu, schemes were built on land previously occupied by 'tanks': reservoirs constructed to hold water to be used for irrigation purposes during the dry season that had become redundant as the land that they served had been built on. In Mumbai, Charkop, the largest scheme, was built on land that had been reclaimed from salt water creeks. Other schemes were located in Navi Mumbai, a new town across the bay to the south-east of Mumbai itself. Land was acquired for the town as a whole and it was then possible to make a small portion available for low-income sites and services schemes. Not surprisingly, given their location on land that previously stored water, the first schemes in Tamil Nadu experienced occasional flooding. Later schemes addressed this problem by deepening one part of the original tank and using the spoil produced to increase ground levels in the area reserved for development.

In order to make plots affordable to low-income people and also to reduce the interest of higher-income groups, both schemes included a high proportion of small plots. The Tamil Nadu schemes offered a range of sizes, initially from 40 m^2 upwards and later from 33 m^2 upwards. The Mumbai plots were smaller. The minimum plot size in Charkop was 25 m^2 while that of schemes in Navi Mumbai plots was only 21 m^2. Following the Bertaud approach outlined in Chapter 3, the schemes also included larger plots, which could be sold at higher prices, with profits used to subsidize the cost of smaller plots. Geometrical layouts, relatively long, narrow plots, and relatively narrow rights of way helped to maximize the land available for development.

Smaller plots were normally located on internal streets or around courtyards, while larger plots were located on the main streets. The small plots opened onto pedestrian paths or courtyards. Paths and courtyards were accessed from roads, typically 7–9 m wide. Plots intended for low-income households were located on pedestrian paths and courtyards and had neither vehicular access nor parking provision. In Charkop, larger plots were provided on primary roads and sold to housing cooperatives for development as multi-storey apartment buildings, each of which accommodated 10–15 higher-income families. Pavements were provided along main roads and car parking spaces were provided to serve the planned apartment buildings.

The small plot sizes and efficient site layouts meant that the schemes achieved high population densities. Planned average densities were 145 households (725 people) per hectare in Mumbai and 70 households (423 people) per hectare in Chennai. Over time the neighbourhoods continued to densify to estimated population densities of more than 1,100 people per hectare in Charkop and 1,200 people per hectare in West Mogappair in Chennai. At 2018 household sizes, these equate to 284 and 318 households per hectare respectively (Owens et al., 2018). While lower than the densities assumed for apartment block schemes planned under the Pradhan Mantri Awas Yojana (PMAY) housing scheme, these densities are higher than those found in most urban settlements and show that schemes based on individual plots rather than high-rise apartments can achieve high densities.

The Charkop design provided groups of plots around long courtyards. Each courtyard provided shared semi-private space. The 46 households grouped round a typical courtyard were organized into a society for the purposes of building their houses and dealing with services. In most cases, basic housing units were constructed by small building firms working on behalf of societies. The standard house design incorporated a roof that sloped up from front to back in order to provide the height required for construction of a mezzanine area at the back of the house. Each plot was provided with a toilet and water and sewerage connections. Plots along through streets were bigger and larger plots were provided on the periphery of the scheme. These were sold to developers and intended for medium-rise apartments, to be sold to higher-income households. Prices were set at levels that allowed cross-subsidy of small plots from the profits made on sale of the larger plots. The New Bombay plots were laid out on a regular grid pattern with narrow back lanes to allow service to the back of plots. The early Chennai schemes were designed by government planners and the layouts proposed were often inefficient. To overcome this problem, the World Bank employed David Gilmore of the UK-based consultants Gilmore Hankey Kirke, a planner steeped in Bertaud's philosophy and methods, to demonstrate how layouts could be redesigned for increased efficiency. He developed modular designs that clustered lower-income housing around pedestrian cul-de-sacs rather than along vehicular streets. The emphasis on producing rational layouts resulted in more efficient use of space and so enabled significantly more land to be used for housing.

As noted earlier in this chapter, one of the problems with early sites and services schemes was the tendency for plots to remain unoccupied for many years. Given the relatively remote location of some of the project sites, it would seem reasonable to expect them to suffer from this problem. Information on the early development of the schemes in both Chennai and Mumbai is anecdotal and inconclusive. In an interview conducted in September 2016, the Project Manager of the Mumbai Urban Development Project stated that the project neighbourhoods appeared underbuilt and under-occupied at the time of project closure (Owens et al. 2018). However, when the author visited the sites in 1991 and 1992, some of the Chennai sites were already well developed. The schemes visited in Mumbai had been started later and were at an earlier stage of development but some plots were occupied. Research on rental arrangements in Chennai, undertaken in the early 1990s, was conducted, at least partly, in project areas, providing an indirect indication that these areas were already well developed (Kumar, 1996). Whatever the exact situation with regard to the early development of the sites, most are now fully developed, with 'build-out rates at or close to 100 per cent' (Owens et al., 2018). As noted earlier, the population densities are higher than those originally envisaged. The build-out rates given by Owens et al. show only two exceptions, with 2015 build-out rates of 50 per cent and 10 per cent for the Manali I and Manali II schemes, north of Chennai.

As already noted, it is difficult to ensure that sites and services schemes benefit the low-income households for which they were intended. Both Tamil Nadu and Mumbai did fairly well in this regard. World Bank evaluation reports from the 1990s show that more than 70 per cent of the project beneficiaries in Chennai were in the low-income group. Similarly, in Mumbai, approximately 60 per cent of residents at project close were low-income. Around 15–20 per cent of plots had been resold. Fieldwork carried out in late 2015 found little evidence of plot consolidation over time. In some cases, households had cooperated to jointly develop rental units on upper floors or invest in shared roofs but the land and ground floors were still held by individual households. Many residents had expanded their properties vertically, using the additional rooms created to either house their extended families or rent (Owens et al., 2018).

Independent assessment of the existing situation in Charkop also provides evidence of project success. Residents interviewed during fieldwork for the Owens et al. study and subsequent household surveys expressed satisfaction with the quality of housing and infrastructure (Adefarasin et al., 2017 quoted in Owens et al., 2018). Earlier, another observer had reported that Charkop was a settled community with houses built from permanent materials, some single and some double storey. More recent images of Charkop provide evidence of further vertical development, particularly along through streets. The observer was particularly impressed by the solid waste collection system, highlighting the role of community members in bringing garbage to the municipal garbage truck when summoned by a man with a bell. She attributed the community cooperation in providing this basic municipal service to the sense of community engendered by the site layout, with its groups of houses clustered around common courtyards (Sharma, 2007). Inspection of satellite images of the Mumbai and Navi Mumbai sites suggests that the open spaces provided in the original schemes have not been encroached and are in reasonable condition.

Owens et al. (2018) conclude that the projects have delivered results that go well beyond their original and relatively narrowly defined goals, offering lessons that are worth emulating. These include the role of varying plot sizes in creating mixed-income neighbourhoods and the tailoring of plot sizes and access street widths to the needs of the specific income groups for which they are intended – car access is not too important where the target group are unlikely to be car owners. Accordingly, there is no need to site small plots, intended for low-income families, on wide roads. Another lesson learned is that access to infrastructure and public transport routes is important. In Chennai in particular, sites developed fairly quickly, even when located in peripheral areas. It is reasonable to assume that transport links facilitated the development process.

Khuda ki Basti: replicating the informal sector

The slow build-out rate experienced in many sites and services schemes is one of the reasons why the sites and services concept fell out of favour from the 1990s on. The problem is often exacerbated by the challenge of providing services to large sites, which often require additional primary infrastructure facilities if they are to be adequately served. In effect, conventional sites and services schemes change the development process from Plan–Service–Build–Occupy to Plan–Service–Occupy–Build. In contrast, the normal practice in the informal sector is that households start with very basic levels of infrastructure – water from wells or vendors, on-site sanitation, and illegal electricity connections – and lobby government to improve these services as the settlement develops. Thus, the sequence in the informal sector can be summarized as Plan–Occupy–Build–Service. Some might question the inclusion of 'Plan' in this sequence but the reality is that some degree of planning goes into almost all informal housing developments.

In Africa, some government schemes have replicated the informal sector approach. For example, in Juba in what is now South Sudan, the government laid out 400 m^2 plots in an area that they named Nimra Talata (number 3 in Arabic). By the early 1980s, most if not all the plots were occupied but services were minimal. Vendors delivered water, drawn from the River Nile since sporadic attempts to sink borewells had yielded very little water. Some households had pit latrines but the rocky ground conditions and by-laws requiring pits to be at least 7 m deep meant that pit latrine construction was difficult and expensive. As a result, many households had no toilet and open defecation was common (information drawn from author's time in Juba 1981–83).

Tanzania instituted a 'surveyed plots' programme at around the same time, aiming to at least ensure that scheme layouts were rational so that no house relocation would be required to allow later infrastructure provision (Mghweno, 1984). These initiatives had the advantage that they did not tie development of sites to the provision of difficult-to-provide infrastructure. On the other hand, they failed to achieve one of the basic objectives of sites and services: to leverage government resources in order to provide basic infrastructure and services. Even this theoretical advantage disappears when informal sector developers set out their schemes with regular layouts and rights of way that approximate to those required by government, as is the case in much of the informal settlement around Karachi.

Another potential problem is the tendency for purchasers to see plots as investments rather than places to live. The Khuda ki Basti scheme near Hyderabad in Pakistan's Sindh Province attempted to overcome this problem. It also aimed to facilitate early infrastructure provision, using the Orangi Pilot Project (OPP) approach, which will be explained in more detail in Chapter 7. The scheme was implemented in part of Hyderabad Development Authority (HDA)'s Gulshan-e-Shahbaz scheme. The scheme had been laid out on desert land starting in 1979 on an extensive site, south of the main Karachi to Hyderabad highway, about 4 km north-west of the town of Kotri and about 10 km from Hyderabad. It provided a range of plots, including relatively small ones intended for low-income houses. Plots were advertised and allotted on payment of a deposit before construction commenced. As already indicated, by 1986 it was following the pattern already described for the Metroville projects in Karachi. Plots were being bought as speculative investments and virtually none were being developed and occupied. Mr Tasneem Siddiqui, the then Director General of HDA, investigated the situation and concluded that plots were not being occupied because poor people could not afford the 25 per cent deposit, were deterred by the length and complication of the application process, and, even if they did apply, were likely to lose out to speculators and investors. His response was to explore new approaches to plot allocation and development on part of the Gulshan-e-Shahbaz site. The resulting scheme was named Khuda ki Basti ('God's settlement' in Urdu). Key elements of the approach were:

- Ease of entry, accomplished by simplifying the plot allocation process, reducing initial costs for allottees, and waiving of standards for building construction.
- Immediate delivery of the plot to the allottee, in advance of infrastructure and service provision.
- Incremental development of infrastructure and services, in line with the financial capacity of residents.

The scheme provided 80 square yard (67 m^2) plots in a conventional layout with rights of way of 30 ft (9.14 m) or more. The total price of an 80 square yard (67 m^2) plot was set at PRs 9,600, equivalent to about $600. This was intended to cover the cost of land and the supply of water to standposts located at intervals within the scheme. Residents would finance and provide 'internal' sanitation facilities, including toilets, sewer connections and sewers themselves, adopting the model already used for the OPP in Karachi (Hassan, 1990).

Initial attempts to use local councillors to identify suitable allottees from existing squatter settlements were unsuccessful. The rate of construction was slow, even when HDA withdrew the plot allocation from households that had undertaken no construction work for three consecutive days. Investigation revealed that the households identified by local councillors belonged to middle-income groups, already had access to services in their current dwellings and were therefore reluctant to move to the new scheme until development had taken place and services had been provided. HDA next recruited three *dallals* (informal sector subdividers) to help with identification of people from low-income settlements in Hyderabad who would benefit from the scheme. To reduce the possibility of speculation, HDA had decided to issue cards on which a schedule of payments was printed. Allottees were required to make an initial payment of PRs 460 (about $30) and then pay PRs 60 per month until the full PRs 9,600 price had been paid off. The *dallals* were each given several cards to issue to the households that they brought in. Unfortunately, one of the *dallals* abused the system, charging as much as double the official price for prime plots on corners and along main roads and making fake cards for choice plots. The *dallals* encouraged better-off households to take plots and start building to give prospective settlers the impression that the settlement was well established, but neglected to say that a plot allocation would be cancelled if HDA found no one living in the house (Aliani and Sheng, 1990).

At this stage, a family on the waiting list and in dire need of shelter arrived at the site with all their possessions and occupied a plot. This showed that a really needy family wants to occupy its plot immediately as it has nowhere else to go. Recognizing this, an area of land within the scheme was set aside as a reception area. Families in immediate need of shelter could bring their possessions and settle in the reception area while waiting to be allocated a plot. Once the family had lived in the reception area for about two weeks, thus demonstrating that it was in genuine need of shelter, HDA gave it a plot. Within 16 days of the initiation of this process, 350 families had moved to their plots via the reception area. HDA therefore made reception area screening a permanent part of the allocation process. Later, it built five one-room housing units, using a mixture of permanent and non-permanent materials, and rented them at PRs 200 per month to those who could afford them. This overcame objections from some potential allottees that the reception area afforded insufficient privacy for the women in their families.

By 1990, the down payment had been revised to PRs 1,000. The development charge had been reduced to PRs 50 in 1986, with the intention that it would increase by PRs 20 per year until 1989. In fact, the increase was not implemented. The development charges were deposited into a separate account for each block of the scheme. HDA arranged for water delivery by tankers and provided a concrete slab on each plot, designed to take a pour-flush toilet. Residents were responsible for constructing a leach pit to take waste from the toilet. Once sufficient funds were in the account, HDA called a meeting of all block residents to decide what infrastructure was to be provided using the money in the account. By 1988, 72 per cent of the residents had piped water in their lanes, and 24 per cent had access to a sewer. Following the OPP approach, sewer construction was managed by residents themselves, with block leaders taking overall responsibility for supervision. The approach to sewer provision was strongly influenced by that of the OPP. Unfortunately, many sewers functioned poorly due to the use of poor quality pipes, some of which broke before they had been installed, and the employment of inexperienced contractors, who were unable to lay sewers to the correct falls. In 1990, the main collector sewer to serve the area had still to be laid, with the result that sewage was discharging locally and collecting in ponds. Electricity connections took some time, partly because residents were unwilling to pay the usual bribes to Water and Power Development Agency (WAPDA) officials to facilitate the connection process (Aliani and Sheng, 1990).

Photo 6.2 Part of the Khuda ki Basti scheme

Photo 6.2 was taken by the author during a visit to Khuda ki Basti in the mid-2000s. It illustrates the rather rural feel of the scheme, with most houses only a single storey high. At the time of the visit, all services were in place and roads were paved to a fairly basic standard. Comparison of satellite images with layout plans given in early papers on Khuda ki Basti show that there has been some encroachment on public spaces but the scheme remains essentially as planned. There is a little development to the north of the area reserved for Khuda ki Basti but this looks slightly irregular and may well be encroachment. The area to the south is fully developed, linking Khuda ki Basti with Kotri. Again, the layout is slightly irregular, suggesting the possibility of encroachment by informal development. Whatever the situation with regard to this area, most of Gulshan-e-Shahbaz remains undeveloped.

In 1991, Tasneem Siddiqui set up the non-profit organization Saiban to replicate the Khuda ki Basti approach elsewhere in Sindh. It implemented schemes in Gharo, near the city of Thatta, in the Taiser Town area of Karachi in collaboration with Malir Development Authority, and near Kalu Shah Kaku, near Lahore in Punjab. The model was also adopted by Ansaar Management Company (AMC), which describes itself as a socially driven private sector business that develops and implements high-quality, affordable housing solutions. The Taiser Town, Kalu Shah Kaku, and AMC schemes received financial support from the Acumen Fund, a US-based social venture capital fund, which describes itself as a global community changing the way the world tackles poverty. The Sindh Katchi Abadis Authority, of which Mr Siddiqui was the Chairman, launched four similar schemes in the interior of Sindh (Siddiqui, 2014). By 2004, an estimated 35,000 people had benefited from the 6,000 housing units provided under schemes using the Khuda ki Basti approach. A further 35,000 people were expected to benefit from schemes then in preparation (Asfar and Rahman, 2004).

The formal title of the Kalu Shah Kaku scheme (near Lahore) is Khuda ki Basti 4. It was launched in 2006 and provided a total of 460 plots each of 100 square yards (83.6 m^2). It is located about 1 km off the main Lahore to Islamabad road, about 16 km north of the centre of Lahore in an area in which many informal settlements have developed along the road. The many factories that have been built along the road provide employment opportunities. The scheme differs from its informal neighbours in its wide streets and generous provision for open space (Photo 6.3). The clustering of houses around public open spaces creates a pleasant ambience. The distance from the main road must have reduced the cost of land acquisition and the relatively low cost of land may have had a positive impact on the affordability of the scheme, despite its rather inefficient use of land. Siddique (2013) describes a similar procedure to that used in Hyderabad, with beneficiaries required to relocate their families to a reception area for a period of 6 weeks before being awarded a plot. The scheme offered core houses, consisting of one room, a kitchen, a bathroom, and a boundary wall. Beneficiaries were required to make a down

Photo 6.3 Street in Khuda ki Basti, Lahore
Showing generous public space provision and OPP-style sewer manholes

payment of PRs 90,000 ($1,125) and could take a loan from the House Building Finance Corporation (HBFC), a 'semi-private' housing finance facility, to cover the balance of the purchase price. The loan was payable over a 10 year period with an interest rate of 15 per cent (Rahman and Hassan, 2009).

The scheme reserved about 25 per cent of all plots to be sold on the open market. It was intended that sale of these plots, which were located in 'prime' locations along the main street and around a central services and business area, would cross-subsidize the cost of the plots intended for low-income households (Rahman and Hassan, 2009). In this respect, the scheme was similar to the World Bank-funded schemes described earlier in this chapter. Comparison of the scheme layout, photographed by the author during a visit in 2010, with the 2020 Google Earth satellite image of the site shows that hardly any of these plots have been developed. While it is possible that people have bought them as an investment, the more likely explanation for the lack of development is that the location is unattractive to higher-income purchasers so that the plots have not been sold.

The Khuda ki Basti initiative received an Agha Khan Award for Architecture in 1995. It has clearly influenced the thinking of other organizations with a commitment to expanding the housing options available to the urban poor. Unfortunately, its impact to date has been limited. One reason for this is undoubtedly the failure of government and other formal sector stakeholders to embrace its approach. Its main strength, its adoption of the informal sector practice of providing houses before services, is arguably also its greatest weakness. Where good quality groundwater exists, it can be accessed via borewells. However, water supply will be problematic where groundwater is either absent, unsafe or unpalatable, for instance because it is saline. Some of the Khuda ki Basti schemes depended on tankered water, at least in their early years. Wastewater disposal is particularly problematic. Even where people have combined to build their own sewers, using the OPP model, the results have often been unsatisfactory because of poorly defined levels, poor construction, and the lack of collector sewers to which community-built sewers can be connected.

Core housing

As stated earlier in this chapter, the core housing concept dates back to the mid-20th century. Early attempts to apply it had limited success but the concept re-emerged in the 1970s and 1980s as a version of sites and services development. Some sites and services schemes, including some of the Tamil Nadu schemes, included a 'wet' core, providing a water tap and toilet facilities, on every plot. Napier (2002) gives other examples of core housing and suggests that these initiatives can be grouped into three main categories:

1. Those providing units that are inhabitable from the outset.

2. Those providing houses with one or more major built components missing, and therefore requiring some input from residents before they are habitable.
3. Those providing service cores designed to deliver water supply, sanitation, drainage, and perhaps electricity supply services.

During the 1970s, the World Bank funded the private non-profit foundation Fundacion Salvadorena de Desarrollo y Vivienda Minima (FUNDASAL) to implement a sites and services programme in El Salvador. Begun in 1973, the project was an early example of the core housing approach. Its aim was to provide adequate shelter and a minimum package of services at a price that was affordable to households with incomes down to the 17th percentile of the urban income distribution. To achieve this, it offered three options, a serviced plot with a sanitary core, the sanitary core and an 18 m^2 core unit, and the sanitary core with 36 m^2 of additional construction. Participation in mutual help construction groups was a requirement for acceptance in the project. In order to promote and support community cohesion, many plots were grouped around common open spaces, which provided semi-private space. The approach evolved over a number of years as discussions with government planners led to the adoption of lower and hence more affordable standards, particularly those for plot sizes and rights of way. Plot sizes, typically 125 m^2 in early schemes, were reduced to as small as 45 m^2 in later schemes. Gaining approval for reduced levels of vehicle access proved to be particularly difficult, despite the fact that most households had monthly incomes that excluded the possibility of owning vehicles other than, perhaps, motorcycles. In total, 6,600 units were co-financed by the first World Bank loan and produced over a five year period, albeit with delays of more than 2 years in some cases because of land acquisition problems. At least 85 per cent of households included in the project had incomes within the target range of the 17th to the 65th percentile of the national urban income distribution. The fairly wide target range and the fact that a small number of families came from below the 20th income percentile suggests that the households benefiting from the programme were mainly in the lower-middle to middle-income groups (Bamberger and Harth Deneke, 1984). FUNDASAL continues to operate, despite the difficult political and social conditions in El Salvador. However, by the late 1980s, it was clear that the programme had been unable to influence national housing policy (Stein and Vance, 2008).

Other examples of core housing initiatives include Charles Correa's Artist's Colony project in the Belapur area of Navi Mumbai and Balkrishna Doshi's Aranya township in Indore, Madhya Pradesh. The Belapur project dates from 1987. It provided complete housing units but was designed with the explicit intention that householders could and would extend those units incrementally. Plot sizes varied from 45 m^2 to 75 m^2 and Correa's design was intended to ensure that the family incomes of the richest occupants would be no more than five times those of the poorest. The scheme was thus deliberately intended to create social cohesion across a range of household income levels. Based on his observation of traditional Indian settlements, Correa's design reflected his belief that cities should be developed using a spatial hierarchy, ranging from the private world of the individual dwelling, through the 'doorstep', to the communal court and the *maidan* (an open public ground used for public gatherings), and finally to the larger public spaces open to all the community (Davey, 1985). Houses were arranged in groups of seven around communal open spaces. These clusters, in turn, were located in groups of three around larger open spaces, which opened into a central open space. External house walls were brick and roofs were pitched, with wooden shingles. In order to minimize problems when people came to extend their houses, there were no party walls. Each house had a private yard with a lavatory block, with lavatories paired in order to minimize service runs (Ravishankar, 2014). One of the claimed benefits of the project was that it provided high housing densities. The scheme provided about 550 plots on an area of about 5.4 ha, giving a housing density of just over 100 units per hectare. These figures suggest that plots covered about 50 per cent of the total area, the exact coverage depending on the distribution of plot sizes.

The Aranya scheme in Madhya Pradesh dates from the late 1980s and was awarded an Agha Khan award in the 1993–95 cycle (see Photos 6.4 and 6.5 for illustration). It is much larger than the Artist's Colony project, providing 6,500 plots on an 85 hectare site, which gives an overall housing density of 76.4 units per hectare. It is located about 8 km from Indore's central business district and was fairly isolated when built, although the city has since grown around it. Through roads, running east-west and north-south, divide the scheme into six sectors and in addition generous provision is made for open space. The scheme was designed to meet the needs of low-income households, with 65 per cent of its plots intended for households falling within the Indian Government's economically weaker section (EWS) category. These plots were 35 m^2 in area, connected to water and electricity services and provided with a plinth, a service core (a latrine and water tap or bath), and the option of a kitchen (Mollard, 2019). In the Aranya scheme, as in some of the sites and services schemes in Mumbai referred to earlier in this chapter, service cores, and the water mains and sewers that served them, were located at the back of plots (MIT, n.d.). Larger plots, located along main streets and in the south-eastern sector of the scheme, did not include a service core (Turlapati, 2013). Plots were initially allocated on a first-come first-served basis, but as people came to know about the scheme, applicants had to enter a lottery system.

In 1989, 80 model houses were constructed on small plots, using load-bearing brick on a concrete plinth with walls plastered and painted. These were intended to provide a model that residents of core plots could follow when constructing their own houses. The mid-1990s report prepared when assessing the project for the Agha Khan award noted that few of the 80 model houses remained in anything approaching their original condition. Anecdotal

Photo 6.4 Aranya: regimented toilet blocks

Photo 6.5 Aranya: waiting for water

evidence to the project assessors suggested that many of the original plot owners had sold their plots, in some cases because they could not afford to pay the instalments on their plots (Mollard, 2019).

From 1986 onwards, the author was involved in the planning and implementation of another core housing scheme, the St Michael's Housing Society scheme in Peshawar, Pakistan. At the time, it was not uncommon for Catholic churches in Pakistan to form housing societies with the aim of providing affordable housing to their parishioners, many of whom were sweepers (garbage collectors) who were both poor and socially marginalized. The society in Peshawar had purchased land near brick workings on the outskirts of the city and the challenge was to develop a scheme that could provide affordable housing with services. The society members had been promised 5 *marla* (125 m^2) plots. In practice, allowance had to be made for land for access and the standard plot dimensions were set at 7 m × 14 m, giving a plot area of 98 m^2. Street widths were 5 m and 3 m. The core provided a 3.5 m × 3.5 m room, and separate toilet and bathing compartments on each plot. These were situated at the front of plots to define streets. Locating the toilet and bathing area at the front of the plot also enabled wastewater from the plot to be discharged through a single connection to a sewer in the street. The society members also asked for a boundary wall around each plot to be included in the 'core' construction. This request stemmed at least partly from their feeling of vulnerability. The site was relatively remote, well away from other Christian communities, a particularly important consideration for an underprivileged minority with origins in Punjab rather than Pakhtunkhwa and speaking Punjabi rather than Pushto. Access lanes were brick-paved. All houses had a single water connection from a piped system supplied from an artesian well. The scheme grew over the years as more land was bought and additional plots were demarcated, eventually providing around 250 houses.

Many residents added two additional rooms at the back of the plot, leaving a central courtyard area, typically around 4 m × 4 m in extent. Some took their government pension, one of the few benefits enjoyed by sweepers, in a lump sum to cover the cost of construction. All built in burnt brick, with concrete roofs, ignoring the example of a demonstration building using pressed mud blocks that had been built on one of the plots. Inspection of 2019 satellite images shows that many plots are almost completely developed, with courtyards either eliminated or greatly reduced. The situation is similar in Charkop, Belapur, and Aranya Town schemes. Photographs of Charkop suggest that most of the original single storey units with mezzanine have been replaced, with most houses now having two storeys or more. Similarly, satellite images of Aranya Town show that many houses now occupy most or all of the plots on which they are located. The service cores, located at the back of the plot, appear to have been subsumed into house structures, and water mains and sewers must run under a number of buildings unless they have been relocated. Many of the plots in the Belapur scheme have been similarly redeveloped, with the original external toilet facilities relocated inside houses. In Belapur particularly, it seems that the architect's vision of how the scheme should look has been superseded by that of the residents. Nevertheless, all three schemes have retained their basic layout. The lesson is perhaps that, where provided, the core should provide the minimum facilities required to encourage people to move onto a site and should be planned in a way that maximizes the possibilities for future building expansion.

Guided land development and land pooling

The 1980s saw considerable interest in guided land development (GLD), which required local government to plan and implement efficient road layouts to serve sparsely developed land on the urban fringes. Landowners were to give up land for the roads without compensation, but they would then benefit from the increased value of their land. Basic infrastructure was to be provided in the first instance and improved incrementally over time. The theory was that the GLD approach facilitates assembly of large areas of land, much of which can be assigned to low-income housing. In effect, it is sites and services on a large scale, designed to provide a mix of housing types and development options. A GLD scheme covering 26,000 ha was proposed for Jakarta in 1980 and the concept was included in a Master Plan for the city produced in 1985. It was also incorporated in the wider context of the Integrated Urban Infrastructure Development Programmes (IUIDP) (Marulanda and Steinberg, 1991).

Marulanda and Steinberg refer to three schemes to be implemented under the GLD umbrella. Two of these, each covering about 50 ha, were to have been implemented under the Asian Development Bank-supported Botabek Urban Development Project. The third, the Klender Guided Land Development Project, covered 61 ha, 30 ha of which was already occupied by low-density *kampungs* (traditional villages). The project aimed to create an integrated and coordinated development with efficient land use, using existing resources. Forty per cent of the land was to be used for high-income housing and the remainder for middle- and low-income housing. Relocation of existing residents was to be avoided where possible, and where unavoidable, was to be achieved within the project area. Local government was to play the role of promoter and facilitator, but the project was to be implemented by a specially created body, consisting of representatives of local and provincial government and the development consultants, who were to act as intermediaries with other parties, including the private sector, concerned NGOs, and the local community. Private sector developers were to be invited to participate in a co-development process, which would pool the resources of government, local landowners, and private developers in a way that shared the benefits arising from the physical and economic development of the area. The project was to be implemented in three phases, the first taking the form of a Kampung Improvement Programme, the second focusing on land development, with a particular emphasis on the supply of serviced land to low-income households, and the third involving provision of the major infrastructure required to encourage development of commercial and recreational facilities within the project area. Marulanda and Steinberg recognized that implementation of the approach depended on political will and it seems that this was lacking, because the scheme was not implemented. The proposed project area is now occupied by a high-income housing estate (Harjoko, 2009: Figure 5).

GLD can be considered a variation on the concept of land pooling or land readjustment, whereby land owned by a number of individuals is consolidated by the transfer of ownership rights to a land pooling agency, which then prepares a plan for the whole area. Land required for access, infrastructure, and social amenities is retained in public ownership and the remainder is transferred back to the owners as serviced land ready for development. A betterment charge is levied on the owners to cover the cost of infrastructure development.

The concept of land pooling was first used to obtain the land required to build Washington, as the USA's capital city. However, modern practice originated with the Lex Adickes, a city planning law devised by Franz Adickes, the Mayor of Frankfurt, Germany, in 1893, and enacted in 1902 (Deuskar, 2013). More recently, it has been implemented in Japan, Korea, and India among other countries. In India, the land readjustment/pooling mechanisms were incorporated into the 1915 Bombay Town Planning Act, which also drew on England's 1909 Housing and Town Planning Act. This was first used for the development of a 3 hectare site on Salsette Island, part of what is now Mumbai. The act was soon extended to the Bombay Presidency, which included parts of what are now Gujarat and Maharashtra states. Some planners argued that land pooling was preferable to land acquisition because it is more participatory. A larger Town Planning (TP) scheme for Pune, covering over 600 ha, followed soon afterwards. Ahmedabad's first scheme was prepared in 1917 and further schemes followed over the years, continuing after Indian independence in 1947. By the mid-1980s land pooling had fallen out of favour. Delays were the norm, with some schemes taking more than 20 years to complete, and schemes were far from being self-financing. In 1986, the World Bank estimated that 50–90 per cent of the total cost of schemes was subsidized by government (Deuskar, 2011). The 2000s saw renewed interest in the land pooling mechanism, particularly but not exclusively in Gujarat. Between 2000 and 2009 Ahmedabad Municipal Corporation (AMC) and Ahmedabad Urban Development Authority (AUDA) developed more than 200 sq km of land using town planning land adjustment schemes. Between 2005 and 2010, AUDA claimed to have built over 11,000 low-income housing units on land obtained through such schemes (Nair and Ahluwalia, 2010, quoted by Deuskar, 2011).

Other Indian states and towns, including Delhi, Punjab, and Haryana, have introduced legislation to allow land pooling and the development of TP schemes. In Andhra Pradesh, land pooling was used on a large scale to secure the land required for its new capital city of Amaravati. By June 2018, around 12,650 hectares had been consolidated on land previously owned by about 25,000 farmers (Ravi and Mahaduvan, 2018). In Nepal, the 17 June 2017 edition of the *Himalayan Times* reported that 12 land pooling projects, covering 260 ha, were being implemented and that 11 schemes, covering 405 ha, were in the pipeline (Himalayan News Service, 2017).

The question for this book is not whether such schemes can be used to facilitate urban expansion, but rather whether they can do this in a way that supports the development of low-income housing initiatives that can provide an alternative to the informal sector. The Gujjarpura scheme in Lahore, referenced earlier in this chapter, used a form of land pooling and was certainly intended to provide housing for low-income households. However, the available evidence suggests that land pooling has generally benefited higher-income rather than low-income households. Using figures originally produced by Shirley Ballaney, Deuskar (2011) showed that of the 153.78 km^2 of TP schemes prepared by AUDA from 2002 to 2010, only 4.52 km^2, less than 3 per cent, had been reserved for affordable housing. He went on to cite Joshi and Sanga's (2009) finding that only 6 per cent of the 172 plots, covering 136 ha, reserved by AMC for low-income housing between 1976 and 2006 was actually occupied by low-income housing. He made the further point that TP schemes had led to the displacement of the low-income populations in existing informal settlements, even on occasion requiring the demolition of informal settlements that had previously been upgraded through AMC's Slum Networking Project.

Overall, the experience in Gujarat suggests that land pooling schemes have the potential to overcome the land constraints that have led to the failure of many sites and services schemes. However, they are not a panacea since there is no guarantee that landowners will wish to join land pooling initiatives. ASCI (2016: 4) suggested that 'a dedicated and sufficiently staffed department, policy changes to incentivise the people to join the mechanism voluntarily and a minimum voluntary proportion of people to avoid conflict may greatly contribute to the successful implementation of the strategy'. They also noted that legislation in Japan and Korea provides for different parties to initiate land pooling procedures, whereas all Indian land pooling models had been initiated by government. Their response to this situation was to argue that government should adapt the legal framework and institutionalize systems, procedures, and monitoring systems in order to encourage others to initiate bottom-up land pooling models. This will require commitment to institutional change, with a particular emphasis on developing institutional commitment to action to address the needs of the urban poor. The implications of this will be further explored in Chapter 10.

References

Adefarasin, A., Spiegel, M., Villasenor, F. and Weniger, M. (2017) *Analysis of sites-and-services approach in Charkop, India*, NYU advanced project in international development Final Report. World Bank Group, Washington, DC.

Administrative Staff College of India (ASCI) (2016) *Study on Land Acquisition vs Land Pooling*, Report sponsored by National Housing Bank. https://nhb.org.in/wp-content/uploads/2017/03/Land-Acquisition-vs.-Land-Pooling.pdf (accessed 16 August 2020).

Aliani, A.H. and Sheng, Y.K. (1990) The incremental development scheme in Hyderabad: an innovative approach to low-income housing, *Cities*, May, 133–48. https://doi.org/10.1016/0264-2751(90)90068-I

Arandel, C. and El Batran, M. (1997) *The informal housing development process in Egypt*, Report prepared For Centre Nacional dela Recherge Scientifique (CNRS), Bordeaux, France. https://www.ucl.ac.uk/bartlett/development/sites/bartlett/files/migrated-files/WP82_0.pdf (accessed 17 April 2019).

Arku, G. (2009) The economics of housing programmes in Ghana 1929–99, *Planning Perspectives*, 24(3): 281–300. https://doi.org/10.1080/02665430902933952

Asfar A. and Rahman A. (2004) *Housing the Urban Poor*, Acumen Fund. https://acumen.org/wp-content/uploads/2013/03/Saiban-Study.pdf (accessed 20 November 2019; no longer available).

Bamberger, M. and Harth Deneke, A. (1984) Can shelter programmes meet low-income needs? The experience of El Salvador, in G.K. Payne (ed.) *Low-income housing in the developing world, the role of sites and services and settlement upgrading*, Wiley, Chichester.

Bamberger, M., Sanyal, B. and Valverde, N. (1982) *Evaluation of sites and services projects: the experience from Lusaka, Zambia*, World Bank Staff Working Paper Number 548, IBRD/World Bank, Washington, DC. http://documents.worldbank.org/curated/en/844131468766180804/pdf/multi-page.pdf (accessed 15 April 2019).

Baum, W.C. and Tolbert, S.M. (1985) *Investing in development: lessons of World Bank experience*, Oxford University Press. http://documents.worldbank.org/curated/en/316461468141895022/pdf/multi0page.pdf (accessed 28 May 2019).

Collective for Social Science Research (2005) *Afghans in Karachi, migration, settlement and social networks*. The Afghanistan Research and Evaluation Unit (AREU). https://old.researchcollective.org/Documents/Afghans_in%20Karachi_CS.PDF (accessed 4 August 2025).

Davey, P. (1985) Belapur Housing in Navi Mumbai, India by Charles Correa, *The Architectural Review*, 19 October 1985. https://www.architectural-review.com/essays/belapur-housing-in-navi-mumbai-india-by-charles-correa/8684855.article (accessed 29 April 2020).

Davidson, F. (1984) Ismailia: combined upgrading and sites and services projects in Egypt, in G. Payne (ed.) *Low-income housing in the developing world, the role of sites and services and settlement upgrading*, Wiley, Chichester.

Davidson, F. and Payne, G. (1983) *Urban projects manual*, 2nd ed., Liverpool University Press, https://forbesdavidsonplanning.com/wp-content/uploads/2020/11/urban-projects-manual.pdf

Deuskar, C. (2011) *A better way to grow? Land readjustment through town planning schemes in Ahmedabad*, Master's thesis, Massachusetts Institute of Technology. https://dspace.mit.edu/bitstream/handle/1721.1/66885/758256692-MIT.pdf?sequence=2&isAllowed=y

Deuskar, C. (2013) George Washington and land readjustment, *World Bank blogs*, 31 July. https://blogs.worldbank.org/en/sustainablecities/george-washington-and-land-readjustment (accessed 19 September 2025).

Harjoko, T.Y. (2009) Urban acupuncture: an alternative, *Informal Settlements and Affordable Housing 2009*. https://www.irbnet.de/daten/iconda/CIB_DC25384.pdf (accessed 8 August 2020).

Hassan, A. (1990) Evaluation of the HDA's Khuda-Ki-Basti Incremental Housing Scheme, 30 September. http://arifhasan.org/wp-content/uploads/2012/09/AH18_HADs-KKB-scheme.pdf

Jere, H. (1984) Lusaka: local participation in planning and decision-making, in G.K. Payne (ed.) *Low-income housing in the developing world*, Wiley, Chichester.

Joshi, R. and Sanga, P. (2009) *Land reservations for the urban poor: the case of town planning schemes in Ahmedabad*, Working Paper 4. https://cept.ac.in/UserFiles/File/CUE/Working%20Papers/Revised%20New/04CUEWP4_Land%20reservations%20for%20the%20urban%20poor%20The%20case%20of%20town%20planning%20schemes%20in%20Ahmedabad.pdf

Keare, D.H. and Parris, S. (1982) *Evaluation of shelter programs for the urban poor: principal findings*, World Bank Working Paper No.547, World Bank, Washington, DC. http://documents.worldbank.org/curated/en/951611468759907426/pdf/multi-page.pdf (accessed 4 June 2019).

Khoury, Z. (1996) Implementing the new urban agenda: the case of Ismailia, Egypt, *Environment & Urbanization*, 8(1). https://doi.org/10.1177/095624789600800109

Kool, M.L., Verboom, D. and van der Linden, J.J. (1988) *Squatter settlements in Pakistan*, Vanguard Books, Lahore.

Kumar, S. (1996) *Subsistence and petty-capitalist landlords: an inquiry into the petty commodity production of rental housing in low-income settlements in Madras*, PhD dissertation, Development Planning Unit, University College London.

Himalayan News Service (2017) Land pooling projects gaining momentum in Kathmandu Valley, *The Himalayan*, 17 June. https://thehimalayantimes.com/kathmandu/land-pooling-projects-gaining-momentum-kathmandu-valley

Marulanda, L. and Steinberg, F. (1991) *Land management and guided land development in Jakarta*, IHS Working Paper Series No. 1, Institute for Housing and Urban Development Studies. https://www.ihs.nl/sites/corporate/files/IHS_WP_001_Land_Management_and_Guided_Land_Development_in_Jakarta_1991.pdf (accessed 17 May 2020).

Matteucci, C. (2006) Long-term evaluation of an urban development project: the case of Hai el Salaam. *7th N-Aerus Conference*. N-Aerus, Darmstadt. https://forbesdavidsonplanning.com/wp-content/uploads/2021/03/ismailia-matteucci-2006.pdf (accessed 4 August 2025).

Metwally, M. (1987) Self-help communities: Ismailia experience, an evaluation of outcomes, in *Proceedings of the XIV IAHS World Congress on Housing, Berlin, 13–17 October*.

Mghweno, J. (1984) Tanzania's surveyed plots programme, in G. Payne (ed.) *Low-income housing in the developing world*, Wiley, Chichester.

MIT (no date) Aranya community housing, Indore, India. http://web.mit.edu/incrementalhousing/articlesPhotographs/pdfs/aranya-3-Details1146.pdf (accessed 21 November 2019).

Mollard, M. (2019) Revisit: Aranya low-cost housing, Indore, Balkrishna Doshi, *The Architectural Review*, 14 August. https://www.architectural-review.com/buildings/revisit-aranya-low-cost-housing-indore-balkrishna-doshi/10044061.article (accessed 29 April 2020).

Napier, M. (2002) The origins and spread of core housing, excerpt from M. Napier, *Core housing enablement, enablement and urban poverty: the consolidation paths of households living in two South African settlements*, PhD thesis, University of Newcastle upon Tyne. http://web.mit.edu/incrementalhousing/articlesPhotographs/pdfs/Origins-Spread-CoreHousing.pdf

Owens, K.E., Gulyani, S. and Rizvi, A. (2018) Success when we deemed it a failure? Revisiting sites and services projects in Mumbai and Chennai 20 years later, *World Development*, 106 (2018): 260–72, https://doi.org/10.1016/j.worlddev.2018.01.021

Pugh, C. (1995) The role of the World Bank in housing, in B.C. Aldrich and R. Sandhu (eds.) *Housing the urban poor: policy and practice in developing countries*, pp. 34–92. Zed, London.

Rahman, A. and Hassan, B. (2009) *The challenges of expanding Saiban: scaling affordable housing for low-income communities in Pakistan*, Acumen Fund. https://web.archive.org/web/20220320202220/https://acumen.org/wp-content/uploads/2013/03/Challenges-of-Expanding-Saiban.pdf (accessed 19 September 2025).

Rakodi, C. (1989) Self-help housing: the debate and examples, upgrading in Lusaka, Zambia and Hyderabad, India, *Habitat International*, 13(4): 5–18. https://doi.org/10.1016/0197-3975(89)90034-9

Rakodi, C. and Leduka, R. (2004) *Informal land delivery processes and access to land for the poor: a comparative study of six African cities*, DFID Policy Brief 6, International Development Department, School of Public Policy, University of Birmingham, UK. https://assets.publishing.service.gov.uk/media/57a08cd6ed915d622c0015f1/R8076-Comparative_land_delivery.pdf (accessed 17 May 2019).

Ravi, R.R. and Mahaduvan, S. (2018) Case study: Amaravati land pooling scheme, *Urban Solutions* 13. https://www.clc.gov.sg/docs/default-source/urban-solutions/urb-sol-iss-13-pdfs/10_case_study-amaravati-land-pooling-scheme.pdf (accessed 8 August 2020).

Ravishankar, R. (2014) *Belapur incremental housing - a case study* [slides]. https://www.slideshare.net/rithikarockingravishankar/belapur-incremental-housing-a-case-study?from_action=save (accessed 29 April 2020).

Seymour, T. (1975) Squatter settlement and class relations in Zambia, *Review of African Political Economy*, 3(May–Oct): 71–77. https://www.jstor.org/stable/3997825

Sharma, K. (2007) The great garbage rush [op-ed], *India Together*, 27 February 2007. http://www.indiatogether.org/2007/feb/ksh-slumclean.htm (accessed 23 March 2019).

Siddiqi, I. (1983) The implementation of the Metroville 1 Project in Karachi, in J. Schoorl, J. van der Linden, and Y.K. Sheng (eds.) *Between Basti dwellers and bureaucrats: upgrading in Karachi*. Pergamon Press, Oxford.

Siddique, M.H. (2013) Khuda Ki Basti, Lahore – NGO Initiative in Low-Income Housing, *GMSARN International Journal*, 7: 115–120.

Siddiqui, T. (2014) Pakistan's urbanization challenge: houses for the low-income, in M. Kugelman (ed.) *Pakistan's runaway urbanization: what can be done*, The Wilson Centre, Washington, DC. https://www.wilsoncenter.org/publication/pakistans-urbanization-housing-for-the-low-income (accessed 4 August 2025).

Stein, A. and Vance, I. (2008) The role of housing finance in addressing the needs of the urban poor: lessons from Central America, *Environment and Urbanisation*, 20(1): 13–30. https://doi.org/10.1177/0956247808089146

Turlapati, L. (2013) Aranya Housing Project: Indore, India [online], Architecture in Development. https://www.architectureindevelopment.org/project.php?id=401 (accessed 21 November 2019).

CHAPTER 7
Upgrading

Upgrading is the term used to describe efforts to improve the quality of slum housing and related services *in situ*. As explained in Chapter 5, it is sometimes used to mean replacement of existing houses with completely new units, often in the form of apartment blocks and often in new locations. But this is redevelopment rather than upgrading. Upgrading recognizes that informal development represents significant social capital and sunk investment by residents and, following Turner, that this investment should be seen as positive assets rather than a problem. Over the years, most upgrading initiatives have focused on service improvements, perhaps with some efforts to upgrade the housing fabric and limited adjustments to the settlement layout to facilitate service provision and rationalize the use of space. Many initiatives have also included efforts to provide residents with secure tenure.

Along with sites and services, upgrading featured prominently in the project portfolios of the World Bank and other international agencies from around 1970 to the late 1980s. The two were often linked with efforts to upgrade existing settlements featuring alongside the provision of new serviced sites. So, for instance, the Lusaka, Ismailia, Chennai, and Mumbai projects described in Chapter 6 all had an upgrading component. Other projects focused mainly or wholly on upgrading. Examples include the World Bank's upgrading projects in Calcutta, the Kampung Improvement Programme (KIP) in Indonesia, also partly World Bank funded, and various slum improvement projects in India funded by the British Overseas Development Administration (ODA), the forerunner of the then Department for International Development (DFID).

Early projects were 'technically driven' in the sense that key decisions were made by professionals on technical grounds. In the best projects, these decisions were made on the basis of observation of what was already happening on the ground and there was some recognition of the need for use of community involvement in decision-making. The mid to late 1980s brought an increased emphasis on integration of informal areas into the overall fabric of the city, most notably through Himanchu Parikh's concept of slum networking (Diacon, 1997). By the early 1990s, the need for user participation, a concept that has already been discussed in Chapter 4, had become a major concern. As will become clear from the examples explored in this chapter, this concern with participation was sometimes at the expense of the wider vision that had characterized the previous generation of projects, at least in theory. The 1990s also saw an increased emphasis on livelihoods, defined as the capabilities, assets, and activities required for a means of living. The aim was to make livelihoods 'sustainable', in other words able to cope with and recover from stresses and shocks and to maintain or enhance capabilities and assets into the future (Chambers and Conway, 1992). To achieve this objective, some urban upgrading projects included components relating to health, education, and employment generation. By the end of the 1990s, international agencies were attempting to link upgrading initiatives to efforts to bring about municipal reform.

This chapter uses examples of typical upgrading projects to illustrate the development of thinking on upgrading since the 1960s. It first looks briefly at early projects, focusing particularly on World Bank-funded interventions in Kolkata and the KIP in Indonesia. The North-east Lahore Upgrading Project is then examined in some detail, as an example of a primarily 'engineered' approach to infrastructure. Condominial sewerage in Brazil and the work of the Orangi Pilot Project in Karachi, Pakistan, provide examples of Schübeler's functionally based approach to infrastructure upgrading. Next, attention turns to the Faisalabad Area Upgrading Project (FAUP), also in Pakistan, which provides an example of a project with a strong participatory ethos, at least in its early years. Information on initiatives that attempted to combine upgrading with urban reform and so go beyond a project-based approach to upgrading is provided in Chapter 8.

Early initiatives: Kolkata

Kolkata illustrates the way in which early upgrading projects often grew out of city planning exercises. A comprehensive urban development plan for the city was produced in 1966 with assistance from the Ford Foundation. This was influenced by the ideas of Otto Koenigsberger and took the form of a 20-year action plan rather than a conventional master plan (Rosser, 1970). The Calcutta Metropolitan Development Authority (CMDA) was created to plan and implement the wide range of projects identified in the action plan. The plan's recognition of the need to improve living conditions in low-income areas led to the implementation of the Bustee Improvement Program (BIP). (*Bustee* is a variation on *basti*, which is the term used in northern India for a low-income informal development). Most were *thika* tenancies, a system under which individual *thika* tenants had rented land from large landowners (*zamindars*) and been given the right to build hutments on the land to provide accommodation to poor people. Following independence, government had taken the land from the *zamindars*, but *thika* tenants retained the right to build hutments on their land. Recognizing that removing existing *bustees* and replacing them with walk-up apartments was an unaffordable option, the CMDA and its international advisers focused on upgrading existing *bustees in situ*. Government was to be given easement rights to acquire land for improvements in rights of way. One water tap was to be provided for each *thika* tenancy holding or per 100 people. Pour-flush toilets were to be installed to replace the existing insanitary conservancy system (bucket latrines). Streets and paths were to be paved and open drains provided for sullage and storm water. Security lighting and bathing areas were to be installed. Drains were to be connected to a nearby sewer if available or, failing this, to a septic tank. In practice, most toilets discharged to a leach pit located directly under the toilet (Thomas, 1997). The author's visits to upgraded areas in Howrah, one of the municipalities covered by the BIP, in the late 1990s revealed that it was common practice to provide two toilets per holding above a common pit or tank, although the *thika* tenant often reserved one of those two toilets for the use of his or her family.

With World Bank assistance, the programme aimed to provide these basic services to 1 million *bustee* dwellers at an average cost of Rs. 100 per head, equivalent to about US$14 at the exchange rate prevailing at the time. The programme provided physical improvements, which were sustained for some time despite poor maintenance. The author's visits to BIP *bustees* in the late 1990s revealed that many of the pits and tanks were full and in urgent need of emptying. Brick paving was in reasonable condition, as were open drains, although the latter were often partially blocked. However, the overall impact of the project was limited. Governments and the residents of the 'formal' city still perceived informal settlements as slums and the basic relationship between these areas and the rest of the city remained unchanged. Thomas (1997) suggested that the improvements achieved through the BIP were fairly modest. He noted that the dilapidated state of many of the 'improved' *bustees* was attracting criticism. Sanitation standards remained low and many of the *bustees* were still unhygienic and poorly lit. The BIP had not tackled the issues of ownership and so most *bustee* dwellers were still tenants, in theory protected from eviction by the 1981 Thika Tenancy Act but in practice still vulnerable to exploitation and eviction.

As World Bank assistance drew to a close, the UK's ODA started its Calcutta Slum Improvement Project (CSIP). The scope of this was similar to that of the World Bank-supported schemes. In 1997, ODA was replaced by the DFID and in 2001, Calcutta was officially renamed Kolkata. Subsequent UK-supported upgrading projects in Kolkata, as in India as a whole, placed increased emphasis on participation and good governance, as explained later in this chapter and in Chapter 8.

Early initiatives: the Kampung improvement programme in Indonesia

The KIP was a Government of Indonesia initiative to improve living conditions in rapidly growing villages and informal settlements, known as kampungs in Indonesia. It was not a completely new initiative, the first efforts to upgrade conditions in kampungs having started in 1924. The first phase of KIP ran from 1969 to 1974 with funding from the Jakarta city government. The World Bank provided support through four projects, Urban I to Urban IV, which ran from 1974 to the early 1990s. Upgrading work undertaken under these projects began in Surabaya in 1976 and in other urban centres outside Jakarta in 1978. In all cases, the objective was to provide basic services with the minimum possible use of technical and administrative resources. By 1979, the programme was covering 1,000 hectares per year. Schemes provided improved access, water supply via public standpipes, sanitation in the form of public toilets, drainage and solid waste management services, and community buildings, including health centres and community centres. Per capita expenditure, expressed in 1993 prices, varied from a maximum of US$118 in Jakarta to $23 in Denpasar with a mean figure of about $100 (World Bank Operations Evaluation Department, 1995). Most of the expenditure was on roads and footpaths, with the latter predominating.

In most cases, community participation in planning and construction was limited. Plans and designs were prepared by local government and implemented by contractors. Communities had a role in monitoring construction and were responsible for subsequent maintenance of facilities. This responsibility was discharged through Kampung Committees (LKPMDKs), which were tasked with organizing maintenance squads from community members, to be paid out of voluntary community funds. Individual households were to be responsible for the maintenance of the footpaths and drains directly in front of their houses. The Surabaya programme, which won a World Habitat Award in 1992, was an exception to this general rule in that efforts to involve the community from the outset led to increased community involvement at later stages in the upgrading process. These efforts were facilitated by the Institut Teknologi Surabaya and involved initial contacts with community leaders, followed by regular consultation between KIP staff, local officials, and community representatives. A claimed outcome of the consultation process was restriction of the width of most access pathways in order to limit vehicular access and thus reduce the likelihood of 'invasion' by middle-income households. Evaluation of the programme showed that the average community contribution was Rp500,000 (about US$19,300) for every Rp1 m (about $38,600) contributed by government (Silas, 1992). It appears that most of this contribution was in kind rather than in cash.

In addition to improvements in housing and infrastructure, the comprehensive KIP (C-KIP), which started in 2000, sought to reduce poverty by providing loans for small- and medium-sized businesses, distributed from a revolving fund. Access to the fund was through community groups, typically consisting of 5 to 10 people. In this respect, C-KIP was similar to contemporary upgrading initiatives in other countries that will be described later in this chapter. As with earlier KIP initiatives, community participation was implemented through existing government structures and assigned a leading role to the chairmen of the RW (Rukun Warga – Community Board) and RT (Rukun Tetangga – Neighbourhood Board). Kampungs supported by C-KIP were required to establish a Yayasan Kampung (Kampung Foundation) and Koperasi Serba Usaha (Diversified Business Cooperative). The role of the former usually ended with the completion of physical upgrading, typically after about one year. The business cooperative, on the other hand, was expected to operate for as long as it had revolving funds to lend to the community. The success of C-KIP varied from kampung to kampung, depending on the experience and commitment of those charged with managing its implementation (Santosa et al., 2010).

The author visited some areas upgraded under KIP in the early 1990s and found that paving and drainage facilities improved over 20 years previously were still in good condition. Interestingly, work carried out under later projects, with greater community participation but less attention to technical detail, had not fared so well.

Integration with the city? North-east Lahore

Lahore is Pakistan's second city and the capital of Punjab, the country's most populous province. In the late 1980s, it was growing at an average rate of around 3.3 per cent per annum, reaching a population of just over 5 million by 1998. The city divides very clearly into formal and informal areas, with the latter found mainly in the north of the city, along its western fringe and across the River Ravi in the area known as Shahdara. Most informal developments are unregulated subdivisions, built on agricultural land, which has been purchased legally but then developed without reference to formal planning and building standards.

A planning study, carried out with World Bank funding in 1979–80, led to efforts to upgrade services in part of Lahore's historic Walled City and the Gujjarpura sites and services project that has already been referred to in Chapter 6. A follow-up study produced an action plan for North Lahore, which identified an area in the north-east of the city as a potential upgrading area and this became the location for the North-east Lahore Upgrading Project. The project covered about 400 ha of which about 270 ha had already been developed, mostly through a process of informal land subdivision. This had produced roughly equally sized plots fronting onto fairly regularly spaced lanes. The area also contained many industrial premises, most of which were involved in iron and steel production. The built-up area was expanding onto adjacent agricultural land and pockets of previously undeveloped land. Throughout the area, plots and access roads and lanes had been raised by up to about 1 metre to remove the risk of frequent flooding. In the case of roads and lanes, this fill material included solid waste. Most houses were of brick and concrete construction and owned by their occupants.

The project area was bounded to the south and east by two major roads, the GT road and Bund road. Their wide rights of way provided potentially good access to the project area, although the condition of the Bund road was poor. The main access roads within the project area were typically 6–10 metres wide. Many had been surfaced but in most cases the surfacing was in poor condition. These roads had to carry the traffic generated by a total population in excess of 100,000 together with the traffic generated by the many foundries and other industries, and it is not surprising that traffic speeds were low. Most public transport within the area was provided by horse-drawn *tongas* (two-wheeled carts). Access lanes were typically 1.5–3 metres wide. In more established areas, many were paved with bricks, with brick and cement-built open drains running along one or both sides of the lane. These drains carried wastewater during dry weather and acted as rather inadequate storm drains during heavy rain. In the north of the project area, the drainage system discharged to open fields while the larger system in the south discharged to the Shalimar Escape Drain, which also drained a large area to the south. There were virtually no sewers in the area and those WCs that existed discharged their effluent to the open drains, sometimes but not always via household septic tanks. Areas close to the GT road had a piped water supply but most households relied on groundwater accessed through open wells and tubewells located on their plots. Most households had an electricity supply although the electricity distribution system left much to be desired. Where streetlights existed, the bulbs were often missing or broken. Solid waste collection services consisted, at most, of occasional forays into the area by a small pick-up truck to pick up waste from points along the through roads. In all these aspects, the area was typical of informal areas throughout Lahore.

Apart from one community centre, the project's focus was on physical infrastructure improvements. Project interventions covered tertiary and some secondary infrastructure. Off-site infrastructure was to be the responsibility of the Lahore Water and Sanitation Agency (WASA). There was no explicit attempt to improve the housing fabric or to provide toilets and other in-house facilities.

The project was implemented by the Metropolitan Planning Wing (MPW) of Lahore Development Authority (LDA). This reflected both MPW's previous role in planning activities and a belief that municipalities, in this case the Lahore Municipal Corporation, lacked the capacity to implement 'integrated' upgrading projects. A special project unit with its own director was set up within the MPW to implement the project. The institutional arrangements were typical of internationally funded urban projects implemented at the time. Because the MPW lacked expertise in the field of infrastructure upgrading, staff were either seconded from other government departments or recruited on temporary government contracts. During project preparation, international consultants were employed as advisers to the government but it soon became clear that they would have to do more than advise if the project was to be completed on schedule. From 1989 onwards there was a change of approach as a team of local and international consultants was employed to produce detailed designs and provide overall guidance during implementation.

Overall, it could be said that the project took a technical approach that dealt with infrastructure provision in an integrated way, using design standards and details that were intended to be both affordable and appropriate to the conditions found in the area. The original project documents made some reference to consultation with local people, and the first project manager employed by the consultants, an architect with experience of participatory approaches to housing provision, did attempt to develop at least basic levels of community participation. However, there was little interest in (and indeed some suspicion of) participation within LDA and the project quickly settled into a conventional 'supply-driven' approach.

One interesting and, for a World Bank-funded project, unusual aspect of the project was its incremental nature. It was prepared under one World Bank-funded project, the Lahore Urban Development Project (LUDP), and largely implemented under another, the Punjab Urban Development Project (PUDP). In order to test and demonstrate technical options, two lanes were upgraded in early 1987. Implementation of a pilot scheme to serve a 7 hectare area in Mahmud Buti, an old village engulfed by informal development, followed in 1988. Implementation of the main project began in 1989. This 'incremental' approach provided opportunities for learning during the first two years of implementation and the results of that learning were used in the design of subsequent contracts.

Engineering designs sought to retain what was good in existing practice, while introducing the improvements required to ensure that the facilities provided under the project fulfilled their intended functions over the course of their intended lifetimes. Design and construction standards took account of the location and intended function of facilities. This led to some differences from conventional standards, which often assume very different conditions from those found in low-income areas. For instance, since most lanes in the project area were not wide enough to allow vehicular access, concrete sewers in narrow lanes were laid with a minimum cover of about 250 mm rather than the 900 mm or more specified by conventional standards. This allowed small chambers, accessible from above, to be used rather than conventional manholes, reducing the cost of local sewers to about PRs1100 ($63) per household (Orangi Pilot Project, 1995).

Drawing on local practice, brick paving was used to surface small lanes, with bricks laid on edge on 20 mm sand cement mortar over 25 mm of compacted sand and grouted with mortar rather than sand. Subsequent inspection showed that the paving had performed well and that the slight increase in cost resulting from the use of cement mortar grouting had been justified by the increased durability of the surfacing. Through roads were provided with a 50 mm pre-mixed asphalt carpet over a 100 mm stone base and 100 mm broken brick sub-base.

Experience in the Mahmud Buti pilot area led to the decision to allow storm flows to run on the surface along smaller roads and lanes. The thinking was essentially the same as that of Himanchu Parikh, who independently promoted the idea of using roads as drains in his 'slum networking' projects in India. This 'road as drain' approach was possible because of the use of hard brick and concrete lane surfacing and the provision of separate sewers to carry sewage flows and so avoid the possibility of diluted sewage flowing on street road surfaces during heavy rainfall. It replaced the insanitary open drains along the sides of lanes carrying both wastewater and stormwater, which are found throughout South Asia. However, its success depended on careful engineering to ensure a continuous fall towards the points at which storm flows could be discharged to newly constructed storm drains. These were normally laid along the wider streets on the routes taken by the pre-existing open collector drains.

The project design assumed that upgrading efforts within the project area would be linked to off-site infrastructure improvements carried out by line agencies through other components of the PUDP. Sewers would connect to a new trunk sewer on the eastern boundary of the project area. The water distribution system would be supplied by new tubewells provided with PUDP funding. Solid waste collection services were more problematic. Existing services in the area were sporadic at best and Municipal Corporation Lahore (MCL) had no plans to improve secondary collection in and around the project area. Meetings were held with officials at the MCL zonal office serving the project area and local ward councillors with a view to introducing improved solid waste management services within the project area, but these did not lead to action.

Two technical innovations were tested in the pilot lanes. Water was supplied through galvanized steel water mains laid along the sides of lanes and existing open drains were covered to act as shared connections. The thinking was that this would overcome the sometimes intractable difficulty of ensuring that people make connections to new sewers. The covered drain arrangement worked reasonably well at first but proved to be expensive as many of the existing drains were in poor condition and had to be replaced rather than rehabilitated. Also, many houses had two or more waste outlets, each of which had to be connected to the drain. Lack of clarity about responsibility for maintaining the covered drains presented a more serious problem. Over time, drain slabs were broken, often as householders made a new connection into the drain, and remained unrepaired because no household or government department took responsibility for them. In response to this problem, designs were developed and tested for shared connections using pipes rather than the open drains. While these worked well and were cheaper than the covered drains, they were not implemented on a large scale. In a situation in which professionals were often reluctant to diverge from perceived orthodoxy, the covered drain approach had become the new orthodoxy, at least for those working on the project.

The most obvious overall impact of the project was the clear improvement in the physical appearance of the areas that had been upgraded, particularly in those that had lacked paving prior to the project. The carefully designed and generally well executed paving, both brick and concrete, proved to be long-lasting. The author visited the area in June 2008 and found that much of the brick paving was still in place. Asphalt paving in lightly trafficked streets was still in place but had not survived in heavily trafficked streets. In retrospect, it would have been better to have specified a thicker asphalt carpet for streets carrying traffic in these locations. Regardless of this, the poor condition of through streets does point to the failure to make funds available for ongoing repair and maintenance.

The extension of water mains into the project area gave residents access to the Lahore WASA water supply system. However, WASA did not provide all the additional tubewells assumed in the project design, with the result that improvements in system pressure and water availability were limited. Similarly, a long delay in constructing a new trunk sewer along the eastern boundary of the project area led to problems with wastewater disposal. A temporary pumping station, included under the project to lift wastewater into the existing Shalimar Escape Drain was poorly maintained by WASA, largely because they appeared to have little interest in a facility constructed by others.

The shallow sewers were structurally sound but blockages were a problem. The key point here is the importance of ensuring that sewers function as closed conduits so that bulky objects cannot enter and block them. One causative factor was the chamber cover design. Covers were light to facilitate removal but this meant that it was easy for residents to lift them and residents certainly did so to sweep street litter into the sewers. The closed conduit concept was also undermined by the lack of traps on house connections, which meant that there was no barrier to prevent solid waste and other objects being flushed through house connections into sewers.

A survey carried out during the course of the project showed an increase in the number of households with flush sanitation, from around 36 per cent in 1986 to around 84 per cent in 1990. The latter figure was found both in areas that had already been upgraded and in those awaiting action, suggesting that the increase in toilet coverage was happening despite rather than because of the project. A survey carried out in 1991 as part of the World Bank/Swiss Aid funded Pakistan Shelter study showed that property values had increased in areas that had been upgraded. Apart from this, the only evidence as to the attitudes of residents to the upgrading initiative is anecdotal. During the visit in June 2008, people remembered the 'World Bank' activities and were generally appreciative of the work that had been carried out.

Unfortunately, the integrated approach to service provision adopted within the project area did not extend beyond it. This had both physical and institutional dimensions. The physical aspects have already been referred to and are indicative of a common problem with upgrading projects, the difficulty of ensuring that off-site services will be provided to match on-site improvements. Without appropriate off-site action, on-site improvements will not provide their intended benefits, at worst providing no benefit at all. The author observed drainage problems similar to those in North-east Lahore when visiting an area in Indore, India, upgraded under Himanchu Parikh's slum networking approach.

The root causes of such problems are often institutional. The North-east Lahore project was implemented by a special unit within LDA but dealt with services that were the responsibility of MCL (street paving, storm drainage, and solid waste collection) and Lahore WASA (water supply and sewerage). The efforts of the project team to engage with these organizations were not very successful. WASA's lack of involvement resulted in a situation in which they had no budget for the operation and maintenance of facilities when the time came for these facilities to be handed over to them. The emphasis on developing appropriate engineering standards, while necessary, aggravated the problem. The consultants had sought a dialogue with WASA on the approach to water supply and sewerage without success. In retrospect, it is clear that some of the innovative design standards and details used in the project were misconceived, and that others, while technically perhaps justified, should not have been introduced without the agreement of those who would subsequently be responsible for their operation and maintenance. The use of covered side drains as house sewer connections and above-ground galvanized water mains are examples of the first and second respectively. Conversely, the use of shallow sewers, with small chambers rather than large manholes was the only realistic option in the narrow lanes found throughout the project area. The failure to engage WASA in the project reduced the likelihood of these standards being adopted more widely within the city. More immediately, it contributed to WASA's failure, at least in the short term, to take responsibility for operating water and sewerage facilities provided through the project. Problems with solid waste management were particularly acute.

The project's impacts on Pakistan government institutions were similarly limited. Early attempts to develop an in-house design capacity within the MPW were soon abandoned and subsequent design was carried out by consultants. Site supervisory staff were mostly hired on temporary contracts and so their project experience was dissipated when their contracts were terminated at the end of the project. LDA had no statutory responsibility for providing upgrading services and ceased its involvement with upgrading once the World Bank-funded project had ended.

The project design assumed that cost recovery for upgrading would be achieved partly through the imposition of user tariffs and partly by raising property taxes. Since LDA had limited control over the first and no control over the second, it is doubtful whether either was achieved to the level envisaged by project planners. The lesson to be learnt from this is the need to make a realistic assessment of institutional relationships and responsibilities and the ways in which they will facilitate or constrain project proposals on issues such as cost recovery and maintenance.

Functionally based approaches to infrastructure improvement

Peter Schübeler's functionally based approach to urban upgrading was introduced in Chapter 4. Unlike the integrated approach adopted for the North-east Lahore project, this focuses on improving a single infrastructure service, at least in the first instance. Two well-known initiatives, one in Brazil and the second in Pakistan, are used here to illustrate the approach. The main focus of both is on construction of sewers to provide improved sanitation services.

Condominial sewerage in Brazil

The condominial concept was developed by Jose Carlos Melo, an engineer from Pernambuco State in Brazil. Its advocates claim that it differs in two important ways from conventional approaches to service provision (Melo, 2005):

1. *It redefines the unit to which service is provided.* Unlike conventional systems, which provide services to individual housing units, condominial systems deliver services to groups of dwellings constituting neighbourhood units or 'condominiums'.
2. *It involves a close relationship between service providers and service users.* The two parties have to come to agreement on roles and responsibilities in order to facilitate service expansion and adaptation to local needs and constraints. On the community side, the condominium becomes both a physical unit of service provision and a social unit for facilitating collective decision-making and organizing communal actions. Members of the condominium must select the appropriate design of the condominial service and commit themselves to complementary actions ranging from sanitary education to direct participation in the construction and/or maintenance process.

The concept can be applied to both sewerage and water supply but has mainly been used for the former. The first condominial systems were installed in Natal in the state of Rio Grande Do Norte in 1980. Within three years, the system had also been introduced in the town of Petrolina in Pernambuco State, Melo's home state. By 1995, there were around 75,000 condominial connections countrywide and condominial sewerage had become the norm in Brasilia, the nation's capital, Recife, and Petrolina. The World Bank-funded PROSANEAR (Programa de Saneamiento de Aguas Residuales or Low Income Sanitation Technical Assistance Project) had adopted the condominial approach. In all, condominial connections represented around 6 per cent of the connections made between 1980 and 1995, including most connections in poor urban neighbourhoods (Watson, 1995). In Salvador, the state capital of Bahia, condominial sewerage had reached over 1 million people living in dense and 'chaotic' informal areas, many with challenging topography by the early 2000s (Melo, 2005).

An important aspect of Brazil's condominial approach is its emphasis on the use of what is commonly referred to as 'simplified sewerage'. This is essentially conventional sewerage, designed to carry faecal solids, urine, toilet flushing water, and grey water from other household appliances, but with some changes from the conventional design methodology and assumptions. Key features of the technical approach developed by Melo include reduction in the minimum sewer diameter to 100 mm and the use of tractive tension theory to allow flatter minimum gradients than those calculated using conventional sewer design methods. The design approach requires that storm water is excluded from the sewer. The reduced minimum depth at the head of the sewer (typically 30–40 cm according to Watson, 1995) and flat gradients reduce the depth of the sewer throughout its length. The reduced depth means that small inspection boxes and chambers can be used rather than conventional manholes and this greatly reduces the cost of the sewerage (Bakalian et al., 1994). Full consideration of the implications of the 'simplified sewerage' approach is beyond the scope of this book. However, it should be noted that excluding storm water from sewers is difficult. Failure to do so may lead to sewage flooding during wet weather. It may also result in reduced sewer capacity as grit carried into sewers with storm run-off settles and has an adverse effect on the hydraulic performance of those sewers. Watson (1995) notes that the proportion of household rainwater connections in Natal had risen over time from around 4 per cent shortly after implementation to nearly 20 per cent by the mid-1990s.

Neder (2000) sets out the planning, design, and implementation process for condominial sewerage. The professional designer is responsible for surveying the area to be sewered and identifying natural drainage paths. The results of the survey are plotted on a 1:2,000 plan showing existing ground levels. Once this is available, it will be possible to produce a preliminary sewer plan, showing the likely routes of public sewers, proposed condominial blocks and the most likely discharge point from each block. Attention then turns to individual condominial blocks. Social mobilizers work with the residents of each block to introduce the condominial approach, ensure that there is an effective community organization in place, and explore the condominial options. The main choices relate to:

- *The sewer route.* This may run through either front or back yards or under a sidewalk.
- *Responsibility for operation and maintenance.* If users opt to undertake routine sewer maintenance themselves, they receive a 50 per cent discount on their sanitation fee, which generally equates to 100 per cent of the water bill.

A condominial 'pact', negotiated and signed by all parties, helps to ensure that the rules governing cooperation and the technical and financial obligations of each party are established in a democratic manner. Where it works, this is a good example of coproduction in practice. To support the approach, some service providers have developed relevant expertise, creating multidisciplinary teams in which social workers and engineers work together as equal partners (Neto and Ily, 2013). To facilitate action to deal with blockages, each block should select a condominial manager. In Natal, these block representatives were given a long length of wire to be used in blockage removal (Watson, 1995). Once decisions have been made on the routes of local sewers in condominial blocks, the preliminary public sewer design can be adjusted as necessary and completed. Construction of condominial systems may be carried out by conventional contractors or, if effort is put into organizing the community, the community itself (Neder, 2000). As with conventional approaches to sewer provision, individual households are responsible for providing their own sanitary facilities and connecting those facilities to the condominial sewer.

Melo (2005) and others claim that the back yard and, to a lesser extent, the front yard options reduce the total length of sewer required. Where existing or proposed toilets are located near the back of the lot, the back yard option also reduces the length of individual house connections. Melo recognizes that back yard routing makes sewers inaccessible to utility company staff and places the responsibility for maintenance on households. Another potential problem is that sewer blockages caused by deposition of bulky objects in the sewer are likely to occur some way downstream of the point where the objects were deposited. In the absence of very good community relations, this is likely to lead to tensions between neighbours and breakdown in the cooperation required for community management. This possibility increases if inspection chambers and connection boxes are left open or damaged. Watson (1995) quoted earlier investigations that revealed that this was the case for 18 per cent of collection boxes in Natal and 21 per cent in Petrolina. She noted that project planners in Brasilia had avoided these problems by leaving a connection pipe stub attached to the connection box in order to facilitate future connections. This, of course, assumes that the location of future toilet and bathroom facilities is known.

Regardless of the theoretical merits of the various routing options, it appears that most condominial sewers in Brazil are laid at the front of plots, often under sidewalks. Melo (2005) quotes figures from CAESB (Companhia de Saneamento Ambiental do Distrito Federal, the Brasilia water utility company) which indicate that only 6 per cent of the 22,020 condominial connections that were operational in 1996 were to back yard sewers. The remaining connections divided roughly equally between the front yard and sidewalk options. The situation is likely to be similar elsewhere in Brazil and in other countries. The author's experience with an attempt to replicate the Brazilian approach in Phnom Penh, Cambodia, was that buildings in back yards made it all but impossible to adopt the back yard option.

The planning process described by Neder (2000) is comprehensive but rather long and complicated. There must be some doubt as to whether it is always followed in full. Once both the teams charged with implementation and the communities with which they engaged had become familiar with an often-repeated process, it would seem quite likely that they shortened and simplified it.

Nance and Ortolano (2007) investigated the involvement of communities in seven condominial projects in Northeast Brazil, three in Recife, and four in Natal. Their investigation involved interviews with both service users and agency staff. Performance was assessed in relation to 27 indicators,

20 relating to operational effectiveness and the remaining 7 to impacts, using information obtained from direct observation and interviews with residents, sanitation agency engineers, and sanitation agency maintenance staff. Information relating to the level of community participation was based on 31 measures of participation and was further analysed in relation to community involvement at four stages in the project cycle:

1. *Mobilization* – involving provision of information about the project and group formation.
2. *Decision-making* – on the service level (in effect the role of the community and the service provider in ongoing operation and maintenance of condominial sewers).
3. *During construction* – involving actions ranging from paying plumbers to make connections, through providing materials to be installed by the service agency to doing all the work themselves.
4. *In carrying out maintenance* – in all seven cases, it was initially assumed that communities would be responsible for maintaining their own condominial sewers.

Six of the seven projects investigated had performed well. In the case of the one poorly performing project, the community had been involved with construction but had been minimally engaged during mobilization (involving providing information about the project and group formation) and decision-making. In all the other projects, analysis of the indicators revealed a moderate level of participation, generally rather higher for construction and maintenance than for mobilization and decision-making. Nance and Ortolano noted the positive relationship between participation during mobilization and decision-making but found little or no correlation between performance and involvement in construction and maintenance. While based on a fairly small sample, their findings were consistent with the overall findings quoted in the literature on demand-responsive projects. They suggest that good results can be achieved with moderate levels of participation.

User maintenance worked reasonably well when the public line functioned properly, problems were limited in size and easy to resolve, and blockages were on the affected household's lot. Maintenance was much more difficult when systems started to break down. When faced with difficult tasks, such as clearing blocked sewers, users often reneged on maintenance commitments and turned to sanitation service operators for help. In response to this situation, Natal set up a specialized multi-disciplinary team to carry out maintenance (Watson, 1995). A later study, covering Recife, Salvador, and Brasilia, concluded that community-based management had failed (Neto and Ily, 2013). Reasons for the failure included the following:

- Community organizations lacked structure and organization.
- Some maintenance tasks required resources and know-how that were not available in communities.

- Neighbourhood disputes arose when a user failed to follow good practice and blocked the sewer.
- Lack of support and awareness-raising mechanisms.
- High residential turnover. In Natal, only about 4 per cent of residents could identify their block representative 10 years after sewer construction.

Watson noted the need for continual education and technical orientation to ensure that the newcomers to sewered neighbourhoods understand the 'dos' and 'don'ts' to be observed when using sewers. In Natal, the operations division of the state water company had created a permanent educational campaign, distributing 'comic strip' fliers, explaining how to use the system and avoid damaging it during building expansion/construction work. Since the operator and local authority in Natal were no longer using the condominial approach by 2013, there must be considerable doubt as to the longevity of this initiative (Neto and Ily, 2013). Watson suggested that one reason for this state of affairs is that neighbourhood blocks are not necessarily a natural form of association and cooperation in urban neighbourhoods. When faced with problems, people are much more likely to solve those problems individually, either acting themselves or calling in a private sector specialist such as a plumber to solve the problem for them.

In practice, it appears that the move in Brazil has been towards *saneamento integrado*, an integrated approach that involves working across sectors such as stormwater management, solid waste management, water and electricity services, and road surfacing and in close alignment with land use and housing improvement or social development and security policies (Neto and Ily, 2013). The extent to which this is an example of Schübeler's process-based approach depends on the degree to which the community participates in the process. Where community involvement is limited, it would appear to represent an essentially technical approach, similar to the North-east Lahore process described earlier in this chapter.

Technical aspects of the condominial approach have been incorporated into official Brazilian standards and, in this respect at least, have thus been formalized. In Brasilia, it has been adopted as the standard approach for the whole city. In other cities, although invented to provide universal access, it has too often been viewed as a low-cost system, suitable only for use in poor districts (interview with J.C. Melo, reported in Neto and Ily, 2013). It has influenced practice in other Latin American countries, with references to condominial sewerage included in the national standards of Colombia, Paraguay, Peru, El Salvador, and Bolivia. However, there must be doubts as to the depth to which the condominial concepts have penetrated sewerage system designs in these countries. It is perhaps significant that none of the universities in Brazil include condominial sewerage in their curricula (Neto and Ily, 2013).

Condominial concepts have been piloted in some African and Asian countries, often with support from the World Bank and WSP (the Water and Sanitation Program, part of the World Bank's Global Water Practice).

The author was part of a team charged with designing a pilot condominial sewerage scheme to serve an area in Phnom Penh, Cambodia. The intention of the World Bank staff member who introduced the initiative and his Brazilian adviser was to replicate the Brazilian approach in its entirety. Unfortunately, most houses in the area already discharged sewage flows and run-off from back yards and roofs to an existing crude combined sewer system through connection pipes that were at least 200 mm in diameter. The scheme was not implemented but the experience points to the need to adapt any approach to service provision to the local context. It also highlights a technical issue with the condominial approach. Brazilian condominial sewers are not designed to carry stormwater. While it is possible that storm flows from relatively small areas can be allowed to run on suitably paved streets and lanes, there will be a need at some point to provide storm drains. Residents can then connect grey water to the drains rather than the sewers and divert black water flows into drains when faced with the need to clear sewer blockages. Discharge of all wastes to drains will, in any case, continue unless all residents connect to the sewer. Another danger, particularly acute where sewers run through front and back yards, is that households will direct run-off from roofs and yards into the condominial sewers, leading to hydraulic overloading and grit accumulation. Nance (2005) notes that, regardless of the cause, poor sewer performance that leads to the use of open ditches for disposal, can be just as bad for public health as no sewer service at all, even if all of the homes are connected to the sewer system.

The Orangi pilot project (OPP): supporting the people's process?

Origins and approach

Orangi Town is a large, mainly informal settlement on the outskirts of Karachi, the largest city in Pakistan. Its population at the time of the last Pakistan census was just under 724,000. By 2013 its population had grown to an estimated 977,000 (Zafar et al., 2017). Dr Akhter Hamid Khan, who had previously been the director of the ground-breaking Comilla Academy for Rural Development in Bangladesh, established the Orangi Pilot Project (OPP) in 1980. OPP's aim was to develop models of community participation and local resource mobilization that could overcome the problems faced by government programmes in upgrading low-income settlements and alleviating poverty. Dr Khan initiated action on four issues faced by the inhabitants of Orangi: sanitation, health, education, and employment. However, sanitation quickly became the main focus of OPP's work and is the sector for which it is best known. In 1988, OPP set up its Research and Training Institute (OPP-RTI) to take responsibility for its sanitation-related work.

From the start, the OPP saw itself as a research organization whose objective was to analyse problems in Orangi and develop viable solutions to those problems through prolonged action research and extension education.

It identified four barriers to the development of improved services in informal areas:

- *The social barrier.* The tendency of community members to operate individually, without a vision of the possibilities available to them if they act as a group.
- *The psychological barrier.* The belief that the community has no power to change its environment and should rely on the government to provide utilities and services.
- *The economic barrier.* Caused by the fact that services provided using conventional engineering standards and organizational methods are unaffordable to most low-income people.
- *The technical barrier.* The lack of the technical and organizational skills necessary to implement community managed development.

OPP provided no project funding. Rather, it saw its role as providing the advice and training required to overcome the four barriers. In response to the social barrier, it supported the development of local organizations in order to establish a sense of community feeling and the conventions of mutual help and cooperative action. To overcome the psychological barrier, it stressed the need for communities to recognize that it is unrealistic to expect government to provide services as a 'free gift'. It developed 'appropriate' standards for facilities and services, which significantly reduced the cost of service provision and hence the height of the economic barrier. Costs were further reduced because communities managed sewer projects themselves, thus removing the need to pay contractor's profit and 'commissions' paid to government engineers. The latter practice is illegal but was and is widespread in Pakistan. To overcome the technical barrier, it trained local people, tradesmen, and petty contractors in the skills required for sewer construction.

An important aspect of OPP's approach was its distinction between 'internal' and 'external' services. In the case of sewerage, internal services included toilets and other on-plot facilities, lane sewers, and neighbourhood collector sewers. External services included trunk sewers and treatment plants. Communities should be responsible for all aspects of internal service provision and management while external services should be the preserve of government (Hasan, 2006). This division of responsibilities, which OPP refers to as component sharing, is similar to the condominial approach's distinction between condominial and public services. By making a clear distinction between the responsibilities of communities and government, it presents an apparently simple approach to co-financing. In practice, responsibilities are less clear than suggested by OPP since financial sustainability may be compromised unless communities contribute towards any cost incurred in pumping the wastewater that they generate. Similar issues arise with other services, particularly solid waste collection and water supply.

Early OPP quarterly reports gave figures for the number of sewers laid and houses connected in Orangi with and without OPP assistance. These showed that, from the outset, many people in Orangi were building sewers without direct OPP assistance. It is possible that some of these people were influenced by what they saw of the OPP model. However, community-led initiatives to build sewers in informal areas are common throughout Pakistan and there is no doubt that OPP built on processes that were already in existence. This suggests that OPP's significance lies in the technical improvements and social strengthening that it promoted rather than its introduction of a completely new approach to sanitation.

Rather than setting up community organizations, OPP works through 'lane managers', respected individuals who are accepted and trusted by the lane residents. There should be at least one lane manager for each lane although, where agreed by the community, there may be more. In Pakistan, the lane manager is invariably a man. Once the community has agreed to go ahead with constructing a sewer, the lane manager collects the required funds from each household, requests OPP for technical assistance, purchases construction material, and procures tools and shuttering from OPP, to be used during construction. He then manages sewer construction. If required by the lane community, the role of the lane manager may extend to managing subsequent maintenance activities. There are clear similarities with the role of the condominial managers in Brazil.

The role played by government in OPP schemes is somewhat different from its role in Brazil's condominial approach. The condominial concept was conceived by a sanitation professional and condominial projects are normally led by a government department or service provider. Orangi had few government services in the early 1980s and there was no immediate prospect of connecting OPP sewers to government trunk sewers. The impetus for change came from communities (with OPP's support) rather than government. The component-sharing concept recognizes the need to work with government but OPP's publications always assume that it and the communities that it supports should take the lead in planning the system and deciding standards and that government departments should accept these standards.

OPP's approach was perhaps more incremental than that adopted in Brazil. It focused first on the action that community members could take to improve local sanitation facilities and only later seeking to respond to higher-level sanitation needs. Orangi's hilly topography helped in this respect, allowing lane sewers to discharge by gravity to the nearest natural drainage channel. There were places where direct discharge to a drainage channel was not possible and this led to the next stage, the construction of collector sewers to carry the flow from several lane sewers to the nearest drainage channel. This left foul flows running in the many drainage channels running through the settlement. OPP's next move was to argue for the construction of box culverts to replace these drainage channels and carry both foul and storm water out of the settlement. Thus, the system that developed in Orangi was a combined system, carrying both foul and storm water. In this respect, it was completely different from the Brazilian model, which depends on complete separation of foul and storm water. The difference was reflected in the sewer diameters used in Orangi. Talpur (2011) gives figures of 6″ (15.24 cm) for lane sewers and 9″–12″ (22.86–30.48 cm) for collector sewers. In practice, most people who build their own sewers use 9″ sewer pipes.

Technical issues

OPP's main technical innovation was the use of cylindrical steel shuttering to cast concrete manhole walls *in situ*. It also produced standard concrete manhole covers to fit the circular manholes produced by this technique. In all other aspects, its procedures and standards were similar to those routinely adopted by the informal sector in Pakistan. For instance:

- *Sewers were sometimes laid at very flat gradients*. Talpur (2011) states that OPP laid pipes with a drop of one inch (2.54 cm) in every 30 feet (914.4 cm), giving a fall of 1 in 360. This is similar to the quarter inch in every 100 ft (1 in 400) quoted by informal sector *mystries* (small contractors) in Pakistan in conversations with the author. This is significantly flatter than the minimum gradient recommended in Brazil and is not theoretically self-cleansing. Some deposition of grit and silt is inevitable.
- *Sewers were laid using plain-ended spun concrete pipes manufactured in local casting yards*. These did not meet formal standards and were often of poor quality (Alam and Parkinson, 2002).
- *Pre-cast manhole covers had no frame*. They were placed on top of the manhole walls, usually without any form of containment to prevent lateral movement.

The resulting product is cheap but susceptible to failure. One way of reducing the frequency of blockages is to install small interceptor tanks, which the OPP refers to as *haudis*, on individual house connections. Unfortunately, this does not eliminate problems associated with the crude pipe jointing method and solids entering the sewer through broken and missing manhole covers. Photos 7.1 and 7.2 illustrate the point that the lack of frames and absence of containment mean that manhole covers are susceptible to

Photo 7.1 OPP-style manhole in Khuda ki Basti scheme on outskirts of Lahore Showing absence of frame and containment

Photo 7.2 Close-up of broken manhole cover

breakage. Broken fragments of cover may drop into the sewer and partially block it, as may other bulky objects if there is no cover to keep them out. An unpublished OPP document from the late 1980s reported the findings of a survey which found that about 25 per cent of manhole covers in Orangi were either broken or missing.

An unpublished study of the situation in Orangi from the late 1990s found that many lane managers ceased to take an active role once initial construction was complete (Siddiqui and Rashid, 1997). It may take several years for a sewer to block completely. In the absence of an active lane manager, the most likely response is that a group of residents collects the money required to hire a worker to clear the sewer. Using the crude methods available to them, removal of all the blocking material will be almost impossible and the problem will usually recur, often at increasingly frequent intervals. Observation and anecdotal evidence suggests that this is the case with many self-built sewers in Pakistan, including those built with OPP assistance.

Replication outside Orangi

OPP's initial attempts to replicate its sanitation programme outside Orangi were unsuccessful because OPP lacked the capacity to replicate the role it played in Orangi.[1] It quickly recognized that the way forward lay in encouraging other organizations to replicate its approach. One of the drivers for the formation of OPP-RTI was the need to train local activists to replicate its approach (Hasan, 2006). From the late 1980s, OPP was attracting interest from NGOs in in other areas in Karachi and Pakistan as a whole. This interest led to efforts to replicate the OPP approach throughout Pakistan. Hasan (2006) states that 41,900 households in 11 towns in Pakistan, excluding Orangi, have built their internal sanitation within existing external sanitation systems, in some cases putting pressure on government to build external facilities. In addition, two replication projects had included provision of water supply on an internal-external basis. Organizations involved in the replication included Anjuman Samaji Behbood (ASB) in Faisalabad, Anjuman Falahi Behbood in Rawalpindi, and the Lodhran Pilot Project (LPP) in southern Punjab. In some cases, for instance Taraqee in Quetta and Youth Commission for Human Rights (YCHR) in Lahore, OPP withdrew support for organizations because they adopted a cost-sharing rather than a component-sharing approach. Despite this difference of opinion and subsequent lack of contact, the author's site visits and personal contacts suggest that both these NGOs were successful in implementing sanitation programmes, at least for a time. The LPP replicated the OPP approach in small towns (Anwar and Sami, 2009). However, the most successful replication of the OPP approach was arguably that in Faisalabad, Pakistan's third largest city. Here, ASB, under the leadership of its founder, Mr Ahmad Nazir Wattoo, applied the OPP principles in implementing both sanitation and water supply projects. It also innovated, using the regular pattern of agricultural land subdivision to provide a framework within which to map the large area of informal development lying south-east of the centre of Faisalabad. Other innovative activities included efforts to develop effective street and house numbering systems and simple technologies for sewer cleaning. Box 7.1 sets out ASB's experience in implementing a water supply project in some detail, highlighting the difficulties that it faced during implementation and illustrating the combination of formal and informal practices used to overcome these difficulties.

Box 7.1 Water supply to Hasanpura

One of ASB's early activities was to plan for the extension of the piped water system into Hasanpura, an informal area that was then on the outskirts of Faisalabad. The nearest Faisalabad Water and Sanitation Agency (FWASA) water main was over 300 metres from Hasanpura on the other side of a main road. With technical assistance from OPP, ASB convinced Hasanpura residents of the benefits of connecting to the FWASA line rather than relying on individual wells and tubewells. It then facilitated the formation of a Hasanpura Water Supply Committee (WSC). ASB then approached FWASA, which initially rejected ASB's proposals but eventually agreed to provide a no-objection certificate (NOC) for the scheme. Construction work on the connecting main and branch mains began in November 1995, about two months before receipt of the NOC from FWASA, funded by a Rs. 200,000 loan from WaterAid. Feedback from junior staff at Faisalabad Municipal Corporation (FMC) suggested that getting permission to cross the road could take a long time and, after discussion with the Area Councillor, ASB and the WSC decided to carry out the work clandestinely, without permission. Accordingly, preparations were made and the 34 m long road crossing was completed over one night. Those opposed to the scheme raised a case with the Area Magistrate but failed to halt it because the scheme enjoyed the support of FMC executives and the Area Councillor. The connection to the FWASA main was also made clandestinely, by two FWASA fitters, who had been hired informally to carry out the work. The line was then extended, using funds provided by those who wished to connect. The cost for those who connected was Rs. 600 per household for tertiary mains, plus Rs. 1,175 for the FWASA connection charge, Rs. 1,300 to the WSC to pay back the WaterAid loan for the connection line, plus a Rs. 100 service charge to the WSC.

Shortly after the main line had been completed, conflicts arose within the WSC and two disaffected members approached the Member of the Provincial Assembly (MPA) for the area. The MPA started to lay his own water main, promising free connections to the community. ASB countered this initiative by pointing out the poor quality of the work being carried out by the MPA's contractor and the MPA's initiative quickly ground to a halt. A more serious threat to the integrity of the ASB scheme followed, as opponents of ASB made 65 illegal connections to the ASB line. Not surprisingly, those who had paid their share of the cost of the line were extremely unhappy about this. ASB persuaded them that their response should be through the legal channels, first requesting FWASA to disconnect illegal connections and then obtaining a court ruling that no water connections could be made without ASB's approval and a payment to the WSC. Opponents continued to lobby politicians. In response, ASB made a presentation to the MPA and the MNA (Member of the National Assembly) representing the area. The MPA then gave his support to the programme and issued a directive to the Managing Director (MD) of FWASA that no new connections should be made without a payment to the WSC. Despite this, FWASA continued to issue connection notices to people who had not paid WSC charges. This situation was eventually resolved when ASB issued a writ against the FWASA MD in the Punjab High Court. This led to a meeting at which the Vice-Chairman of the FWASA Governing Board directed the MD that no new connections should be made without consulting ASB. Following this, the writ was withdrawn and work on the scheme progressed smoothly.

Source: Based on Alimuddin et al., 2001

Impact on thinking of government and international agencies

OPP's approach attracted the attention of the Sindh Katchi Abadis Authority (SKAA) and international agencies. The Director General of SKAA from 1993 was Mr Tasneem Ahmed Siddiqui, who had initiated the Khuda ki Basti scheme in Hyderabad when Director General of the Hyderabad Development Authority. Under his leadership, the SKAA embraced OPP ideas, not least the concept of component sharing.

In the late 2000s, OPP's concepts underpinned the Changa Pani Programme, a strategic initiative of the Government of Punjab involving partnership between the local community, civil society in the form of ASB, Lahore WASA, and the Urban Unit (an urban sector policy and management unit that had been set up in the Punjab Government's Planning and Development Department). The first phase of the programme was implemented in Badar Colony, a poorly serviced peri-urban settlement on the outskirts of Lahore. The population of the project area was about 21,000. The programme covered both water supply and sewerage, with Lahore WASA taking responsibility for trunk sewers and external water supply mains while residents of the area were responsible for all aspects of internal services. The original intention was to achieve a continuous 24/7 water supply but this was not achieved. As with similar areas of Lahore, water was provided two or three times per day. One factor contributing to the failure to achieve 24/7 supply is likely to have been Lahore WASA's failure to install water meters, as intended in the original project design. A follow-up programme, Changa Pani II was initiated but little information is available on its progress.

The author has visited two unsuccessful attempts to replicate the OPP approach with international support. In both cases, OPP acted as adviser. The first was the UNICEF-supported Urban Basic Services Programme (UBSP) in Sukkur, northern Sindh, the project aimed to improve sanitation and drainage in three low-lying settlements, Gor Takri, New Pind, and Boosa Lane, which together covered an area of about 126 hectares. The area contained a wastewater pond, which already covered more than 10 hectares and flooded adjacent residential areas during heavy rain. This was to be drained, with the reclaimed land made available for public open space and community facilities. The scheme would not be possible without pumping and it was agreed that government and UNICEF would pay the capital cost of collector sewers, a pumping station, and a rising main to convey wastewater to a discharge point on the Indus river. OPP would mobilize the residents of the target areas to finance and build their own lane sewers. The 'external' elements of the scheme were completed by late 1993 and residents of 14 lanes constructed sewers, which served a total of 155 houses and operated satisfactorily for about six months, after which the scheme failed, largely because the pumping arrangements were unsatisfactory, resulting in frequent pump breakdowns. Because of rather bureaucratic government procedures, these were not dealt with immediately and the pond quickly reformed. In the absence of prompt government action, community activists hired a local pump repair 'specialist' to improve the pumping set-up. The revamped system worked for a short time but failed again when the transformer burnt out. It was repaired but Sukkur Municipal Corporation still failed to respond to requests to fix the faults in the overall system and by 1995 OPP had concluded that the project had failed (based on Hasan, 1997). By the time of the author's visit in July 2007, no trace of the community built sewers remained. The residents had reverted to open drains to dispose of their wastewater. The pumping station was in poor condition but still apparently operated intermittently and the wastewater pond remained.

The second unsuccessful initiative was the Collaborative Katchi Abadi Improvement Programme (CKAIP) in Hyderabad, the second city of Sindh. This was a pilot project, supported by the World Bank and the Swiss Development Corporation, which was designed to test and demonstrate an approach to upgrading services in low-income areas in Pakistan. It was to involve SKAA and the Hyderabad Municipal Corporation (HMC), with OPP providing advisory inputs. The overall objective was to provide a range of services, including roads, water supply, and street lights, but following the standard OPP model, the initial emphasis was on sewered sanitation. In view of the flat topography and the distance from the nearest possible discharge point, it was decided that construction of an off-site sewer must precede that of lane sewers. The Hyderabad Water and Sanitation Agency (HWASA) prepared a design for off-site sewerage involving pumping. OPP, quite rightly given the experience in Sukkur, argued that a pumped scheme was likely to be problematic and produced an alternative design involving gravity sewers laid to flat gradients and discharging to the nearest collector drain. The author has seen the OPP drawings for this sewer and also visited the site. Sewer gradients averaged about 1 in 1,500, and were flatter in places. Rather than following the normal convention of indicating sewer invert levels on longitudinal sections, ground levels were indicated, together with a depth to the sewer invert. Levels were only given to the nearest 3" (76 mm). There is no way that this crude method of defining invert levels could have given accurate results in the field. Even if it could, there was little chance that masons could lay sewers accurately to the required flat gradients, which in any case were much too flat to provide self-cleansing. At the time of the author's visit, the sewer was in place and some open drains had been connected to it. Given the likelihood that the flows in these drains would carry silt during storm events and the absence of an effective solid waste collection service in the area, silting and blockages were inevitable and the sewer was already non-operational.

OPP has influenced national sanitation policy in Pakistan. When a new policy was required in the mid-2000s, Pakistan's Federal Government appointed Arif Hasan, OPP-RTI's Principal Adviser, as the national consultant to draft the document. The policy, which was approved in September 2006, included references to the need for mapping prior to any intervention and sharing of internal and external infrastructure development between citizens and the government (Pervaiz et al., 2008, p. 40).[2] The sanitation policies of the

Punjab and Sindh provincial governments, enacted in 2015 and 2017 respectively, both refer to the component-sharing approach. The Punjab policy states that it 'will be adopted for all urban and rural areas'. One challenge now will be to ensure that those working in the field are aware of the policy, accept it, and are willing to implement it. Another challenge will be to address the technical issues experienced in various OPP projects that have been raised earlier in this section.

Faisalabad area upgrading project: integrating the people's process?

Faisalabad is Pakistan's third city with a population now well in excess of 2 million. In 1989, the British and Pakistani governments agreed to support an upgrading project in the city, the Faisalabad Area Upgrading Project (FAUP), with the objective of promoting the economic and social welfare of 240,000 people living in the city's informal settlements. This was to be achieved by improving community level physical and social infrastructure, including health and education, and providing income-earning opportunities for informal settlement inhabitants. Specific interventions were to be identified and developed through a participatory process based on the establishment and involvement of self-reliant community groups. The project was not particularly successful. However, its approach was strongly participatory, at least in its first years, and it is described in detail here because of the lessons that can be learnt from it.

On the British side, the project was administered by the ODA. The Pakistan partner was the Faisalabad Development Authority (FDA), the body with overall responsibility for planning and new development initiatives in Faisalabad city. Consultants were appointed to manage the project on behalf of ODA, with the author acting as Project Director for the consultants from 1993 to 1999.

The FAUP was to be implemented in two phases. The first, lasting two years, was to cover four pilot areas with a total population of about 60,000 people, while the second would extend project activities to further areas which would be identified in the course of the first phase. In fact, the project, which ran from 1994 to 2003, did not progress beyond the four pilot areas. The project design envisaged the formation of self-reliant community groups, which would take the lead in identifying and meeting needs. Social organizers, employed through a Project Management Unit (PMU), would work with these groups to identify a broad menu of options from which the communities themselves would then identify priorities. Tertiary level infrastructure sub-projects were to be funded 50 per cent by the communities themselves and 50 per cent by the project. Once a sub-project had been approved, the community would deposit its share of the cost into a joint bank account, specially set up for the sub-project. The government would then deposit its share in the account. To ensure accountability, the account signatories were to be a social organizer and a member of the community. Secondary infrastructure facilities would be wholly funded by government and implemented using standard government procedures.

Development of the participatory approach

The project design drew on the experience of both the OPP and the Agha Khan Rural Support Project (AKRSP) in Pakistan's northern areas. However, it differed from the former in important details. Rather than concentrating on one priority problem in the first instance, as strongly recommended by OPP, it set out to tackle multiple issues from the outset. The project provided 50 per cent of the funds required to implement tertiary infrastructure schemes, thus breaking OPP's golden rule that the supporting organization should neither provide nor handle the funds required to implement community infrastructure. Shortly before the project commenced, ODA requested that Participatory Rapid Appraisal (PRA) methods should be used in the development of the project. As has been discussed in Chapter 4, one of the basic features of PRA is its emphasis on reversing roles so that local people rather than professionals take the lead in analysis and project planning (Chambers, 1994).

From late 1993 onwards, trainee social organizers went through a period of intensive training, focusing strongly on the PRA ethos and methods. As a result, the participatory ethos was deeply embedded when intensive fieldwork began in mid-1994. After making contact with local residents, social organizers sought to involve them in community mapping exercises, which normally took place at the level of the 'lane' or housing cluster, typically covering 20–30 households. These provided some information on residents' concerns and perceptions but, more importantly, helped to build rapport between community members, particularly women, and PMU team members.

In some areas, it soon became clear that residents had immediate concerns that might provide useful 'entry points' for project activities. The most common concerns related to drainage and there was considerable interest in the provision of tertiary sewers. Indeed, the first sewer project was implemented in a lane in which the residents had already started to collect money to build a sewer. These early project activities and procedures had much in common with those that already existed in the informal sector. In this respect, the overall approach represented a genuine attempt to involve the government in the people's activities. Other needs identified at this early stage included improvements to school infrastructure, particularly improved water supply and sanitation facilities, and employment opportunities. When assessing the options for women's employment, local residents, particularly men, identified the need for 'sewing centres', following what seemed to be the received wisdom on this subject, even though there was little evidence that there was any real demand for the products of such sewing centres.

There was some discussion at this stage around the means/end distinction that was first discussed in Chapter 4. The consultant's project manager had brought in two advisers from the National Rural Support Programme (NRSP) and one of these argued strongly that the focus on specific local infrastructure schemes, for instance the construction of a lane sewer, would give community members a narrow vision of the objectives of the project. It would then be impossible to move towards a more holistic approach to participation. Those who opposed this view argued that it was unlikely that people would be prepared to sit through long participatory meetings unless they could see the potential for those meetings to lead to concrete benefits. In the end, the project took the view that the confidence gained from involvement in a successful scheme would strengthen community organization and encourage community members to seek further challenges.

Over the first two years of the project, the participatory concept was developed and conceptualized in terms of multi-purpose community organizations (MPCOs). These would provide the channel through which community members within project areas could cooperate with the project to find and implement solutions to their problems. The initial focus would be on forming MPCOs at the lane level (typically serving 20–30 households) and efforts would then be made to develop representative MPCOs at the neighbourhood and district levels. The intention was not just to implement 'projects'. Rather, it was hoped that people's engagement with the development process would help communities to develop confidence in their abilities and a greater awareness of their responsibilities and rights. This 'tiered' approach to community organization is quite common and has been institutionalized in some countries, for instance in the Indian Community Development Society (CDS) system, which was developed in Kerala and later adopted in other Indian states (see also Chapter 4). In the CDS system, membership at the grass roots level is open only to women, but in other countries, for instance Indonesia, tiered participatory systems reach down to local communities and are dominated by men.

Problems and responses

Problems emerged in the course of the project. It proved difficult to sustain lane level organizations, which often formed around a particular infrastructure project and then became inactive when the project had been completed. This experience supports the general principle that community organizations are only likely to endure if there is a reason for them to do so. Ongoing maintenance of infrastructure assets is a poor basis for developing continued community cohesion because maintenance requirements are usually low at first and rarely provide enough reason for an organization to stay together over the years that may elapse before major maintenance and repairs are required.

In practice, the best results were often obtained when social organizers deviated from the rigid tiered approach to community organization. During the period 1995 to 1997, good progress was made in Shadab Colony, one of the four pilot areas. Initial successes were based on contacts between FAUP social organizers and an existing community organization, which operated in one neighbourhood, containing around 150 of Shadab Colony's 1,150 households. The FAUP team convinced the leaders of the society to change their focus from providing welfare, in essence doing things for people, to working with people to initiate and implement development activities in their area. Within six months of initial contacts with the society, it was undertaking a wide range of activities and similar arrangements and activities were being initiated in other parts of Shadab Colony. Some activities, for instance brick paving in tertiary streets and the construction of tertiary sewers connected to sewers already laid by the Faisalabad Water and Sanitation Agency (FWASA), took place at the street or lane level. However, others, including the very visible conversion of seven open spaces within the settlement into community parks, involved whole neighbourhoods. After 1997, the number of new initiatives in Shadab Colony declined, partly because members of the strong social organizer team left the project, were promoted or transferred but also perhaps because the obvious needs had been met. The main focus of project activities shifted to Chak 7, one of the other three project areas, where the social organizers had coalesced into a strong team. Here, as in Shadab Colony, the range of activities was wide and action was sometimes taken at the level of the neighbourhood, typically around five streets or lanes, rather than within a single lane.

The experience in Shadab Colony and Chak 7 illustrates the importance of finding social organizers with initiative and vision. Without these qualities, the Shadab Colony team would not have deviated from the 'official' line and adopted the approach that quickly proved to be successful. It also illustrates the importance of identifying 'change agents', people who want change and are willing to work for it, within communities.

Quality of workmanship emerged as an important issue as the project progressed. For instance, in Chak 7, the FWASA provided secondary water mains on the understanding that tertiary mains and house connections would then be provided through the FAUP with benefiting communities providing 50 per cent of the funding. In addition, individual households would pay the standard WASA connection charge. WASA fitters, working privately, laid the tertiary mains and connections. However, their work left much to be desired and some leaks were evident as soon as the mains had been commissioned. A more general problem was the desire of community groups to reduce the capital cost of schemes, which often led them to adopt low standards. For instance, brick paving was invariably laid directly onto the ground surface without any form of bedding. The result was that, in marked contrast to the paving provided in North-east Lahore, the paving usually deteriorated fairly quickly. Local sewers were laid at shallow depths, with conventional manholes replaced by OPP-style inspection chambers, with covers contained in a steel band and set into a steel-rimmed concrete surround. The government engineers working on the project initially accepted these 'improved' OPP standards but reverted to more conventional standards before the end of the project. One reason for this may have been their fear that they would be sanctioned by the government audit if they diverged from officially recognized standards.

Despite local successes, overall progress was slow. Even where a community had invested in a specific service improvement, for instance laying a new sewer or water main, there was no guarantee that it would go on to undertake other improvements. The project management team concluded that this was largely because the requirement that community members paid 50 per cent of the cost of tertiary infrastructure meant that many residents could not afford the full range of required improvements. It may also have been due to the fact that, while some of the proposed improvements were beneficial to the community as a whole, they had less obvious attraction for individual households, which therefore did not prioritize them. The extreme slowness of government procedures also contributed to the lack of progress. This was particularly obvious whenever there was a need for a line agency to take action to provide secondary infrastructure. This slowness was not due to lack of resources since finance for secondary infrastructure to serve project areas was provided through the project. There are clear parallels here with the experience of OPP in Sukkur. One other point is that the bottom-up approach to sub-project choice may have resulted in a rather disjointed and hence inefficient response to service needs.

In order to achieve coverage, a more conventional integrated area-based approach to infrastructure provision, with all activities controlled by the PMU, was adopted in the last 18 months or so of the project. Community members were required to contribute 15 per cent of the cost of the whole scheme, rather than the original 50 per cent contribution for tertiary infrastructure. By this stage, the project had moved some way from its initial strongly community-led approach. Even with this late effort to increase the rate of progress, the overall physical impact of the project was limited. More significantly, the processes initiated through the project did not become the norm within government. The team of social organizers was disbanded when DFID funding ended in 2002. No firm evidence is available but it is likely that most of the community organizations set up through the project ceased to function once the support of the social organizers had been withdrawn.

Institutional factors and initiatives

Despite its emphasis on participation and process, the management structure of the FAUP is conventional. The project design gave a central place to the PMU which was given responsibility for all sectors of the project, with line agencies and other specialist providers being given very much a secondary role. The specialists within the PMU were to work with the social organizers and communities to design and prepare community projects. For secondary infrastructure works, they were to prepare fully detailed and costed proposals in liaison with the appropriate line departments. Secondary infrastructure work was to be carried out by line departments in the Faisalabad Municipal Corporation (FMC) and FDA or by contractors engaged under Government of Punjab rules. Tenders were to be examined by a Tenders Committee chaired by the project manager and comprising the relevant specialist, the finance director and the consultant's project coordinator. Thus, the tender process, which would normally be managed by the senior officials of the relevant line department, was controlled by the PMU, and the role of the line departments was basically to provide services as required by the project management. Although the PMU was to take overall responsibility for implementation, it was assumed that line departments would be responsible for managing facilities once they were complete. FWASA would be responsible for managing water supply, sewerage, and main drainage facilities while FMC would manage roads, local drainage, street lighting, and solid waste collection. Not surprisingly, line departments were less than enthusiastic about these arrangements and often slow to respond to project needs. At the same time, it proved difficult to enter into dialogue with line agencies about important issues such as the development of standards appropriate to the conditions found in low-income areas.

Eventually, the funding agency and their consultants recognized the need to draw line departments from the periphery to the centre of the project process. Some progress in this direction was achieved by making sure that proposals for secondary infrastructure were in accordance with the wider plans of the line agencies, even if this meant that the scale of provision was greater than needed for immediate upgrading needs. More significant progress was achieved through efforts to provide assistance directly to WASA and FMC solid waste management activities. In the case of solid waste, FMC's positive response to the recommendations of a specialist consultant led to significant improvements in the operation and maintenance of secondary collection equipment. FWASA received specialist advice on community infrastructure and the project encouraged it to create a specialist Community Infrastructure Unit. This received considerable support from the consultants and helped to broker the links between FWASA and ASB referred to earlier in this chapter. The project developed pro forma agreements defining the roles of government and community organizations in participatory initiatives and the tariffs payable by owners of self-managed tertiary infrastructure connected to WASA facilities. It also carried out work on appropriate standards and procedures for water supply and sanitation facilities in low-income areas. Unfortunately, FAUP's dependence on consultants and the fact that it remained outside the main FWASA structure meant that these initiatives did not continue after the withdrawal of external funding.

Notes

1. However, a year later (1997) OPP-RTI started to work outside Orangi by documenting and mapping settlements and infrastructures systems all over Karachi; and increased its level of engagement with concerned government departments and agencies such as the Karachi Metropolitan Corporation (KMC) and Sindh Katchi Abadis Authority (SKAA), as well as Karachi community-based organizations (CBOs) (see Pervaiz et al., 2008).
2. The second, and presumably final, draft of the policy is available at http://www.asb.org.pk/sanitationpolicy.pdf.

References

Alam, S.M.K. and Parkinson, J. (2002) *Appropriate design standards and construction specifications for tertiary sewerage systems*, FAUP/GHK, Faisalabad. https://www.ircwash.org/sites/default/files/Alam-2002-Appropriate.pdf (accessed 20 July 2019).

Alimuddin, S., Hasan, A. and Sadiq, A. (2001) *Community-driven water and sanitation. The work of the Anjuman Samaji Behbood and the larger Faisalabad context*, IIED Working Paper 7 on Poverty Reduction in Urban Areas. https://pubs.iied.org/pdfs/9073IIED.pdf (accessed 29 July 2019).

Anwar, F. and Sami, F. (2009) *The Lodhran Pilot Project implementation toolkit: a participatory model for low-cost sanitation*, Water and Sanitation Program. https://documents1.worldbank.org/curated/en/654651468314690251/pdf/722220WP0Box370UBLIC00lodhran0pilot.pdf (accessed 19 September 2025).

Bakalian, A., Wright, A., Otis, R. and de Azevedo Netto, J. (1994) *Simplified sewerage: design guidelines*, UNDP-World Bank Water and Sanitation Program, Washington, DC. http://documents.worldbank.org/curated/en/676741468227353807/Simplified-sewerage-design-guidelines (accessed 18 July 2019).

Chambers, R. (1994) The origins and practice of participatory rural appraisal, *World Development*, 22(7): 953–69. https://entwicklungspolitik.uni-hohenheim.de/uploads/media/Day_4_-_Reading_text_8.pdf (accessed 29 July 2019).

Chambers, R. and Conway, G.R. (1992) *Sustainable rural livelihoods: practical concepts for the 21st century*. IDS Discussion Paper No. 296. Institute of Development Studies, Brighton. https://www.ids.ac.uk/files/Dp296.pdf (accessed 6 July 2019).

Diacon, D. (1997) *Slum networking: an innovative approach to urban development*, Building and Social Housing Foundation, Coalville, UK. https://www.world-habitat.org/wp-content/uploads/2016/03/Slum-Networking.pdf (accessed 4 March 2019).

Hasan, A. (1997) *Working with government: the story of OPP's collaboration with state agencies for replicating its low-cost sanitation program*, City Press, Karachi.

Hasan, A. (2006) Orangi Pilot Project: the expansion of work beyond Orangi and the mapping of informal settlements and infrastructure, *Environment and Urbanization*, 18(2): 451–80. https://doi.org/10.1177%2F0956247806069626

Melo, J.C. (2005) *The experience of condominial water and sewerage systems in Brazil: case studies from Brasilia, Salvador and Parauapebas*, World Bank, Washington, DC. https://documents.worldbank.org/en/publication/documents-reports/documentdetail/505601468226737476/the-experience-of-condominial-water-and-sewerage-systems-in-brazil-case-studies-from-brasilia-salvador-and-parauebas (accessed 4 August 2025).

Nance, E.B. (2005) Multistakeholder evaluation of condominial sewer services, *American Journal of Evaluation*, 26(4): 480–500. https://doi.org/10.1177/1098214005281324

Nance, E. and Ortolana, L. (2007) Community participation in urban sanitation: experiences in northeastern Brazil, *Journal of Planning Education and Research*, 26(3): 284–300. https://doi.org/10.1177/0739456X06295028

Neder, K.D. (2000) *Condominial sewerage design and implementation manual*, Brasilia. https://aquadoc.typepad.com/files/neder-2000-condominial.pdf (accessed 26 November 2019).

Neto, A. da C. M. and Ily, J-M. (2013) *Choosing and implementing small-bore sewers case study Brazil*, Programme Solidarité Eau, Paris, https://www.pseau.org/sites/default/files/fichiers/r_d/case-study_non-conventional-sewers_brazil.pdf (accessed 22 July 2019)

Orangi Pilot Project (1995) NGO Profile, *Environment and Urbanization*, 7(2): 227–36. https://doi.org/10.1177/095624789500700216

Pervaiz, A., Rahman, P. and Hasan, A. (2008) *Lessons from Karachi: the role of demonstration, documentation, mapping and relationship building in advocacy for improved urban sanitation and water services*, International Institute for Environment and Development, Human Settlements Discussion Paper Series, Theme: Water – 6. https://pubs.iied.org/pdfs/10560IIED.pdf (accessed 30 July 2019).

Rosser, C. (1970) Action planning in Calcutta: the problem of community participation, *Journal of Development Studies*, 6(4): 121–39. https://doi.org/10.1080/00220387008421339

Santosa, H.R., Faqih, M. and Cahyadini, S. (2010) Comprehensive Kampung Improvement Programme to support better settlement and poverty reduction, paper presented at the *18th CIB World Building Congress, May 2010, Salford, United Kingdom*. https://www.irbnet.de/daten/iconda/CIB18951.pdf (accessed 16 July 2019).

Siddiqui, T. and Rashid, A. (1997) 'The Orangi Pilot Project: a low cost sanitation model', unpublished paper prepared for workshop on the Strategic Sanitation Approach in Dhaka, Bangladesh, UNDP-World Bank Water and Sanitation Programme.

Silas, J. (1992) Government-community partnership in kampung improvement programmes in Surabaya, *Environment and Urbanization*, 4(2): 33–41. https://doi.org/10.1177/095624789200400204

Talpur, M. (2011) *Component sharing: technical and social guidelines for a low-cost urban sanitation model*, WaterAid, London and Islamabad.

Thomas, F.C. (1997) *Calcutta poor: elegies on a city above pretense*, M.E.Sharpe, Armonk, NY.

Watson, G. (1995) *Good sewers cheap? Agency-customer interactions in low cost urban sanitation in Brazil*, World Bank Water and Sanitation Division, Washington, DC. https://coilink.org/20.500.12592/q2v9nz (accessed 3 August 2025).

World Bank Operations Evaluation Department (1995) *Indonesia impact evaluation report, estimating the quality of life in urban Indonesia: the legacy of Kampung Improvement Programme*, World Bank, Washington, DC. http://documents.worldbank.org/curated/en/927561468752367336/pdf/multi-page.pdf (accessed 16 July 2019).

Zafar, S., Qaisar, M., Sohail, Z. and Zaidi, A. (2017) Development of government schools based on GIS: a case study of Orangi Town, Karachi, *Journal of Geoscience, Engineering, Environment and Technology*, 2(4): 235–41. https://doi.org/10.24273/jgeet.2017.2.4.348

CHAPTER 8
Acting city-wide?

To date, few initiatives have provided housing that is affordable to poor people at a scale that will reduce the need for informal responses to their housing needs. In the case of new housing, as discussed in Chapter 5, the formal housing provided has usually been unaffordable to the urban poor without high levels of subsidy. Sites and services projects, as we have seen in Chapter 6, have rarely gone to scale and, even where they have, their impact has been limited when compared with the growth of informal settlements. Some upgrading initiatives have achieved wide coverage, the most obvious example being the various Kampung Improvement Programme interventions in Indonesia, and while worthwhile, successful initiatives have only achieved fairly limited improvements to living conditions and have not usually resulted in secure tenure.

This chapter examines past and ongoing efforts to move beyond the level of individual projects and looks at the housing and shelter needs of cities as a whole. It covers initiatives and strategies with an explicit focus on eliminating slums, especially those that combine this focus along with a recognition of the need for improved municipal governance and that seek to remove the constraints to adequate living conditions for the urban poor. Thus, this chapter also examines efforts to address the major constraints represented by both a lack of housing finance and a lack of suitable land.

Large-scale government schemes

The Egyptian and Indian experiences described in Chapter 5 are examples of centrally initiated attempts to meet housing needs through country-wide new-build housing programmes. As noted above, these have produced housing that is unaffordable and/or unsuitable for the poorest households. South Africa provides another example of government investment in a large-scale 'affordable' housing initiative, and in 2014 the South African government announced its intention to phase out smaller low-cost housing projects of a few hundred units and focus exclusively on new megaprojects made up of thousands of units. Champions of this approach believed that large-scale projects could deliver more houses quicker and would reduce administrative burdens by focusing government's attention on a few dozen projects rather than the 11,000 human development projects that were then at various stages of development across the country. Politicians liked the approach because large schemes are much more visible than diffuse small-scale projects.

When announcing the policy, the then Minister of Human Settlements, Lindiwe Sisulu, stated that megaprojects would help deliver 1.5 million units by 2019. The Gauteng provincial government was particularly attracted to the idea of creating new 'post-apartheid' cities, strategically located to promote growth in underdeveloped areas and with urban spaces designed to avoid the inequalities and inefficiencies that beset existing cities. The proposed changes to be achieved through the projects were so great that government referred to them as 'catalytic' projects.

Some critics of the approach noted that the high price of land in reasonable proximity to existing urban centres meant that the new towns would almost inevitably be poorly located. They pointed to the historical evidence that poorly located new towns experience great difficulties in generating enough jobs for the people that live in them. Others noted the high cost of constructing new towns, not least that of providing new infrastructure, and the long planning and construction period required for such large projects. Even if the new town approach were to be successful, it would take years to deliver affordable housing at scale. In 2018, the Minister for Human Settlements stated that, while catalytic projects 'worth more than half a million rand' had been initiated, the programme's budget had suffered a massive cut as a result of the fiscal challenges faced by the state (Ballard and Rubin, 2018).

The issues with a new town or new settlement approach could have been foreseen if the South African planners had taken account of Egypt's experience with its new towns. Similarly, lessons could perhaps have been learnt from both Egypt and India's difficulties in ensuring the availability of the financial, institutional, and human resources required to implement ambitious programmes within relatively short time frames. The UK's council housing initiatives, particularly its experiences in the decades after the Second World War, provide a more positive example of government attempts to build new housing units to address housing problems. As noted in Chapter 2, these were not without problems, but they did achieve significant improvements in overall housing conditions. The problem with the South African programme lies not so much in either its objectives or its origin in a political imperative to meet the housing demands of a recently enfranchised but economically disadvantaged majority population. Rather, it lies in government's failure to recognize the challenges that would inevitably arise in meeting those demands and the consequent adoption of poorly conceived strategies and programmes.

The cities alliance: 'Cities Without Slums'?

The Cities Alliance is an international alliance of local authorities, donors, and private sector actors, launched by the World Bank and UNCHS (Habitat) in 1999.[1] Its vision statement states that it is 'a global partnership to help cities meet the urban challenges of the 21st century: pro-poor policies; good urban governance; and prosperous cities without slums'. Its two clearly defined aims are to:

1. Facilitate local stakeholders to define their vision of the city and formulate a City Development Strategy (CDS), focusing particularly on economic and social needs; and
2. Make unprecedented improvements in the living conditions of the urban poor by developing city-wide and nationwide slum upgrading programmes (Cities Alliance, 2006).

These general objectives were pursued through two linked activities: the promotion of CDSs and the Cities Without Slums initiative. The Cities Alliance defined CDSs as 'action-oriented processes, developed and sustained through participation, to promote equitable growth in cities and their surrounding regions to improve the quality of life for all citizens' (Cities Alliance, 2006: 8). It went on to argue that 'a CDS helps cities integrate a strategic development approach and a long-term perspective into their urban planning. With a CDS, cities move beyond planning around the short-term political or donor-funding cycles to considering where they should be in 20 or 30 years, and the steps that need to be taken to achieve those goals' (ibid: 12). The Cities Without Slums action plan, produced in July 1999, was subsequently endorsed by the 150 heads of state and government attending the UN Millennium Summit in September 2000. Its aims were reflected in Target 11 of the Millennium Development Goals, to achieve a significant improvement in the lives of at least 100 million slum dwellers by 2015.

The limited budget available to the Cities Alliance meant that, at best, it has acted as a catalyst, using its resources to fund initiatives that might stimulate a process leading to city-wide change. In 2016, it provided about US$6.4 m to support 38 projects, most of which were in Africa. Expenditures in Asia were only just over $0.5 m (Cities Alliance, 2016), and the levels of funding provided in previous and subsequent years were similar. The Cities Alliance is funded by national and international donors, including private donors such as the then Bill & Melinda Gates Foundation (BMGF). Grants from donors may support activities over a number of years. For instance, in 2009, BMGF provided Cities Alliance with a $15 m grant to fund a new, comprehensive, and programmatic approach in five developing countries faced with rapid urban growth and poverty. By 2016, the Cities Alliance had active country programmes in the original five countries, Burkina Faso, Ghana, Mozambique, Uganda, and Vietnam, and two additional countries, Liberia and Tunisia. It claimed that the original $15 m grant had leveraged over $700 m in investments from major development organizations and just over $9 m in co-financing from Country Programme partners. Another Cities Alliance initiative, the Future Cities Africa programme, ran for 24 months to November 2016. The UK's Department for International Development (DFID) provided financial support. The $7.5 m budget supported activities in 2 cities in Ethiopia and Ghana, 3 cities in Mozambique, and 14 cities in Uganda

(Cities Alliance, 2016). Its focus was more on resilience and economic growth rather than housing and informality. Based on the evidence collected in the course of the programme, Cities Alliance (2016) concluded that:

- There was little evidence of transformational change in any of the four countries.
- Government capacity to manage urbanization processes was severely deficient and planning processes paid insufficient attention to gender.

The first conclusion raises questions about the impact of the programme, and by extension the Cities Alliance itself. The second conclusion is hardly surprising and it raises the question of why this reality was not recognized from the outset.

The Cities Alliance has provided support to some initiatives involving the slum dwellers organizations introduced later in this chapter. For instance, its 2016 Annual Report states that 'a grant to the City of Harare was responsible for fostering a strong and lasting relationship between informal resident dwellers, Dialogue on Shelter, and the municipal government' (Cities Alliance, 2016: 49). The BMGF was the main external funder of the Harare initiative and residents of areas to be upgraded were represented by the Zimbabwe Homeless People's Federation, an affiliate of Slum/Shack Dwellers International (SDI).

Overall, it is clear that the Cities Alliance has fallen far short of its stated objective of stimulating city-wide and nationwide slum upgrading programmes. Parsons (2010) notes that its aim was to strengthen institutions and partnerships for slum upgrading at the level of the city rather than to 'end slums' within a specific timeframe. Cities Without Slums is therefore a normative idea, providing a broad conception of what the world should look like, rather than a causal idea with operational targets. Parsons goes on to suggest that governments have wrongly interpreted the normative idea – that cities should not have slums – as an actual target requiring eradication of slums, and have used this to validate large-scale slum demolition projects. He gives examples of illegal mass evictions in Zimbabwe in 2005 and in Abuja, Nigeria in 2006, and the passing of slum 'elimination' legislation in South Africa in 2007. In response, Parsons quotes Marie Huchzermeyer's argument for an official policy of recognition, that seeks to manage and understand slums and informal settlements instead of clearing them away and trying to prevent them from re-emerging. In this respect, she suggests that the Cities Without Slums campaign would be more appropriately named 'Cities Recognizing Slums' (Huchzermeyer 2006).

Cities Alliance literature makes it clear that it views CDSs as economic tools that allow cities to allocate limited resources strategically to the areas in which they will make the most impact. As such, it views improved housing and services as a means to an end rather than an end in itself. This leaves it open to criticism from those on the left. For instance, Gruffydd Jones (2010) argues that the orientation of the Cities Alliance approach around the principles and logic of the market, commodification, competition, and private investment indicates an underlying neoliberal philosophy. To support her argument, she cites the statement in the 2008 Cities Alliance Annual Report that 'Poor people's purchasing power, estimated at more than $5 trillion, represents an uncaptured market for the formal private sector' (Cities Alliance, 2008: Box 2, p. 3). The Cities Alliance statement echoes Hernando De Soto's thinking in its emphasis on the economic gains to be achieved by formalizing the informal sector. Gruffydd Jones's critique, in particular her identification of what she describes as the financialization of housing and urban development, has clear parallels with the thinking of Rod Burgess. She argues that this financialization is made manifest through a considerable expansion in home ownership, the widespread, routine, and normalized treatment of housing as a financial asset, and the growing integration of housing finance with national and international housing markets. The emphasis on the need to involve residents in the planning and design of upgrading projects is evidence of a neoliberal approach that downgrades the role of government from that of a service provider for the public good to that of acting to facilitate the creation of relationships between a multiplicity of actors – specifically, between the private sector, community groups, and municipalities.

Gruffydd Jones's critique extends beyond the Cities Alliance to include UN-Habitat and in particular its Slum Upgrading Facility. She argues that, by working with local actors to make slum upgrading projects 'bankable', it is paving the way for the entry of international capital markets into the housing sector in low-income countries. This might be true in theory, but, as already explained, the Cities Alliance has had very limited impact, and thus one consequence is that it has not been the Trojan horse for global financial interests feared by Gruffydd Jones.

City-wide alliances and groupings of low-income communities

Despite its references to the need for inclusive planning approaches, the Cities Alliance is fundamentally a top-down response to urban issues. However, it does recognize the need for all 'stakeholders' to participate in efforts to develop strategies and action plans. This recognition is reflected in the inclusion of SDI on its Management Board. SDI is one example of organizations representing low-income communities coming together with the aim of implementing city- and country-wide responses to slum conditions. Another is the Asian Coalition for Housing Rights (ACHR). Both SDI and ACHR operate outside government, although both stress the need for cooperation with state authorities. In Thailand, the Community Organizations Development Institute (CODI) is similar to SDI and ACHR, but is a Thai Government institution. All of these organizations have similar philosophies and approaches, and all start with the creation of community savings groups, the promotion of peer-to-peer exchanges between communities, an emphasis on the importance of enumeration and mapping, and a belief that residents of informal settlements should take the lead in deciding how to improve those settlements.

Not surprisingly, there are strong links between these organizations, as we shall see in the following sections.

Slum dwellers international

SDI is a transnational social movement of the urban poor, operating in more than 30 countries in Africa, Asia, and Latin America (SDI, 2018). Its origins lie in the National Slum Dwellers Federation (NSDF), formed in Mumbai, India in 1975. In 1984, a second organization, the Society for the Promotion of Area Resource Centres (SPARC), was formed in Mumbai. Its work with the women residing on the pavements of Mumbai led to the formation of Mahila Milan (MM), a network of women's collectives. In 1986, SPARC, NSDF, and MM came together to form an Indian Alliance, with SPARC acting as the legal institutional entity and NSDF and MM working with communities. The underlying philosophy was that poor people living in informal settlements should take the lead in their own development, relying on their own efforts rather than waiting for external entities – professionals, NGOs, and consultants – to solve their problems (Patel, 2014).

From 1991 onwards, peer-to-peer exchanges between Indian and South African slum dweller movements resulted in the formation of the South African Homeless People's Federation and People's Dialogue for Land and Shelter. Several similar organizations were formed in Southern Africa, while ACHR worked with the Indian Alliance to develop and strengthen federations of slum dwellers in Asia. In 1996, nine federations from Asia and Africa came together to form Slum and Shack Dwellers International, the organization that is now known as SDI (Patel, 2014). By 2015, SDI had affiliated federations in 33 countries (Beukes, 2015), bringing together over a million slum dwellers in over 30 countries. It seeks to inform and support local initiatives to provide alternatives to eviction, to transform slums into resilient neighbourhoods, and to promote inclusive cities. These aims are to be achieved through women-led, bottom-up change agendas for securing tenure and increasing access to basic services, housing, and livelihoods (SDI, 2018). SDI stresses the need to build partnerships with other stakeholders and institutionalize tested practices in order that they can be scaled up (SDI, 2013).

SDI's governance structure consists of a Secretariat, a coordinating team, a Board and a Council of Federations, which is made up of nominated grassroots leaders from affiliated Federations. The Secretariat has administrative and management functions and is accountable to a Board and a Council of Federations. It facilitates, and sometimes resources, horizontal exchange and information-sharing programmes among member Federations. It also seeds precedent-setting projects, which are designed to catalyse change processes at all levels. The Board nominates the members of the coordinating team, which serves as an executive and is responsible for overseeing the implementation of SDI programmes.

SDI provides a set of core principles and practices, around which national federations of the urban poor can mobilize. These include:

- *Mobilization of resources through savings groups*. These groups provide a basis for community self-organization and building trust within slum/informal settlement communities.
- *Recording information on informal settlements* through participatory enumeration, mapping, and profiling exercises. These activities are undertaken by settlement residents with support from federations and SDI (Beukes, 2015). Although undertaken for individual settlements, the intention is that the results of these exercises should be combined to provide city-wide information.
- *Dialogue with the state* on issues relating to tenure and alternatives to eviction.
- *Community-to-community learning exchanges*, which allow people from poor communities to learn from people like themselves.

SDI's long-term vision is one of a transformed built environment, in which erstwhile slums become inclusive and resilient neighbourhoods, fully integrated into the city. In the short term, the aim is that partner communities demonstrate integrated settlement planning and incremental upgrading through precedent-setting projects and partnerships with local government.

Most descriptions of the work of SDI and its affiliates emphasize its role in enumerating and mapping settlements. The information collected is used to inform the dialogue with the municipal authorities and others on tenure and eviction. Box 8.1 summarizes key points on the process followed by an SDI affiliate in Uganda.

In the Uganda case, community members were mainly involved in enumeration rather than spatial mapping, and this is likely to be the most common case. There are examples of community members being involved in mapping exercises prior to the incorporation of both enumeration data and mapping information into GIS databases beyond Uganda. For instance, community members were involved in house numbering, collection of household data, and spatial mapping in the Mrima settlement in Mombasa, and one perceived outcome of this involvement was that people would develop a familiarity with maps and area-based representations of their communities. This would increase their ability to evaluate externally produced maps and negotiate more knowledgeably on proposals for their communities. The process did not involve all community members, rather, an 'inclusive and representative' team was chosen from among community members in an open forum. Training, including exchange visits to participate in mapping exercises in other settlements, was facilitated by members of Muungano wa Wanavijiji, the Kenyan alliance of slum dwellers affiliated to SDI. The first step was to number each household, using a numbering code formulated and agreed during training. The trained teams then moved through the settlement, picking up all features and representing them as shapefiles on

Box 8.1 Enumeration and mapping in Uganda

The National Slum Dwellers Federation of Uganda (NSDF-Uganda) was formed in 2002, following a visit by Federation leaders from other countries and support NGO staff. In 2003, it undertook an enumeration and mapping exercise, covering 27,000 households in Kisenyi, a mixed residential and commercial area in central Kampala. Kisenyi III, the most residential area of Kisenyi, subsequently became the core of the federation and the focus for most of its work. By 2010, it was strong enough to take a lead enumeration and mapping role in the Ugandan government's Transforming the Settlements of the Urban Poor in Uganda (TSUPU) project. This was implemented in five secondary cities with support from the Cities Alliance. NSDF-Uganda undertook this five city enumeration to support the TSUPU initiative. Key steps in the process included:

1. Initial contacts with municipal leaders and politicians to introduce the proposed enumeration process and ensure their support.
2. Settlement profiling, based on discussions with municipal official and groups of residents and intended to obtain an initial estimate of settlement sizes and infrastructure levels.
3. Training for enumeration teams (more people were trained than was strictly necessary in order to spread understanding and ownership of the process throughout the community).
4. Shack counting and numbering – required in order to plan for the implementation and monitoring of the enumeration.
5. Enumeration, conducted concurrently in five cities and taking about one month to complete.

The enumerations revealed problems with lack of access to sanitation and safe water, and NSDF-Uganda responded by constructing shared standpipes and water points. Following the enumeration, NSDF-Uganda created detailed maps that could be used along with enumeration data to produce GIS records of the low-income settlements in the five cities. This was done using the GIS platform known as the Social Tenure Domain Model, which had been developed by the Global Land Tools Network (part of UN-Habitat).

Source: Based on Makau et al., 2012

plain white paper. (More recent information on the Muungano wa Wanavijiji website shows that enumerators now make increased use of electronic devices such as tablets.) The information collected was then transferred into the GIS database and analysed using GIS software in order to highlight key points from the situational analysis. The maps were then presented to the community in a meeting that allowed all community members to see the results of the mapping of their settlement. The aim was that community members would be challenged to own the map and use it as a negotiating tool for service provision and future planning, as well as general well-being of the community (Simiya and Mbaka, 2011).

Collecting, recording, and analysing the information required for detailed mapping requires considerable resources. Even where funding is available to carry out a detailed household level survey, it is unlikely that funding will be available for the regular updates that would be required to ensure that the survey results remain relevant over time. When asked to carry out a city-wide settlement mapping process in Cuttack, Odisha, as part of the Indian Government's Rajiv Awas Yojana (RAY) programme, the Indian Alliance implemented a two phase survey process. In the first phase, a team consisting of one staff member from the Urban Development Resource Centre, SPARC's partner organization in Odisha, two experienced federation leaders, and one new federation member, all from Cuttack, collected settlement-level information. This included information on settlement locations, settlement boundaries, population, the number of houses, infrastructure services, and the risk of flooding. The team visited several settlements each day, meeting community leaders and residents to obtain the information required to fill out a settlement profile form. The second phase focused on the household level and involved collection and recording of detailed cadastral information, including precise plot boundaries, and information on house size and household income is collected. This information was only collected for settlements identified for interventions on the basis of information obtained during the first phase. A SPARC technical assistance team worked with this group to create the mapping process and then provided technical support, taking the lead in converting information collected in the field into shape files and recording them into the GIS database. Settlement boundaries were agreed with community leaders in the field and recorded using hand-held GPS devices (Livengood and Kunte, 2012).

Mapping and enumeration activities raise awareness and provide useful information, but their full value will only be realized when they are followed by actions to improve conditions in low-income settlements. The available information suggests that there is still some way to go before the scale of mapping and enumeration activities is matched by that of follow-upgrading (where, following an initial phase of basic upgrading, additional measures are introduced to further improve the facilities and conditions). For example, in 2018, the South African SDI Alliance reported that it had supported residents in 1,420 settlements to prepare community profiles (52 per cent of all settlements nationally), 100 communities to enumerate themselves, and 23 upgrading projects, in seven municipalities. However, its initiatives had leveraged only R20 m (about $1.4 m) from local governments for incremental upgrading (Hendler and Fieuw, 2018).

In order to increase their impact, SDI affiliates have sought to influence the political sphere. Again, the case of the South African SDI Alliance is instructive. Following the ending of Apartheid in 1994, the African National Congress (ANC) government had committed itself to improve access to housing, enshrining the right to housing in the 1996 Constitution. However, its main strategy for achieving housing objectives was to subsidize large-scale contractor-built housing, a strategy that led to the megaproject approach referred to earlier in this chapter. The South African government did recognize the need to support community-driven self-build activities, launching the People's Housing Process in 1998. The South African SDI Alliance had previously lobbied ANC ministers to secure government support to build capacity for people-led housing development, and it used the R10 m received as a result of this lobbying, together with some donor funding, to start the uTshani (grassroots) Fund as a not-for-profit company. A legal agreement with the National Housing Board allowed this to become a conduit for housing subsidies. Provincial housing boards, officially the developer of housing projects, were to pay the beneficiary's subsidy into the uTshani Fund, allowing the member to self-build as part of a community project. Between 1996 and 2001, the Fund had administered 4,500 subsidy applications, offering bridging loans to beneficiaries while their housing subsidy was being secured. Unfortunately, these short-term loans often became long-term debts, largely because government agencies were slow in releasing moneys to the Fund to cover the subsidies that it had agreed. At the same time, government concerns about the poor standard of houses constructed by developers led to stricter standards above those of some of the existing uTshani Fund-subsidized houses, making it impossible for the Fund to claim the subsidies for 'pre-financed' work. This led to a drastic slowdown in output, with only 300 houses constructed between 2004 and 2007. The resulting tensions led to a break-up in the South African Homeless People's Federation, one of the two social movements included in the Alliance. The breakaway group retained the original name while the majority renamed themselves the Federation of the Urban and Rural Poor (FedUP). In 2006, six provinces agreed to ring-fence subsidies for 1,000 residences for FedUP groups. The provinces agreed to pay subsidies for house construction upfront and provide serviced greenfield plots. However, the Free State was the only province to make the agreed upfront payments. Elsewhere, the uTshani Fund continued to pre-finance construction and retrospectively claim back subsidies. Federation leaders claimed that FedUP houses are of significantly better quality than contractor-built houses and are larger, typically 50 m^2 compared to 35 m^2. However, the overall impact of the South African SDI Alliance's efforts appears to have been limited, with only 11,825 houses completed between 1995 and 2015 (Fieuw and Mitlin, 2017).

A similar picture emerges in relation to urban settlement upgrading in South Africa. In 2010, the Office of the President signed a performance agreement with the Minister of Human Settlements to upgrade 400,000 informal settlement dwellings by 2014, with a further 750,000 dwellings to be upgraded between 2014 and 2019. In the years before this, the Alliance had supported the formation of the Informal Settlement Network (ISN), which aimed to create a social movement of mainly existing settlement-level residents' organizations. By 2010/11, the ISN had networked with 600 settlements in the five major cities of South Africa: Johannesburg, Ekurhuleni (East Rand mining belt), eThekwini (Durban), Nelson Mandela Bay Metro (Port Elizabeth), and Cape Town, and was active in smaller towns, including Stellenbosch and Midvaal. Its predecessor, the Coalition of the Urban Poor, had profiled almost all the informal settlements in Johannesburg and Cape Town, hoping to use the information gathered as the basis for partnerships with local governments. This did not always work, as local governments disputed the validity of the information collected by communities.

In 2010, the Alliance responded by collaborating with others to set up the Community Upgrading Finance Facility (CUFF), with the objective of catalysing communities to engage with government around collaborative upgrading and livelihoods projects. The focus was on demonstrating the possibilities for settlement upgrading through projects that would act as pilots for subsequent action. The similarity in name and remit suggests that CUFF was inspired by the Community Led Infrastructure Finance Facility (CLIFF), which has already been described in Chapter 5. The board of CUFF consisted of 60 per cent shack dwellers and 40 per cent supporting NGO professionals. CUFF adopted a 're-blocking' strategy, through which existing shacks were improved and rearranged in accordance with a community-designed layout that provided for adequate access to streets and services and safe public spaces. By 2018, six re-blocking projects, affecting 864 households, had been completed, five in Cape Town and the sixth in Johannesburg. Cape Town officials had developed and adopted a law on re-blocking informal settlements, which allowed the city council to provide engineering and planning support and to ensure alignment with other public works initiatives. In 2013, the largest of the projects, Mtshini Wam, was awarded a Gold award at the Impumelelo Social Innovations awards. Also, in 2013, the Alliance established a people's led finance facility in Cape Town. The aim was to provide a facility in which community savings and donor funding would leverage municipal finance for community-led upgrading initiatives. It was hoped that, by bypassing lengthy bureaucratic requirements, this would allow organized urban poor communities to quickly access the necessary funds to upgrade their settlements in partnership with the municipality (Hendler and Fieuw, 2018).

Overall, perhaps the biggest challenge for SDI affiliates in various countries is to develop good working relationships with municipal governments. The preferred SDI approach is to sign a Memorandum of Understanding (MoU) with a city government. Shand (2018) and Hendler and Fieuw (2018) describe examples from Zimbabwe and South Africa respectively. Shand notes that, while MoUs are not legally enforceable and do not fundamentally alter institutional conditions outside the project, they can help to reinforce the legitimacy of non-state groups as development actors and contributors to the co-production of services. One possible issue is their time-limited nature. Hendler and Fieuw describe the MoU between Stellenbosch Municipality and the Community Organization Resource Centre (CORC), a non-profit organization that fulfils a similar role in South Africa as that of SPARC in India. This arrangement was for three years, ending in 2015, at which time cooperation between CORC and the municipality reached a hiatus, and it was necessary to seek another arrangement for completing work started under the MoU.

Overall, it is clear that SDI is some way from achieving city-wide impact in any of the cities in which it is involved. Individual projects have generally been small and many have fallen behind schedule, in some cases becoming moribund before completion. Possible reasons for this situation include:

- *Limited reach of SDI and its affiliates.* This is perhaps inevitable. SDI initiatives are rooted in specific communities and its lack of presence in other communities makes it difficult to operate effectively on a wider scale. As already noted in Chapter 7, this is a problem that the OPP faced in Pakistan.
- *Limited capacity to plan, implement, and manage interventions.* In Cape Town, the city's requirements for technical input into re-blocking projects increased over time, exceeding CORC's capacity to either appoint or fund the required staff.
- *Limited local government commitment to the partnership approach.* After successes in Cape Town and Stellenbosch up to 2014, the partnerships in these two municipalities became significantly strained (Hendler and Fieuw, 2018).
- *Slow and bureaucratic government responses to community initiatives.* For instance, Hendler and Fieuw note that it took the Cape Town council two years to appoint a service provider for re-blocking projects in Mfuleni, one of the areas identified by SDI. They went on to note the need for 'quick, light and cheap interventions to start changing the way government thinks about informal settlement upgrading projects' (Hendler and Fieuw, 2018: 100).
- *Limited government commitment to upgrading and re-blocking.* The City of Cape Town's approach to upgrading informal settlements is now guided by a re-blocking policy (Hendler and Fieuw, 2018), but it has been slow to provide the resources needed to support this policy. At a national level, as explained earlier in this chapter, the South African government has chosen to pursue a strategy based on the mass provision of subsidized housing and has provided few resources for community-based upgrading initiatives.

SDI and its affiliates have had more success in influencing the approach of international organizations. As noted earlier in this chapter, the Cities Alliance has provided funding for some SDI-led initiatives. The links between the two organizations are strengthened by the fact that the Cities Alliance Management Board includes an SDI representative. A related success concerns the positive impact of SDI thinking on points such as the importance of enumeration and mechanisms for raising community involvement, as well as on starting upgrading processes.

The Asian coalition for housing rights

ACHR is a coalition of Asian housing professionals, NGOs, and community organizations, all with a commitment to find ways of promoting people-driven housing solutions. Formed in 1988 to provide a forum for grassroots and community groups, urban social activists, NGOs, and professionals, it initially focused on housing rights and the problem of evictions. As it developed, ACHR increasingly sought to explore new ways of enabling grassroots organizations to have a stronger voice on urban development issues. Adopting a similar approach to SDI, it promoted regional community-to-community exchanges across Asia. From 2000 onwards, it introduced community savings and credit activities and established community development funds, influencing development processes in Lao PDR, Cambodia, Vietnam, Nepal, Mongolia, Sri Lanka, Thailand, Philippines, and India. It claimed that city- and country-wide slum upgrading in Thailand and India has been used to boost and support learning for structural change in other countries.

From 2008, ACHR channelled much of its effort through the Asian Coalition for Community Action (ACCA) programme. Initially a three-year programme, this aimed to catalyse and support city-wide upgrading and partnerships between community organizations and local government. After an initial city-wide community survey, the design envisaged grant support to individual communities to finance implementation of small-scale infrastructure schemes, followed by provision of loans to support larger housing projects, and. each city was to establish its own community development fund to provide support for these activities. The process was to be led by communities, with support provided by 'community' architects and planners. By January 2013, city-wide community surveys had been or were being conducted in 165 cities in 19 countries. These surveys provided the information required to identify, prioritize, and plan settlement upgrading projects, which were then carried out by the communities in partnership with their city governments. Almost 1,200 small-scale upgrading projects – typically involving some combination of walkways, drains, toilets, water supply, community centres, and solid waste management – had been completed or were in progress. Some 110 ACCA-supported 'big' housing projects had been or were being implemented and almost 43,000 urban poor families had already benefited from these projects. Most of the 'big' projects involved partnerships between communities and governments. City development funds were operating in 98 cities, with a total capital of $5.8 m, less than half of which came from ACCA and the rest mobilized from communities, local governments, and other sources.

ACCA's $11 m budget was funded by a BMGF grant. This was used to fund ACCA expenditure of up to $58,000 per city, with allocations of:

- $15,000 for at least five small upgrading projects in five different communities;
- $40,000 for one big housing project, with a maximum of 7–8 housing projects per country; and
- $3,000 for process support, to cover activities such as surveying and mapping, network-building, support for savings activities, local meetings, and exchanges.

ACCA allocated an additional $10,000 per country per year for national level expenditure to cover meetings, exchange visits, and advocacy. The aim was that this relatively small level of expenditures, amounting to only about 6 per cent of total project value, would leverage larger contributions from communities and government. These contributions amounted to 13 per cent and 78 per cent respectively of the total $97,667,623 budget, with most of government contributions being in kind in the form of land (Buckley et al., 2014).

In addition to funding specific projects, the $40,000 for big projects was also used to seed or contribute to a city-level community development fund. By 2012, funds operated in 167 cities in 19 countries. The total held in the funds was $5.8 m, of which 48 per cent had been provided by ACCA, 31 per cent by the people themselves, 11 per cent from government, and 10 per cent from other sources. Although government contributions were relatively small, ACHR saw them as an important signal of government support.

Buckley et al. (2014) give examples of changes in government policies, standards, and attitudes to informal development that have been influenced by ACCA activities. These include a new national housing policy in Cambodia, based on city-wide, community-driven, and partnership-based community upgrading strategies. Unfortunately, the impact of this policy appears to have been limited. Like other government actions referred to earlier in this book, the Cambodian government has continued to prioritize the construction of apartments for sale, many provided by the formal private sector. Despite their low-cost designation, these units are only affordable to middle- and higher-income households (Hutt, 2018). Other government actions that can be at least partly attributed to the influence of ACCA include provision of free land for housing the poor, including land that they already occupy, and the inclusion of urban poor coalitions in some planning and budgeting bodies.

The ACCA programme ended in 2015 and was followed by the similar but smaller ACHR-SELAVIP project. This was implemented with support from the SELAVIP Foundation (Servicio Latinoamericano, Africano y Asiatico de Vivenda Popular [Latin American, African and Asian Social Housing Service]), which was founded in the 1970s and seeks to promote initiatives to address the most urgent habitat needs of the urban poor. Like ACCA, this initiative incorporated both small upgrading schemes and larger housing initiatives.

Overall, it seems that ACHR's ability to achieve city-wide impacts has, similar to that of SDI, been disappointing. It has influenced the thinking of international agencies but has been less successful in changing the attitudes of governments and professionals. The further implications of this, together with possible ways forward, will be explored in Chapters 9 and 10.

Government efforts to support community-led action

CODI and Baan Mankong

In the 1960s, Thailand was a low-income country but its economy has since grown steadily and the World Bank now classifies it as upper-middle income. In 2019, the World Bank's Thailand Overview stated that poverty levels had declined from 67 per cent in 1986 to 7.8 per cent in 2017, as measured by the poverty line of $5.5/day. Despite this overall economic improvement, a significant proportion of Thailand's population was still housed in informal settlements, and a 2008 survey by CODI and the urban poor community networks around the country found that more than 1.6 million low-income families (out of 20 million) were living in about 6,300 urban poor communities throughout the country, with over 720,000 of those families in need of secure, permanent housing (CODI, 2019).

In 1992, recognizing that Thailand's economic success during the 1980s and early 1990s had brought limited benefits to the poor, the Thai Government set up the Urban Community Development Office (UCDO). The government provided initial funding equivalent to $50 m to support urban community development activities and to provide low-interest loans to community organizations for emergencies, housing, and income generation. Though technically falling under the National Housing Authority, UCDO had its own development process and a separate board of directors. Its remit was to support community organizations with loans for new housing, housing improvement, settlement upgrading, and income generation. Recognizing the benefits that ensue when people work collectively and the importance of the relationship between low-income groups and government, UCDO established and worked through representative and accountable local citizens' organizations. It provided loans, which were channelled through community-based savings and loan groups. As the number of groups increased, UCDO found it increasingly difficult to provide support to individual groups. To address this problem, it encouraged individual groups to form networks at various levels, including the city level, where the network could negotiate with the city or provincial authorities, or simply to work together on shared problems. Loans could be made to individual groups or through networks, but the latter increasingly became the channel through which UCDO funds (and later CODI funds) were made available to low-income groups.

By 2000, 950 community savings groups had been established and supported in 53 of Thailand's 75 provinces; housing loans and technical support had been provided to 47 housing projects involving 6,400 households; grants for small improvements in infrastructure and living conditions had been provided in 796 communities benefiting 68,208 families, and more than 100 community networks had been set up. Also in 2000, UCDO was merged with the Rural Development Fund to become the Community Organizations Development Unit (CODI). CODI's central guiding principle was that communities have the desire and capability to bring about change and should have the opportunity to determine what they need and set the direction of their own development processes. Unlike UCDO, which had been located within the National Housing Authority, CODI was (and is) an independent public organization, able to apply to the annual government budget for funds. This gave it greater flexibility and wider linkages. Like UCDO, it works through networks of community-based savings and loan groups and its board includes representatives from both government and community organizations (Boonyabancha, 2005). Recognizing the gap between the larger economic and political forces that determine development and the reality of people's lives on the ground, CODI supported the formation of community councils to represent the various communities within a sub-district (ward). These were initially organized on an informal basis, but the 2008 Community Councils Act gave them a legal status.[2]

In January 2003, CODI initiated its Baan Mankong (secure housing) programme. This sought to:

- go beyond individual projects to address low-income housing problems across whole cities; and
- stimulate changes in social structures and managerial systems, increase community confidence, and change the relationship between communities and local government.

The process was to be demand-driven, with community organizations undertaking most of the construction work. Government funds were to be channelled directly to poor communities. By working together rather than individually, these communities would be empowered to plan and undertake improvements to their housing environment and basic services.

Increased tenure security was and remains a central CODI objective. Communities are encouraged to explore a range of tenure options, but about 80 per cent involve either cooperative land ownership with land title or a long-term lease (Boonyabancha, 2009). Communal land ownership is the preferred option where land can be transferred to the community. Long-term leases are negotiated where the land is owned by a third party, in most cases the government. Communities are also heavily involved in funding the programme, as they are required to save 10 per cent of the amount they borrow in a community savings account in order to qualify for a Baan Mankong loan. The loan charge to community cooperatives is 4 per cent per annum. Cooperatives then on-lend to their members, increasing the interest rate as required to cover administrative expenses (Bhatkal and Lucci, 2015). The assumption is that the resulting interest rates will still be no more than that available from commercial lenders.

CODI gives four upgrading options (Bhatkal and Lucci, 2015).

- *On-site upgrading* – improvement to housing and services without changes in the site layout.
- *On-site re-blocking* – as on-site upgrading but with the overall layout rationalized, which will require that some houses are moved.
- *On-site reconstruction* – complete demolition of the existing settlement, with residents rehoused on-site, typically in apartments. This may be combined with *land sharing*, in which part of the site is reserved for slum dwellers and the other part allocated to the owner for construction of apartments for sale. This is an option where slum residents have squatted on private land.

- *Relocation* – complete resettlement of the community to another location.

Direct benefits resulting from involvement in the Baan Mankong programme include increased tenure security, improved housing conditions (including an increase in the use of permanent materials), and increased access to utility services. Indirect benefits include greater access to credit and increased investment in businesses, increased access to formal sector employment, and an increase in time that children spent studying (Bhatkal and Lucci, 2015).

The Baan Mankong process, as explained by Boonyabancha (2005), starts with meetings to explain the Baan Mankong approach. These include both 'network' meetings, which may be attended by people from other cities, and meetings in poor communities. The latter should, if possible, involve municipal staff. The next step is to establish a joint committee, including representatives of low-income communities, network leaders, local government officers, and representatives of academia and NGOs. Its first task is to organize a city meeting with representatives from all urban poor communities in order to introduce the proposed programme and the process to be followed. It then organizes a survey of all low-income communities in the city in order to gather information on the number of households and family members, housing security status, land ownership, infrastructure problems, community organizations, savings activities, and other existing development initiatives. The survey process gives people opportunities to meet with and learn from each other. Its results are used to produce a community upgrading plan, covering the whole city, and community-driven plans should be integrated with other aspects of the city's development. At this stage, pilot projects are identified, prepared, and implemented on the basis of need, community willingness to implement them, and the learning possibilities that they provide. Taking account of the lessons learnt from these pilots, the process is then extended to cover all other communities identified in the city-wide plan. Throughout this process, Baan Mankong supports community collective savings groups in order to mobilize local resources, strengthen local groups, and build collective management skills. It also emphasizes the need to build community networks around common land ownership, shared construction, cooperative enterprises, community welfare activities, and collective canal maintenance.

Figure 8.1 shows the key features of CODI's operational structure. It illustrates the importance that CODI places on networks of community organizations and its role in providing a link between secondary stakeholders, including local authorities, and communities. CODI shares its emphasis on community-based financial mobilization through savings groups, the need for community-led city-wide surveys, and the role of community networks with both SDI and ACHR schemes. As with the other organizations, the surveys appear to focus mainly on collecting quantitative information and do not include detailed physical surveys of individual low-income

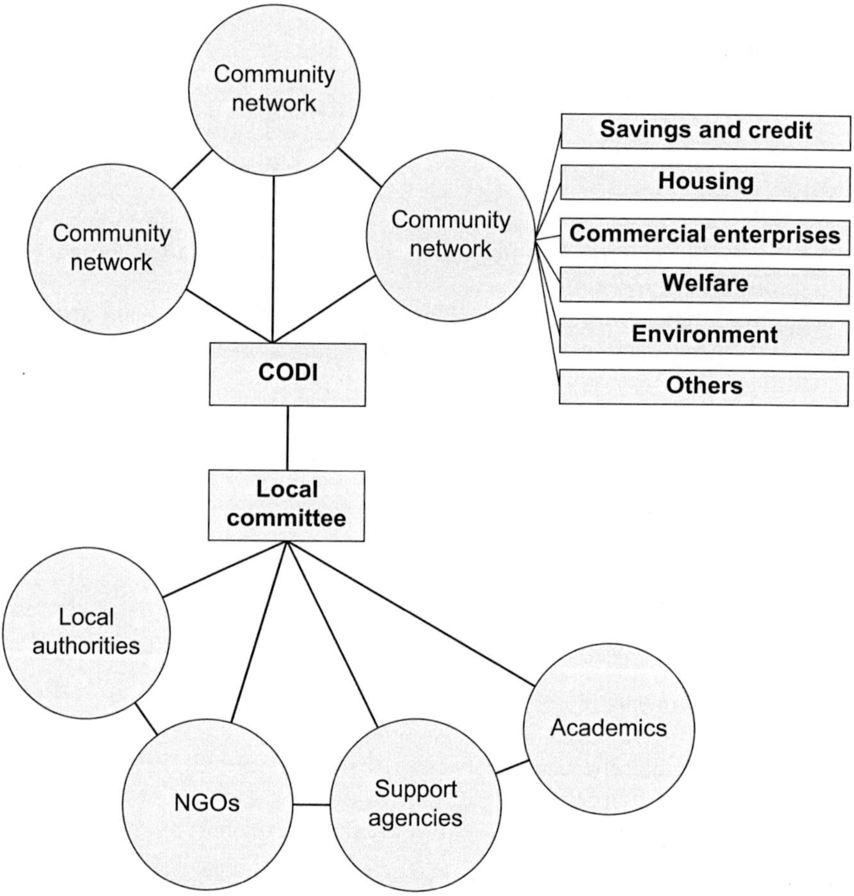

Figure 8.1 CODI organizational structure
Source: Adapted from Figure 2 in Nadkarny and Anderson, n.d.

communities. In order to access Baan Mankong loans, communities must form cooperatives and develop housing in a collective way, and loans are extended collectively to the community cooperative rather than to individual households.

The original Baan Mankong target was to improve housing and living conditions and tenure security for 300,000 households in 2,000 poor communities in 200 Thai cities within five years. A pilot phase involving 10 communities and a total of about 1,500 households was to be implemented in 2003. In 2004, this was to be expanded to cover 174 communities with 15,000 households in 42 cities, with expansion to 285,000 units in 200 cities in 2005–2007, covering at least half the urban poor communities in Thailand. Boonyabancha and Kerr (2018) report Baan Mankong activities in 370 cities around the country, covering 105,000 families in 2,557 communities (with the average community having 91 households). The Thai Government had supported these activities with policy initiatives, nominal leases on public land, housing and land loans amounting to $266.5 m, and housing subsidies totalling $221.6 m, channelled through the CODI fund. While impressive, these figures show that Baan Mankong's achievements have fallen some way short of its original targets. Boonyabancha and Kerr (2018) suggest that the reasons for this included:

- *Financial constraints*. By 2009, the city-wide upgrading process was being implemented in some 260 cities and towns, and housing projects covering 80,000 households had been approved. The large scale of the programme led to cash-flow problems. The CODI fund had been almost completely drained, with most of its capital tied up in long-term Baan Mankong programme housing loans. Despite a modest infusion of fresh capital brought about by an experimental link between CODI and the Government Housing Bank, followed by government infusion of an additional $94 m into the CODI fund, the programme began to slow down. Further infusions of $60 m in 2011 and $30 m in 2012 had not been delivered by November 2012 (Wangkiat, 2012).
- *Capacity constraints*. In the early years of CODI, much of its urban work, including the Baan Mankong programme, was managed from its Bangkok office. By 2013, it was clear that the increased size of the programme had created a need for decentralization, but the new decentralized teams lacked the knowledge of the city-wide community-driven processes that the central management team had acquired over the years.
- *Erosion of the programme's ethos*. The release of government funding was conditional on CODI teams providing proof that targets were being met. Inexperienced teams tended to look for quick answers to these demands and in the process lost sight of the people's delivery mechanisms. The paradoxical result was that the increased focus on targets and outputs led to a reduction in the rate of production of houses and services.
- *A tendency for horizontal networks to morph into more hierarchical systems*. Experienced national leaders became the main supporters of country-wide housing projects and took leading roles in both national and regional committees.
- *Reduced interaction with city governments*. The existence of a strong national network and availability of CODI funds reduced the need to build consensus and work with local government and other stakeholders. As a result, the original collaborative city-wide development concept faded and was replaced by an increased focus on identifying and implementing projects. Some housing projects could not be completed and there were cities in which there was no follow-up to the first project.
- *Diversion of resources to other CODI programmes*. These included community councils, city funds, community welfare and insurance

programmes, the healthy communities project, disaster rehabilitation, and housing for the poorest.

After collective reflection, CODI concluded that the focus on a few pilots had resulted in many communities being left behind. There was a need for a renewed emphasis on city-wide partnerships, leading to the preparation and implementation of city-wide plans. Once community networks had surveyed all the slums, the aim should have been to ensure that as many communities as possible would quickly start to work on solutions to their housing problems. The community networks should have developed clear plans for solving all of their city's housing problems within three to five years. Each city should have set up a joint city committee, with representatives from the local authority, communities, and other actors. This committee would then discuss and approve every single housing project, and review the city-wide survey information and city-wide upgrading plans. The overall aim would be to use these mechanisms to institutionalize a city-wide co-productive approach to slum upgrading (Boonyabancha and Kerr, 2018).

Given the constraints listed above, the obvious question is how to provide the human, organizational, and financial resources required for implementation of the proposed accelerated and expanded programme. One possible answer on the question of finance is provided by the 20-year National Housing Development Strategy, approved by the Thai Government in 2016 and covering the period 2017–2036. This finance aims to build on CODI's progress and provide permanent housing for 1 million urban and rural poor families by 2036 (CODI, 2019). It requires that every province set up a multi-stakeholder committee to oversee the planning process. This was to be chaired by the provincial government and include representatives of the National Housing Authority, local government and private sector actors, and two representatives of poor communities, one rural and one urban. Boonyabancha and Kerr (2018) noted that, while there was still uncertainty about the government's commitment to the new policy, it could lead to increased coordination between the various public land-owning agencies and create room for many poor people to negotiate secure tenure for the land they occupy.

One of CODI's greatest challenges is to provide an effective link between a community's own organizational systems, which are usually informal and often messy, unpredictable, and constantly in flux, and government systems, which tend to be bureaucratic, hierarchical, and inflexible. CODI must report to the Ministry of Finance, the Budget Bureau, the Ministry of Social Development and Human Security, and the National Audit Office, all with different rules, regulations, procedures, and hierarchies. It has also faced challenges caused by the frequent shifts in Thailand's political landscape over the years. Boonyabancha and Kerr (2018) stress the need to cultivate political support, but this support is not always easy to sustain, as evidenced by the experience with the Million Houses Programme in Sri Lanka.

Urban partnerships for poverty reduction (Bangladesh) and its successors

The Urban Partnerships for Poverty Reduction (UPPR) project ran from 2008 to 2015 and covered 23 towns and cities in Bangladesh. It built on the experience of the earlier Local Partnerships for Urban Poverty Alleviation Project, which had run from 2000 to 2007. Both projects were UNDP initiatives, located within the Bangladesh Government's Local Government Engineering Department, with much of the external funding provided by the British Government's DFID. The project was supported by a central team, based in Dhaka, and town-level teams led by 'town managers'. Like CODI, it emphasized the importance of savings groups and community involvement in mapping. Its approach to community organization was similar to that of the Community Development Society (CDS) model, developed in Kerala in the early 1990s and subsequently adopted in other Indian states. The model involves:

- *Primary groups*, typically drawn from around 20 households. These were the equivalent of Kerala's neighbourhood groups (NHGs).
- *Community development committees* (CDCs), equivalent to Kerala's Area Development Societies. These operate at the settlement level and typically represent seven or more NHGs, Every CDC had four leaders, elected from NHG leaders.
- *Cluster committees*, each representing several CDCs. In some cities there was also a Federation, representing CDCs in all wards of the city. Each Federation is governed by a 7–9-person board of directors, elected from the CDC and CDC cluster leaders, who form the general body of the Federation.

UPPR had a strong focus on livelihoods, encouraging saving and providing loans to be used for productive purposes, for instance starting a small tea shop or purchasing a cycle rickshaw. Most of its shelter-related activities involved local infrastructure upgrading but it also supported some efforts to improve housing. Post-project assessment revealed that both communities and institutional key informants viewed savings and credit activities and mobilization of poor and extremely poor communities as the most successful aspect of the project. Key informants also ranked support to improvement in housing conditions and improved access to healthy and secure living environments fairly highly. Communities were less sure about the impact of efforts to improve housing conditions. This probably reflects the limited involvement of the project on housing improvement and provision activities. The much quoted example of the housing project to rehouse evicted households in Gopalganj only provided about 260 new houses. It is not clear whether respondents ranked activities on what they thought should be their impact rather than the impact that they actually achieved. Respondents in both groups ranked the project's success in achieving higher-level institutional and poverty reduction objectives much lower (Spora Sinergies, 2016).

The post-project assessment said little about the lasting impact of the changes wrought by the project. The author was a member of a World Bank team that visited UPPR project areas in five municipalities in 2013 and 2014 during project preparation for what subsequently became the Low Income Communities Housing Support Project (LICHSP). These visits revealed that infrastructure upgrading was almost always local and self-contained. Lane paving schemes were largely on-site. In most cases, water supply was from tube wells fitted with handpumps. The project provided some simple systems for removing iron from drinking water but at least some of these had been abandoned by 2019. Some settlements had local distribution networks supplied by tube wells powered by electrical pumps but there were few, if any, connections to the municipal water supply. Observation and interviews with local residents suggested that one reason for this was the poor level of service provided by municipal systems, which provided poor quality water at low pressure. In almost all cases, sanitation facilities provided through the project took the form of shared pour-flush toilets discharging to twin leach pits. The theory of this configuration is that one pit is used until it is full, with the flow from the toilet switched to the second pit and the contents of the second pit are left to decompose. After about a year, they degrade into a humus-like material that is inoffensive and pathogen free. It can then be safely removed and used as a fertilizer or soil conditioner. The system requires that users understand the system and use pits alternately, as required by the design. It makes the implicit assumption that people will empty the pits themselves and that there is a local use for the humus removed from pits. In practice, it was clear that none of these conditions existed. People invariably used both pits simultaneously and called a specialist pit emptier if and when they needed to empty their pits. There were few if any working arrangements for disposal of the faecal sludge removed from pits. In Sirajganj, for instance, desludging vehicles and a faecal sludge treatment plant had been provided under an Asian Development Bank project, but a visit in 2018 revealed that the treatment plant had never been used and was now inaccessible since access to it was blocked by solid waste. Similarly, the poor or non-existent state of municipal solid waste collection services meant that UPPR had had little impact on solid waste collection services.

These findings are consistent with the difficulties that other upgrading initiatives have experienced in making connections with municipal services and thus linking upgraded settlements with the fabric of towns and cities as a whole. They also tie in with the findings of Spora Sinergies (2016) that, as a general rule, local governments had been insufficiently involved in UPPR as a whole, with the result that there had been 'low appropriation of the project by the political sphere' (Spora Sinergies, 2016: 40). Their review did find that there were places, for instance Sirajganj, where good relations between CDC leaders and councillors meant that the latter were more responsive to community demands. Indeed, it gave the example of the creation of a dedicated slum development unit in the municipality as an example of an initiative arising from the good relationship between CDC leaders and the councillors. There was no evidence that this unit was active in 2017 when consultants for the LICHSP started working in Sirajganj. LICHSP intended to work through the UPPR CDCs but found that many of these had become inactive following closure of UPPR in 2015.

One positive aspect of UPPR was its city-wide Settlement and Vacant Land Mapping. Maps showing the location of low-income settlements and vacant land were produced for all 27 project towns. A team from the Dhaka-based Centre for Urban Studies (CES) led the mapping process, which used a participatory methodology involving the UPPR project team, the community, and 'stakeholder/users' (Nazem and Hossain, 2012). CES used satellite images to produce the base maps required for settlement mapping. Information collection work in the field was assigned to teams consisting of field research assistants and CDC leaders. In each town, CES provided training through a two-day programme. In the course of the surveys, poor settlement communities were asked questions on 16 issues, covering land ownership, tenure status, housing conditions, services, education, employment, income, savings and credit activities, risk and vulnerability, and social problems. Communities rated their current situation with regard to each question on a scale of 1 to 4. CES used the survey results to divide settlements into four categories, extreme poor, very poor, moderately poor, and marginally poor and produced city maps showing settlements in each category in a different colour. These maps show the extent of each settlement but provide limited information on internal layouts.

Nazem and Hossain (2012) identify some limitations in the approach. Field teams found that it was difficult to define poor settlements. Field workers sometimes faced difficulties in defining settlement boundaries and obtaining information. The score card approach relied on rather arbitrary judgements on the answers to the various questions and trained surveyors reported that community members were sometimes 'conceptually weak' in conducting surveys and obtaining data efficiently. The last is not surprising, given the short duration of the training that they received. Despite these limitations, the author's impression, based on extensive visits to low-income settlements in Comilla in 2013 and other towns in 2014, was that the maps were spatially accurate and that the categorization was reasonably in line with actual settlement conditions.

UPPR established the first Community Housing Development Fund (CHDF) in Gopalganj under the guidance of ACHR. This channelled funds from the ACCA programme to finance construction of 260 houses for members of a community that had been evicted from their homes by the district administration. UPPR had identified 52 parcels of vacant government and privately owned land and in 2010 the Ministry of Land allocated 4.16 acres (1.68 ha) to Gopalganj municipality to be used for the project. The Comprehensive Disaster Management Programme (CDMP-II) provided BDT 61 m ($0.87 m) to fund the construction of 260 houses through a CHDF established by the

Gopalganj CDCs and clusters. The initiative was clearly influenced by CODI, which was the focus for a study tour to Thailand, organized by UPPR in December 2010 and involving a member of parliament, senior central and local government officials, a lawyer, a journalist, and community leaders (Juhasz and Rahman, 2013). The CHDF helped to negotiate a 99-year lease on the land and provided loans to target households at 10–12 per cent interest rates and with a payback period of 5–7 years. CHDFs were subsequently established in other cities, including Sirajganj, Rajshahi, and Chittagong, but the total number of households benefiting from them had only reached 300 by 2019 (Rahman, 2019). In terms of city-wide impact, this level of activity was negligible.

In August 2018, Government of Bangladesh approved the World Bank funded Livelihoods Improvement of the Urban Poor Communities Project (LIUPCP), which builds on the experience of UPPR and uses much the same approach. LIUPCP forms part of the National Urban Poverty Reduction Programme and as such has a wider remit, including objectives relating to climate change resilience and strengthened pro-poor urban management, policy, and planning. The project design includes provision for the construction of 5,000 new housing units for extremely poor families in secondary cities and a housing finance facility to provide financial support for a further 15,000 families to build their own houses (Rahman, 2019). At the time of writing, the information required to assess the effectiveness of the project is not available.

The design of the World Bank LICHSP, approved in April 2016 and scheduled to run until December 2021, drew on the experience of CODI and ACCA and sought to build on the 'organized and cohesive' community groups established by UPPR. LICHSP operated in three municipalities, Sirajganj, Cumilla, and Narayanganj, all of which were previously UPPR towns. Its outputs included both:

- urban community improvements and upgrading, to be achieved through a community-driven planning process; and
- housing improvements, financed through micro loans advanced through the Palli Karma-Sahayak Foundation, an umbrella organization for microfinance NGOs.

Community improvement and upgrading was to benefit 24,000 urban poor living in informal and low-income settlements while the target figure for housing loans was 40,000 beneficiaries.

At the project design stage, it was hoped that the successor project to UPPR would be operational and that LICHSP could work through the already existing CDC structures. In practice, anecdotal evidence from LICHSP consultants and field staff suggests that many CDCs had become inactive after the withdrawal of UPPR support. Nevertheless, LICHSP used aspects of the UPPR approach, including the formation of women-only primary groups, and the production of community-led plans at the settlement level. The project's efforts initially focused on Sirajganj, where the first project area was a low-income settlement on government land, part of which flooded during the wet monsoon months. The solution adopted was to re-block the whole settlement after bringing in fill to raise all parts of it above the flood level. This required the agreement of all community members to dismantle their houses, saving transportable elements to be used in the construction of new houses in the re-blocked settlement. All subsequent interventions were on land that was, in some sense, already owned by individual community members, and as a result there appeared to be no interest in even the minimal re-ordering of house locations to allow widening and straightening of rights of way.

Community needs and priorities were identified during 1–2 day workshops facilitated by community organizers. Engineers were then brought in to design schemes to meet community needs. Their proposed interventions typically included shared toilets with septic tanks, covered drains, new tube wells with handpumps, and community centres, among others. Few community members showed any interest in linking to municipal water networks. National competitive bidding was used more extensively than in UPPR projects, particularly for toilet and drainage contracts, leaving only path surfacing and minor works to be carried out by community contracting methods.

Recognizing the importance of good governance

From the mid-1980s onwards, recognizing that change was dependent on the existence of a supportive policy environment, the World Bank placed increased emphasis on the need for policy-based loans. The value of projects lay in their ability to embody policy changes in specific investments (Buckley and Kalarickal, 2006). In the late 20th century, policy-based loans tended to be linked to the World Bank's concern, some would say obsession, with structural adjustment. Even when this was not the case, success was likely to be assessed in terms of overall economic performance rather than changes related to the specific sector to which the loan applied (Dubey, 1985). The World Bank's approach to shelter for the poor emphasized action to improve financial systems, focusing particularly on the introduction of mortgages and other financial instruments. This approach has been criticized as representing an unnecessarily financialized approach to shelter needs (Van Waeyenberge, 2017).

Regardless of ultimate objectives, policy loans were usually linked to requirements that beneficiary countries implemented institutional changes required to ensure that policy changes would be implemented and sustained over time. Experience in the field revealed a need for improved governance at all levels, not least at the municipal level. In order to provide services for poor people, local governments needed to have the ability to plan for change, to have reliable revenue resources sufficient to support planned activity, and to have sound financial management practices. These in turn required that they have competent and committed staff with capacity to plan, deliver, manage, and maintain services. From the mid-1990s to the mid-2000s, the UK's DFID increasingly focused on the need for improvements in the legal, policy, and enabling environment. This led it to embedding its support for settlement upgrading in projects that had a strong governance dimension (DFID, 2001). Two DFID projects in India from this period, the Andhra Pradesh Urban Services for the Poor (APUSP) and the Madhya Pradesh Urban Services for the Poor (MPUSP) are examined below. These represent the second and third stages in DFID's efforts to move from a focus on slum upgrading, through municipal strengthening and reform, to a concern with higher-level governance systems (Oxford Policy Management Asia, 2013).

Andhra Pradesh urban services for the poor

APUSP, with funding from DFID, started in 2000 and initially covered the 32 Class 1 municipalities (those with a population of more than 100,000) in Andhra Pradesh. A further 10 municipalities were added later to take account of the results of the 2001 census. The project sought to integrate micro-level initiatives targeted at specific low-income communities into a municipality-wide planning and development process, in parallel with a process of municipal reform. The focus on this reform took account of the devolution of responsibilities to municipalities required by the Constitution of India 74th Amendment Act of 1992. To achieve its objectives, the project incorporated three complementary components:

- C1, Municipal reform – designed to bring about improvements in the financial, planning, and implementation capacity of municipalities.
- C2, Environmental services – intended to provide environmental infrastructure improvements in low-income areas.
- C3, Strengthened civil society – intended to build a more vocal and informed civil society, with increased ability to lobby municipalities to improve services.

The C3 component was initially separated from the other two components but about two years in the project was integrated with them under the control of a single project coordinator.

The project's physical activities were intended to address the needs of low-income 'slum' areas. While the main emphasis was 'in-slum' infrastructure, up to 35 per cent of the total infrastructure spend was earmarked for the higher-level infrastructure improvements required to support 'in-slum' upgrading. The state government initially insisted that upgrading efforts should be confined to officially recognized 'notified' slums. This excluded recently developed slums, which often suffered from the worst environmental conditions and housed the poorest and most vulnerable people. Eventually, following pressure from both the project consultants and DFID, the state government agreed to extend project activities to non-notified slums.

Guidelines for assessing and prioritizing the needs of non-notified slums were developed and piloted in late 2003.

The key instrument for implementing components C1 and C2 of the project was the Municipal Action Plan for Poverty Reduction (MAPP). This was designed to enable poor people to express their needs and the municipality to incorporate these needs into its plans and budgets. It also provided a framework within which the municipality could identify the measures required to improve its performance and request state level action in sectors that were state responsibilities. MAPPs were to be rolling plans, regularly updated to reflect the lessons learnt as implementation progressed. They were to be produced at the municipal level and to include proposals for municipal reforms and investment in slum and slum-related infrastructure. Because of capacity constraints, it was decided that a basic MAPP (BMAPP) should be produced for each town in the first instance. It was envisaged that each town would later produce a comprehensive MAPP (CMAPP), for which funding would be provided once municipalities had met specified performance criteria relating to the progress on reform and infrastructure development. The intention was that CMAPP should be a medium-term rolling plan covering 3-year cycles. It should provide detailed guidance for the first cycle and indicative guidance afterward. Within the MAPP, there were to be three separate plans, a Municipal Reforms Action Plan, a Municipal Infrastructure Action Plan, and a Social Development Action Plan (Centre for Good Governance, 2008).

To produce the MAPP, the various stakeholders came together in two working groups. Working Group 1 focused on improvements in municipal performance and Working Group 2 on poverty, paying particular attention to the infrastructure needs of low-income settlements. The municipal reform component responded to the Government of India's municipal reform concerns, as set out in its Eighth and Ninth Five-Year Plans. These included:

- introduction of accrual-based double entry accounting systems;
- property tax rationalization;
- improved financial management, leading to an improved cash balance and improved investment capability;
- introduction of improved budgeting methods;
- introduction of e-governance systems;
- institutional capacity-building;
- measures to reduce municipal expenditure in relation to value of services delivered.

The list shows the strong focus on improved financial management and performance. Some reforms had lasting effects, for instance, energy studies carried out under the project led to the creation of the Andhra Pradesh State Energy Conservation Mission, which regularly wins awards for implementing improved energy conservation measures. However, these outcomes had neither relevance to nor impact on government policies on informality and action on housing needs. And land reform was noticeably absent from

Poverty →

Environmental infrastructure deficiency ↓

SCORE	1	2	3
1	1/1	2/1	3/1
2	1/2	2/2	3/2
3	1/3	2/3	3/3 (Priority settlements)

Figure 8.2 3 × 3 matrix for ranking low-income settlements

the municipal reform agenda (Oxford Policy Management Asia and CRISIL Infrastructure Advisory, 2013). The project did have a strong emphasis on municipal capacity-building, with training materials prepared for municipal planners and engineers, which were delivered in conjunction with state and national training institutions based in and around Hyderabad, Andhra Pradesh's then capital.

Working Group 2 placed all eligible low-income settlements into a 3 × 3 matrix, increasing levels of poverty indicated along one axis and decreasing levels of infrastructure provision indicated along the other, as shown in Figure 8.2.

Settlements with the highest poverty levels and greatest infrastructure deficiencies were selected for inclusion in the BMAPP. Before final selection, they were screened to ensure that the planning process had been objective and had not been subjected to political pressures, and the project team then facilitated a micro-planning exercise in each of the chosen settlements. The matrix approach was far from perfect. In the first instance, at least, rankings were based on secondary information, which was not always accurate. Nevertheless, it did provide a simple format for representing the relative needs of different settlements. Stakeholders liked it for its transparency, despite the fact that some raised questions about the data and indicators being used. However, its greatest benefit was arguably its role in channelling available funds to areas of greatest need rather than distributing them evenly across all settlements and thus diluting their impact (Dove, 2004).

One weakness related to the scope of interventions. The government project director initially insisted that sanitation should be excluded from the project on the grounds that it was already covered by the Government of India's Integrated Low-cost Sanitation (ILCS) programme. The reality was that there were significant problems with the ILCS programme. For instance, many of the latrines were not being used, others were not being used as designed, and many poor people, particularly women, had no access to conveniently located sanitation facilities (Tayler, 2005).

Project interventions did lead to significant investment in slum infrastructure, particularly water supply. Between 2001 and 2007, 2,720 km of water main was laid and more than 20 water tanks were constructed, benefiting a population of about 2.7 million. The project evaluation also refers to the provision of protected water supply to 265,000 slum residents. It is not clear what this relates to, but it may mean provision of water from local tube wells, with or without local distribution systems. APUSP schemes aimed to provide individual house connections at a subsidized fee of Rs.1,200 (about $27), with water in the system for at least 2–3 hours per day (Centre for Good Governance, 2008). This limited aim reflects the reality of the appalling levels of service provided by many municipal water supply schemes in India. The author's visits to APUSP towns revealed that many towns provided water for even shorter periods as well as many operational problems. Treatment was often ineffective, with clarifiers silted and sand filters mixed with mud. Chlorinators were invariably broken, and staff had to inject chlorine directly into the water to be treated, leading to the release of free chlorine, which had a deleterious effect on the system's concrete structures. Few towns metered their water and bulk water meters were either absent or non-functional. These deficient operational practices in municipal water systems raise serious doubts about improving local water supplies by relying on these systems.

The project did make considerable efforts to support improved planning, design, implementation, and management of municipal infrastructure services. The consultant team produced training manuals and efforts were made to incorporate these into the curriculum of local training institutions, including the Engineering Staff College of India, but, unfortunately, these institutions tended to be rather academic and it proved difficult to find lecturers with practical rather than theoretical understanding of municipal water supply systems. In parallel with training, municipalities were encouraged to collect and record information on their assets, develop an asset register and produce an operation and maintenance plan, incorporating comments for stakeholders (Centre for Good Governance, 2008). The approach reflects mainstream thinking in its emphasis on registering assets. In the case of water supply, the impact of the operation and maintenance plans may have been limited by:

- The lack of information on water production and flows through the system, which are impossible to determine accurately without metering.
- The poor condition of many facilities, which makes it difficult or impossible to operate them correctly.
- The tendency for municipal engineers to focus on new works rather than operation and maintenance of existing systems, leaving day-to-day operational decisions to operational staff, who have practical knowledge but limited powers, for instance, to order consumables and replacement parts.

There is little information on APUSP's impact on sanitation and wastewater disposal systems, but given the initial reluctance of the project director to include sanitation in the project, it is likely to have been limited. One exception was the town of Ramagundum, where APUSP facilitated the construction of localized shallow sewer systems in 13 low- and lower-middle-income communities over the period 2002–2008. The sewers discharged to communal septic tanks and served around 3,800 households in total, with a population of about 22,500. A review of the scheme in 2012 found that the systems were working well 4–6 years after construction, with residents taking responsibility for occasional maintenance tasks (Nema, n.d.). It seems that municipality engineers were involved in the designs.

Turning to APUSP's long-term impact on the practices and procedures of the Andhra Pradesh government, Centre for Good Governance (2008) stated that the preparation of a MAPP every five years was mandatory for all municipalities in Andhra Pradesh. This requirement was to be incorporated into Andhra Pradesh's Model Municipal Law. A Government Order issued by the State of Andhra Pradesh mandated all urban local bodies (ULBs) to follow the matrix process for allocation of all types of funds, with each ULB allocating 40 per cent of its budget for pro-poor service delivery. Projects in Andhra Pradesh funded by the World Bank and the Government of India were to follow the matrix methodology. The Bank's Social and Environmental Assessment and Management Framework for Andhra Pradesh Municipal Development Department confirms that the project used the CMAPP process to identify sub-project investments, but it notes that sub-projects were identified by town-level committees and that the strategies prepared by these committees had not trickled down to the general community.

Overall, it seems that APUSP's impacts have mainly related to wider governance issues and provision of water supplies, with little impact on the approach to housing. As in other Indian states, housing policy is strongly influenced by the national housing policies and programmes that have already been described in Chapter 4.

Madhya Pradesh urban services for the poor

MPUSP ran from 2006 to 2012. It initially worked in the four largest cities in Madhya Pradesh, Bhopal (Photos 8.1–8.3), Indore, Jabalpur, and Gwalior (Photos 8.4–8.5), but later expanded to cover a further 10 towns. It was located within the Urban Administration and Development Department (UADD) of the Government of Madhya Pradesh. The DFID consultants for the project had also been consultants for APUSP. It is therefore not surprising that MPUSP mirrored APUSP in its use of MAPPs, the 3 × 3 neighbourhood identification matrix, and a pyramidal social organization structure based on neighbourhood self-help groups. It differed from APUSP in its increased focus on facilitating change at the state government level and its emphasis on helping cities to meet their commitments under the Federal Government's Jawaharlal Nehru National Urban Renewal Mission (JNNURM). In the first four cities, MPUSP was implemented in parallel with the ADB-funded Urban Water Supply and Environmental Improvement Project (UWSEIP). The project design assumed

Photo 8.1 Bhopal: leaking pipe. Author's own

Photo 8.2 Bhopal: second resettlement area. Author's own

Photo 8.3 Bhopal: upgraded slum. Author's own

Photo 8.4 Gwalior: urban fringe informal development. Author's own

Photo 8.5 Gwalior: vertical expansion. Author's own

that UWSEIP's city-wide infrastructure improvements would support MPUSP efforts to improve in-slum infrastructure.

As with APUSP, the focus of municipal reforms was on improving financial performance, e-governance, and energy efficiency. The project also developed training materials, which were used as part of its capacity-building remit. Training courses covered engineering, planning, and social development aspects of slum upgrading. At the State level, the project aimed to assist government in developing supportive public policy, but there is no evidence that this extended in any significant way to policies for dealing with informal development. Action on land reform and secure tenure was absent and slum upgrading efforts largely catered for settlements in which residents had already been issued with *pattas*, a land deed issued by the government (Oxford Policy Management Asia and CRISIL Infrastructure Advisory, 2013). The introduction of an automated building permission approval system should have, in theory, helped to remove obstacles to formalizing building construction. No information is available on this, but it is likely that the benefits were experienced in unregulated developments rather than slums. DFID's Project Completion Review for MPUSP refers to its role in developing slum databases for participating cities. This MPUSP upgrading plan suggested three intervention options:

- *In situ upgrading and improvement* – appropriate for slums on land designated for residential use, with most houses constructed from permanent materials.

- *In situ redevelopment* – appropriate for slums on land designated for residential use in which existing housing and infrastructure conditions are poor.
- *Relocation* – appropriate for slums on land that is either unsuitable or not designated for residential use, and for households whose continued residence is considered untenable, despite the fact that the slums in which they live are on land designated for residential use.

The plan is dated May 2013 and was produced by the JNNURM cell in Indore Corporation and is not, therefore, directly attributable to MPUSP, but it is reasonable to assume that MPUSP had a role in preparing the ground for the plan exercise.

MPUSP did engage with slum upgrading on a significant scale, with 130 slum settlements upgraded in the four cities. Nevertheless, it is likely that the project had limited influence on policies for dealing with informal settlements. Early in the project, government officials arranged site visits for the consultants to supposedly informal areas but all of these were either redevelopment or resettlement sites. The assumption that redevelopment and resettlement are the best 'upgrading' options probably persisted, despite the best efforts of the MPUSP consultants.

Considerable efforts were made to develop women-only community groups in the project towns. As with APUSP, the building blocks for these efforts were neighbourhood groups, known as Basti Vikas Samiti or BVSs, and 130 BVSs were registered across the 14 project towns. These were involved in articulation of needs, development of needs-based plans, and monitoring of slum development. As in other similar projects, BVSs were expected to take responsibility for the management of solid waste collection services and maintenance of in-slum infrastructure. The Project Completion Review, produced in December 2012, stated that it was too early to say whether BVSs would continue to practice their core roles post MPUSP. However, experience elsewhere, described in earlier chapters of this book, suggests that effective community management structures are difficult to sustain in the absence of significant and continued institutional support. The Project Completion Review's observations that no BVS federation had been established at city level, and that peer-to-peer communication was weak, lend support to the view that community structures may have struggled to outlive MPUSP.

The project had a limited impact on water supply services in slums. The DFID Project Completion Review does state the finding of an independent evaluation that households in MPUSP were 32 per cent more likely than those in non-MPUSP slums to have access to piped water. However, the overall hours of supply in MPUSP slums remained similar to those in the rest of the city, with 57 per cent of households receiving water for less than one hour daily. The short supply periods and poor water pressures show that there were problems with integrating in-slum improvements implemented under MPUSP with off-site improvements implemented through UWSEIP. Yet again, these problems point to the need to integrate slum upgrading efforts with wider municipal service improvements. They are perhaps also indicative of a belief, widespread in India, that intermittent water supplies can provide an acceptable level of service.

The Project Completion Review states that 5,619 households accessed improved sanitation under MPUSP. Around 25 per cent of these improvements were toilets that were constructed by households themselves, with the remainder constructed by contractors hired by self-help groups. As with water supply, the issues with sanitation are likely to relate to connections with wider municipal systems. It might be assumed that such connections are not required for on-site facilities such as pour-flush toilets connected to either leach pits or septic tanks, but these facilities will depend on the availability of reliable sludge emptying and removal systems. The review found no significant impact on sewerage and drainage facilities in MPUSP slums as compared with their non-MPUSP counterparts. Taken together, the findings on water supply, drainage, and sanitation suggest that the project had limited success in linking improvements in individual settlements into wider municipal systems.

Later projects such as MPUSP and Support Programme for Urban Reforms attempted to solve this problem by diverting focus to the state government level and setting up Technical Assistance Support Teams, which would directly support the host department responsible for municipal reform. However, now, a different problem arose. This arrangement diverted the focus of implementation largely to the state level, neglecting actual implementation at the level of the municipalities. Municipal bodies would thus often have little idea about how to proceed with a reform, and sometimes conditions were not conducive to promote these reforms. In response, the financial assistance component offered by DFID also sought to place 'city support units' covering one or more cities to assist cities in implementation, but results have largely been mixed.

One of the project aims was to set up a municipal training centre, but this did not materialize. It was intended that community funds would be used for day-to-day maintenance work but there was pressure from elected representatives for the funds to come under their own discretionary funds. Also, elected representatives resisted the increased role for professional staff, who they perceived as a challenge to their discretionary powers.

It should be noted that APUSP and MPUSP both facilitated the setting up of dedicated poverty alleviation units with the urban local authorities to coordinate and take forward all urban poverty programmes. These organizations have been sustained beyond the project periods and have helped the state to engage with communities.

A follow-on phase, sometimes referred to as MPUSP 2 but also as Madhya Pradesh Urban Infrastructure Investment Programme (MPUIIP), included a Madhya Pradesh Urban Investment Fund and support to efforts to set up a Public/Private Sector Partnership cell in the UADD. It covered 14 towns and cities. Reference is made to this follow-on phase having aided poor women to access land/title, and also to having secured access to improved drinking water for 90,000 poor people through service level benchmarking-related interventions. Also it was intended to provide linkages with JNNURM, including implementing a participatory approach to provision of basic services to poor communities, the earmarking of pro-poor funds, and support to the preparation of city development plans, as well as the strengthening of urban poverty cells.

Notes

1. The Cities Alliance was anchored at the World Bank in Washington until 2013, at which point it came under the auspices of the UN Office of Operational Services and its headquarters was moved to Brussels.
2. General information about CODI activities can be found on its website: https://en.codi.or.th

References

Ballard, R. and Rubin, M. (2018) Why megaprojects to deliver houses in South Africa might not work, *The Conversation*, 24 May. https://theconversation.com/why-megaprojects-to-deliver-houses-in-south-africa-might-not-work-94139 (accessed 19 December 2019).

Beukes, A. (2015) *Making the invisible visible: Generating data on 'slums' at local city and global scales*, IIED/SDI Working Paper, IIED, London. https://sdinet.org/wp-content/uploads/2016/02/10757IIED-1.pdf (accessed 6 July 2025).

Bhatkal, T. and Lucci, P. (2015) *Community-driven development in the slums: Thailand's experience*, Overseas Development Institute, London. https://media.odi.org/documents/9668.pdf (accessed 19 August 2025).

Boonyabancha, S. (2005) Baan Mankong: going to scale with 'slum' and squatter upgrading in Thailand, *Environment and Urbanization*, 17(1): 21–46. https://doi.org/10.1177/095624780501700104

Boonyabancha, S. (2009) Land for housing the poor – by the poor: experiences from the Baan Mankong nationwide slum upgrading programme in Thailand, *Environment and Urbanization*, 21(2): 309–329. https://doi.org/10.1177/0956247809342180

Boonyabancha, S. and Kerr, T. (2018) Lessons from CODI on co-production, *Environment and Urbanization*, 30(2): 444–460. https://doi.org/10.1177/0956247818791239

Buckley, R. and Kalarickal, J. (2006) *Thirty years of World Bank shelter lending: what have we learned*, Washington, DC: World Bank. https://documents1.worldbank.org/curated/en/958091468159898471/pdf/362170PAPER0re10 1OFFICIAL0USE0ONLY1.pdf (accessed 19 August 2025).

Buckley, R., Kallergis, A. and Deusk, C. (2014) *The Asian Coalition for Community Action's Approach to Slum Upgrading*, East Asia and Pacific Sustainable Infrastructure Unit, The World Bank. http://documents.worldbank.org/curated/en/892901468027633257/pdf/902680WP0ACCA000Box385309B0 0PUBLIC0.pdf (accessed 20 January 2020).

Centre for Good Governance (2008) *Lessons learnt document on municipal service delivery for the poor in Andhra Pradesh*. https://www.cgg.gov.in/wp-content/uploads/2017/07/08050158_CG_BK01_120p.pdf (accessed 19 August 2025).

Cities Alliance (2006) *Guide to city development strategies: improving urban performance*, Washington, DC. https://www.877gethope.org/generated/uploads/frankel/Repurposing%20Strategies/Strategies%20-%20Catalytic%20Redevelopment/Comprehensive%20Redevelopment%20Strategies/Cities%20Alliance%20Redevelopment%20Guide.pdf (accessed 17 August 2025).

Cities Alliance (2008) *Cities Alliance annual report 2008*, Washington, DC. https://www.citiesalliance.org/resources/publications/annual-reports/annual-report-2008 (accessed 19 August 2025).

Cities Alliance (2016) *Cities Alliance annual report 2016*, Washington, DC. https://www.citiesalliance.org/resources/publications/annual-reports/annual-report-2016 (accessed 19 August 2025).

Community Organizations Development Institute (CODI) (2019) *Baan Mankong, Thailand's national, people driven, collective housing program*. https://web.codi.or.th/wp-content/uploads/2019/05/baan-mankong-280959.pdf (accessed 19 August 2025).

Department for International Development (DFID) (2001) *Meeting the challenge of poverty in urban areas*, paper in the series 'Strategies for achieving the international development targets'. https://alnap.org/help-library/resources/meeting-the-challenge-of-poverty-in-urban-areas/ (accessed 24 August 2025).

Dove, L. (2004) Providing environmental urban services to the poor in Andhra Pradesh: developing strategic decision-making, *Environment & Urbanization*, 16(1): 95–106. https://doi.org/10.1177/095624780401600108

Dubey, V. (1985) *Policy based lending and the World Bank*, Washington, DC: World Bank Group. http://documents.worldbank.org/curated/en/418021487215433223/Policy-based-lending-and-the-World-Bank (accessed 27 December 2019).

Fieuw, W. and Mitlin, D. (2017) What the experiences of South Africa's mass housing programme teach us about the contribution of civil society to policy and programme reform, *Environment and Urbanization*, 30(1): 215–32. https://doi.org/10.1177/0956247817735768

Gruffydd Jones, B. (2010) 'Cities Without Slums'? Global architectures of power and the African city, in K. Bakker (ed.), *The African city centre (re) sourced*, pp. 57–68. Pretoria: University of Pretoria.

Hendler, Y. and Fieuw, W. (2018) *Exploring partnerships with local government: A people's led approach to informal settlement upgrading*. CORC, Cape Town. https://www.sasdialliance.org.za/wp-content/uploads/2018/11/Upgrading_Publication_CORC_2018_SML.pdf (accessed 19 December 2019).

Huchzermeyer, M. (2006) How to improve the lives of 100 million slum dwellers by 2020, *UN Chronicle*, 43(2).

Hutt, D. (2018) The trouble with Cambodia's affordable housing plan: the effort is neither affordable nor well-planned, *The Diplomat*, 14 November. https://thediplomat.com/2018/11/the-trouble-with-cambodias-affordable-housing-plan/ (accessed 21 January 2019)

Juhasz, A. and Rahman, A. (2013) *The Gopalganj Model: a way forward for community driven affordable urban housing*, UNDP. https://web.archive.org/web/20200109053230/https://www.undp.org/content/dam/bangladesh/docs/Projects/UPPR/Gopalganj%20Housing%20Brochure%2020.08.13.pdf (accessed 19 September 2025).

Livengood, A. and Kunte, K. (2012) Enabling participatory planning with GIS: a case study of settlement mapping in Cuttack, India, *Environment and Urbanization*, 24(1): 77–97. https://doi.org/10.1177/0956247811434360

Makau, J., Dobson, S. and Samia, E. (2012), The five-city enumeration: the role of participatory enumerations in developing community capacity and partnerships with government in Uganda, *Environment and Urbanization*, 24(1): 31–46. https://doi.org/10.1177/0956247812438368

Nadkarny, S. and Anderson, M. (no date) Slum Upgrading in Thailand: CODI, http://healthycities.berkeley.edu/uploads/1/2/6/1/12619988/thailand.pdf (accessed 21 January 2020; no longer available).

Nazem, N.U. and Hossain, A. (2012) Mapping poor settlements in 27 cities and towns of Bangladesh, UPPR experience. *CUS Bulletin on Urbanization and Development* No. 60–62.

Nema, A. (no date) *Performance assessment of off-grid simplified sewerage systems in Ramagundam municipality*, PSeau. https://www.pseau.org/sites/default/files/fichiers/r_d/case-study_non-conventional-sewers_india.pdf (accessed 27 February 2020).

Oxford Policy Management Asia and CRISIL Infrastructure Advisory (2013) *Research into lessons learnt from DFID India urban investments over 20 Years. Final report.* Oxford Policy Management Asia, New Delhi; CRISIL, Mumbai. https://assets.publishing.service.gov.uk/media/57a08a0b40f0b652dd00052c/India_Urban_Review_Final_Report.pdf (accessed 17 January 2019).

Parsons, A. (2010) *The seven myths of 'slums': challenging the prejudices about the world's urban poor*, Share the World's Resources, London. https://www.sharing.org/sites/default/files/images/PDFs/7_myths_report%20%282%29.pdf (accessed 22 March 2019).

Patel, S. (2014) *South-South Knowledge Creation and Transfers to Address the Challenges of Inclusion for the Urban Poor: India and South Africa*, Institute of Development Studies, Brighton. http://www.mspguide.org/sites/default/files/case/3_web.pdf (accessed 5 April 2019; no longer available).

Rahman, A. (2019) *Housing solutions for the urban poor in Bangladesh* [Blog] LIUPCP, 6 March. https://www.undp.org/bangladesh/press-releases/housing-solutions-urban-poor-bangladesh (accessed 31 August 2025).

Shack/Slum Dwellers International (SDI) (2013) *Strategic Plan 2013–2017*, SDI, Cape Town, South Africa. https://sdinet.org/wp-content/uploads/2015/08/2013-17_SDI-Strategic-Plan.pdf (accessed 19 December 2019).

SDI (2018) *Strategic Plan 2018–2022*, SDI, Cape Town, South Africa. https://sdinet.org/wp-content/uploads/2018/05/SDI_StrategicReport_Pages_422.pdf (accessed 19 December2019).

Shand, W. (2018) Making spaces for co-production: collaborative action for settlement upgrading in Harare, Zimbabwe, *Environment and Urbanization*, 30(2): 519–536. https://doi.org/10.1177/0956247818783962

Simiya, E. and Mbaka, N. (2011) Mapping process in Mrima-Mombasa [blog], 18 October. Muungano wa Wanavijiji, Nairobi. https://www.muungano.net/browseblogs/2011/10/18/mapping-process-in-mrima-mombasa (accessed 5 February 2020).

Spora Sinergies (2016) *Urban poverty reduction in Bangladesh: The UPPR experience, documentation of UPPR learning and good practice, abridged version*, United Nations Development Programme (UNDP) Urban Partnerships for Poverty Reduction project. http://www.spora.ws/wp-content/uploads/2016/05/2016.eng_.-Urban-Poverty-Reduction-in-Bangladesh-The-UPPR-Experience-Spora1.pdf (accessed 12 February 2020).

Tayler, K. (2005) Two participatory projects in South Asia, *Proceedings of the Institution of Civil Engineers, Municipal Engineer*, 58(1). https://doi.org/10.1680/muen.2005.158.1.37

Van Waeyenberge, E. (2017) Crisis? What crisis? A critical appraisal of World Bank housing policy in the wake of the global financial crisis, *Environment and Planning A: Economy and Space*, 50(2): 288–309. https://doi.org/10.1177%2F0308518X17745873

Wangkiat, P. (2012) Govt urged to free up B3bn, *Bangkok Times*, 9 November. https://www.bangkokpost.com/thailand/politics/320277/govt-urged-to-free-up-b3bn#google_vignette (accessed 17 August 2025).

CHAPTER 9
Review: Challenges and possibilities

Previous chapters have shown that informal settlements and poor-quality housing continue to be important features of urban development in the South. Attempts to deal with this situation, whether originating with governments, international agencies, the private sector or non-governmental organizations (NGOs), have had only a limited impact on the housing conditions of the poor. Not only this, but over the decades the number of people living in slums and informal settlements has been increasing, very often at rates higher than country averages for urban population growth.

There is clearly a need for new thinking, leading to new strategies and action plans. But how should such new thinking be defined and developed? Nothing is to be gained by going back to failed policies and approaches and attempting to implement them as in the past. On the other hand, there is much to be learnt from our past experience. To take one example, Chapter 6 showed that some sites and services projects were effective in providing good quality housing at a reasonably affordable price. The alliances of the poor described in Chapter 8 may not have achieved city-wide change, but their impact could expand if basic constraints could be overcome. Similarly, it is reasonable to ask whether lessons from the Community Led Infrastructure Finance Facility (CLIFF) could inform new approaches to financing housing for the poor.

In other words, new strategies must take account of the lessons from past experiences and the factors that influenced project and programme outcomes, prominent among which are constraining factors. These lessons must then be considered in the light of the existing situation. Too often, housing initiatives have started from where their instigators would like to be rather than where they actually find themselves and have then either ignored or glossed over the institutional and other constraints that stand in the way of successful implementation.

With these points in mind, this chapter draws on the theoretical thinking outlined in Chapters 3 and 4 and the lessons from the project and programme experience described in Chapters 5–8 to identify key factors in any situation. It pays particular attention to constraints. Points emerging from this chapter are then used to inform the proposals for action set out in Chapter 10.

The varied nature of informal development

Any responses to informal development must recognize that informal settlements are not all the same. A basic distinction is that between settlement on land belonging to others and settlements created by subdivision and sale of privately held land without reference to official slum and building regulations. Most settlements in the first category are built on government-owned land, much of it marginal. Settlements in the second category include unregulated subdivisions carried out by farmers with plots sold piecemeal, schemes laid out by 'developers', who assemble the land, subdivide it, provide minimal services, and then sell the plots to individual householders. But this dichotomy does not begin to describe the rich variety of types of informal settlements and the ways they grow and evolve.

For example, settlements differ from each other physically. Many are clearly identifiable by their irregular site layouts and narrow rights of way. Others reproduce the patterns found in their more formal counterparts but with smaller plot sizes, reduced rights of way and limited provision of public facilities and open space. Some settlements are distinguishable by their use of poor-quality building materials, while others use similar building techniques to those used by their formal sector counterparts. In most cases, open space is at a premium, but some developers leave open space for parks, as was the case in Shadab Colony in Faisalabad, described in Chapter 7. In other cases, privately or publicly owned land is present but is unavailable because it is flooded. The following paragraphs show examples of these patterns of informal settlement.

Korail is one of the largest informal settlements in Bangladesh, covering about 36 ha and housing an estimated 20,000 families. It includes both houses and small businesses, almost all built from corrugated metal sheets on a wood or precast concrete framework. Rights of way are extremely narrow and fires occur fairly frequently. The long, relatively narrow shapes of the buildings are typical of those containing rows of single room dwellings, built for rent. The buildings can rise to a height of two or occasionally three storeys. Korail is just across the water from Gulshan, perhaps the wealthiest area in Dhaka, and the contrast is obvious.

Borobag forms part of a large unplanned area lying south of the centre of Mirpur, Pakistan. This area extends up to 3 km in most directions and covers an area of around 900 ha. Most of the houses are built from permanent materials and many are large but the layout has no regularity. Access is by a maze of narrow lanes, many less than 3 m in width with occasional 5-m 'streets'. There is no way that this area could be labelled a slum but its development can certainly be classed as informal.

In Cairo an informal area, *Boulaq el Dakrour*, lies next to part of the high-income Dokki District with the main railway line from Cairo to the south running between them. Both are regularly laid out and contain mainly medium-rise apartment buildings, built using reinforced concrete frame with brick or blockwork infill walls. The obvious difference between the two lies in the space standards adopted. Like the Borobag, Boulaq el Dakrour is best described as an unregulated subdivision rather than a slum. The rights of way and space allowed between buildings is much greater in Dokki District than in Boulaq el Dakrour.

The three examples illustrate another important distinction: that between houses occupied by their owners and those built specifically for rent. Korail contains many units built for rent, as do similar informal areas in other cities, for instance Kibera in Nairobi. The medium-rise and occasional higher-rise buildings in Boulaq el Dakrour are subdivided into apartments, most of which are sold but many are rented out. The situation is complicated by the fact that, as already noted in Chapter 6, many 'owner-occupiers' in informal settlements build additional rooms for rent. In any event, a key point is that John Turner's ideas were based on the situation in Peru, where informal settlement took forms closer to those found in Boulaq el Dakrour and Borobag than in Korail. He might have reached rather different conclusions if confronted with the situation in poor-quality units built specifically for rent.

It is not necessarily the case that informal housing built with permanent materials is structurally inferior to formal housing. Almost all the building collapses during Cairo's 1992 earthquake occurred in either dilapidated historic parts of the city or in formal developments such as Heliopolis and Nasr City rather than in informal areas (Sims, 2010). The buildings in the Mirpur unregulated subdivision appear to be reasonably sound. In contrast, Korail's buildings are of poor quality and built from materials that will have a limited life.

Not only are there wide variations between informal settlements, it must also be recognized that informal settlements change over time. The author worked on environmental improvement proposals for informal settlements in Howrah in the mid-1990s, under the Calcutta Environmental Management Strategy and Action Plan. At that time, it was obvious that private developers were replacing low-rise *thika* tenancy holdings with medium-rise apartment blocks. Through this strictly illegal process, existing tenants were rehoused in small, dark apartments on the ground floor while apartments on higher floors were either sold or rented for profit.

These comparisons illustrate two key points. First, that conclusions based on the situation in one city or neighbourhood may not apply to all cities and neighbourhoods in or beyond the country in which the city is situated. Second, conditions should be expected to change over time. In an area such as Boulaq el Dakrour, this change may amount to nothing more than an increase in building heights and hence an increase in housing density. The example of Howrah shows that, given the right set of social and economic circumstances, the change can be much more fundamental. Some changes take place gradually. Others take place fairly rapidly, following cataclysmic events. For instance, Kolkata's informal settlements include both slums that formed as a result of industrialization and those developed to house refugees after partition in 1947 and the Bangladesh war of independence in 1971 (Schenk, 2010).

The important point to take from this review of possible physical, institutional, and social arrangements is that any attempt to engage with informal development must start from an understanding grounded in local realities and the way that they change over time. Other points to be taken into account are summarized below.

Formality and informality

As noted in Chapter 3, a binary division between formal and informal systems and procedures simplifies what is often a much more complex reality. Nevertheless, the examples included earlier in this chapter show that there are often clear physical distinctions between areas developed through essentially formal and informal means. These examples illustrate the further point that informal settlements are often physically separated from their formal neighbours. In Cairo, the railway separates Boulaq el Dakrour from Dokki and there is only one linking bridge between the two. In a similar way, Korail is separated from Gulshan by a lake. Although directly abutting onto formal areas to the north and west, Korail can only be accessed by one road and a pedestrian path along the side of the lake.

Social separation may be less visible but is no less prevalent. Take for instance the example of Cairo. The views of the character Abdallah in the extract from the short story *Dregs of the City* (Chapter 2) are not untypical of the way in which middle class Cairenes view informal areas. Few have ever visited them and most have only a hazy notion of what life is like within them. In the 2000s, the author accompanied a public official with responsibility for fire services into the informal areas lying west of the Cairo to Upper Egypt railway line. A highly educated man with a PhD from a French university, he worked from an office located no more than 800 metres as the crow flies from the informal settlements in Boulaq el Dakrour. Cairo's informal areas can hardly be described as slums and yet he was genuinely shocked to find that some of his fellow citizens were living in what he viewed as terrible conditions and repeatedly asked how this could be allowed to happen.

The combination of lack of knowledge and preconceived notions about life in informal areas gives rise to the prevailing idea in 'respectable' society that informal settlements should be demolished and replaced with proper housing. Even when the concept of *in situ* upgrading is accepted, the tendency is to treat individual informal settlements as separate entities in isolation from the surrounding urban fabric. This can affect infrastructure choices, with on-site options such as handpumps and on-site sanitation preferred to connections to municipal water mains and sewers.

Some organizations and concepts, for instance the Orangi Pilot Project (OPP) and Himanchu Parikh's slum networking concept, stress the need to tie informal areas into the wider city. Their focus is on infrastructure rather than the less tangible subject of how informal areas are viewed by the city authorities and society as a whole. There is little doubt that most government officials and people living and working in the formal sector see informality as something other. Yusuf Idris's fictional judge Abdallah, introduced in Chapter 2, certainly started with this attitude. However, the evidence suggests that attitudinal and socio-economic factors are often as important as physical barriers in keeping people apart. Mardhotillah and Gamal (2018) studied the interaction between an informal settlement and its formal neighbours in Cikini, an area located close to the centre of Jakarta with good transport links. A wall separated the informal settlement from an adjacent formal area with only a single gate allowing pedestrian access. The real significance of the wall lay in its role as a physical symbol of segregation in Cikini, based on differences between economic and social classes. The formal part of Cikini had benefited from its location, with land values and commercial activity increasing over the years. In contrast, the informal area still suffered from poor housing conditions and services, conditions made worse by densification as people seeking cheap housing moved into the settlement. The economic opportunities available to its residents were limited to low-income jobs and street vending on sidewalks. Likewise, a study in Mexico found that, while segregation levels at the macro level were not becoming more polarized, boundaries between adjacent neighbourhoods had hardened as people turned to forms of gated communities, largely for security reasons, and access between adjacent neighbourhoods housing people of different classes was becoming ever more restricted. The differences between higher- and lower-income communities could be attributed, at least in part, to differential access to land markets (Ward, 2009).

The main point to take from these examples is that there are significant barriers to the integration of informal areas into the city as a whole. These are attributable not so much to informality itself but to socio-economic factors and preconceived notions. One key lesson is that integration within the growing city will only be possible when the area of land designated for lower-income residential areas is greatly increased.

Existing housing and service production systems

The statistics and examples given in this book illustrate the important role played by the informal sector in housing production. This role is exercised predominantly but not exclusively in the low-income housing market segments and mostly involves owner-builders and petty contractors, producing what Rod Burgess described as 'manufactured housing'. The housing produced varies considerably and not all housing is easily upgradable. For instance, a 2001 study of Mumbai slums found that 42 per cent of slum dwellings had an area of less than 10 m^2, 38 per cent between 15 and 20 m^2, and only 9 per cent above 20 m^2 (Montgomery and Yuva, 2001, quoted by Repestro, 2010). It is true that Burgess's industrialized form of housing production dominates formal sector provision in many countries, such as in Egypt where large real estate companies include SODIC, Emaar, Talaat Moustafa, Roya, and Orascom (Sims, 2010). Searches of the websites of these and similar companies active in other countries reveal that they almost always target higher-income customers. Many market their housing schemes as idealized communities, emphasizing their green surroundings and modern lifestyle amenities. None provide housing that is affordable to the lower half of the urban household income distribution and it is clear that they do not offer an alternative to informal development.

The situation with regard to building materials is more nuanced. Processes that require expensive specialized plant, including production of cement and the galvanized corrugated steel sheets that are widely used in informal sector production, are dominated by large-scale companies. The same cannot be said of brick production, which in many countries takes place in a large number of relatively small brick factories, using predominantly manual production methods. The precast concrete components that are commonly used in house and infrastructure construction are produced in small, often informal, casting yards. However, distribution systems for these components, as for brick and indeed cement, are relatively small scale and informal. As with housing production, the existing situation bears little relation to the housing production processes identified by Burgess. Informal systems play a major role in both housing and building materials production and there is no evidence that this is likely to change in the foreseeable future.

Formal utility services do exist in some informal areas, although again there is much variation. Cairo's informal settlements enjoy water supply, sewerage, and electricity coverage levels that are almost identical with those in formal areas, although the quality and reliability of these services are much lower (Sims, 2010: 106). However, this high level of coverage for all three services is the exception rather than the rule and most informal areas suffer from service deficiencies, even after upgrading. Electricity is usually the first service to be provided and coverage is usually higher than that of either water supply or sanitation. Drawing on data from the 2004–2005 Indian Human Development Survey (IHDS), which covered 40,000 households across India, Aklin et al. (2015) found a 93 per cent electrification rate among slum households. It is not clear whether this figure refers to the availability of electricity or to connections but it is only marginally lower than the 95 per cent rate that they found for general urban areas. The situation regarding continuity of supply was less satisfactory, with electricity only available for an average of about 15.5 hours each day. Electrification rates in African informal areas are likely to be much lower. Regardless of availability, electricity services in informal areas are often unsatisfactory, with frequent blackouts and fluctuating voltage. These deficiencies are attributable partly to lack of system capacity, which impacts disproportionally on informal areas, and partly to the frequently haphazard way in which distribution systems are extended into informal areas.

Where groundwater is available, residents of informal areas often obtain water from wells and boreholes. Water mains may extend into unregulated subdivisions, but the supply from those mains is likely to be intermittent and at low pressure. Extension of municipal systems into so-called slum areas is less common. In most cases, water is delivered to shared stand pipes rather than individual house connections. Supply periods may be very short, and some informal settlements in India receive water at intervals of three days or more. 'Pit taps', located below ground level in order to access water delivered at extremely low pressure, are not uncommon in South Asia. In the absence of adequate municipal services, many informal settlement residents rely on private sector providers, almost all operating informally. Many transport water in vehicles and carts but there are examples of privately constructed water supply and distribution systems, mainly in places where groundwater can be accessed fairly easily. Collignon and Chaponniere (2011) described the situation in peri-urban areas of Maputo, Mozambique, where around 450 informal businesses were providing water to about 500,000 people through about 55,000 house connections and 450 standpipes. About 50 of these enterprises maintained systems with more than 200 connections, together sharing about 48 per cent of the private sector market. Conan (2004) found that small-scale water providers served around 44 per cent of households in Jakarta, Indonesia and 36 per cent of households in Cebu, the Philippines. Where individual households and local systems are served from deep boreholes, the water quality at source will not necessarily be worse than that provided through municipal systems, although contamination is likely during distribution and transport.

Many studies have shown that water purchased from private suppliers is more expensive than that obtained from public networked systems. This is not necessarily because private sector suppliers, most of which operate informally, make excessive profits. Rather, their charges are high because the unit cost of water supplied by water carriers and standpost operators is invariably higher than that supplied via an individual connection to a networked system. A study in Nepal found that poor households were likely to pay much more for water and one important factor was access: charges were higher in areas where narrow rights of way restricted access for water tankers (Raina et al., 2020).

Residents of newly established informal areas often depend on on-site sanitation systems, discharging toilet wastes to on-site soakaway pits and water from bathrooms and kitchens either to the same pits or to open drains. It is not uncommon for landlords, local elected representatives or community members to construct local sewers. Photo 9.1 shows an informally built sewer in Kamrangir Char, an informal area on the outskirts of Dhaka. The lane shown in the photograph is representative of the whole area, almost all of which is informally sewered. The sewers are of poor quality, are laid with minimal fall, and discharge untreated wastewater to the nearby river. However, they exist and provide a service, albeit one that is rather unsatisfactory. The author's investigations revealed similar arrangements in other parts of Dhaka, including those such as Korail that are viewed as slums. In contrast, formal sewerage rarely extends into informal areas. As already noted in Chapter 7, OPP encourages residents of informal areas in Pakistan to plan and construct their own sewers. Although OPP's philosophy is that these community-built 'internal' sewers should discharge to the 'external' government-managed systems, the latter do not always exist. The same is true in Indore, India, where at least some of the sewers required to implement the slum networking approach were not built. Similarly, the impact of infrastructure improvements in North-East Lahore was limited because the complementary off-site water supply and drainage improvements were either delayed or cancelled.

Photo 9.1 Informally built sewer in Kamrangir Char

Few informal areas are served by municipal solid waste collection services. Informal systems, such as Cairo's *zabaleen* system, rely on income from recycling and reuse of waste material and for this reason operate mainly in higher-income areas, where people are more likely to throw away recyclable items.

These examples illustrate the point that service levels in informal areas vary widely. Rather than relying on general assumptions, it will always be best to thoroughly check the existing situation on the ground. The absence of formal systems does not mean that services do not exist but it will often mean that those that do exist are of poor quality, have poor interface with formal trunk networks, and cannot be optimized without connections to wider municipal networks.

The importance of the rental sector

Most government and international agency interventions in the housing sector have focused on housing for sale. Early Egyptian public housing schemes did include a high proportion of rental apartments, but most of these were subsequently sold off, as explained in Chapter 5, and more recent schemes provide few if any apartments for rent. Sunil Kumar's research in Chennai, already referred to in Chapter 6, revealed thriving rental arrangements in World Bank-financed sites and services schemes. His subsequent research in Bangalore and Surat found similar rental arrangements in incrementally built housing. The research found that the production and provision of urban rental accommodation was primarily undertaken by individuals and households and that large-scale landlordism was an exception. A large proportion of the landlords were as poor as or even poorer than their tenants (Kumar, 2001). Similarly, Stein and Vance (2008) found a flourishing tenancy market in self-help settlements in Latin America. Low-income households built rooms for rent and so generated additional income while at the same time offering a flexible form of shelter for those who could not purchase housing units. The income generated by building additional rooms for rent provided an important survival mechanism for low-income families, while access to affordable and well-located rental housing helped new migrants to secure an economic foothold in the city. And a good supply of affordable rental units provides the urban poor with mobility and locational choices.

Investigations in the city of Guwahati in India's Assam state found that a range of informal land development processes were creating a variety of rental 'submarkets'. The study looked at five submarkets, with varying degrees of tenure security and accessibility. Not surprisingly, the poorest settlements, located alongside railway tracks and other sites with minimal tenure security, provided very few rental units. Conversely, many residents of settlements with higher de facto security had invested in rental units. As a general rule, the best rental accommodation, which was also that commanding the highest rental charges, was in settlements that were well located, with good access and services. In such situations, rental units represented either a step in the owner's process of consolidating his or her own housing or the process by which he or she gradually sought higher profits from their land. Tenancy also played a significant role in protecting the land of absentee owners from occupation or encroachment by others (Desai and Mahadevia, 2014), particularly those in the early stages of developing their properties.

These examples show that the rental sector flourishes in informal settlements. The variety of rental arrangements and the ways in which these are used by both landlords and tenants support Turner's thesis that the autonomy and variety provided by the informal sector are essential to meeting the diverse housing needs of low-income people. The range of processes and their dependence on location and situation suggest a need to tailor responses to local conditions. This will require an understanding of how land is converted informally to housing, who is building for rent, who is renting, and the dynamics of the market.

The impact of poverty

Michael Stone's (1993) work, summarized in Chapter 3, showed that poverty is a significant barrier to housing access even in high-income industrialized countries such as the USA. In the UK, subsidized council housing played an important role in providing affordable housing for lower-income households from the mid-1920s, reaching a peak in the 1950s and 1960s. There were problems with this programme, as briefly described in Chapter 2. Regardless of this, it is doubtful whether this experience is at all directly transferable to lower-income countries, with their limited financial and institutional resources and general fiscal constraints. If rich countries have consistently failed to provide affordable housing for low-income households, it is not surprising that the countries of the Global South have faced and continue to face similar difficulties. The evidence presented in earlier chapters shows that conventional housing, whether built by government or the private sector, is unaffordable to the poorest households (or even to modest income households) unless it is subsidized, and high land prices exacerbate this problem. It has been estimated that only 1 per cent of the 'affordable' housing units built by India's private sector between 2007 and 2013 cost less than Rs400,000 (about US$8,000), while the calculated affordability ceiling based on median household income was about Rs300,000 (about $6,000) (Bhan et al., 2014). Any serious attempt to respond to informality must recognize that it exists partly because of the inability of formal housing systems to provide housing that meets the aspirations and requirements of poorer households at a price that they can afford. Failure to do so will inevitably lead to promotion of policies and programmes that have little or no chance of success.

Previous chapters have described efforts to reduce the cost of housing, provide subsidies to low-income households, and create lending instruments aimed directly at the urban poor. All of these have a part to play in helping poor households to access improved housing, but none of them addresses the underlying issue of poverty. Some upgrading initiatives have addressed the need for improved livelihoods by promoting small and medium enterprises (SMEs). For instance, the Faisalabad Area Upgrading Project had an SME component, but this had little lasting impact. In addition to providing a basis for community self-organization, the savings groups promoted by Slum/

Shack Dwellers International (SDI), Community Organizations Development Institute (CODI), and Urban Partnerships for Poverty Reduction (UPPR) among others, provide loans with which members can start small businesses. While a useful resource for some, it is doubtful whether these loans have a significant impact on overall poverty levels.

The sustainable livelihoods approach (SLA), which became a central feature of the British Government's Department for International Development (DFID) policies in the early 2000s, offered a more systematic approach to tackling poverty. The SLA used the Chambers and Conway definition of a livelihood as 'the capabilities, assets and activities required for a means of living' (DFID, 2001). To be sustainable, a livelihood must be able to 'cope with and recover from stresses and shocks and maintain or enhance its capabilities and assets both now and in the future, while not undermining the natural resource base' (DFID, 2001). The framework emphasized the importance of livelihood assets, which it divided into five types of capital: human, social, natural, physical, and financial. It argued that the extent to which these were present helped to determine the vulnerability of poor people to shocks, trends, and the effects of seasonality. Although initially developed in a rural context, DFID also claimed that the approach was applicable in urban areas. Secure housing was recognized as a valuable asset for the urban poor, both in itself and as a means of facilitating access to other resources (Farrington et al., 2002). The weakness of the SLA arguably lies in its inability to provide guidance on how the requirements for a sustainable livelihood can be met in practice. In particular, it provides little guidance on the changes in economic and political structures required if the livelihoods of the poor are to be truly sustainable. Whatever the truth of this view, the literature contains few references to sustainable livelihoods after around 2003 and it seems that the concept was sidelined, in practice if not in theory, not long after this date.

In the early 21st century, the International Monetary Fund (IMF) and the World Bank promoted Poverty Reduction Strategy Papers (PRSPs), an apparently more comprehensive approach to poverty reduction. Highly indebted countries were required to prepare a PRSP in order to receive foreign aid and debt relief from Western donor agencies and international financial institutions. The process involved two stages. First, a country would prepare an interim PRSP (I-PRSP), which was intended to provide a roadmap for preparation of the full PRSP, which was itself updated every three years. The IMF website lists the PRSPs produced for each country. The most recent produced by African countries date from the period 2010–2015. Asian countries seem to have abandoned PRSPs by 2010 and some populous countries, including India and Indonesia, never produced one. This reflects the fact that one of the main objectives of PRSPs was to unlock aid under the Heavily Indebted Poor Countries (HIPC) Initiative, which applied mainly to African countries. Whitfield (2010) found that Ghana's PRSPs had had limited impact. They did increase the allocation of resources to social services but did little to move forward a strategy of long-term poverty reduction. PRSPs were intended to be participatory, although the extent of genuine participation in their preparation is questionable. For example, Quadri (2018) found no 'quality' involvement of civil society and NGOs in Nigeria's PRSP process and no evidence of a reduction in poverty as a result of the PRSPs prepared for Nigeria and Benin. She suggested that this could be at least partly explained by the neoliberal ideology that guided the formulation and implementation of the PRSPs.

The limited impact of the SLA and PRSPs points to the difficulties of dealing with poverty in the absence of strong political commitments to reduce inequality. An analysis of 18 PRSPs by Grant and Marcus (2009) found that, although all discussed governance issues, details of political analysis were generally absent. All the available evidence shows that, in the absence of radical political and socio-economic change, poverty will continue to have a significant impact on people's access to housing and services. Approaches to housing and informality that ignore this evidence cannot be successful.

The role of market forces

Chapter 3 outlined a range of views on the role of market forces in housing provision. At one extreme stand those such as Kristian Niemietz, Peter King, and Karol Boudreaux, who argue that too much government is hampering the efforts of free markets to meet housing needs. The limitations of their arguments were discussed in Chapter 3. In essence, they are right that the wrong kind of regulation can inhibit formal markets but they seem to ignore the reality that completely unregulated markets have rarely if ever provided adequate shelter conditions for the poorest in society.

Chapter 3 also summarized the disagreement between John Turner and Rod Burgess on the relative importance of the utility versus market values of housing. What does the evidence reveal about the true picture? Property sales certainly take place in informal settlements but they appear in most cases to be fairly infrequent, suggesting that residents are more concerned with the use value than the exchange value of their houses. Sales to outsiders are rare (see for instance Perlman 2016; Mardhotillah and Gamal, 2018). However, Turner's analysis appears to draw general conclusions from his description of specific cases. For instance, his car painter with his 'supportive shack' was dependent on the good will of the comrade who allowed him to build his shack in her back yard. A more common scenario is likely to be that women, like the comrade, see their back yards as commercial assets, to be exploited by actions such as using the space to build additional rooms for rent. The rows of single rooms and small housing units, clearly intended for rent and that are found in informal settlements in most cities, are clearly market driven, as are the 15-storey high-rise blocks found in prime locations in some of Cairo's informal developments.

At a more strategic level, formal providers of higher-income housing are likely to outbid residents and informal sector providers for land that has a high market value, particularly where they have government support, as in the cases of the Maspero Triangle in Cairo and Dharavi in Mumbai. The changes in the Howrah *thika* tenancies, described earlier in this chapter, show that the commercial interests of landlords can lead to developments that adversely affect the living conditions of their tenants.

These examples illustrate the reality that informal settlements in commercially attractive locations are subject to market forces, regardless of the use value of the housing that they provide to their inhabitants. Where this is the case, there is a need to protect the interests of poor informal sector communities against the efforts of powerful developers, both formal and informal, who seek to gain access to their land. Hernando De Soto fails to address this issue in any meaningful way. However great the capital tied up in an area like Dharavi or the Maspero Triangle, and whatever the rights of their residents, governments and property developers will still view them as sites to be redeveloped. Similarly, there is a need to ensure that piecemeal redevelopment of sites such as the Howrah *thika* tenancy holdings takes place in a way that protects the rights of existing tenants. Efforts to engage with such informality that ignore the economic and political context are bound to fail. As pointed out by Buckley and Kalarickal (2004), a targeted and limited public role is a *sine qua non* for a well-functioning housing sector. At the same time, there is no mysterious, straightforward market-oriented panacea that can address all of the shelter problems faced by low-income families in developing countries.

The relative merits of 'top-down' and 'bottom-up' responses to housing need

Previous chapters have examined a wide range of responses to housing needs, some initiated by governments, some promoted by international agencies, and some resulting from actions by national and international NGOs and organizations of the urban poor. Views on the value of these initiatives vary widely. Not surprisingly, the organizations with responsibility for specific approaches and initiatives tend to emphasize and promote the value of those initiatives, sometimes commenting unfavourably on the initiatives of others. Government officials often criticize NGO initiatives, arguing that their small scale means that they are irrelevant to overall housing needs while their adoption of informal procedures and standards is extra-legal and prevents them from providing adequate housing and services. Many NGOs are similarly dismissive of government efforts and, in some cases, receive strong support from academics and development organizations. As described in Chapter 8, international organizations have sometimes tried to bring governments, NGOs, and organizations of the urban poor together. However, wide differences of opinion regarding the merits and effectiveness of different approaches to housing and service provision remain. Where does the truth lie among such widely differing approaches and opinions?

Annamalai et al. (2016) examined the evidence on the impact of what they termed 'top-down' and 'bottom-up' approaches to water supply, sanitation, and electricity services in low-income and informal areas. They used the term top-down to mean services provided by public or private agencies through centralized planning and implementation. Bottom-up initiatives were those led by NGOs, community-based organizations (CBOs), and other small-scale service providers and characterized by a high degree of decentralized planning and implementation. They recognized that most programmes fall somewhere between these two poles but classified initiatives as top-down or bottom-up, depending on which type of organization had played a dominant role. They analysed the findings of 104 studies, covering six geographical regions, 34 countries, and 103 cities. Studies of Asian cities were the most numerous with Dhaka the most studied city, followed by Mumbai, Ahmedabad, Jakarta, and New Delhi. They concluded that:

- While there were individual cases of effective service provision through centralized planning, top-down efforts were generally ineffective in connecting populations to centralized services.
- Bottom-up approaches were effective in the provision of individual toilets, but, overall, they were no more successful than top-down approaches in improving access to safe water.
- Even where successful, bottom-up approaches had proved difficult to scale up. In particular, it had proved difficult to ensure the sustained participation of community members in maintaining the infrastructure created.

Poor performance of top-down approaches stemmed from institutional deficiencies, including government mismanagement and lack of clarity regarding government agency responsibilities. Other factors included the lack of a pro-poor policy, poor finances, the lack of a strong legal mandate for network expansion in slums, and inappropriate pricing policies. Initiatives were more likely to be successful if they included mechanisms for interacting with benefiting communities and provided opportunities for them to contribute time, effort, and money to the project.

The case studies included in previous chapters support these conclusions. Neither government nor NGO-led initiatives have been very successful in connecting upgraded informal areas to centralized services. In many cases, project planners have abandoned efforts to make connections to municipal services, focusing instead on on-site solutions to service deficiencies, which does little to promote the integration of informal settlements into the wider urban fabric. Even where connections to municipal systems exist, services to low-income areas are often compromised by the poor performance of those systems. The experience in Brazil and Pakistan confirms that community involvement in infrastructure maintenance is difficult to sustain.

The findings of Annamalai et al. (2016) relate specifically to services. However, the case studies included in Chapters 5 and 6 suggest that similar conclusions can be drawn with regard to efforts to provide affordable housing. Government housing programmes rarely provide accommodation that is accessible to and suitable for the poorest households. NGOs and their supporters have repeatedly drawn attention to this fact but none of their efforts to develop alternative housing supply mechanisms have gone to scale.

Addressing constraints to appropriate housing

The case studies included in previous chapters illustrate a range of constraints on efforts to develop formal systems for providing affordable housing. These constraints include the following, which we discuss below:

- land, which is expensive, even when it is available;
- the gap between formal standards and informal sector practices;
- unnecessarily strict and complex formal rules and procedures, which reduce the ability of the formal sector to respond to housing needs, particularly those of the poor;
- vested interests of politicians, government officials, and others;
- lack of information as few informal areas are accurately mapped and necessary socio-economic information is often very inaccurate;
- political and institutional constraints leading to a lack of capacity to deliver and/or regulate formal development.

Land

This book has emphasized the fact that, in city after city, a high proportion of the population is squeezed into informal settlements that occupy a tiny portion of the available urban space. This land is often marginal, in the sense that it is either low-lying and subject to flooding or steeply sloping. This situation is partly explained by high land prices, which make lower-density development unaffordable to low-income households. Shams et al. (2014) cited residential land values in prime locations of Dhaka in the range US$30–60 per sq ft ($325–650 per m^2), similar to prices reported in other regional cities such as Hyderabad, Kuala Lumpur, and New Delhi. These prices were comparable with those in the United States, where land prices rarely exceeded $60 per sq. ft. Segregation between richer and poorer households may be exacerbated as financial crises force the lowest income households to sell their land to higher-income households and move to less desirable sites (Thirkell, 1996). It is arguable that poverty is the root cause of this situation although it is unfortunately true that most governments do little to ensure that suitable land at anywhere near the volume required is made available to house poor households. Regardless of the causes of the situation, any strategy for improving housing conditions for low-income households must address the issue of land.

As was pointed out in Chapter 8, CODI claims that it has successfully used a community-based approach to the identification of development land. However, its literature gives few details of how this is intended to work and it seems that the land parcels identified are fairly small and certainly fall well short of meeting city-wide demand for land to house the urban poor. The UPPR project in Bangladesh followed CODI's approach to land identification, marking both existing informal settlements and potential development land on maps of project towns. Development land areas were small and inspection revealed that many had been encroached by informal development.

The example of the Extension of Municipal Services (EMS) project in Greater Cairo (Chapter 6) shows that, even where suitable development land is in government ownership, policymakers are likely to prioritize the needs of high-income groups over those of the urban poor. Providing land for low-income housing clearly needs a fundamental shift in attitude.

Planning, building, and infrastructure standards

Planning standards exist to ensure that all premises enjoy adequate access, light, and ventilation and that fire hazards are not increased by the close proximity of buildings. Building standards and regulations should ensure that buildings are safe and provide acceptable living conditions, but existing standards often go beyond these basic requirements to define the form and appearance of both settlements and individual buildings. Like planning and building standards, existing formal infrastructure standards often go beyond the basic requirement to ensure that services are delivered to specify the way in which they should be delivered. For instance, by-laws in some African countries recognize no sanitation option other than sewerage.

There is no doubt that formal standards sometimes exceed those required to ensure that these conditions are met. For instance, a modelling exercise in Brazil, using statistics on Brazilian urbanization for the period 1980 to 2010, concluded that the imposition of strict planning and building regulations and standards, some federally mandated and some locally imposed, was the largest single factor contributing to the growth of informal settlements (da Mata, 2013). Brazilian federal law required a minimum lot size of 125 m^2 but allowed municipalities to produce their own amended planning standards in the light of local conditions. Da Mata's research revealed that no less than 1,183 out of a total of 1,482 municipalities had amended their lot size requirements, in all cases opting for an increased minimum. And the problem of unrealistically high planning standards is not confined to Brazil. In African countries, formal schemes can have standard plot sizes as high as 400 m^2. In Asian countries, minimum plot sizes for individual houses are typically of the order of 75 m^2. Access standards often assume the need for vehicles and few require road widths of less than 6–10 metres. They are based on the often implicit assumption that every household owns a car and that vehicle access is required to either individual plots or designated parking areas, an extremely unlikely requirement in informal areas, where car ownership is usually very low, with motorcycles providing the most common form of motorized transport.

If unnecessarily high standards were the only problem, the proponents of deregulation and leaving everything to the market would have a point. Unfortunately, this is not the case. Most informal settlements are not laid out or built in ways that meet basic access, light, ventilation, and fire safety standards. Take, for instance, the case of Korail, the Dhaka informal settlement referenced earlier in this chapter. The use of corrugated sheet cladding on timber frames and the extremely narrow access paths mean that the settlement presents a severe fire safety hazard. For example, in December 2016, 526 houses in Korail were destroyed in a fire, and another fire, in January 2017, destroyed about 5,000 houses in the settlement (Hasan and Mollah, 2017). The fire-affected areas have since been rebuilt with slightly wider rights of way but the area is still susceptible to catastrophic conflagrations.

Light and ventilation conditions in informal areas can also be problematic, particularly in the cases of medium- to high-rise development. In Cairo's informal settlements, buildings invariably extend to the plot boundary limits and air and light for rooms that do not face onto the street are provided by inadequately sized 'light wells' (Sims, 2010). Box 9.1 summarizes the findings of a theoretical research exercise on light conditions in typical Cairo informal settlements. It shows that even the rooms facing onto the street do not receive adequate light if they are located opposite a tall building. Given that streets in the city's informal settlements are often narrower than the 4 m minimum considered in the study, there seems to be no way that satisfactory light conditions can be achieved in the four storeys and upwards buildings that are the norm in Cairo's informal settlements.

Box 9.1 A study of light conditions in Cairo's informal settlements

Wagdy et al. (2015) calculated spatial daylight autonomy (sDA) and annual sun exposure (ASE) figures for a 6 m deep by 4 m wide by 3 m high south-facing room for a range of window to wall ratios (WWR), road widths, and building heights opposite from one to nine storeys. sDA is an annual daylighting metric that quantifies the fraction of the area within a space that receives at least 300 lux for at least 50 per cent of the annual occupied hours. It should be at least 5 per cent and preferably above 75 per cent. An sDA of at least 55 per cent is normally required if the lighting to a room is to be considered satisfactory. ASE measures the percentage of floor area that receives at least 1,000 lux for at least 250 occupied hours per year. It is a proxy for glare that is intended to help designers limit excessive sunlight in a space. The WWR is the area of window in the front wall divided by the area of the wall. The exercise assumed a south-facing façade and no window openings other than those in the front wall. For a 4 m street, rather wider than some in Cairo's informal sector, the study found that a WWR of 90 per cent was required if the bottom apartments facing a nine-storey building were to meet sDA requirements. Reducing the WWR to 85 per cent and 60 per cent gave satisfactory sDA figures for building heights opposite of six storeys and four storeys respectively. To put these figures into perspective, most apartments in Cairo's informal settlements have a WWR of much less than 50 per cent and few face streets that are wider than 4 m. The implications are clear: existing apartments in Cairo's informal areas do not receive sufficient light to meet generally accepted minimum norms.

Rules and procedures

Whatever the merits of other aspects of his argument, De Soto's analysis of formal procedures in a number of countries reveals their cumbersome length and complexity. There is no doubt that unwieldy procedures play a part in pushing developers, builders, and the households into informality. This does not mean that there are no common procedures within the informal sector. Previous chapters have provided ample evidence of this. For instance, in Lahore, Pakistan, in the 1980s, the author observed 'estate agents' operating out of small offices located in recently subdivided areas. De Soto's thesis is that removal of onerous rules and procedures would encourage such actors to move into the formal sector. This is true but he pays little if any attention to the barriers that stand in the way of change. The most important of these is an inbred resistance to change, rooted in the persistence of inappropriate modern models and, in many cases, the existence of vested interests. As with norms and standards, responses to informality cannot ignore the need to change or by-pass the institutions that have created restrictive rules and procedures.

Vested interests

Informal settlement is invariably affected by vested interests. Those with such interests include:

- Politicians who promise services in exchange for votes.
- Government officials, who take bribes in return for turning a blind eye to the illegality of informal settlements.
- The 'slum mafia,' which can be described as unelected people who control many informal settlements. They typically act as the conduit between residents and politicians and government officials but in turn extract rents in the form of bribes and protection payments.
- Developers in both the formal and informal sectors who covet informal land because of the high profits that can be made through its redevelopment.

People in different groups often collaborate. An obvious example is the collaboration between slum mafia, politicians, and officials to facilitate delivery of services to informal settlements. Such activities can bring benefits but are often ad hoc and therefore poorly planned. They can 'produce exclusionary and discriminatory outcomes, while being characterised by unbalanced power structures and sometimes even patron–client relationships' (Hackenbroch and Hossain, 2012: 398). At worst, they have resulted in the murder of activists who seek increased understanding of the ways in which informal land markets work and promote a more transparent and equitable approach to those markets. OPP's Parween Rehman was murdered in Karachi in 2013, almost certainly because her work on improving land records for informal areas had threatened the vested interests of the land mafia and, perhaps, their political allies.

Information

Few informal settlements are accurately mapped, and many appear as blank spaces on city maps, in contrast to neighbouring formal settlements. Thus there is a complete lack of accurate cadastral information. Both CODI and SDI emphasize the role of slum dwellers in collecting information but, as noted in Chapter 8, their emphasis is on enumeration rather than spatial mapping.[1] Enumerations provide information on whole settlements and are thus useful for making an initial assessment of the issues to be addressed, and community mapping exercises can provide information on how residents view their living environments. With targeted facilitation, they can also provide information on people's ideas about how their communities might develop, for instance providing ideas on how the road network might be improved. However, enumerations and community mapping exercises are unlikely to provide the information on conditions inside the settlement required for detailed planning. The SDI experiences in South Africa show that the information they collect is not always accepted by government departments.

Satellite imagery has been used as a basis for producing digital cadastral maps, but mostly for rural areas, where individual land holdings are relatively large (see for instance Kohli et al., 2018). Small plots and complex layouts make extraction of information from satellite imagery difficult, even with image data with 0.5 m spatial resolution, a situation exacerbated by shadows and tree coverage. Most studies have focused on determining the extent of informal areas, with fewer aiming to extract specific objects such as roofs and roads. Most of the latter have been from African cities, where informal settlements are often of lower density than in other regions. Because of the high cost of acquiring and processing commercial and up-to-date high-resolution imagery, most studies have covered small areas (Kuffer et al., 2016).

One response to the limited spatial resolution of satellite imagery is to use aerial imagery from Unmanned Aerial Systems (UAVs), commonly called drones. Because these fly low over settlements, they can capture data at a high resolution, and the spatial resolution can be as high as 3 cm (Gevaert, 2018). Maps produced using drones can provide accurate information on building locations and plot boundaries. Each plot can then be numbered and the map information can be linked to socio-economic information on the household and the services provided on the plot and recorded in a GIS system. One exercise in Kenya obtained information on three settlements, ranging from 1 ha to 16 ha in area. The imagery was used to produce digital maps, which provided a base for socio-economic and cadastral surveys and improvement plans, developed in consultation with the communities (Onyango, 2019). The government of India's Odisha State worked with Tata Trusts and the Omidyar Network to map around 250,000 slum households across the state, using drone imagery. The information collected was verified on the ground in consultation with community members. Tape measurements were used to determine the space actually occupied by each household. The information collected in this way was used to make lists of occupants, which are verified by community members. Lists were then handed over to municipalities, while the digital data was transferred to a GIS-based state map (Mishra and Murali, 2018).

While the use of drones does reduce the effort required to map informal areas accurately, it is not without problems. One is the reluctance of governments to authorize the use of drones for mapping purposes. In the early stages of the Low Income Communities Housing Support project in Bangladesh, the consultants used drones to map two informal settlements but they were prevented from taking the approach further because it was deemed to be in violation of government regulations. Another potential problem is that, while reducing the need for field surveys, the use of drones does not eliminate it. The Odisha initiative clearly involved a fair amount of measurement on the ground. A potential related problem is lack of agreement between households on where plot boundaries lie.

Another information-related constraint is the absence of street and house numbering systems in many informal settlements. Without such systems, it is impossible to identify individual plots and define their location and to ensure that they can be integrated into wider city systems. In particular, the lack of street and house numbers hampers efforts to deliver and bill for essential services, deliver mail, and respond quickly to emergencies and service breakdowns (Farvacque-Vitkovic et al., 2005).

Political and institutional constraints

Political will and institutional capacity are both essential to the success of efforts to house the urban poor. The failure of the EMS project in Greater Cairo illustrates the importance of such political will. The project was intended to provide plots suitable for the development of affordable housing on desert land, mainly to the east of Cairo, in order to stem the growth of informal settlements on agricultural land. All desert land in Egypt is in government ownership, albeit in many cases it is controlled by the military. With political will, gaining access to suitable sites should not have been a problem. In fact, the Governor of Cairo, an ex-military general, never accepted the EMS approach, referring to the threat posed by low-income neighbourhoods and claiming that he did not want to be known as having built slums (David Sims, personal communication). The EMS project (Chapter 6) was never implemented and the area in which it was located has since been developed into middle- and high-income apartment blocks. The introduction to Douglass North's thinking on institutions in Chapter 3 emphasized the importance of the attitudes, assumptions, and perceptions that determine institutional approaches to the issues that confront us. Clearly, the Cairo Governor's response to EMS was conditioned by his mental models, which drew on the values and attitudes engendered by his experience as a member of the Egyptian elite and his military training.

This is one, albeit extreme, example of the attitudes to informality of politicians, officials, and indeed large parts of the general public in Egypt and beyond. As illustrated by examples earlier in this book, government recognition of informal sector activity is invariably retrospective and rather grudging. Recognition of the values of informal development has come mainly from international institutions such as the World Bank or from slum dwellers themselves and the NGOs that support them. Government recognition has been slow to materialize and its support unreliable at best. Even where national policies theoretically recognize the importance of informal settlements, the resources provided for improvement have usually been very limited. One study found that responses to informal slums in Chennai exhibited an underlying continuity of approaches that has extended over decades. Although political philosophies evolved, from paternalistic socialism in the 1970s through an emphasis on cost recovery and affordability in the 1980s, and a neo-conservative emphasis on 'beautification' of slums in the 2000s to slum-free 'smart city' discourse in the late 2010s, the predominant response to informality remained demolition and replacement by some combination of *in situ* tenement construction and relocation to peri-urban resettlement sites (Saharan et al., 2018). This is consistent with Chapter 5's findings on the continued emphasis on replacing informal development with tenement blocks in Mumbai and Egypt.

The difficulties associated with distorted or unrealistic mental models are often accentuated by weaknesses in government systems and lack of capacity. In many countries in the Global South, these difficulties include weak municipal governments with very limited investment budgets and planning capacities, and with inadequate service providers. The lack of planning systems and technical capacities is likely to be particularly problematic in smaller towns and in peri-urban areas lying outside official municipal boundaries. Plans, if they exist, are often old and likely to have been produced by a specialist planning department housed in a national or regional ministry. Many include little or no information on informal settlements and most have a limited impact on the direction and form of urban development.

Since the early 1990s, international agencies have promoted and national governments have, perhaps reluctantly, accepted the view that government should act as an enabler rather than a direct supplier of housing and other services. For instance, the Dhaka Structure Plan 2016–2035 recommends that the public sector should facilitate private sector housing provision rather than providing housing itself (RAJUK, n.d.). The examples given in Chapter 5 show a similar emphasis on private sector provision in both Egypt and India. The underlying assumption is that, while lacking the financial and institutional capacity to provide housing itself, government has the capacity to oversee the activities of private sector developers. The reality is that, in many countries across the Global South, government capacity to regulate the activities of others is extremely limited. Poor-quality work by private sector contractors is often accepted without question, with the result that the finished quality of housing units is often poor (see for instance Mukhija, 2001). Even when recognized, capacity limitations are often ignored. For instance, the Dhaka Structure Plan report identifies poor control over private developers and lack of capacity of public agencies as system weaknesses, but then it goes on to recommend precisely such a system to exert control over those developers.

Government inability to either provide affordable housing at the scale required or to regulate formal sector activity and its limited ability to enforce its own policies together have the perverse effect of contributing to the continuance of informal sector activity. For example, Egypt has banned residential development on agricultural land from at least the 1980s but this has not prevented continuing massive informal encroachment on agricultural land (Masri and Abdelaty, 2018). In February 2019, Pakistan's Punjab province banned the development of new housing on agricultural land (Mustafa, 2019). Planning systems in Punjab are weak, particularly in smaller towns and it is unlikely that this legislation will be enforced any more effectively than that in Egypt.

One constraint faced by NGOs and organizations of the urban poor is their dependence on a small number of leaders. These leaders are often charismatic, with a clearly defined philosophy and approach, and their leadership roles are widely recognized and rarely contested. However, it can also lead them to reject ideas from outside and refuse to accept constructive criticism. When Robert Neuwirth attempted to question Jockin Arputham, the leader of the National Slum Dwellers Federation in India and key figure in SDI, on the barriers to the achievement of full-scale slum dwellers' rights, he quickly found himself shut out, with the conversation rapidly brought to an end (Neuwirth, 2006: 138–39). This lack of willingness to question can lead to a focus on one approach or technology to the exclusion of all others. For example, OPP invariably advocates sewerage with connections to individual households, in contrast to the Indian Alliance, which almost always recommends communal sanitation facilities.

The concentration of power and resources at the centre of an organization can constrain efforts to innovate and expand initiatives. In 2013, after several years of managing the Baan Mankong Programme from Bangkok (see Chapter 8), CODI decided that it was time to decentralize its management systems to give more decision-making power to regional CODI offices. This proved more difficult than anticipated because the regional CODI teams, whose staff came mostly from rural backgrounds, lacked the deep historical knowledge of the city-wide and urban community-driven processes that had accumulated over years in the central management team. A long period of adjustment and transferring capacity to the regional offices was necessary. While struggling with this knowledge and capacity deficit, the regional teams came under pressure to meet targets set by government. Lacking the experience of the processes developed in Bangkok, they lost the balance that was so crucial in CODI's role, and opted instead for quick responses to government demands. The result was that the Baan Mankong Programme became more and more like a conventional, project-based housing delivery programme. At the same time, the much greater strength of the national network enabled it to access CODI funds directly. This reduced its motivation to work with local governments and build partnerships and consensus with other local stakeholders. In the absence of effective city committees and joint mechanisms, the original collaborative, city-wide development concept faded, and the Baan Mankong Programme became a more in-house, network-driven process that was less about co-production and more about producing projects. Without the involvement of city governments and other local partners, the process became fragile. Some housing projects could not be completed, and many cities implemented a single project, with no subsequent follow-up (Boonyabancha and Kerr, 2018).

Note

1. See http://knowyourcity.info/explore-our-data/ for information on the SDI 'mapping' process.

References

Aklin, M., Bayer, P., Harish, S. P. and Urpelainen, J. (2015) Quantifying slum electrification in India and explaining local variation. *Energy*, 80, 203–12. https://doi.org/10.1016/j.energy.2014.11.063

Annamalai, T.R., Devkar, G., Mahalingam, A., Benjamin, S., Rajan, S.C. and Deep, A. (2016) *What is the evidence on top-down and bottom-up approaches in improving access to water, sanitation and electricity services in low-income or informal settlements?* EPPI-Centre, Social Science Research Unit, UCL Institute of Education, University College London. https://assets.publishing.service.gov.uk/media/5832d330e5274a7022000015/SR_-_Q7_Final_Draft_for_Publication.pdf

Bhan, G., Anand, G. and Harish, S. (2014) *Policy approaches to affordable housing in urban India: problems and possibilities*, IIHS-RF Policy Paper, Indian Institute for Human Settlements, Bangalore. https://iihs.co.in/knowledge-gateway/policy-approach-to-affordable-housing-in-urban-india/ (accessed 13 August 2025).

Boonyabancha, S. and Kerr, T. (2018) Lessons from CODI on co-production, *Environment and Urbanization*, 30(2): 444–60. https://doi.org/10.1177/0956247818791239

Buckley, R.M. and Kalarickal, J. (2004) *Shelter policies for the urban poor: idiosyncratic and successful but hardly mysterious*, Policy Research Working Paper 3427, World Bank, Washington, DC.

Collignon, B. and Chaponniere, E. (2011) PPP with local informal providers aimed at improving water supply in the peri-urban areas of Maputo, Mozambique, paper presented at *35th WEDC International Conference, Loughborough*. https://wedc-knowledge.lboro.ac.uk/resources/conference/35/chaponniere-e-1138.pdf

Conan, H. (2004) *Small piped water networks: helping local entrepreneurs to invest*, Asian Development Bank, Manila. https://www.adb.org/sites/default/files/publication/28569/small-piped-water-networks.pdf

Da Mata, D. (2013) *Disentangling the causes of informal housing*, preliminary draft. https://editorialexpress.com/cgi-bin/conference/download.cgi?db_name=UEA2013&paper_id=143 (accessed 2 May 2019).

Desai, R. and Mahadevia, D. (2014) Diversity and dynamics of informal rental housing in a mid-sized city in India, *Environment and Urbanization Asia*, 5(2): 285–301. https://doi.org/10.1177/0975425315577173

DFID (2001) *Sustainable livelihoods guidance sheets*. https://www.livelihoodscentre.org/documents/114097690/114438878/Sustainable+livelihoods+guidance+sheets.pdf/594e5ea6-99a9-2a4e-f288-cbb4ae4bea8b?t=1569512091877 (accessed 25 August 2025).

Farrington, J., Ramaut, T. and Walker, J. (2002) *Sustainable livelihoods approaches in urban area: general lessons, with illustrations from Indian case studies*, Working Paper. ODI Global, London. https://odi.org/en/publications/sustainable-livelihoods-approaches-in-urban-area-general-lessons-with-illustrations-from-indian-case-studies/ (accessed 13 August 2025).

Farvacque-Vitkovic, C., Godin, L., Leroux, H., Verdet, F. and Chavez, R. (2005) *Street addressing and the management of cities*, The World Bank, Washington, DC. http://documents1.worldbank.org/curated/en/573071468142795481/pdf/329230Street0Addressing01not0external1.pdf (accessed 8 December 2020).

Gevaert, C.M. (2018) *Unmanned aerial vehicle mapping for settlement upgrading*, PhD thesis, University of Twente, Netherlands. http://dx.doi.org/10.3990/1.9789036546355

Grant, U. and Marcus, R. (2009) *Background paper for the chronic poverty report 2008–09: Chronic poverty and PRSPs: a desk study*. Chronic Poverty Research Centre, London. https://assets.publishing.service.gov.uk/media/57a08bc2ed915d622c000e99/prs-grant_marcus-prsps-desk-study.pdf (accessed 13 August 2025).

Hackenbroch, K. and Hossain, S. (2012) 'The organised encroachment of the powerful'—Everyday practices of public space and water supply in Dhaka, Bangladesh, *Planning Theory & Practice*, 13(3): 397–420. https://doi.org/10.1080/14649357.2012.694265

Hasan, R. and Mollah, S. (2017) Design for disaster, *The Daily Star*, 10 July, Dhaka. https://www.thedailystar.net/frontpage/dhaka-korail-slum-designed-disaster-14307280

Kohli, D., Unger, E-M., Lemmen, C., Bennett, R., Koeva, M., Friis, J. and Bhandari, B. (2018) Validation of a cadastral map created using satellite imagery and automated feature extraction techniques: a case study of Nepal, paper presented at *FIG Congress 2018, Istanbul, Turkey*. Template - FIG Congress 2010 (accessed 8 December 2020).

Kuffer, M., Pfeffer, K. and Sliuzas, R. (2016) Slums from space – 15 years of slum mapping using remote sensing, *Remote Sensing* 8(6): 455. https://doi.org/10.3390/rs8060455

Kumar, S. (2001) *Social relations, rental housing markets & the poor in urban India*, Final Report to DFID. https://assets.publishing.service.gov.uk/media/57a08d64ed915d622c00197b/R6856.pdf (accessed 9 January 2020).

Mardhotillah, H. and Gamal, A. (2018) Segregation and gentrification of an informal settlement in a city center, *International Journal of Technology* 7: 1346–54. https://doi.org/10.14716/ijtech.v9i7.2519

Masri, L. and Abdelaty, A. (2018) Egypt's poor bear brunt of crackdown on farmland building, *Reuters*, 27 November. https://www.reuters.com/article/us-egypt-agriculture-housing/egypts-poor-bear-brunt-of-crackdown-on-farmland-building-idUSKCN1NW163 (accessed 16 December 2019).

Mishra, P. and Murali, A. (2018) Drone-mapping for land titling – one pixel at a time, *Factor Daily*, 28 May. https://factordaily.com/orissa-drone-mapped-slum-titling-project/ (accessed 6 April 2020).

Mukhija, V. (2001) Enabling slum redevelopment in Mumbai: policy paradox in practice, *Housing Studies*, 18(4): 213–22. https://dx.doi.org/10.1080/02673030120090548

Mustafa, W. (2019) Pakistan's Punjab province bans farmland use for towns, *Reuters*, 1 March. https://www.reuters.com/article/us-pakistan-housing-land/pakistans-punjab-province-bans-farmland-use-for-towns-idUSKCN1QI5CO (accessed 16 December 2019).

Neuwirth, R. (2006) *Shadow cities: a billion squatters, a new urban world*, Routledge, New York and Abingdon.

Onyango, F.A. (2019) UAV mapping for informal settlements planning [blog], *Africa Goes Digital*, 1 May. http://www.afgoesdigital.com/uav-mapping-for-informal-settlements-planning/ (accessed 5 April 2019).

Perlman, J. (2016) The formalization of informal real estate transactions in Rio's favelas, in E.L. Birch, S. Chattaraj, and S.M. Wachter (eds), *Slums: how informal real estate markets work*, University of Pennsylvania Press, Philadelphia.

Quadri, M. (2018) Neoliberalism and the paradox of poverty reduction: a synthesis of the poverty reduction strategy paper experience in Benin and Nigeria. *Journal of Pan African Studies* 11(7): 186–203.

Raina, A., Gurung, Y. and Suwal, B. (2020) Equity impacts of informal private water markets: case of Kathmandu Valley, *Water Policy*, 22(S1): 189–204. https://doi.org/10.2166/wp.2018.138

RAJUK (no date) Housing for all, in *Draft Dhaka Structure Plan 2016–2035*. https://www.academia.edu/31508051/_Draft_Dhaka_Structure_Plan_Report_2016_2035_Full_Volume_ (accessed 13 August 2025).

Repestro, P. (2010) Moving in-selling out: the outcomes of slum rehabilitation in Mumbai, *International Conference on Applied Economics*, pp 641–648. https://online.fliphtml5.com/vgtx/tata/#p=1 (accessed 13 August 2025).

Saharan, T., Pfeffer, K. and Baud, I. (2018) Shifting approaches to slums in Chennai: political conditions, policy discourses and practices, *Singapore Journal of Tropical Geography*, 39(3): 454–71. https://doi.org/10.1111%2Fsjtg.12244

Schenk, C. (2010) Slum diversity in Kolkata, *Columbia Undergraduate Journal of South Asian Studies* I(II): 91–108. http://www.columbia.edu/cu/cujsas/Volume%20I/Issue%20II/W%20Collin%20Schenk%20-%20Slum%20Diversity.pdf

Shams, S., Sohal, M. and Ahsan, A. (2014) Housing problems for middle and low income people in Bangladesh: challenges of Dhaka megacity, *Environment and Urbanization ASIA*, 5(1): 175–84. http://dx.doi.org/10.1177/0975425314521538

Sims, D. (2010) *Understanding Cairo: the logic of a city out of control*, The American University in Cairo Press, Cairo.

Stein, A. and Vance, I. (2008) The role of housing finance in addressing the needs of the urban poor: lessons from Central America, *Environment and Urbanisation*, 20(1): 13–30. https://doi.org/10.1177/0956247808089146

Stone, M.E. (1993) *Shelter poverty: new ideas on housing affordability*, Temple University Press, Philadelphia, PA.

Thirkell, A. (1996) Players in urban informal land markets; who wins? who loses? A case study of Cebu City, *Environment and Urbanization*, 8(2): 71–90. https://doi.org/10.1177/095624789600800213

Wagdy, A., Abdelghany, A. and Hegazy, M.A. (2015) Daylighting optimization for informal settlements in Cairo, Egypt, in A. Gasparella, M. Baratieri, F. Patuzzi, and V. Corrado (eds.) *Building simulation applications, BSA 2015: 2nd IBPSA-Italy Conference*, pp. 483–90. Free University of Bozen Bolzano, Italy. https://eprints.qut.edu.au/203350/1/62623994.pdf (accessed 30 November 2020).

Ward, P. (2009) Unpackaging residential segregation: the importance of scale and informal market processes, *Investigaciones Geográficas, Boletín del Instituto de Geografía, UNAM*, 70: 114–134. (PDF) Unpackaging residential segregation: The importance of scale and informal market processes (researchgate.net) (accessed 30 November 2020).

Whitfield, L. (2010) The state elite, PRSPs and policy implementation in aid-dependent Ghana, *Third World Quarterly* 31(5): 721–37. https://doi.org/10.1080/01436597.2010.502692

CHAPTER 10

Thoughts on a strategy for change

This final chapter uses the concepts and practical lessons explored in earlier chapters to suggest an outline for future shelter strategies, covering both housing and related services. It first considers objectives and then moves on to explore strategic options for achieving those objectives, which must be guided but not necessarily determined by Sustainable Development Goal 11 (SDG 11) and its associated targets. Attention then turns to ways of responding to the challenge presented by the difference between formal and informal sector standards. The place of the responses to informality set out in Chapters 5 to 7 is then considered. Previous chapters have shown the importance of institutions and the constraints that are often associated with existing institutional arrangements. A review of institutional options and constraints leads into an assessment of innovative institutional options. The chapter concludes with thoughts on lessons for international organizations and an argument for the need for a new professionalism.

Objectives

Almost all international organizations define their objectives, at least loosely, in terms of the Sustainable Development Goals (SDGs). There are 17 goals in total and each is accompanied by a series of targets and indicators. The United Nations states that 'the SDGs are a bold commitment to finish what we started, and tackle some of the more pressing challenges facing the world today' (UNDP, n.d.). The reference to finishing what was started refers to the earlier Millennium Development Goals (2005). The SDG with most relevance to the concerns of this book is SDG 11, which is to 'make cities and human settlements inclusive, safe, resilient and sustainable' (United Nations, 2015). And this goal has two targets, each of which implies a whole range of rather vaguely worded sub-goals:

Target 11.1 'By 2030, ensure access for all to adequate, safe and affordable housing and basic services and upgrade slums' (ibid.).

Target 11.3 'By 2030, enhance inclusive and sustainable urbanization and capacity for participatory, integrated and sustainable human settlement planning and management in countries' (ibid.)

And there are other SDG targets that are relevant to the challenges faced by the urban poor. In particular, SDG 1 is to 'end poverty in all its forms everywhere' and SDG 6 is to 'ensure access to water and sanitation for all' (ibid.). Other SDGs refer to the need for good health systems, quality education, accessible transport, gender equality, affordable and clean energy, improved air quality and waste management and decent work, improved social and environmental links between urban and peri-urban areas, and support to efforts to introduce sustainable and resilient buildings using local materials.

The SDGs and their associated targets are certainly aspirational, presenting visions of what the future should be. But are they realistic? The governments and international agencies that signed up to the SDGs and their associated targets believe that they are attainable, although most would probably accept that it will be difficult or impossible to achieve them by 2030. The alternative view, which is not confined to Marxists such as Rod Burgess, is that poverty and its associated problems, including poor housing, cannot be eliminated without significant changes in the way in which the world's economy is structured. Others would argue that the challenges of poverty and poor housing can at least be mitigated by social market systems that combine regulated capitalist economic activity with some form of welfare state. As already noted in Chapter 3, yet others reject both views and argue that the problem is too much regulation. Whatever the merits of these different viewpoints, there is no doubt that poverty has been stubbornly hard to eradicate in both advanced and developing nations and in both free-market and nominally socialist systems. Stone's work on the persistence of shelter poverty in the United States (Chapter 3) provides eloquent confirmation of this fact.

This book takes the view that, regardless of the arguments about the causes of poverty, there is a need for actions to improve housing conditions. This is true, even where political and institutional structures are deeply flawed, and the challenge is to identify actions that have the potential to bring about improvements within the constraints presented by existing institutional structures, systems, capacities, and attitudes. The focus should be on what is realistically possible rather than some theoretical but unattainable ideal.

Previous chapters in this book, particularly Chapter 4, have shown that the formal sector has consistently failed to provide housing that is both of acceptable quality and affordable to low-income households, and Chapter 8 identified the weakness of urban planning systems in many countries. Efforts to eliminate informal development are thus constrained by the inability of formal sector systems to provide housing that is affordable and the inability or unwillingness of governments to prevent the growth of informal settlements in contravention of formal plans. Taken together, these findings point to a need to recognize and engage with the informal sector rather than trying to eliminate it, with the objective of ensuring that all citizens, including the poor, have access to adequate housing and services. The term adequate must cover both physical and social aspects of housing provision. An appropriate overall objective might be to *ensure that all have access to adequate housing and services in neighbourhoods that are socially and physically integrated into the city.* This will require action to:

- Reduce and eventually eliminate informal practices that produce completely unsatisfactory results.

- Engage with informal practices that have the potential to produce results that are at least reasonably satisfactory.
- Explore ways in which formal practices can be made more responsive to the needs of the urban poor. This might involve 1) streamlining procedures and modifying norms and standards, as appropriate, to increase access; and 2) increasing the scale and scope of formal affordable housing provision.

The first two bullets raise the question of what should be considered satisfactory. An appropriate answer might be that, to be widely accepted and integrated into the overall urban fabric, low-income settlements must be transformed into durable and decent neighbourhoods (Coelho, 2016). Full integration implies that residents pay formal taxes and user charges sufficient to cover the sustained delivery of municipal services. Since many resident households are poor, there are likely to be situations in which some form of cross-subsidy from higher-income households is appropriate. The experience with the Basic Urban Services Programme in Sukkur, examined in Chapter 7, points to the problems that can result if the need to contribute to the ongoing costs of off-site services is ignored.

In order to achieve the objectives set out above, it will be important to:

- *recognize the realities set out in Chapter 9*, paying particular attention to the constraints identified in that chapter;
- *respond to the causes of poor housing*, not least poverty, inadequate institutions, and deficient assumptions and practices in both the formal and informal sectors;
- *provide responses to the various forms of informality*, recognizing that action that is appropriate for one type of informality in one set of circumstances will not be appropriate for another type;
- *identify intermediate objectives*, chosen to provide staging points on the journey towards achievement of the overall objectives.

One specific issue to be addressed is that of standards. The problem is not just that formal standards are unnecessarily high, although they often are. Rather, the unfortunate reality is that informal development often falls far short of the minimum standards required to ensure a safe and healthy living environment. When considering possible responses to informality, one key challenge is that of framing an appropriate response to the informal sector's often unsatisfactory standards. This challenge is considered in the following paragraphs.

The challenge of standards

Informal settlements cannot be considered satisfactory if they fail to provide an environment that is both safe and healthy. Since the 19th century, the standard measure for assessing whether settlements meet this requirement has been the degree to which they comply with planning, building, and infrastructure standards. Unfortunately, as already noted in earlier chapters, few informal areas meet even the most basic formal standards, let alone the sometimes-inflated standards promulgated by some governments. Despite this, governments frequently extend services into informal areas, thereby affording them some degree of de facto recognition.

Examples of standards developed specifically for use in low-income developments exist. However, many of these were developed in the context of projects supported by international agencies and very few have been incorporated into national planning standards. The adoption of appropriate sewerage standards in Brazil for condominium schemes is one possible exception to this general rule, but it seems that some municipalities never used these approaches while others have moved away from them. Pakistan's National Sanitation Policy incorporates elements of Orangi Pilot Project (OPP) thinking but this has not been accompanied by any review of standards. Even where government bodies attempt to introduce appropriate standards, there will often be a gap between the minimum standards deemed necessary to provide acceptable living conditions and sustainable services and what is routinely practised by the informal sector.

One approach to bridging the gap between formal planning standards and informal planning norms is to review existing standards in the light of the objectives that they are designed to achieve. For example, car ownership in informal areas is usually low, with motorcycles providing the most common form of motorized transport. If it is accepted that this situation is unlikely to change greatly in the future, critical requirements can be reduced to:

- streets that simply allow emergency vehicles to reach points a maximum specified distance from every house;
- streets that are not required for emergency vehicles are made wide enough to allow pedestrian, motorbike, and perhaps rickshaw access; and
- streets that are wide enough to ensure adequate light and ventilation conditions in adjacent buildings and to minimize fire risk.

Planning standards from Western industrialized countries provide a starting point for assessing what these requirements might mean in practice. For instance, in the UK, the building regulations require that no part of a building should be more than 45 metres from a point reachable by a fire hydrant. Roads designed for fire vehicle access must be at least 3.7 m wide and provision for turning vehicles must be made at the end of any cul-de-sac more than 20 m long. Given that fire vehicles do not vary greatly from country to country, a similar standard might be appropriate in other countries.

Unfortunately, many existing informal areas fail to meet even these standards. One possible response to these situations is to encourage households to take an incremental approach to improving access standards. The GTZ-funded Nasriya Upgrading Project in Aswan attempted to do this by requiring that any householder who wanted to rebuild their house had to set its façade back a maximum of 1.5 m to an agreed line. The intention was that this would lead to the gradual realignment of house façades to provide the desired street width, typically 6 m. It was hoped that house owners would agree to this because the proposed street widths were not excessive and improved access would benefit everyone in the community (Eweida, 2000). Analysis of 2019 satellite images of Nasriya reveals street widths typically in the range 3–4 m, suggesting that the initiative had limited success. However, the approach might repay further investigation and refinement, particularly in settlement in which housing, unlike that in Nasriya, is constructed mainly from non-permanent materials.

If building standards are to reflect informal practices, they must permit the use of materials, such as corrugated sheets, while ensuring that buildings provide a safe, healthy, and comfortable living environment. Using John Turner's terminology, the aim should be to proscribe materials and practices that cannot provide this environment rather than to prescribe those that must be used. The example of Ismailia, among others, shows that governments and the professionals who advise them are often reluctant to accept and act on this principle. It is true that non-conventional materials have drawbacks. Mud blocks require regular maintenance and corrugated sheets are susceptible to rust and have poor sound and heat insulation properties. It is therefore important that standards for such materials should include guidance on how their drawbacks can be minimized. Decoray (2017) provides such guidance for the use of corrugated galvanized iron (CGI) roofing sheets. India's National Building Code includes brief references to the use of stabilized mud blocks but these are insignificant and all but lost in a large document that goes into great detail on every aspect of conventional building construction.

Brazil's experience shows that it is possible to produce infrastructure standards that respond to the conditions found in low-income informal areas. There is clearly a need for other countries to follow its example. And appropriate standards do not have to be low standards. For instance, sewers can be laid at shallow depths where house connections are short and narrow street widths preclude entry of heavy traffic. Where the networks provided are to connect to the services of a formal service provider and/or are to be maintained by that service provider, it is essential that they are acceptable to the provider, and this may require dialogue and pilot-scale initiatives to demonstrate the viability of the standards. It is worth pointing out that many service providers in Western industrialized countries allow standards similar to those used in Brazil for services on private land and lightly trafficked streets. While lessons on what constitute appropriate standards can be learnt from other cities and countries, it will always be important to take account of the ways in which local conditions differ from those in the other locations. The attempt to transfer Brazilian standards to Phnom Penh in Cambodia, described in Chapter 7, provides a good example of the difficulties that ensue if this principle is ignored.

Perhaps the greatest barrier to the formalization of informal sector activities is the need to deal with the implications of incremental development. As explained in Chapter 6, informal development reverses the sequence to Land – People – Housing – Infrastructure, rather than the Land – Infrastructure – Housing – People sequence of conventional housing projects. Plots are occupied when infrastructure services are at an early stage of development and unlikely to provide required minimum levels of service. Buildings may also fail to meet basic standards as plot owners construct basic accommodation, which they seek to improve or add to incrementally over time. Following Turner's proscriptive principle, an appropriate response to this situation might be to ensure that:

- Services meet basic public health needs in the short term but have the potential to be upgraded in the future. This will require specification of minimum standards in terms of water availability and quality, access to toilet facilities, and provision for removal and safe disposal of wastewater and solid waste.
- Housing provides adequate shelter, regardless of the construction materials and methods used, at least in the initial stage of housing construction.

The unfortunate reality is that many settlements will fail to meet even the most reduced standards that are acceptable to formal sector decision-makers. In Bangladesh, during project preparation for what became the World Bank-funded Low Income Communities Housing Support Project (LICHSP), the consultants worked with the National Housing Authority (NHA) to produce revised building and planning standards for low-income areas. The standards proposed 3 metres minimum clearance in front of newly constructed single and two storey buildings, reduced to 1.2 metres for single storey buildings and 1.8 m for two storey buildings in existing settlements. Similar attempts to amend access standards have been made elsewhere but few have resulted in changes in legislation. Even if accepted, the unfortunate reality is that many existing informal settlements do not comply with even such reduced standards.

If it is accepted that there is limited scope for improvements in access, the response to fire risks in existing informal areas will have to be multi-faceted. A framework for addressing fire safety in informal areas might include mitigation, preparedness, response, and recovery (Arup, 2018). Ideally, mitigation would include the provision of adequate space around buildings, multiple escape routes from those buildings, and fire breaks. In practice, poverty and the lack of alternatives forces people into informal housing that meets none of these conditions. In such cases, it might still be possible for organizations that support communities to coordinate their efforts in order to deliver consistent fire safety messages.

Many planners and engineers assume that narrow lanes and irregular site layouts make it impossible to upgrade utility services in informal areas to provide acceptable levels of service. While this may be true of services provided to conventional standards, the examples of North-east Lahore and condominium systems in Brazil, among others, show that networked services can be delivered to informal areas if they are built using standards that are tailored to suit local conditions. For instance, sewers laid in pedestrian lanes do not need to be as deep as those under main roads because the external loading on them is much lower. Such 'appropriate' standards will tend to be cheaper than those built to arbitrary standards developed in the light of very different conditions.

The key point to emerge from this discussion is the need to recognize that:

- the standards adopted should relate to function and location; and
- they should take account of the possibility that levels of service can be improved over time.

Without acceptance of these principles, it is hard to see how incremental approaches such as that of Khuda ki Basti (see Chapter 6) can be formalized and widely adopted. The second implies the need for an increased emphasis on processes, and this in turn will require significant changes in official thinking, in both governments and international agencies. A good starting point for achieving these changes will be to explore the implications of the de facto recognition of informal settlements, something that governments frequently do by providing services to those settlements.

Bearing these points in mind, a generalized low-income housing strategy can be elaborated, based on the responses to informality introduced in Chapters 5–7, as follows:

Construction of complete housing units

Chapter 5 showed that governments still assume that construction of complete housing units is the best response to informality. Housing units may be located on greenfield sites on the outskirts of towns and cities or may replace existing informal housing *in situ*. The latter is often referred to as upgrading but a more accurate term is reconstruction. Most schemes provide apartments in medium- or high-rise blocks, as described in Chapter 5. As already noted, such schemes provide few opportunities for residents to extend their houses to provide additional accommodation. Low-rise housing schemes that provide one housing unit per plot are more flexible but less common. Charles Correa's Belapur scheme in Navi Mumbai, described in Chapter 6, is an example of a low-rise scheme designed to allow both horizontal and vertical expansion.

The World Bank-funded sites and services schemes in Tamil Nadu and Chennai, described in Chapter 6, show that low-rise schemes can achieve housing and population densities of over 300 units and 1,200 people per hectare respectively, after vertical expansion. While these densities would be considered high in most situations, there are cities in which existing informal settlement densities easily exceed 2,000 people per hectare, such as in Egypt. At such densities, low-rise development is only possible if plot sizes are extremely small. To achieve a target population density of 2,000 people per hectare, with an average household size of 5 and 40 per cent of the land occupied by roads, public spaces, and public facilities, the 400 plots required per hectare would occupy 6,000 m^2, giving an average plot size of 15 m^2, which is too small to be viable.

In such situations, as shown by the examples in Chapter 5, many governments seek to redevelop existing informal areas, providing housing units in medium- and high-rise apartments. The Indian Alliance's Rajiv Indira/ Suryodaya scheme illustrates a situation in which redevelopment appears to be the only viable approach. The scheme's three blocks reserved for low-income families occupied a plot of about 1,900 square metres and were designed to provide 208 housing units. If the scheme had used single storey development, the land available would have been only 9 m^2 per housing unit, clearly too small to be viable.

Even where the primary aim of redevelopment is to benefit poor people, the housing provided is often unaffordable to the current inhabitants, who cannot afford the rents on the new properties and so are forced out. This has been a recurrent theme, from the Boundary Estate in East London, described in Chapter 2, onwards. Construction costs tend to increase with increased building height. The author's analysis of construction costs given in Community Led Infrastructure Finance Facility (CLIFF) annual reports revealed the following approximate costs for CLIFF projects implemented in the early 2000s:

- For high-rise (typically around seven storeys) schemes, Rs260,000–310,000 (US$6,000–7000) per apartment.
- For schemes with blocks up to three storeys in height, Rs100,000–130,000 ($2,300–3,000) per unit.

The difference is likely to be greater where poor ground conditions lead to increased foundation costs for tall buildings. Supporters of the apartment block approach to housing provision will no doubt argue that its reduced land requirement and hence saving on land cost will more than compensate for increased construction cost. This may be true where schemes designed to reduce land costs will tend to have very high densities, a point illustrated by the analysis in Chapter 5. Taken together, the high densities, relatively high cost, and lack of flexibility of apartment schemes mean that they should be used sparingly. Options that allow for incremental development should be preferred where they are viable. In most cases, this will mean that upgrading, perhaps involving some re-blocking, and sites and services and core housing schemes will be better options.

The Indian Alliance schemes (Chapter 5) illustrate the important point that those who will be affected by that action should have a voice. This requirement is all too often missing in government and private sector attempts to redevelop informal settlements. Where existing economic forces are driving redevelopment processes, as for instance in the case of Howrah's *thika* tenancies described in Chapter 9, the only response open to those seeking to protect poor people's rights may be to work to minimize the adverse impact on existing low-income residents.

Sites and services and core housing

As explained in Chapter 6, sites and services schemes were a central feature of approaches by international agencies to low-income housing from the 1970s to the 1990s but then fell out of favour because of their apparent lack of impact. The success of the schemes described in Chapter 6 suggests that the decision to abandon them completely was premature. Accepting this, the questions to be answered are:

- What role should they play in an integrated low-income housing strategy?
- What constraints prevented them from being more successful in the past?
- How might those constraints be overcome?

Sites and services schemes should certainly have a role in replacing unregulated subdivisions. The advantages flowing from this include rational layouts and provision for at least minimal services. The example of Khuda ki Basti suggests that they also have the potential to reach down to those who would otherwise find it difficult to access housing markets for ownership. That of the Tamil Nadu schemes shows that they can reach lower-income households indirectly as householders construct additional rooms for rent. In a similar way, Ismailia shows the potential for serviced sites to develop over time.

An obvious constraint on the sites and services option is the apparent shortage of developable land close to the places where low-income households live and work. In the 1980s and 1990s, many sites and services proposals were not implemented because government departments were unable to assemble the land required for the schemes. Successful schemes, including Ismailia and the Tamil Nadu and Mumbai schemes described in Chapter 6, relied on land that was already in government ownership. However, land cannot be an absolute constraint. Private sector actors, in both the formal and informal sectors, routinely assemble, subdivide, and sell land. In Pakistan development authorities have implemented large-scale programmes to provide sites for middle- and higher-income housing. The first task of those seeking to reintroduce the sites and services approach must therefore be to develop mechanisms for accessing land that benefit society as a whole rather than simply land developers and corrupt government officials.

Costs will be reduced if land is assembled in large parcels. While working in Peshawar, the author helped to design and implement a small housing scheme on land purchased by the St Michael's Housing Society, an initiative started by one of the Catholic parishes in Peshawar. The scheme involved construction of core houses and the provision of water supply, sewerage, and street paving. Land had been purchased for what became the core of the scheme but more land was purchased as houses were built, people moved in, and more people joined the society. Land prices rose sharply as farmers realized that the land was in demand for housing. If the land had been purchased as one large parcel at the beginning, rather than incrementally, the price would have been quite acceptable. Government or a proxy such as a public land development company would have the resources to purchase, hold, and eventually develop the land. As with upgrading, the key to effective action will be the introduction of appropriate and effective institutional arrangements.

Peripheral land will normally be cheaper and easier to assemble than that located close to urban centres, and, in many cases, such peripheral land will also be beyond the limits of transport corridors and existing networked services. Informal sector land subdividers and developers sidestep this problem by selling parcels and/or buildings first, and assuming that residents or government will then step in to provide services, perhaps over time. Both Khuda ki Basti and Ismailia mimicked this approach by creating plots and providing basic services in the first instance. As indicated earlier in this chapter, widespread adoption of this approach will only be possible if ways can be found to amend service delivery standards to allow initial basic service provision, followed by incremental improvements.

At root, all of these constraints are, at least partly, institutional. At one level, government institutions appear to be less effective than private sector actors in gaining access to land. However, the real problem arguably lies deeper in the attitudes and assumptions of politicians and government officials. Both governments and private sector developers have often succeeded in finding land for higher-income housing in cities in which assembling land for sites and services schemes aimed at the urban poor has proved to be impossible. There is a large element of self-interest here. The profits to be made from land assembly and sale for higher-income development are certainly greater than those that can be made from providing land for the urban poor. The Maspero Triangle scheme in Cairo bears witness to this, as does the development pressures on Dharavi. There are genuine issues with the standards adopted by informal sector builders, but governments are rarely willing to enter into dialogue on amendments to unnecessarily high standards. We will return to institutional matters later in this chapter. For the moment, it is sufficient to note that the perceived failure of the sites and services concept was more to do with attitudes, assumptions, and institutional capacities than with any fundamental flaws in the concept itself. It is time to examine the concept again, recognizing the need to deal with the tension between formal and informal practices and to overcome institutional constraints.

Upgrading

The great strength of upgrading is its acceptance of the existence of informal development. It starts from where people are rather than where politicians and administrators would like them to be. Some upgrading projects have achieved widespread coverage. However, as noted in previous chapters, most of these projects, for instance the Kampung Improvement Programme (KIP) in Indonesia and Urban Partnerships for Poverty Reduction (UPPR) in

Bangladesh, have had limited objectives, relating mainly to improvements in street paving, on-site sanitation, and local drainage. Where water supply improvements have been included, they have tended to rely on ground water. While relatively easy to achieve, such improvements are likely to have limited impacts on the living conditions of the residents of the upgraded areas. This is particularly true of schemes that are built to low standards, using poor quality materials, as is often the case with ad hoc improvements funded by politicians, NGOs, and communities themselves. In the case of drainage schemes, failure to see local improvements within their wider context may actually make conditions worse. For instance, the common practice of raising roads and paths above the plinth levels of adjacent houses blocks drainage paths and directs storm flows into residential space.

One consequence of this situation is that politicians, government officials, and 'respectable' society tend to view upgrading as a temporary, one-off response to housing problems, to be replaced by 'real' housing in due course. To induce a more sustainable response, upgrading should ideally seek to bring about more process-oriented and staged changes. These changes should ideally involve:

- Rationalized and improved layouts, which facilitate movement, improve light and ventilation conditions, reduce fire risk, and improve access for emergency vehicles.
- Improved services in stages, ideally linked to municipal systems.
- Progressive Improvements to the housing stock.

Where existing layouts are convoluted, with narrow rights of way and limited open space, one option will be to re-create a completely new layout through what is commonly referred to as 're-blocking.' Re-blocking has been carried out successfully by Community Organizations Development Institute (CODI) in Thailand and Slum/Shack Dwellers International (SDI) in South Africa, in conjunction with measures to improve tenure security (CODI, 2019; Hendler and Fieuw, 2018). A specific aim of re-blocking in South Africa was to reduce fire risk (Gontsana, 2016). Most if not all of the CODI and SDI schemes have been located in areas where residents lack legal tenure. Gaining tenure recognition can be a strong motivation to agree to wholesale re-blocking. This can be seen in the experience of the LICHSP project in Bangladesh, which suggests that residents are less amenable to re-blocking where they can already claim ownership of the land that they live on.

Previous chapters have identified the constraints on the extension of municipal services into informal areas, and one obvious constraint is the inadequacy of existing off-site networks and service systems. These can be considered supply-side constraints. Water and sewerage networks and solid waste collection services often have limited coverage and lack the capacity required to allow extensions into informal areas. Electricity supply networks are more likely to penetrate informal settlements but often deliver electricity intermittently and at low voltage due to low system capacities. Schools, health facilities, and other social services are likely to be inadequate in terms of both quality and quantity. On the demand side, low-income residents may be unwilling to pay for municipal infrastructure services, particularly when the service quality is low.

Examples provided throughout this book show that many governments' preferred response to perceived deficiencies in informal buildings has been to demolish and replace existing structures with either apartment blocks or standardized single-storey housing units. In true upgrading, as opposed to redevelopment, the approach would support the incremental improvement processes commonly found in the informal sector. What this might mean in practice will depend on local conditions and existing construction methods. Where existing buildings already use permanent materials such as brick and concrete, the greatest demand is likely to be for vertical or horizontal building extensions. Where buildings use poor quality materials, there is likely to be an equal demand on improvements to the building fabric. To date, few upgrading schemes have enjoyed much success in responding to either demand.

Taken together, these points suggest the need for a more ambitious and holistic approach to upgrading existing informal settlements. The aim should be, as far as is possible, to improve settlement layouts, facilitate residents' access to municipal services, and improve the quality and size of their housing. The big question is how to achieve these aims. Possible answers to this question will be explored later in this chapter. For the moment, the following points can be made:

- Municipalities and the local government departments that support them must be involved in upgrading initiatives. Without them, it will be very difficult to ensure that upgrading initiatives are integrated into wider municipal plans.
- Similarly, service providers must be involved in planning and implementing service improvements. They should be encouraged to explore options for adapting their standards to facilitate service extensions into informal areas.
- Efforts to improve settlement layouts will require action to record existing land ownership arrangements, convince community members of the benefits of re-blocking, and facilitate agreement on any land transfers required to facilitate re-blocking.
- Housing finance institutions (particularly microfinance companies) can provide the financial support required by individual households and groups of households that wish to improve their housing conditions.

In an ideal world, the municipality would take a leading role and coordinate the activities of other stakeholders. Unfortunately, many municipalities are weak financially, have severely limited planning and service delivery capabilities, and few have people with the knowledge and skills required to engage with communities on the complex issues that surround the land adjustments required for re-blocking initiatives. The Department for International

Development (DFID) was right in the 1990s and 2000s to emphasize the need to strengthen municipal systems and capacities. However, as already noted in Chapter 8, the impact on informal settlements would have been greater if its approach had focused more directly on the efforts to strengthen responses to informality. Where local government lacks the human and organizational resources required to support innovative approaches to upgrading, the institutional options introduced earlier in this chapter should be explored, always bearing in mind the aim of integrating informal settlements into the overall urban fabric to the greatest extent possible.

Integration will best be achieved if informal settlements are viewed in their overall context rather than individually. DFID's 3 × 3 matrix worked against this, prioritizing settlements that ranked lowest on both infrastructure deficiencies and poverty and vulnerability, regardless of their relationship to each other, and thus downplaying the need to see settlements in their context. UPPR's approach was similar, with priority given to the poorest settlements identified through a weighted settlement living conditions index (SLCI) approach (Fortuny et al., 2011). Although aimed at helping the poorest, neither approach recognized the possibility of dealing with clusters of contiguous low-income settlements, including both settlements ranked lowest in the matrix or index and those with a higher ranking. A cluster-based approach would have allowed a more rational approach to off-site infrastructure provision and this would have facilitated efforts to integrate informal settlements into the overall fabric of the city. Such an approach would be similar to Himanchu Parikh's slum networking approach, without going so far as to assume that all slums will always be located along natural drainage paths.

Some informal settlements, particularly those on the urban fringe, are located some distance from the nearest functioning municipal services, and resource constraints will often mean that such areas are unlikely to receive municipal services in the near future. One response to this situation is to provide self-contained and locally managed services to serve individual settlements and housing schemes. The Lusaka Water Trust model is a good example of this approach. Established with the help of CARE International in the early 2000s, Water Trusts (WTs) are community-owned and managed water and sanitation service providers. By 2014, there were 12 WTs, all supplying water to informal settlements. Some were also managing public toilets and some had taken part in pilot faecal sludge management schemes initiated by Water and Sanitation for the Urban Poor (WSUP). A 2014 review of three of the early WTs (Nkonkomalimba and Mumba, 2014) found that they had expanded their services over the years, providing a generally good water supply service. All three were meeting their operational costs from revenue, albeit with some subsidy in the form of services provided to them by the Lusaka Water and Sanitation Company (LWSC). The largest, Chipata WT, also claimed to be able to meet system expansion costs. Both LWSC and Lusaka City Council (LCC) provided support to these WTs. LWSC monitors water quality, provides technical assistance, and helps WTs to deal with outbreaks of water-related disease, assists with the design of new facilities, and provides training for board members and managers. These services were initially provided free of charge but by 2014 human and financial resource constraints led to pressure for new service contracts that would require WTs to pay for some of these services. LCC support took various forms, including provision of office space in community-based LCC offices and assistance with preparation of legal documents and land procurement.

The Water Trust model has some similarities to the independent water provider model on the outskirts of Maputo, which was described in Chapter 9. Its management structure is, of course, different in that it involves the community and enjoys support from a formal service provider. To what extent might these models be replicable? The answer to this question must take account of existing institutional arrangements. The Lusaka initiative would not have been possible without the support provided by LWSC. In the case of Maputo, it is possible that a similar model might be introduced to both support and regulate existing private sector water providers.

Institutional change: options and constraints

The most important lesson to emerge from this book is that the biggest constraints on better engagement with the informal sector are institutional. Chapter 3 introduced the thinking of Douglass North and others on institutions, with North stressing the importance of both internal and external factors on what he terms 'institutional path dependence'. Failing to adequately allow for such institutional concerns, international development agencies have repeatedly attempted to address housing needs through government agencies that are inadequate, inappropriate or both. Their assumption has been that their interventions will lead to institutional change, but time and time again, partner organizations have reverted to their old ways once the international agency has ended its assistance. In fact, change requires organizations that are open to new ideas and therefore able to incorporate alternative views, theories, and ways of working. Where this condition is not met, a donor can promote and facilitate change but it is unlikely that it will be sustained once the donor withdraws their support. Lasting change will be particularly difficult to achieve where attitudes to informality are both negative and deeply ingrained, as earlier chapters have shown is the case in many countries.

One response to such situations is to focus on the role of 'champions', individuals within organizations who are committed to changing those organizations for the better. Unfortunately, many of the initiatives described in this book show that the changes resulting from the efforts of such individuals tend to erode over time, since institutions are often remarkably resistant to change and tend to revert to the status quo when left to their own devices. The change management literature emphasizes the need to convince individuals working within organizations of the need for fundamental reform. In doing so, it pays insufficient attention to the fact that individuals are strongly influenced by the culture of the organization within which they work. Thus, for instance, if rent-seeking is a fundamental aspect of an organization's culture, it is very difficult to insist that individuals act honestly and transparently. Their choices often boil down to leaving the organization or becoming part of the corrupt culture. Whether or not undesirable practices such as rent-seeking are present, perverse incentives may create a barrier to change. Partly to reduce opportunities for corruption and nepotism, many government systems require strict adherence to rules and procedures, regardless of whether they are relevant and useful. The sanctions imposed on those who transgress discourage innovation and lead to a situation in which it is safer to do nothing than to develop new responses to challenges. All these factors act as a break on urgently needed institutional change.

The need for institutional change and development is not confined to government departments and agencies. The examples given in this book show that national and international NGOs and even international development agencies can also be fixed in their ideas and can be resistant to the possibility of change. However, there is little doubt that government attitudes to informality continue to be a major constraint on efforts to develop effective responses to the housing needs of the urban poor.

Marxists like Burgess argue that real change cannot be achieved without radical political and economic reform. This view is closer to the truth than that of those who talk glibly about the ability of 'development' to end poverty or at least significantly reduce it. Unfortunately, there is little evidence that governments are queuing up to make radical changes in their systems of governance. This being so, the immediate challenge is to introduce improved institutional arrangements within the constraints imposed by existing political systems. The options can be grouped into those that:

- strengthen existing government systems;
- support direct action by residents of informal settlements, typically through organizations of the urban poor and with support provided by national NGOs;
- create new institutions, with the intention of overcoming the limitations of existing government responses to informality.

The first is normally the preferred choice of international development agencies. They typically require that a project management unit (PMU) be created to manage a project and that consultants are hired to provide support to the PMU and government implementing bodies. The expected outcome is a strengthened government body, but unfortunately the practical outcome is usually quite different. The consultants and PMU remove any direct need for the government body to respond to the situation that the project is designed to address, and in fact they mostly operate to by-pass the deficiencies found in these bodies. Even where a government agency or department appears to change its approach to meet the requirements of a supporting international agency, the change will often be one of rhetoric rather than genuine conviction. With the end of international support, the PMU almost always is disbanded, the consultants depart, and the agency or department slips easily back into its old ways. Resistance to change is likely to be particularly problematic in countries with authoritarian governments, dominated by members of an elite who have no wish to challenge the status quo and hence their own interests.

Support to direct action by residents of informal settlements has obvious merits but, as illustrated by the examples given in Chapter 8, has fallen well short of having a city-wide impact. The lack of impact is attributable to the fact that governments view NGOs and alliances of the poor as outsiders and sometimes troublemakers. As a result, they struggle to gain government recognition, and this, even when gained, is more often than not transitory. Dealing with this situation certainly requires a change in the way government views organizations of the urban poor. It also requires that NGOs and alliances of the urban poor review the extent to which their own attitudes and assumptions create barriers to the partnerships required to move from local to city-wide action. There is, for example, a need for dialogue on the details of the infrastructure standards and details promoted by organizations such as OPP. As noted in Chapter 7, sewers built to OPP's standards are cheap but also inadequate and prone to premature failure.

Many would oppose the option of creating new institutions on the grounds that it creates unnecessary complexity and diverts attention away from the task of strengthening existing systems. This is a valid argument where existing government bodies are reasonably flexible and open to change. Unfortunately, it is clear from the cases described in this book that this is often not the case. There is little point in pouring resources into organizations that are dysfunctional and riven with personal interests. Where this is the reality, the creation of new institutions can be a catalyst for change, as was the case in the creation of the Ismailia Land Development Agency in Egypt (Chapter 6). Success will depend on the attention paid to staff selection, pay and conditions, financial independence, training, and the introduction of incentives to ensure transparency. There is a danger that the effectiveness of new institutions will erode over time, but this danger is arguably less than for the other options.

The best course of action in any situation will thus depend on the openness to new ideas of existing political and administrative systems.

- Where existing organizations are open to change, the best option will normally be to work through them while encouraging them to foster closer links with NGOs and organizations of the urban poor. It may be appropriate to create new permanent organizations to provide niche support.
- Where there is at least some recognition of the need for change among senior politicians and senior administrators, but where existing institutions are dysfunctional and resistant to change, the possibility of complete new institutional arrangements should be explored.
- Where politicians and government officials do not recognize the need to engage with the informal sector, direct action by organizations of the urban poor and the NGOs that support them may be the only option.

If so, the organization or organizations leading the process should constantly seek opportunities to engage with government and, where appropriate, formal sector developers.

OPP's influence on the approach taken by the Khuda ki Basti initiative and the Sindh Katchi Abadis Authority (SKAA) from the late 1980s onwards provides an example of the way in which government bodies can be influenced by NGO thinking. The OPP approach had a strong champion in the person of Mr Tasneem Siddiqui in his roles of Director General of both Hyderabad Development Authority (HDA) and later the SKAA. Unfortunately, there is no evidence that HDA continued to use the approach after Mr Siddiqui's departure. The SKAA was still using it in 2008 but on a small scale (Hasan, 2008). This illustrates the important point that NGOs must influence institutions, rather than individuals, if they are to bring about lasting change.

Some institutional options

CODI is perhaps the best example of the creation of a new government institution to facilitate development activities in informal settlements. Its website refers to its role in strengthening communities and their organizations and acting as a bridge between formal and informal systems. Ismailia provides another example of the creation of new government agencies. CODI has developed over the years, through several changes of government. However, as already noted in Chapter 8, organizations like CODI are ultimately dependent on political support, and this support is not always easy to sustain. The Ismailia Planning and Land Development Agency lost its relevance as centralized thinking in the Egyptian government and lack of continued support by international agencies undermined the philosophy that underpinned it. Mumbai's Slum Rehabilitation Authority has fared better and still plays an active role in slum redevelopment in the city. In theory, it is an autonomous body with planning powers, but in practice its approach is closely tied to that of the Maharashtra Government as a whole. It functions purely as an approving authority, scrutinizing developers' proposals and approving or rejecting them (Zhang, 2016).

Its experiment with a new Dharavi Community Land Trust, to be governed by former landowners, community members, and neighbourhood associations, never materialized (Carr, 2015), even though it echoed on a large scale the concept of small community land trusts (CLTs) which emerged in the USA during the civil rights movement in the 1960s and became firmly established in the 1990s. The concept was adopted in the United Kingdom in the 2000s. CLTs have been established in other countries, including Belgium, France, Italy, and Australia.

How might the CLT model be adapted to deal with the larger and more complex challenges of informal settlements such as Dharavi? Any organization working in such settlements will require good planning and engineering capabilities, combined with both ability and willingness to engage in dialogue with the communities located within the areas for which they were responsible. In order to resist commercial pressures from those with little interest in the well-being of the inhabitants, it would need strong legal powers. These requirements do not appear to have been seriously considered in the proposal for Dharavi (Mumbai). It would seem that, while CLTs offer an option for organizing at the local level, there is also a need for institutions that operate at a higher level to provide support to community organizations and to mediate with government as a whole. One option for meeting this need would be to use a modified version of the development corporation model, such as was created in the 1980s in the UK under Margaret Thatcher. These urban development corporations (UDCs) were to revitalize run-down industrial and inner-city areas, and their specific remit was to develop a strategic vision for an area and then secure the public and private investment required to implement that vision. The UDC model was criticized for its lack of local accountability as local government was sidelined and the model tended to prioritize economic development over the interests of the existing inhabitants of the UDC area.

However, it is possible to envisage a model that retains the strengths of the UDC model, while providing a central role for the community and local government institutions. This would focus on the needs of informal areas and the options for integrating them into the city as a whole. It might be constituted as a public company, with a board including representatives of residents' groups, local NGOs with relevant knowledge and experience, local government, other government departments, the private sector, and academia. Staff would be recruited from both government and the private sector. The core team should cover a range of disciplines, providing knowledge and expertise relating to land, housing, services and infrastructure, community development, and institutional development, among others.

The main disadvantage of the UDC model is that it removes any direct role for city-wide municipalities. In theory, this disadvantage could be overcome by designing interventions so that the UDC-style organization could eventually be absorbed into the municipality, preferably as a specialist 'informal settlements unit'. However, the model does nothing to strengthen the municipality itself and so the long-term effectiveness of the unit cannot be guaranteed. Another option is to create an organization within a national, provincial or state local government department to provide support to municipalities. The DFID-supported upgrading initiatives in India described in Chapter 7 attempted to provide such support, but as noted there, did not have a strong focus on the issues surrounding informality. They also suffered from the fact that they were conceived as projects, so that the supportive institutional arrangements did not necessarily continue beyond the end of donor funding. A potentially more interesting model is Pakistan's Punjab Urban Development Project (PUDP) in Chapter 7. This was created as a public sector company in 1998 to support the World Bank-funded Punjab Municipal Services Improvement Project (PMSIP). Registered under the Companies

Ordinance 1984, it aims to incorporate the expertise and efficiency of the private sector, while aligning itself with the development vision of the local governments as well as that of the provincial government. The PMSIP closed in 2013 but PMDFC continues to play an important role as the technical arm of Punjab's Local Government and Community Development Department. Although a relatively small organization, PMDFC offers expertise in municipal planning and infrastructure services including operation and maintenance, GIS systems, contract management, and municipal governance, including financial management. It has developed a range of training materials and provides training to local government staff.

In his role as municipal engineer and planner on the World Bank team, the author interacted closely with PMDFC during PMSIP preparation and implementation. Its effectiveness certainly depended on its ability to identify, recruit, and retain good people, but this cannot be the whole story. One probable reason for the success of the PMSIP approach is its relatively modest scale, since its low profile meant that it was not subject to early political pressures. By the time that such pressures might have been exerted, PMDFC had proved its value and was seen as an important asset by the Punjab Government. Another important factor was the flexibility of the PMSIP process. Individual sub-projects were identified in the course of the project in consultation with local authorities and were then prepared by local consultants. In contrast, the companies created under the Asian Development Bank (ADB)-funded Sindh Cities Improvement Program, with aims similar to PMSIP, were tied to a programme of works determined during a rather inadequate project preparation process. When problems arose with aspects of this programme, it lacked the flexibility to adapt its approach and foundered along with the project itself.

The World Bank's PMDFC's role during PMSIP was primarily advisory, and this meant that it was difficult to ensure that local governments followed through on its recommended operational improvements. Nevertheless, it does suggest a model that could be adapted to provide formal support to municipalities and other government departments on innovative approaches to dealing with informality. The adapted model would have to interact with organizations representing the inhabitants of informal settlements and also to develop expertise in a range of relevant professional disciplines, not least those relating to information systems and land records.

New institutional arrangements will not be successfully implemented without vision and political will and will not be sustained without political support. CODI has endured through changes in government, but there are many examples, for instance Sri Lanka's Million Houses Programme, that were abandoned after a change in government. The central issue here is the need to overcome negative attitudes to the informal sector and recognition of its crucial role in providing affordable and suitable housing. As noted earlier in this chapter, support from politicians and senior government officials is needed if new initiatives are to get off the ground. Unfortunately, initiatives started by such 'champions' of change are vulnerable because the objectives of their instigators often differ from those held by other mainstream decision-makers. Such champion-led initiatives are at significant risk of becoming just one more demonstration initiative that sinks without trace after it has achieved its initial limited objectives. Initiatives that challenge the status quo will be more likely to endure and prosper if they receive support from international agencies, but this support will need to extend considerably beyond the usual five-year duration of a typical project. This point is considered in more detail in the next section.

Lessons for international organizations

Previous chapters in this book have shown that bilateral and multilateral development agencies are generally more open to innovative responses to informality than most governments. However, the overall impact of their support for such responses has been very limited. The sites and services concept, strongly supported by the World Bank, appeared and disappeared without changing the fact that governments continued to build conventional housing schemes that were unaffordable and/or inappropriate for the urban poor. Upgrading projects still receive support but are often unambitious, limiting themselves to incremental improvements in infrastructure provision, which have limited impact on the underlying realities of life in low-income settlements and have little in the way of demonstration effects. Efforts to improve governance have had some success, but the examination of DFID's projects in India in Chapter 8 show that the changes achieved have not had much long-lasting impact on housing systems to serve the urban poor.

Lessons emerging from this experience include the need for:

- *Recognition of institutional constraints*: in particular, there is no point in attempting to implement innovative programmes unless the institutions responsible for them are transparent, functional, and have a commitment to innovation and change.
- *Long-term commitment,* which takes account of the considerable time that will usually be required for changes in attitudes, assumptions, and practices to permeate implementing organizations.
- *Awareness of complexity:* all too often analysis stops at the end of project preparation. But this is precisely the point at which it should really begin.
- *Flexibility in project operations,* which is essential in order to respond to the complexity inherent in informal housing, must be built into project architecture and processes.

Some of the initiatives supported by international agencies failed to meet any of these requirements. The government departments that implemented them had limited capacity and even less interest in responding to the needs of the informal sector. And initiatives were invariably project-based, with individual projects lasting a limited period, typically around five years. This gives insufficient time for the institutional development and change that is essential for long-term success. The widespread use of consultants to circumvent capacity constraints further limited institutional change. Terms of reference often referred to the need to provide training to the staff of host organizations, but such training normally took the form of short workshops, and while these might introduce trainees to the possibilities for change, they cannot provide the in-depth knowledge required for significant changes in working practices. Even where initiatives provided useful on-the-job training, rigid institutional systems constrained trainees from implementing what they had learnt.

Urban projects are invariably complex, with issues emerging in the course of implementation that are sometimes difficult to foresee. The traditional project cycle followed by international development organizations involves an orderly progression through project identification, preparation, appraisal, approval, implementation, and evaluation. Targets are identified during project preparation and there is limited scope to make adjustments in the light of lessons learnt during implementation. The situation is not helped by the procedures required by international agencies to ensure transparency and compliance with social and environmental safeguard requirements. These can cause considerable frustration among local stakeholders, who wonder why decisions and subsequent action take so long. The traditional project cycle can work where there is widespread agreement on objectives and the steps required to achieve them, but it is much less effective where competing interests and visions and a lack of information mean that it is hard to predict the consequences of interventions. Unfortunately, these are the circumstances encountered when dealing with many donor-driven urban initiatives, not least those concerning informal housing.

A better approach in such circumstances is to adopt a process approach in which implementation takes place in stages, with later stages planned in the light of the outcome of initial interventions (ODA, 1992). This approach was the basis for the 'New Project Cycle' promoted by staff from the World Bank's Operations Evaluation Division (OED) in 1994. This emphasized the need for listening, piloting, and demonstrating before mainstreaming (Picciotto and Weaving, 1994). It is reproduced in slightly simplified form in Figure 10.1.

Picciotto and Weaving's approach appears to draw on Denis Rondinelli's 'adaptive' approach to planning, which emphasized the need for strategic planning, incremental analysis, experimental design, and successive approximation in decision-making (Rondinelli, 1993). It also reflects the thinking of Calden and Wildavsky (1974) who argued that learning and adaptability could be fostered by breaking large complex problems into smaller disaggregated ones, which could then be dealt with incrementally. It is interesting to note that, partly due to circumstances, the North-east Lahore Project described in Chapter 7 adopted an incremental approach and was the better for it. Unfortunately, Picciotto and Weaving's thinking has had little influence on the way in which internationally funded projects have been planned and

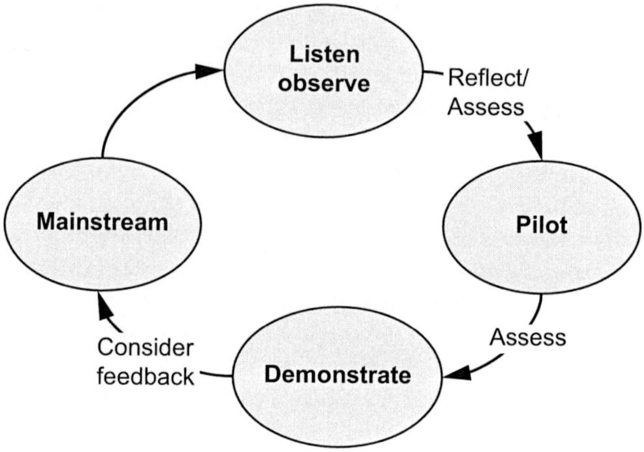

Figure 10.1 New project cycle
Source: adapted from Picciotto and Weaving, 1994

executed in the subsequent quarter century. Funding agencies continue to use the traditional project cycle and the emphasis on outputs rather than process has, if anything, grown stronger over the years. The Faisalabad Area Upgrading Project (FAUP), described in Chapter 7, provides an early example of this. ODA was insistent that the project should take a process approach, but were equally insistent that progress should be assessed in relation to the logical framework produced before the project began. It seemed to be unaware of the inherent contradiction between these requirements.

This brief review of current practice suggests a need to fundamentally rethink the ways in which international agencies approach informal sector challenges in the urban context. This must start from acceptance that development is a learning process very much grounded in local realities, and that this requires a flexible approach to planning and will almost always extend beyond the time limits imposed by the existing project cycle. This will require a commitment to support promising initiatives over periods of 10 years and more. There will often be a need to create new institutions with a specific remit to engage with informal sector stakeholders, including resident associations, NGOs, and, where appropriate, the informal private sector. Ensuring that these institutions are effective will require a renewed commitment to changing attitudes and working practices. There is arguably a need to promote a new professionalism, as explained below, and also for international agencies to have a key role in providing support for new institutional structures and systems.

The need for a new professionalism

Robert Chambers (1993) called for an end to 'normal professionalism', his term for the dominant thinking, values, methods, and behaviour in a profession or discipline (Chapter 4.) He argued that this type of professionalism was conservative and was sustained by a core–periphery structure of knowledge and knowledge generation, linked to education and training systems, organizational hierarchies, and the rewards and career patterns of international development organizations. Chambers noted the inertia in many educational institutions and their tendency to rely on ideas generated in the West, which focus on the needs of rich people but have little to say about the lives and concerns of the poor.

Chambers' arguments were grounded in his rural development experience, but many of the issues that he identified also arise in the urban sector. For instance, planning education in the South is overwhelmingly based on often outdated Western models that focus on Western cities and their suburbs. During the early days of the FAUP, a young social organizer, a planner by profession, proudly showed the author his copy of Lewis Keeble's *Principles and Practice of Town and Country Planning*, the most recent version of which had been published in 1964. In the late 1990s, Keeble's idea of planning as the art and science of creating safe, beautiful living environments still permeated Zambian planning thought (Kazimbaya-Senkwe, 1997). Planning courses started from the underlying assumption that the plan, once produced, was enforceable. This alone was a killer assumption. Resource problems and the existence of the informal sector and the factors that had led to its growth could be blissfully ignored. Kazimbaya-Senkwe argued that planning education should deal with facts on the ground rather than an idealized version of reality. Reflecting Turner's proscriptive thinking, she called for an approach to development control that sought to reduce if not do away with the negative externalities of informal development rather than to prevent informal development altogether. Planning law modules, usually of Western origin, should provide opportunities for critical appraisal of existing laws rather than thrust them unquestioningly at students.

Conventional engineering education similarly provides little guidance on dealing with the technical challenge of providing services to informal settlements. It is often assumed that infrastructure provision for low-income communities is straightforward. In fact, the opposite is frequently the case, partly because of the tendency for informal settlements to occupy marginal low-lying and steeply sloping sites and partly because of the need to deal with the lack or poor quality of off-site services. Narrow rights of way require non-standard approaches to water supply, sewerage, and drainage provision. Few conventionally trained engineers are equipped to deal with these issues, and unfortunately engineers are often more reluctant than their architect and planner colleagues to adapt approaches to take account of informal sector realities.

Chambers' response to professional deficiencies was to advocate 'handing over the stick' from professionals to local people, who should take the lead in analysis and project planning (Chambers, 1994). In effect, he downgraded the role of professionals to that of technicians who faithfully follow the instructions of the community. His approach has some validity in relation to problems that can be dealt with locally, but it breaks down when the issues to be dealt with stretch beyond local communities. Responses to water supply, drainage, solid waste disposal, and electricity supply challenges must involve professionals with specialist knowledge. F. A. Hayek's distinction between universally applicable 'scientific' knowledge and local knowledge provides a basis for a more subtle take on the roles of professionals and community members in initiatives involving urban informality (Hayek, 1945). Community members do have local knowledge, but they are unlikely to be aware of all the options that are open to them, with the result that they will tend to be conservative in their approach to housing construction and service provision. Without access to sound technical advice, they will continue to adopt local solutions to local problems, ignoring the wider implications of their actions. The result will be a fragmented, and therefore unsatisfactory, response to service needs. This suggests a need not to 'hand over the stick' but rather to 'share the stick', with both communities and professionals bringing their knowledge and insights to bear on problems. This will require professionals who both understand the communities with which they work and have a sound understanding of the technical and contextual challenges posed by informal development. It is not true to say, as one social development specialist once said to the author, that it did not particularly matter if an engineer is technically competent as long as he or she understands and is trusted by the community. Yet without technical competence, he or she will quickly lose the trust of the community, and a technically competent professional will be better placed than their less competent colleagues to recognize the positive aspects of innovative community proposals.

Efforts to encourage appropriate forms of professionalism are not new. As early as the mid-1950s, Charles Abrams recognized the need to 'teach or discover an indigenous Turkish architecture' and train professionals and tradesmen to work on the planning and implementation of housing initiatives. His emphasis on training led to the establishment of the Middle East Technical University (METU) in Ankara in 1956 (Abrams, 1964). METU has grown and prospered since then, albeit with a conventional approach to higher education. Another example is in Tanzania, where a surveying training school was established prior to independence, renamed the Ardhi Institute in 1974, and its range of courses was expanded to include building design, building economics, and, later, public health engineering. Since then, it has carried out research into informality and low-income housing, sometimes in collaboration with universities and research establishments from Western countries.

Universities in Northern countries have collaborated with their Southern counterparts to provide in-depth training to government officials and others, mainly those who are involved with upgrading. As already noted, in the late 1980s and early 1990s the author was involved in courses provided by the Water, Engineering and Development Centre (WEDC) at Loughborough University in the UK. These courses covered the engineering requirements for sites and services and upgrading projects, and they were initially provided in Loughborough and lasted about three months. Most of the attendees were

Indian government engineers and planners working on various ODA-funded upgrading projects. Later, the courses were transferred to India and operated in conjunction with an Indian training organization. Another useful example is the collaboration between the University of California's Berkeley Institute of Urban and Regional Development, the University of Nairobi, and various other educational establishments, slum dweller organizations, and NGOs to explore conditions in Mukuru, a large informal settlement in Nairobi (University of California et al., 2017). Some of these collaborations have produced guides to community planning and infrastructure provision at the local level (Hamdi and Goethert, 1997; Cotton and Tayler, 2000).

Another route into a new professionalism is offered by the close links between some NGOs working in low-income informal settlements and educational institutions, mainly schools of architecture. For example, the Asian Coalition for Housing Rights (ACHR) was instrumental in setting up the Community Architects Network (CAN), a regional network of community architects and planners, engineers, young professionals, lecturers, and academic institutes. Established in 2010, with the aim of connecting community architects and technical professionals with community groups that are seeking change, CAN provided both support to and learning from the various ACHR activities. NGOs such as Society for the Promotion of Area Resource Centres (SPARC) and OPP have also developed strong links with young professionals, mainly architects, and the university departments that produce them. The opportunities that such links offer to young professionals have led to profound changes in attitude in some, resulting in a lifelong commitment to a new type of professionalism.

Welcome as they are, post-graduate courses that recognize the importance of the informal sector and collaborations between academics and progressive NGOs do not address the basic problem that planning education does little to prepare the majority of students for the challenge of interacting with the informal sector. The highly motivated professionals that they produce remain a minority and, as is particularly clear from the examples in earlier chapters, have had little or no impact on mainstream thinking. Engineers present a particular problem in that few have the attitudes and design skills to deliver working infrastructure in informal areas, which almost always present physical and institutional difficulties. Attempts to respond to these difficulties have often been led by consultants, as was the case in North-east Lahore. While workable for individual projects, this approach cannot respond to the overall challenge of delivering functioning services to informal areas.

Overall, the situation in the early 2020s is possibly worse than that in the 1970s and 1980s, when the new thinking associated with people like John Turner had a strong influence on many young architects and planners in both the West and the South. There are lessons here for international agencies. They need to rediscover their commitment to radical approaches to addressing urban informality and housing. They also need to recognize the need for new forms of professionalism and be prepared to commit themselves to long-term action to support efforts to develop that professionalism, covering all the disciplines associated with the delivery of housing and services, including social development, architecture planning, and engineering. Support should extend to institutions in both the West and the South and take a work-based approach to learning that combines theory with practical exercises designed to highlight issues that are likely to be encountered when seeking to engage with informality. There should also be a link with support to new institutions that have a specific focus on the challenges presented by informal housing.

References

Arup (2018) *A framework for fire safety in informal settlements*, Arup, London. https://www.arup.com/insights/a-framework-for-fire-safety-in-informal-settlements/ (accessed 18 August 2025).

Calden, N. and Wildavsky, A. (1974) *Planning and budgeting in poor countries*, John Wiley, New York.

Carr, C. (2015) The best idea to develop Dharavi slum? Scrap the plans and start again, *The Guardian*, 18 February. The best idea to redevelop Dharavi slum? Scrap the plans and start again | Cities | The Guardian (accessed 30 December 2020).

Chambers, R. (1993) *Challenging the professions: frontiers for rural development*, Practical Action Publishing, Rugby.

Chambers, R. (1994) Participatory rural appraisal (PRA)—analysis of experience, *World Development*, 22(9): 1253–68. https://doi.org/10.1016/0305-750X(94)90003-5

Coelho, K. (2016) Tenements, ghettos or neighbourhoods? Outcomes of slum-clearance interventions in Chennai, *Review of Development and Change*, XXI(1), January–June 2016, Madras Institute of Development Studies. https://www.academia.edu/37662566/Tenements_Ghettos_or_Neighborhoods_Outcomes_of_Slum_Clearance_Interventions_in_Chennai (accessed 12 May 2020).

Community Organizations Development Institute (CODI) (2019) *Baan Mankong, Thailand's national, people driven, collective housing program*. https://en.codi.or.th/wp-content/uploads/2019/11/Collective-Housing-in-CODI-Oct-2019.pdf (accessed 18 August 2025).

Cotton, A. and Tayler, K. (2000) *Services for the urban poor*, WEDC, Loughborough.

Decoray, E. (2017) *How to build safe roofs with corrugated galvanised iron (CGI) sheeting*, IFRC-SRU. https://preparecenter.org/resource/how-to-build-safe-roofs-with-corrugated-galvanised-iron-cgi-sheeting/ (accessed 18 August 2025).

Eweida, A. (2000) *The institutionalisation of urban upgrading processes and community participation in Egypt*, PhD thesis, Department of Geography and Topographic Science, University of Glasgow. http://theses.gla.ac.uk/1568/1/2000eiweidaphd.pdf (accessed 12 May 2020).

Fortuny, G., Geier, R. and Marshall, R. (2011) *Poor settlements in Bangladesh, an assessment of 29 UPPR towns and cities*, UN-Habitat, Dhaka.

Gontsana, M-A. (2016) Outsmarting shack fires, *GroundUp*, 12 February, Cape Town. https://www.groundup.org.za/article/outsmarting-shack-fires/ (accessed 15 May 2020).

Hamdi, N. and Goethert, R. (1997) *Action planning for cities: a guide to community practice*, Wiley, Chichester.

Hasan, A. (2008) *Financing urban upgrading: lessons from Karachi's Katchi Abadis*. IRC International Water and Sanitation Centre. https://www.ircwash.org/sites/default/files/Hasan-2008-Financing.pdf

Hayek, F.A. (1945) The use of knowledge in society, *The American Economic Review*, 35(4): 519–30. https://german.yale.edu/sites/default/files/hayek_-_the_use_of_knowledge_in_society.pdf (accessed 6 January 2020).

Hendler, Y. and Fieuw, W. (2018) *Exploring partnerships with local government: a people's led approach to informal settlement upgrading*. CORC, Cape Town. https://www.sasdialliance.org.za/wp-content/uploads/2018/11/Upgrading_Publication_CORC_2018_SML.pdf (accessed 19 December 2019).

Kazimbaya-Senkwe, B.M. (1997) Planning education, planning systems and the informal sector in developing countries, paper presented at the *14th Inter-Schools Conference on Development Global and Local Development: New Agendas, New Partnerships, Edinburgh 24–25 March.*

Nkonkomalimba, M. and Mumba, M. (2014) *Sustainability and equity review of CARE Zambia's peri-urban water and sanitation model*, CARE International Zambia. Sustainability and Equity Review of CARE Zambia's Peri-urban Water & Sanitation Model (careevaluations.org) (accessed 28 December 2020).

Overseas Development Administration (ODA) (1992) *The process approach to projects*. Technical Note No. 4, Aid Economics and Social Department, ODA, London.

Picciotto, R. and Weaving, R. (1994) A new project cycle for the World Bank? *Finance & Development*, 31(4): 42–44. https://www.elibrary.imf.org/view/journals/022/0031/004/article-A012-en.xml

Rondinelli, D. (1993) World Bank Working Paper, https://documents1.worldbank.org/curated/en/868391468740679709/pdf/multi0page.pdf

United Nations (2015) *Transforming our world: The 2030 Agenda for Sustainable Development* (A/RES/70/1). United Nations. https://sdgs.un.org/2030agenda (accessed 18 August 2025).

University of California, Berkeley, University of Nairobi, Muungano wa Wanavijiji, Slum Dwellers International, Akiba Mashinani Trust, Strathmore University, and Katiba Institute (2017) *Mukuru, Nairobi, Kenya: Situational Analysis – Mukuru kwa Njenga, Kwa Rueben & Viwandani*. https://static1.squarespace.com/static/58d4504db8a79b27eb388c91/t/5a65fbd653450a34f4104e69/1516633087045/Mukuru+SPA+Situational+Analysis+2017+Phase+2.pdf (accessed 30 December 2020).

Zhang, Y. (2016) Building a slum-free Mumbai, 3 March. Wilson Center Urban Sustainability Laboratory, Washington, DC. https://www.wilsoncenter.org/article/building-slum-free-mumbai (accessed 10 August 2020).